Gadamer and

Continuum Studies in Continental Philosophy

Series Editor: James Fieser, University of Tennessee at Martin, USA

Continuum Studies in Continental Philosophy is a major monograph series from Continuum. The series features first-class scholarly research monographs across the field of Continental philosophy. Each work makes a major contribution to the field of philosophical research.

Adorno's Concept of Life, Alastair Morgan
Art and Institution, Rajiv Kaushik
Being and Number in Heidegger's Thought, Michael Roubach
Badiou, Marion and St Paul, Adam Miller
Deleuze and Guattari, Fadi Abou-Rihan
Deleuze and the Genesis of Representation, Joe Hughes
Deleuze and the Unconscious, Christian Kerslake
Deleuze, Guattari and the Production of the New, edited by Simon O'Sullivan
    and Stephen Zepke
Derrida, Simon Morgan Wortham
Derrida and Disinterest, Sean Gaston
Derrida: Profanations, Patrick O'Connor
Encountering Derrida, edited by Simon Morgan Wortham and Allison Weiner
The Domestication of Derrida, Lorenzo Fabbri
Foucault's Heidegger, Timothy Rayner
Gadamer and the Question of the Divine, Walter Lammi
Heidegger and a Metaphysics of Feeling, Sharin N. Elkholy
Heidegger and Aristotle, Michael Bowler
Heidegger and Logic, Greg Shirley
Heidegger and Philosophical Atheology, Peter S. Dillard
Heidegger Beyond Deconstruction, Michael Lewis
Heidegger, Politics and Climate Change, Ruth Irwin
Heidegger's Early Philosophy, James Luchte
Kant, Deleuze and Architectonics, Edward Willatt
Levinas and Camus, Tal Sessler
Merleau-Ponty's Phenomenology, Kirk M. Besmer
The Movement of Nihilism, edited by Luarence Paul Hemming,
    Kostas Amiridis and Bogdan Costea
Nietzsche's Ethical Theory, Craig Dove
Nietzsche, Nihilism and the Philosophy of the Future, edited by Jeffrey Metzger
Place, Commonality and Judgment, Andrew Benjamin
Sartre's Phenomenology, David Reisman
Nietzsche's Thus Spoke Zarathustra, edited by James Luchte
Time and Becoming in Nietzsche's Thought, Robin Small
The Philosophy of Exaggeration, Alexander Garcia Düttmann
Who's Afraid of Deleuze and Guattari? Gregg Lambert
Žižek and Heidegger, Thomas Brockelman

Gadamer and Ricoeur

Critical Horizons for Contemporary Hermeneutics

Edited by
Francis J. Mootz III
and
George H. Taylor

BLOOMSBURY

LONDON · NEW DELHI · NEW YORK · SYDNEY

Bloomsbury Academic
An imprint of Bloomsbury Publishing Plc

50 Bedford Square	175 Fifth Avenue
London	New York
WC1B 3DP	NY 10010
UK	USA

www.bloomsbury.com

First published by Continuum International Publishing Group 2011
Paperback edition first published 2012

British Library Cataloguing-in-Publication Data
A catalogue record for this book is available from the British Library.

ISBN: HB: 978-1-4411-7599-1
PB: 978-1-4411-5685-3

Library of Congress Cataloging-in-Publication Data
A catalog record for this book is available from the Library of Congress.

Typeset by Newgen Imaging Systems Pvt Ltd, Chennai, India
Printed and bound in Great Britain

Contents

Part III: Extensions

Introduction

George H. Taylor and Francis J. Mootz III

Hans-Georg Gadamer (1900–2002) and Paul Ricoeur (1913–2005) were two of the most important hermeneutic philosophers of the twentieth century. As the chapters that follow attest, they were in significant dialogue with one another, whether in person or in print. The present volume follows their model and brings into conversation Gadamerian and Ricoeurian scholars. The goal is to demonstrate the continuing fruitfulness of Gadamer's and Ricoeur's work and to assess continuing points of similarity and difference in order to refine and extend their legacies. We hope the fertility and acuity of the present contributions will stimulate more thought and dialogue on the rich and enduring value of Gadamer's and Ricoeur's scholarship.

The contributors often highlight differences in theme or accent in the work of Gadamer and Ricoeur, but they also agree that there is much these two philosophers share. As confirmed in a number of the following chapters, Gadamer and Ricoeur both regard *understanding* as the basic posture of human life. We engage in dialogue with others to allow their being to unfold. We try to allow the world around us to speak. Understanding is our primary means of participation in, and belonging to, the world. In the contemporary globalized environment where many people seem different from us, understanding renders the seemingly strange more familiar. The primary task hermeneutics takes for itself is to think through the nature of human understanding.

Gadamer and Ricoeur also share a basic perspective that understanding is always *interpretive*. Understanding is always inextricably informed by the perspective we bring to bear in the act of understanding. Understanding is a product of our language, our history, our traditions. These "prejudices"—these prejudgments—offer us our lens on the world. We do not have available the eagle eye, the Enlightenment's dream of detached reason that is independent in perspective. Understanding is always located within the situated and partial perspective of our prejudices. Our understanding is shaped by the way we belong to the world.

Our *belonging* to the world speaks to the way in which, through our languages, traditions, and cultures, we inhabit something beyond ourselves. Belonging has two consequences. First, as individuals we participate in a larger community;

this community grounds our identity. We are not in a situation of anomie. Second, these larger influences have their own logic that is greater than the action of individuals. Gadamer expresses this as the function of *play*. In play—in language, conversation, music, games—the play has primacy over the players. Players enter into the spirit of the game; they play by its rules. The play has a certain agency of its own. Ricoeur more poetically captures this notion by referring to the "dance."

Finally, judgment arises not only out of perspectival settings, it must be applied in contextual settings as well. *Application* is not a matter of adapting the preformed universal to address a particular case. In application, the principle is itself extended, revised, and recast as it confronts the contours of a specific question. Judgment is an act of practical reason (*phronesis*). Hermeneutics converges with rhetoric in the common emphasis on a situated judgment of persuasion and shared practical wisdom. Pure reason is not available to the interpreter; even if it were available, it would not be sufficient to deal with the interpreted context in which practical questions arise.

The essays that follow relate these general themes to a variety of topics. A number of chapters concentrate on the hermeneutic attention to our belonging to the world. P. Christopher Smith provides some historical context to the discussion. He juxtaposes Gadamer's emphasis on belonging with Martin Heidegger's focus on human displacement, on not-being-at-home. For Heidegger, humanity is located in a fallen circumstance that it fails to recognize. The task of hermeneutics, he says, is to break away from the traditional and predominant ways of exposition and to break through to original sources of true human being. Hermeneutics must proceed by the path of *Destruktion*. Because the community is false, the task of being awake to oneself is radically individual. Gadamer, by contrast, does not find humanity in a situation of estrangement. Rather, the isolated individual needs to recover a sense of participation in a larger community. The task is one of *Konstruktion*, construction of traditional worlds of belonging that have been almost obliterated by technology's calculative rationality. Through dialogue and conversation, the individual constructs the world we share. The individual moves from "I" to "we" through participation in the community of those who understand. Gadamer grants priority to *phronesis*, embedded practical judgment, while in Heidegger *sophia*, wisdom, displaces *phronesis*.

Smith's careful juxtaposition of Heidegger and Gadamer underscores the character of hermeneutic belonging. Heidegger remains more persuasive than Gadamer in emphasizing that understanding is not purified of, but rather remains conditioned by, the pre-rational affect that supplies its background setting. Yet Gadamer has gone beyond Heidegger in his emphasis on the nature of our—rather than my—being thrown into the world. Ricoeur joins Gadamer in shifting the starting point of hermeneutics away from a "self's" relationship to itself and to its relationship with others, but Ricoeur's perspective is limited because it concentrates on the relation of "self" and "other," rather than on the underlying bond of community. For Gadamer, individuals relate on the basis of a third dimension—the "game," the conversation—in which they participate.

Several chapters concentrate on the prominent debate as to whether it is sufficient to regard human reason as a form of understanding and belonging to the world. The charge, leveled particularly by Jürgen Habermas against Gadamer, is that understanding does not allow the distance that permits a critique of its potential distortions. If our norms are based on our understanding, how do we assess our understanding's limits? Does hermeneutics unreflectively perpetuate tradition for tradition's sake? The typical claim is that Gadamer's hermeneutics is descriptively conservative in this sense, and that Ricoeur's hermeneutics mediates between Gadamer and Habermas by introducing the element of critique through explanation, drawn from the analysis of the social sciences.

Merold Westphal argues that Gadamer and Ricoeur do not assume postures of opposition but rather they together bring to light the dialectic of belonging and distanciation. It is true that Gadamer expresses a deep commitment to the existence of belonging. Our prejudices and our traditions make presuppositionless interpretation impossible. It is also the case that Ricoeur emphasizes that the distancing created by explanation is an ineluctable element of interpretation. The autonomy of the text—its separation from the subjective meaning of its author and place of birth—illuminates that textual meaning is a product of its structure, something that can be, and must be, explained. Explanation helps unfold what is at work in the text, both positively in the sense of the world of the text and negatively in the sense of elements of false consciousness and deception. Ricoeur ultimately argues that understanding and explanation are complementary and interpenetrating. Explanation is not imposed on the text, but belongs to the text. The text must be explained in order to be understood; distanciation is a condition of understanding. This interrelation between understanding and distance is also present to some degree in Gadamer. Interpretation is not self-enclosed. Presuppositions may be challenged by the text and require revision. The "fusion of horizons" between reader and text indicates accommodation, not subsumption. Gadamer agrees that distanciation has legitimacy; he wants to distinguish true presuppositions from false presuppositions. Yet in Gadamer this side of the hermeneutical task remains underdeveloped. His emphasis rests in explanation ultimately serving the end of historical belonging. Because the interpreter belongs to history and its traditions, full distanciation is not possible. Ricoeur similarly acknowledges the connection between distanciation and belonging. For both Gadamer and Ricoeur, hermeneutics is dialectical in the sense of an ineliminable tension between belonging and critique.

Andreea Deciu Ritivoi also attends to the tension between belonging and distanciation. She argues that the power of hermeneutics lies less in the assumption of belonging than in its desire to overcome distance. As an example she offers Georgia Warnke's contention that hermeneutics offers a way of overcoming, in arenas of strenuous contemporary debate—such as abortion—the clash of traditions. Ritivoi claims that Warnke's assumptions are too optimistic, and she argues that we should use Ricoeur's development of distanciation as a basis for a reevaluation of Gadamer's conception of tradition. A revised conception of tradition reshapes hermeneutic understanding of what makes change and transformation possible. In particular, Ritivoi maintains that Ricoeur's work on ideology and utopia shows how tradition represents a symbolic system that permits cultural self-transformation, a project of liberation. Ricoeur's hermeneutic theory does not explicitly describe the mechanism by which distanciation from tradition becomes possible, but his work on ideology and utopia does so. Ideology is not necessarily distortive. More fundamentally it is interpretive; it brings together the ideas and beliefs that are foundational to a community. Ideology is not identical to tradition; rather, ideology offers a symbolic system that grounds tradition. Utopia, in turn, projects us outside tradition in identifying the realm of the possible. Utopia distances us from what is, and offers a vantage point from which to critique the given and consider alternatives. Utopia offers the possibility of changing a tradition and so correcting its possible distortions. The fusion of horizons between ideology and utopia helps ensure that the horizon of tradition does not become self-encompassing. The distanciation offered by utopia offers tradition an emancipatory function.

Francis J. Mootz III defends Gadamer against the claim that his hermeneutics only emphasizes belonging and does not incorporate critique. Mootz finds support in a continuing, if under-developed, element in Gadamer's hermeneutics: its interconnection with rhetoric. The rhetorical and hermeneutical aspects of language interpenetrate. The textual interpreter does not act as a passive recipient or all-knowing reader, but rather undertakes the role of rhetorical actor according to the dialogical model of question-and-answer. This creates interpretation's dynamic character and the space for critical reappraisal of a tradition. Further, just as rhetorical speech must be contextualized to a specific audience on a distinct occasion, hermeneutic understanding also arises in application. It is a rhetorical achievement. Situated rhetorical understanding occurs in a context of application after a fusion of horizons in which an interpreter's prejudices are confronted by an "other," whether the other is a text or a partner in conversation. A genuine dialogue disallows both intransigent assertion of one's own prejudices and mere acceptance of the other's opinions.

Mootz contends that Gadamer's hermeneutics gives rise to a more radical form of critique than Ricoeur's mediation between explanation and understanding. Philosophical models of explanation suppress the critical possibilities of rhetorical dialogue by imposing their own criteria. As Gadamer emphasizes, *phronesis* retains primary significance, because it is a social reason rooted in experience within a dialogic tradition in contrast to the claims of cognitive or technical mastery by explanatory models. To maintain a dialectic of belonging and distanciation, Mootz finds Ricoeur's work on ideology more attractive than models of explanation. The tension between ideology and utopia instantiates the dialectical character of hermeneutic experience as rhetorical event. Mootz exemplifies the possibilities of critical hermeneutics through the practice of legal interpretation, where the law as a tradition also offers the textual resources for critique of existing decisions.

George Taylor treats the topic of belonging through evaluation of Gadamer's concept of the fusion of horizons. On a broad level this concept crystallizes many prominent hermeneutical themes. Contemporary horizons are infused by horizons—traditions—from the past. Similarly, our understanding of the past (or of the other) is infused with what we bring from our present horizon. Understanding is not just reproductive, but productive; in the situation of present application, it is ineluctably different from understanding in the original context. Also, our individual perspective is not fixed; a horizon can be tested by, and may expand through, interaction with the horizons of others. Yet Gadamer's delineated development of the fusion of horizons is more troubling. For Gadamer, dialogue presupposes or creates a common language, history, or tradition. He speaks of the availability of a single historical horizon. Understanding, Gadamer says, presupposes that speakers speak the same language; understanding creates a higher universality. The achievement of the fusion of horizons is belonging.

Taylor argues that dialogue is not grounded in commonality—one horizon—and that Ricoeur offers resources for an alternative perspective. Ricoeur's own discussion of the fusion of horizons appears more cautious. Ricoeur writes, for example, of the tension between past and present horizons. His work on translation and on metaphor offers more persuasive characterization of what the fusion of horizons entails. Between two languages—and even between speakers internal to a linguistic community—an impassable difference persists, which translation seeks to bridge but never does completely. No identity of meaning exists because between two sources no third text is available that acts as a common source. Understanding, Ricoeur writes, is translation. Metaphor functions similarly: it creates resemblance—and understanding—across difference; sameness is mixed with difference. Metaphor disallows a common language because difference is always retained. The tensive relationship in translation and metaphor that Ricoeur describes seems to capture better the possibilities of dialogue and understanding than does the fusion of horizons.

Succeeding chapters turn from the dialectic between belonging and distanciation to the role of human agency. John Arthos pursues this issue through inquiry into why Gadamer, in contrast to Ricoeur, did not develop a theory of narrative. Through this lens, Arthos discerns differences in priority between Gadamer and Ricoeur. While Gadamer does not deny individual agency, his hermeneutics insists that the event of meaning—the address of history, culture, and social change—happens to us. The agency of events lies in themselves. Identity is centered in the presence of spirit in history. Arthos is sympathetic to Gadamer's presentation and its concern to break away from the priority granted to subjective experience—which experience limits the openness to the other. Yet Arthos wants to retain a role for individual agency, which he finds in Ricoeur. For Ricoeur, narrative can be broadly understood to offer a relationship between the act of emplotment and the enduring identity found in a person, nation, or culture, but his theory particularly pursues a subject identity and an identity that acts, that has the capacity to initiate. While Gadamer locates agency in language and culture, Ricoeur locates it primarily in human action. The recognition of one's location, stressed by Gadamer, is not interchangeable with the construction of one's location, stressed by Ricoeur. Both are important, but Gadamer's perspective occludes the latter. Ricoeur's privileging of narrative emplotment as a form of temporal order over other hermeneutic forms, such as dialogue and play, grants emphasis to human action, and action places agency in the realm of human choice. Granting weight to narrative does not reduce dialogue and play; these discursive modalities simply function at different levels.

David Vessey takes up the theme of agency by contrasting Gadamer's and Ricoeur's discussions of recognition. For Ricoeur, the recognition granted another demonstrates a form of human connection more basic than social contract. Contract is not the original source of social norms. Also, while Levinas and Husserl claim an originary asymmetry between self and other, Ricoeur demonstrates that asymmetry presupposes a deeper affinity founded in recognition. Mutual recognition is a symbolic mediation that is exempt from both the juridical and commercial orders of exchange. In *Truth and Method* Gadamer invokes recognition to denote the seriousness with which the other—whether a text or an interlocutor in dialogue—should be treated. We should recognize that the other may have something to say from which we can learn. We acknowledge our finitude and may grant the other some authority; the other may have a truth or insight greater than our own. In his later writings, though, Gadamer drops the vocabulary of recognition. In his view, emphasis on recognition of an other mistakenly presumes the independence of subjects and relies too greatly on the agency of individual subjects. What deserves attention instead is a more profound mode of being with others in the common understanding that precedes recognition, that background of shared agreement, the shared being together. A shared background, especially a linguistic one, shapes us to make dialogue possible. Dialogue fundamentally presents not a mode of recognition but of play, and the play has an agency of its own. The agency in a dialogue is social, a form of mutuality that Gadamer develops in the concept of friendship as a shared bond.

David Fisher attends the determination of action by forces other than the intentions of agency, whether individual or communal. He discusses how *phronesis*, practical judgment, must be informed by that which is, in the classic Greek term, *deinon*, the strange, the monstrous, wondrous, uncanny. He uses as a particular vehicle the necessary insight offered to *phronesis* by the tragic. While observing that both Gadamer and Ricoeur treat this subject, he concentrates on Ricoeur's argument. For Ricoeur, the incorporation of the tragic into *phronesis* protects moral conviction from the alternatives of univocity and arbitrariness. The introduction of aporia-producing limit experiences requires ethics to address that which eludes thought—the uncanny nature of human life, including the existence of unmerited suffering. Philosophy must retain its relationship to nonphilosophy. The experience of aporia challenges modern ethical theory's conviction that moral decision can be determined by rules and procedures. A *deinon phronesis* begins in darkness—the experiences of loss and incomprehension—and the aporias created challenge ethics' self-sufficiency. Yet the aporias of the uncanny allow not only for darkness but for light. When informed by tragic *phronesis*, the ethical domain may become open to the horizon of hope, the possibility of a superabundance of meaning as opposed to the abundance of senselessness and destruction. Ricoeur's approach to *deinon phronesis* is informed by both Aristotle and Heidegger. Ricoeur draws much on Aristotle, although he diverges in emphasizing the other-regarding qualities of *phronesis*. Ricoeur is also similar to Heidegger since, for both, uncanniness is basic to being in the world. But Ricoeur ultimately differs from Heidegger, primarily because the latter separates the uncanny from the ethical realm and does not encompass the presence of suffering.

The four final chapters are marked by engagements with Gadamer and Ricoeur that extend their efforts to topics that were not addressed, or remain underdeveloped, in these thinkers' works. Bernard Dauenhauer argues that Ricoeur's model of translation can fruitfully illuminate the nature of political action. Both Gadamer and Ricoeur assert that human being is founded primordially in belonging to the world. Both acknowledge our experiences of the familiar and the strange, but Ricoeur finds the human failures that block or distort understanding are frequent and enduring, while for Gadamer these failures seem more localized and transient. Ricoeur's critical hermeneutics incorporates efforts to comprehend and respond to distortive understandings.

For Ricoeur, action denotes the basic manner in which persons exist and inhabit the world. Action involves not only doing but undergoing. Actions comprise our capabilities, including our limitations. Through our actions we constitute our identity. Politics is the fundamental domain of human action; it is a domain of human agency in which human capabilities and vulnerabilities—including acts of great evil—can flourish. At its most positive, politics offers the potential for redressing distortion and reaching more positive understanding. This arena is rightly one of rhetoric, as the intertwining of consensus and conflict leads to negotiation. Ricoeur's model of translation offers an apt model for political action, because translation requires hospitality, both an openness to learning something new about the other and a readiness to welcome the other. Translation recognizes that distance is not fully overcome; the translation seeks equivalence without establishing identity. Applied to politics, the proper posture is one of a hospitality that welcomes differences even if it does not endorse them. Forgiveness and hope are principles of political action; they express attitudes of trust that it is good for us to live with, and depend on, one another. When applied to politics, the model of translation acknowledges the finiteness and fragility of human action, the practicality of judgment, and the hospitality that should be tendered others and their views.

Louise Derksen and Annemie Halsema assess the contributions Gadamer and Ricoeur may offer to feminist theories of embodiment. They begin by drawing out the fragmentary presentations by each thinker on the body, move to the potential relevance of these approaches to feminist theory, and conclude by noting their limitations and (yet) continuing relevance. Gadamer's work is valuable because he contends that the contextual meaning structures that inform human existence are not just historical, cultural, and linguistic, but include material factors such as climate and the environment. Human health, another example, is the ability to function within the whole. The claim that the body must be understood in context, in light of the whole, entails that understanding the body is a form of hermeneutic understanding. A physician's dialogue with a patient, and then diagnosis, exemplifies this process. The body is a lived experience rather than a mechanical object or mere object of science. For Ricoeur, the body is the involuntary, which stands in a dialectical relation-ship with the voluntary. Maintenance of this dialectic entails rejection of the body as being simply empirical, an object. Instead, the body is a subject body that has capacities to act. Further, understanding the body includes understand-ing the other's body as having its own capacities and aims. The "whatness" and "whoness" of the body demonstrate that it belongs both to the order of "things" and to the order of "self." Both these aspects of embodiment can be narrated, and thus are part of narrative identity. For both Gadamer and Ricoeur, our body constitutes our being-in-the-world, and embodiment is one of the limits of philosophy. Even as embodiment is expressed in language, it also escapes language, as Ricoeur discusses in connection with sexuality and Gadamer in connection with what he calls the enigma of health.

A feminist critique elaborating on the limitations of Gadamer and Ricoeur on embodiment would raise three concerns. First, these thinkers do not suffi-ciently address the way the body is materialized as a cultural product; second, they do not attend the way forms of power in society impose upon the body—particularly the female body. Third, the political implications of dialogue on the body seem little discussed. Gadamer's and Ricoeur's theories nevertheless retain their pertinence. A hermeneutical model of understanding the body remains significant. Gadamer's view of the dialogue between physician and patient might be a model for possible communication about bodily experience, communication that, in its illumination, may have an influence on power structures. Ricoeur's work can also enrich feminist approaches to identity. For him, the self is open to otherness, and the subject not only acts but can suffer because of the acts of others. To understand suffering comprehends disrespect, discrimination, and exclusion. Ricoeur's attention to justice and recognition are also themes central to feminist thought.

David Kaplan evaluates the potential of Gadamer's and Ricoeur's thought to a philosophy of technology. Neither of the two has anything original to say about technology per se, but their hermeneutic theories are pertinent to the analysis of the meaning of artifacts, the reasoning relevant to their use, and the ways they mediate experience and self-understanding. As is well known, Gadamer criticizes technology because of its supposed elevation of a dehumanizing, calculative rationality. His approach is transcendental in the sense of appraising the conditions of technology. Transcendental theories of technology err, however, because they fail to treat human-made things as being similar to other socially constructed realities that reflect human ends and values. They define things solely according to their technical qualities. If we recognize that meaning is inherent in materials, then Gadamer's hermeneutics is helpful in making sense of technology. First, we recognize the interpretive character of understanding technology. Technology is open to interpretation, just as the character of artifacts is dependent on uses, ends, and meanings. Second, technology is bound up with practical reason, with practice. The connection between practical judgment and tact—the sense of appropriateness in a particular context, guided by past wisdom and open to new points of view—often has been missing from contemporary discussion of technology. Third, Gadamer's notion of "play" alerts us that in being interpreted, the work cannot be isolated from the conditions in which it appears. This is pertinent to contemporary approaches to technology and embodiment. The link between play and truth may be hermeneutics' most important contribution to a philosophy of technology. It is not sufficient to understand the meaning of encounters with things, or the uses of tools as functions of embodiment or know-how, for this meaning can be interpreted as a text, informed by social consensus.

Ricoeur's views on technology over his long career are episodic and inconsistent. But, as with Gadamer, themes in his work can contribute importantly to a philosophy of technology. First, Ricoeur's work on capabilities considers both human capacities and vulnerabilities; we both act and suffer. Ricoeur offers a basis for deeper consideration, in the philosophy of technology, of what has been only a recent connection drawn between capability, vulnerability, and technology. Technology may be vital in either expanding or hindering our capabilities. The task for technology policy is not only to enhance capabilities but to reduce contingent vulnerabilities, such as the suffering of the poor. Second, Ricoeur's emphasis on testimony—attestation of personal truths by individuals—allows individuals to tell of the ways that technology may, or does, affect users, environments, and communities. Third, application of Ricoeur's theory of how narratives capture the temporal, historical, and moral character of human experience allows the appreciation that artifacts are capable of narration. We can tell the story of things. These stories pattern the way we relate to technology. Kaplan ultimately finds Ricoeur's approach to technology more beneficial than Gadamer's. It is necessary to say more about technology than that it is—in Gadamer's transcendental sense—the play of history and language. Ricoeur's amenability to, and incorporation of, non-hermeneutic forms of knowledge engenders a hermeneutics that is more than a function of understanding.

In her discussion of the appropriation of Gadamer by the Asian school of New Confucianism, Kathleen Wright shows the breadth of contemporary extensions of hermeneutics. New Confucianism is a neoconservative philosophical movement that claims to be the legitimate contemporary representative of orthodox Confucian values. This school affirms that it is compatible with Western approaches, and yet that it still can maintain the independence of Chinese culture. Some critics have charged that the use of Gadamer by this conservative Confucian school confirms Gadamer's own deep cultural conservatism. Wright urges that the nature of the appropriation must be more carefully delineated before we can evaluate this claim. She examines in particular the creative transformation of Gadamer by Chung-ying Cheng, who has created the first Chinese philosophy that explicitly claims to be hermeneutic. Cheng reconstructs Gadamer in two ways. First, he transforms Gadamer's concept of "horizon" into a broader notion of "vague category" that harmonizes by subordinating differences between the (now horizonless) text and the reader to what they "suppose in common prior to their difference." This eliminates the matter of the text and leaves no grounds for disputing interpretations. Second, and similarly, Cheng changes Gadamer's concept of "understanding another as a fusion of horizons." For Gadamer the fusion of horizons increases both the reader's self-understanding and the text's meaning. Again, Cheng's emphasis on underlying harmony disallows any dispute between reader and text, or between two interpreters. Cheng takes, to an extreme that conflates all difference, the Gadamerian notion of understanding as predicated upon belonging, upon what is held in common. Conflict is subordinated to harmony above all. Despite the charge by critics, it is Cheng's philosophy (and that of other New Confucians) that explains the neoconservative orientation of New Confucianism, and not Gadamer's philosophy on its own. Yet Wright also asks whether it may be fair to raise the question of why Gadamer's hermeneutics, rather than Ricoeur's, recommended itself to Cheng. Calling upon Ricoeur's assessment that a hermeneutics needs to be able to incorporate a critique of distortion and ideology, she poses whether Gadamer's hermeneutics needs supplementation so it does not fall prey to ideological reception or self-deception. Her challenge returns to the debate discussed in a number of early chapters about what a critical hermeneutics might entail, and whether Gadamer's hermeneutics avails itself of these capabilities.

The chapters illuminate, with great depth and sensitivity, numerous themes in the work of Gadamer and Ricoeur: the nature of belonging, the tension between belonging and distanciation (or explanation), agency, dialogue, rhetoric, the fusion of horizons, narrative, human capability and vulnerability, embodiment, ideology and utopia, practical judgment (*phronesis*), recognition, translation, the interpretation of things, and the relation between philosophy and non-philosophy. The chapters also exemplify the nature of the dialogue—and the debate—between Gadamer and Ricoeur, and between Gadamerian and Ricoeurian scholars. Finally, the chapters build upon these themes and begin the construction of hermeneutical philosophy for our current century. We hope these critical horizons engender dialogue and debate with our readers as well.

Part I

History

Chapter 1

Destruktion-Konstruktion: Heidegger, Gadamer, Ricoeur

P. Christopher Smith

In *Truth and Method* Gadamer devotes two entire sections to the uses of Heidegger's thinking for his own hermeneutic theory: "Heidegger's Development of a Hermeneutical Phenomenology" and "Heidegger's Uncovering of the Before-Structure of Understanding."[1] These sections in *Truth and Method* respond directly to Heidegger's early use of "hermeneutics" and thus provide special insight into how the idea of hermeneutics develops from Heidegger to Gadamer. In particular, the expression, "the hermeneutics of facticity," attracts Gadamer's attention (Gadamer, 1986, p. 259). Therefore, in the first of the four parts of this chapter, "*Destruktion*: Heidegger's hermeneutics of facticity and his transition from hermeneutics to philosophy," we will find it useful to focus our investigations on two of Heidegger's earlier studies in which this expression is central: the 1923 Marburg lecture class, *Ontology (the Hermeneutics of Facticity)*, and the 1922 proposal sent to Paul Natorp in Marburg, "Phenomenological interpretations of Aristotle." Our purpose here will be not only to clarify the things that Gadamer found so valuable in these texts, but also to show that the project Heidegger announces in them is already aimed at matters quite different from those Gadamer will pursue. In the second part, "*Konstruktion*: Gadamer's appropriation of Heidegger's hermeneutics of facticity," we will observe the changes that occur when Gadamer moves away from Heidegger's radical concern to take down the layers of falsification that hide an individual *Dasein's*, or human existence's, authentic being from itself, and turns instead to how we, as participants in a community, construe, interpret, and lay out traditional texts as these have been handed down to us. In the third part, "Gadamer on Heidegger," we will measure our conclusions about the differences between Gadamer and Heidegger against what Gadamer himself has to say about his experiences with the young Heidegger. And in the fourth and final part, "Community, affect, and Paul Ricoeur," we will ask to what extent Ricoeur might help us synthesize the strengths of Heidegger and Gadamer while remedying the deficiencies of each. To be specific, Heidegger is much stronger than Gadamer when it comes to incorporating the prerational, somatic, affective setting for all intellection in his hermeneutics. On the other hand, Gadamer recognizes, as Heidegger seems not to, that conversation with others in the community is prior to, and determinative of, any conversation of the self with itself. *Loquimur ergo sum*, not *cogito ergo sum*; "We speak to each other, therefore I am," not "I think, therefore I am."

Destruktion: Heidegger's Hermeneutics of Facticity and His Transition from Hermeneutics to Philosophy

In § 2 of *Ontology (the Hermeneutics of Facticity)* (pp. 9–14) Heidegger explains how the sense in which he means "hermeneutics" differs from the traditional and contemporary uses of the word, which he rejects. He recurs to Aristotle to recover an original sense of the word; for "Hermeneutics," he asserts, much as Gadamer will later, "is presently no longer explication [*Auslegung*] itself . . . but rather *the theory* of the conditions, the object, the means, the communication and practical applications of explication" (Heidegger, 1988, p. 13, emphasis added). In an effort to return hermeneutics to what it once was, namely interpretation, Heidegger takes as his starting point Aristotle's idea of *dêloun*, or making something plain in *logos*, or speech. Aristotle's *Peri hermêneias (On Interpretation)*, he submits, "concerns *logos* in its basic function of uncovering and making us familiar with what *is* (*mit dem Seienden*) (ibid., p. 10). The particular being, entity, or thing that *is*, which Heidegger's hermeneutics seeks to make plain—is *Dasein*, human existence, "there," in the factual world. *Dasein* is to be *ausgelegt*, that is explicated, interpreted or, literally, "laid out" before us:

> Hermeneutics has the task, at each time, of making accessible to human existence itself the character of its own being, of communicating this, and of inquiring about the self-alienation with which human existence is affected. In hermeneutics the possibility takes shape for human existence to become, and to be, understanding (*verstehend*) of itself. (Ibid., p. 15)

Since facticity, Heidegger tells us, characterizes the being of our own existence, the way we *are*, and more specifically names our always being "there" (*da*) in a particular factual situation, the hermeneutics that explicates human existence will be a "hermeneutics of facticity" (ibid., p. 7).

We must be careful, however, for this "hermeneutics of facticity" is not the usual kind of investigation that an unaffected subject applies to an object distinct from itself. Rather, the "hermeneutics of facticity" is an activity belonging to facticity itself and it is carried on from within, and during, its own experience. In other words, the "hermeneutics of facticity" is facticity's own exposition of itself. Moreover, Heidegger tells us "hermeneutical exposition is a possible, special, and characteristic way how facticity can be" (ibid., p. 15). Thus, the "*der*" in "*Hermeneutik der Faktizität*" oscillates ambivalently between an objective genitive, meaning that facticity will be the matter of the hermeneutical exposition, and a subjective genitive or possessive, meaning that the interpretation belongs to facticity, that it is facticity's own way of "laying out," expositing, both itself and its world. What will be important here for Gadamer is that hermeneutics so conceived takes down the traditional idea of a detached subject knowing at a distance a state of affairs it has arrayed before it. Here, knowing—or, better, understanding—is always located within what is experienced, and has no overview of the whole. To put this succinctly, the difference here is between the "facticity" of Odysseus on his raft, trying to make sense of what is happening to him, and the detachment of a modern meteorologist charting storms in the Aegean.

From Heidegger's proposal, "Phenomenological interpretations of Aristotle," we have only an introduction, or preface, entitled "Indication [*Anzeige*] of the hermeneutic situation." Precisely as an introduction, however, it tells us a great deal about Heidegger's understanding of hermeneutics in general, and not just the particular uses he will make of it in treating Aristotle. Here, foreshadowing *Being and Time*'s detailed exposition of *Dasein*, or human existence, Heidegger elaborates in a highly original way the "situation" in which contemporary interpreters of Aristotle find themselves. Hence, for Heidegger, hermeneutics still has the traditional sense of the interpretation of texts, in this case, Aristotle's, and the "hermeneutical situation" most evidently speaks to the situation of the one who would undertake such an interpretation. However, it is already implied in the word "hermeneutical" that not only texts will be *ausgelegt*, "laid out," explicated, exposited, but so also will the situation itself of the interpreter. As Heidegger boldly states in announcing what will become his later project in *Being and Time*, "The object of philosophical research is human existence [*Dasein*] insofar as this research inquires about the character of *Dasein*'s being. The basic orientation of philosophical questioning . . . is to be understood as explicitly laying hold of a basic way factual life moves" (Heidegger, 1989, p. 238). In other words, we are already being pointed towards the "hermeneutics of facticity" (see ibid., p. 247).

The essential point here, for our comparison of Heidegger and Gadamer, is that with hermeneutics we have moved beyond a modern epistemology that posits a static "knower," who knows a static object. The being of both the knower and the thing known are now to be thought of as correlative processes, or *movements*, over a time. Hence, to use a metaphor, however foreign it might be to Heidegger's antitechnological spirit, the event of understanding is like a moon shot in which the motion of the earth, from which the rocket is launched, must be correlated with the motion of the moon for a onetime trajectory to reach its destination. We can see why, accordingly, Heidegger would devote such an extended part of his proposal for an Aristotle project to an exposition of the *Dasein*, the "being there," of the one undertaking such an exposition. The subject matter to be interpreted, Aristotle, no less than *Dasein*'s facticity, is not some timeless, ahistorical object that presents itself to the view of some removed, detached spectator looking on from "nowhere" in the world. Rather, Aristotle only becomes available each particular time, and this only for the interpretation of someone who is situated in the process of existing, who is under way "there" in the world. As we will see, this structure of the correlative motions of both interpreter and interpreted will also figure prominently in Gadamer's appropriation of Heidegger's hermeneutics.

What, then, are the "important elements" of facticity that Heidegger indicates (*anzeigt*)? Just what does he mean by *Dasein*'s "*Bewegtheit*" or being in motion (ibid., p. 240)? How does human existence carry itself out (*sich vollzieht*)? Those familiar with *Being and Time* will recognize in his answers to these questions many of the key expressions of that later work: "Factual life's being in motion has the basic sense of its worry and care [*Sorge*]" in "its going about [*Umgang*]" "taking care [*Besorgen*]" of things in the world by "negotiating, making things ready, producing things, securing itself by making use of things, applying them to something, taking possession of them, conserving them, or letting them get away [from itself]." All this requires circumspection (*Umsicht, Sichumsehen*), or better, "looking around" to "see about" "getting things done [*Ausrichten*]." And this in turn presupposes that things are known and familiar; presupposes, that is to say, their *Bekanntheit* and *Vertrautheit* (ibid., pp. 246–47). In other words, we know the things of the world as they present themselves in our experience "there" in the world, while we are under way among them, and not from some perspective above them, the view from "nowhere."

For his part, Gadamer will argue that in our hermeneutical understanding texts are known to us in this same way, that is, from under way within the tradition of their interpretations, and only insofar as we can bring this tradition to bear on the situation in which we find ourselves. It is striking, however, that, quite unlike anything in Gadamer's hermeneutics, Heidegger begins his own hermeneutical exposition in his "Phenomenological interpretations of Aristotle" with what he will later call a "deficient mode" of human being, there in the world, namely its inclination to shirk the burdensome task of existing, its "tendency to make things easy for itself" (ibid. p. 238). This comment is aimed specifically at contemporary philosophers who divert themselves with accumulating knowledge, and who evade any "intensification of the questionable" that would have an impact on their own existence (ibid., pp. 238–39). However, we are being prepared for a more general exposition of the tendency of any human existence to lose itself (*Aufgehen*) in its preoccupations, to fall away (*Abfallen*) from itself, to fall for and into (*Verfallen an*) the world and into the ruination (*Zerfall*) of itself (ibid., p. 242).

Gadamer will make the point that the development of these themes under the heading of fallenness (*Verfallenheit*) in *Being and Time* is not meant critically despite its sharp edge. Rather, Heidegger is trying to recover the original premetaphysical concomitance of being and not-being and a sense of not-being that is more than the *nihil negativum* of "a cat *is not* a dog." Thus, Heidegger, in addressing the "am" of "I am," starts from who "I am not" in my forfeiture of myself, just as he makes clear the utensil's being by highlighting its not being available when it is broken, misplaced, or in the way.[2] But this, I would argue, is to read Heidegger in retrospect from his later work. The fact that initially he aims what he says here at contemporary philosophers makes plain that at this stage of his thinking, at least, there is indeed a critical motif, however secondary it may be to the ontological one. And, as we will see, it is precisely this critical motif that takes Heidegger in a very different direction from anything we will find in Gadamer.

It is striking, too, that in what would seem to be an indication of another of *Dasein*'s deficient ways of being, Heidegger cites a second tendency in human existence, "there" in the world, to evade altogether genuinely taking care of things. We need to pay particular attention to his account of this tendency, for although he would seem to be elaborating a deficient way that *Dasein* is not itself, he is in fact announcing a program for his future investigations:

> One's going about taking care of things [*der sorgende Umgang*] includes not just a possibility of abandoning care about getting things done, but in fact an inclination to do this, based in a primary way factual life, tends to move. In restraining the tendency to go about taking care of things, the latter shifts to looking *around* without looking *to* carrying anything out, to getting it done. Seeing about doing something takes on the character of merely looking on at something [*Hinsehen auf*]. The world is there for 'care' in this looking on at something, namely in curiosity [*cura, curiositas*], but not as something within which one might go about carrying some particular thing out, but simply in regard to the way it looks [*in der Hinsicht auf ihr Aussehen*]. Looking on at something [*das Hinsehen*] is executed in defining things in regard [to how they look], and it can be organized as science. (Ibid., p. 241)

Foreshadowed in this dense formulation would seem to be a criticism of science as derivative, as well as an explanation of the origins of science in Plato's turn to the *eidos* or, as Heidegger translates it, *das Aussehen,* or the "look" something has about it (ibid., p. 253). Indeed, here science's looking on at things is even equated with curiosity, a "fallen" form of the way we originally see about taking care of things. One might expect, therefore, that Aristotle will emerge as an "earlier" thinker than Plato precisely because, in his *Ethics* and *Rhetoric* at least, he does not engage in Plato's theoretical withdrawal from the world and his abstraction to the "ideas" or mere "looks" that things have about them, but instead develops his concepts out of human existence's—*Dasein*'s—factual being "there" in the world. One might expect, that is, that Heidegger will privilege Aristotle precisely because the latter sometimes reverses the abstraction from

Sich-Umsehen to *Hinsehen*, from "seeing about" doing something to "looking on at" something, and because precisely in such a reversal he provides a prototype of the "hermeneutics of facticity." And one might think that, as a kind of prescientific knowing belonging to our original experience in the world, Heidegger would give priority to Aristotle's *phronêsis*, or discernment in regard to the matters of human practice, over *sophia*, *nous*, and *epistêmê*, over wisdom as a composite of intuitional insight and science. But in the end, as we will see, these expectations would be misplaced for Heidegger, but exactly right for Gadamer.

For there is something else at work in Heidegger, not found in Gadamer. For want of anything better, I will call this other motif in Heidegger, "*Angst*-driven existential intensity." It originates in a sense of total displacement, the not-being-at-home that Heidegger will later call *Unheimlichkeit*, or uneasiness. Though we do not hear much about Heidegger's Plotinus studies, he must have identified strongly with the latter's sense of always being a "stranger in something strange," of being "from away," as native Mainers refer to us Massachusetts people who have fled north.[3] For Heidegger, however, the problem lies not in the alienation itself, but in one's self-deception and failure to recognize it, in one's evading it, in fact, by plunging into an ersatz world in cultivated obliviousness to how fake this world really is. This need not, of course, be as trivial as Mickey Mouse and roller-coasters. As Heidegger himself repeatedly points out, the academic world will do just as well. For Heidegger, genuine philosophy, as opposed to philosophical garrulity, is the necessary corrective to this fallen circumstance. Philosophy, he tells us with singular vehemence, "is the kind of recognition found in factual life itself, the kind of recognition in which factual existence there in the world [*faktisches Dasein*], brings itself back to itself, rips itself free at all costs and remorselessly takes a stand on its own" (Heidegger, 1988, p. 18).

Heidegger does not start with self-recognition. Indeed, "at first and for the most part" one finds oneself already lost to oneself, having always already submersed oneself in the anonymous ways of the mock world. Hence *Wachsein*, being awake to oneself, presupposes the *Destruktion* of anything that diminishes, obscures, or blocks genuine self-knowledge.

To the extent the phenomenological hermeneutics of facticity seeks by its exposition [*Auslegung*] to help find a radical possibility for appropriating today's situation, it sees itself constrained to shake up the traditional and predominant way things have been exposited, with its buried aims, its implicit tendencies, and the hidden routes that the interpretation takes, . . . and to break through to the original sources and aims of the explication. Hermeneutics accomplishes its task only on the path of *Destruktion*. . . . *Destruktion* is, indeed, the proper path on which the present, in its proper and basic ways of being in motion, must be encountered. (Heidegger, 1989, p. 249)

Moreover, since the community is false, being awake to oneself must be radically individual. It is a matter of the self's relating itself to itself by itself, of recovering itself from the open realm of public discussion (*Öffentlichkeit*) (see ibid., p. 243), whose talk Heidegger characterizes as *Gerede* (Heidegger, 1988, p. 31), talk that is mere talk and makes nothing clear. *Wachsein*, being awake to oneself, is "the particular, decisive possibility, *for each individual now*, of concrete facticity [*die bestimmte entscheidende Möglichkeit je der konkreten Faktizaität*]" (my emphasis) (ibid., p. 19). "Concrete" is Kierkegaard's word and indicates here the opposite of abstract philosophical talk. In "abstract" philosophy the self's responsibility to itself is dissipated. On the other hand, precisely for that reason losing oneself to abstract philosophy is soothing, comfortable (*beruhigend*) (Heidegger, 1989, p. 242). Hence, the very prospect of "ripping oneself free" "at all costs" generates the feeling of "the questionableness of things [*ontische Fraglichkeit*], worry, disquiet, anxiety, temporariness" (Heidegger, 1988, p. 17), and the temptation is always to flee this uneasiness.

There is nothing like this motif of displacement and estrangement in Gadamer, for whom the desired progression is not from a falsified community back to the solitary self, but the other way around, namely from the idiosyncratic self back to the cultural community. Hence, the task for Gadamer is not the destruction of a false world, but the construction of a multiplicity of traditional worlds nearly obliterated by technology's forced uniformity. Not *Destruktion* but *Konstruktion*, very much in the classicist's sense of construing a passage of Greek or Latin, becomes the task. Moreover, for Gadamer, hermeneutics, as constructive rather than destructive, is not preparatory for something else that surpasses it, but ultimate. Hermeneutics *is* philosophy.

Not so for Heidegger, however. For if, as Heidegger contends, concrete philosophy is "being awake" to oneself, and if this *Wachsein* is to be achieved via a destructive "hermeneutics of facticity," hermeneutics as such cannot be ultimate: "If I may be allowed a personal comment," Heidegger tells his audience,

> for my part I suspect that hermeneutics is not philosophy, rather something quite preliminary, which, however, has its very own function. It is thus not a matter of finishing up with it as soon as possible, rather of holding out in it for as long as possible. (Heidegger, 1988, p. 20)

Having thus underscored the importance of hermeneutics, Heidegger, in the characteristically sardonic tone we often hear in these lectures, nevertheless goes on to assert bluntly that "[h]ermeneutics is itself not philosophy. Rather, it is meant merely to place before the philosophers of today a matter for their consideration, be they so inclined, that has long since lapsed into oblivion" (ibid., p. 20). This last leaves no doubt that he already intends to move beyond the "hermeneutics of facticity," to something else of which he himself has only a premonition at this point.

Konstruktion: Gadamer's Appropriation of Heidegger's "Hermeneutics of Facticity"

Even so, at the beginning of a crucial section in *Truth and Method* entitled "Heidegger's project of a hermeneutical phenomenology," Gadamer can still take Heidegger's "hermeneutics of facticity" as his starting point:

> Under the heading of a 'hermeneutics of facticity' Heidegger countered Husserl's eidetic phenomenology and the distinction between fact and essence on which it was based, with a paradoxical challenge: not the pure cogito [Descartes's "I think"], as constitutive of typical essential universality, but the facticity of *Dasein*, existence, for which no grounds can be given and which can be derived from nothing prior to it, was to provide the basis of phenomenological inquiry. (Gadamer, 1986, p. 259)

In effect, in making facticity the starting point Heidegger is introducing, not a ground, but a Nietzschean *Ungrund* and *Abgrund*—an opaque, inscrutable non-ground and abyss. He thereby demolishes the idea of a "clear and distinct," secure foundation for any systematic philosophy, be this Descartes's, Hegel's, or Husserl's. As Gadamer puts this in a later study,

> For facticity means precisely the irremovable resistance that the factual puts in the way of all comprehension and understanding. With the particular turn he gave the concept of facticity Heidegger intended to make it the basic determinant of human existence. Facticity is precisely not only consciousness and self-consciousness. Its understanding of being, which differentiates it from all beings and which constitutes its hermeneutical structure, does not fulfill itself in a special condition of spirit/mind [*Geist*] in which it transcends all natural beings. . . . On the contrary, human existence asks about the meaning of its existence and sees itself confronted with the incomprehensibility of its own existence. (Gadamer, 1987, p. 218)

Thus,

> By making the hermeneutics of facticity the ground and foundation Heidegger got beyond classic idealism's concept of spirit/mind [*Geist*], on the one hand, and the limited themes in any phenomenological reduction to a purified transcendental consciousness, on the other. (Gadamer, 1986, p. 262)

This strategy of Heidegger's was definitive for Gadamer's exploration of hermeneutical theory in *Truth and Method*:

> Against the background of such an existential analysis of human existence [there in the world] (*Dasein*), with all the far reaching consequences for

metaphysical issues in general of which even now we have yet to take the measure, the specific issues in the hermeneutics of the human sciences suddenly look very different. The work presented in this volume is dedicated to an elaboration of the new form the hermeneutical problem has assumed. (Ibid., p. 264)

The dependence on Heidegger expressed in this passage notwithstanding, we must note that a shift in the sense and subject matter of hermeneutics as such is also implied. Hermeneutics is still exposition and interpretation, still *Auslegung*, and not the theory of exposition or interpretation; but in Gadamer, hermeneutics is no longer the exposition of factual existence there, in the world. Rather, Heidegger's hermeneutics of facticity will provide the ontological and epistemological structures for Gadamer's hermeneutical interpretation of "texts" taken in the widest sense. Heidegger's hermeneutics of facticity uncovers and exposits understanding (*Verstehen*) as basic to human existence: "Understanding [*Verstehen*]," writes Gadamer, "is the original way in which *Dasein*, human existence there, in the world, carries itself out" (ibid., p. 264). Precisely *Dasein*'s self-understanding, however, has the same structures that we find in the understanding of texts. In short, Heidegger's hermeneutics of facticity provides a new account of understanding in general that explains, in particular, the traditional task of hermeneutics or interpretation: how we are to go about interpreting texts.

The consequences of this difference between the application of hermeneutics in Heidegger and its application in Gadamer are profound. In Heidegger the main treatment of *Verstehen*, or understanding, which was scarcely a concern at all in "Phenomenological interpretations of Aristotle" and *Ontology (the Hermeneutics of Facticity)*, occurs in *Being and Time* within an exposition of *Dasein*'s being in the world (Heidegger, 1960, §§ 31–32). Although it is not stated expressly in the discussion of understanding per se, the background for this discussion is the fact that *Dasein* has lost itself to the world it understands. *Dasein* has lost itself, that is, to the world of tools and implements in their "workshop" interconnectedness, the world in which it understands how to go about taking care of things:

[The] factual existence of *Dasein* [being there in the world] is not just in general and nonspecifically a potential way for it to be in the world it finds itself thrust into. Rather it also has specifically always dissipated itself already in the world of things it is taking care of. In this fallen being-at [someplace while doing something] [*Sein bei*] one flees from an uneasiness [*Unheimlichkeit*] that stays mostly covered up with latent anxiety because the public realm of the anonymous "they" [*das Man*] suppresses it. This flight might be explicit or might not, might be understood or might not. (Heidegger, 1960, p. 192)

But if, as in Gadamer, the exposition of understanding as such becomes the primary concern, there is no critical background to its exposition. Understanding, this is to say, will not be evaluated as either authentic or inauthentic. Consequently the themes of anxiety, displacement, self-alienation—themes so central to the early Heidegger's concerns—vanish, and with them, the existential intensity characteristic of Heidegger's "hermeneutics of facticity." Indeed, *Verstehen*, understanding, in Gadamer has nothing at all to with the individual's recovery of herself or himself from dissipation in a falsified world; in fact, quite the opposite is true. In understanding, as Gadamer conceives of it, the individual moves from private isolation into participation in the community of those who understand. He or she moves from I to we. And he or she does this in conversation, *Gespräch*, with others.

But we are getting ahead of ourselves. Following Heidegger's initiative, Gadamer maintains that "Understanding is the original, primal characteristic of how human life itself is" (Gadamer, 1986, p. 264) and, he continues, "Heidegger disclosed that projection [*Entwurf*] was characteristic of all understanding." We are, this is to say, above all human when we are engaged in understanding something. Drawing upon two German reflexive idioms— *sich auskennen in etwas* and *sich verstehen auf etwas*—Gadamer supplements Heidegger's account with a particular emphasis on the fact that all understanding is not only of some thing, but simultaneously understanding of, and for, oneself. *Sich auskennen in etwas* means to have familiarized *oneself* with something, and *sich verstehen auf etwas* means to know *for oneself* how to go about something. We may infer from these idioms that "in understanding [something] one understands oneself and projects oneself toward possibilities of oneself" (ibid., p. 265), and, with reference to Gadamer's specific concern of understanding the past, "the structure of historical understanding is seen . . . to be grounded in the existential futurity of human existence" (ibid.).

The point, quite in keeping with Heidegger's emphasis on getting clear about oneself, is that the thing to be understood "is" always correlative to the self-understanding of the one who understands it. For the thing, the subject matter, is always understood in relation to the self-projections of the one who understands it, to the way that person "is." Further, both the one who understands and the thing that is understood "are" historically, that is, in the process of unfolding themselves over time, and neither the one who understands nor the thing understood "are" statically present independently of each other. Both "are" in their interactive development. Hence understanding is still *a mensuratio ad rem*, as Gadamer puts it (ibid., p. 266), or, in another traditional formulation, an *adaequatio intellectus ad rem*, except that the "adequation" of the intellect, its measuring and fitting of itself, is never to a timeless thing that always is what it is, some brute fact, "determinable" and independent of the one who knows it: "[N]either the one who knows nor what is known *are* simply there on hand, 'ontically' speaking, rather both have the same sort of being, historicity" (ibid., p. 266). Hence, I suggest that we might better speak of a reciprocal *adaequatio intellectus et rei,* of the temporary adequation of two entities, intellect *and* thing, to each other, each in their particular historical development at a given time—*je,* as Heidegger puts it.

To take an example of which Gadamer is fond, jurisprudence, the construction of a law can never be "strict" in the sense that the law is what it is, in itself, for all time, as those who framed it intended it to be, and in the sense that its interpreters need, therefore, to leave behind their particular situation at a time and place in order to make their intellect adequate to understand that law's static being, what it is in essence. Rather, like a Beethoven symphony, the law only is, exists, in the history of its interpretations to which the interpreter belongs. The law exists only in the history, that is, of the particular correlative interactions of interpreter and law, each in the process of coming to be at a given place and time.

And perhaps most of all, Gadamer relies on Heidegger's exposition of the *circularity* of understanding (see Heidegger, 1960, § 32): "Basic to Heidegger's enterprise," he says, "is his derivation of the circular structure of understanding from the temporality of human existence, and certainly one might inquire what the consequences of this are for the human sciences" (Gadamer, 1986, p. 270). And in yet another adaptation of Heidegger on the structure of understanding, Gadamer explains Heidegger's grounding of the circularity of understanding in the temporality of human existence. He points out that in Heidegger *Geworfenheit,* one's having always already been thrust into a situation, and *Entwurf,* one's thrusting or projection of oneself forward, go together, and he concludes that "[i]f thrusting oneself forward while having been thrust into a situation [*geworfener Entwurf*] is the structure of human existence, and if the way human existence carries itself out is understanding, this [structure] must hold for understanding as it is carried out in the human sciences" (ibid., p. 268).

> Hence, there is never any understanding and interpretative exposition [*Auslegung*] in which the whole of this existential structure would not be functioning, and this however much the intention of the one who would know is to do nothing other than to read "what is there" and to take from the sources "how things actually were." (Ibid., pp. 266–67)

In other words, how anything past is understood or read is inevitably determined by where the interpreters find themselves in their own past of previous interpretations. Moreover, in any present understanding the temporality of *Dasein's* past combines with the temporality of *Dasein's* future; its historicity, this is to say, with its futurity. It is in this combination that we establish the circularity of understanding: *Dasein* "always already" (*je schon*) has an understanding that preconditions the understanding it will have. In looking to the future *Dasein* brings its past to bear. It does this in the "before-structures" of what Heidegger, and Gadamer following him, call *Vorhabe, Vorsicht,* and *Vorgriff.* Originally these words refer, first, to what one intends to do, or what one has in mind *before* or ahead of time, a presumption; second, to caution or literally, precaution, or foresight, but also envisioning something *before* or ahead of time; and, third, to something done in advance in the sense of being proactive but also the conception of something *before*, ahead of time, a preconception.[4] The boundaries between these are fluid, and we must say that each in its own way gives us a perspective on the same thing: *Dasein*'s projections of the past onto the future in coming to understand anything. Hence the idea of some sheer objectivity, wherein we would simply see what's there, the "facts," without having anything in mind before and with no anticipations or expectations, proves to be a fiction.

It might seem, accordingly, that Gadamer takes over from Heidegger the ideas of both circularity and the "before" structure of understanding without modification. But there are important differences. With one difference, I suggest, Gadamer falls behind Heidegger, and with another he advances beyond him. Turning first to how Gadamer falls behind Heidegger, we can say that Heidegger, in contrast to Gadamer, grasps that there is no such thing as an understanding purified of the affective setting that codetermines it. For Heidegger, *Geworfenheit*, one's having "always already" been thrust into the situation "in which one finds oneself" has not so much to do with the way history determines our understandings as with the affective coloring or tone of every experience that has always already come over us without our doing—see Heidegger, 1960, § 30 and § 40 on *Befindlichkeit*, literally, "how one finds oneself *feeling*." At issue here is something for which Gadamer's hermeneutic theory gives no account, namely affect, *pathos*, *Stimmung*, or frame of mind. Heidegger's point—to my mind, a crucial one—is that any knowing, cognition, or understanding is inevitably conditioned by the affect that provides its background setting. The knower, this is to say, has always already been thrust, *geworfen*, into a particular way he or she feels about things, into the "tone" or "tenor" they have about them that determines how they show up (see ibid., § 39). Literally, *Stimmung* means "voicing," and this is the primary concern in Heidegger's exposition of *Geworfenheit*, one's having been thrown. In fact, *Geworfenheit* as *Stimmung* and *Befindlichkeit*, "the way one finds oneself feeling," is at least coeval with any other determination of "facticity": In this sense, *Geworfenheit* tells us that there is no getting around the "fact that" one always already feels a certain way about things. Here, Heidegger, perhaps following Nietzsche most of all, moves decisively beyond the Platonic tradition of a disembodied intellect capable of "pure" knowing, a tradition that gains force with the Stoic idea of *apatheia* or dispassion, that reaches its perfection in Enlightenment science, and that continues to dominate Anglo-American thought with its illusory separation of the cognitive from the emotive. Indeed, Heidegger displays convincingly that pure reason is an illusion, and in this he decisively surpasses Gadamer's cultured intellectualism.

Turning to how Gadamer goes beyond Heidegger, on the other hand, we can say that his rethinking *Geworfenheit* as *our* having been thrown rather than *my* having been thrown, surpasses Heidegger just as decisively. For in Heidegger a different mistake persists: namely that I can be who I am in separation from the community or world. The tradition here is traceable to Plato, too, namely, his idea of the soul's highest state as being "itself by itself" (*autê kath' heautên*) (*Phaedo*, 65c). This way of thinking is reinforced by the New Testament, Johannine idea of *ho kosmos*, or the "world" into which we have fallen, to which we do not belong, and from which we must ultimately be saved. Heidegger's talk of "being in the world" is surely traceable in part to these Gnostic ideas in John. In applying Heidegger's idea of *geworfener Entwurf*, the thrust forward that has already been thrust, Gadamer, however, introduces language quite opposed to Heidegger's assumption that *Dasein* has lost itself to the "world." In particular, *Überlieferung, Sitten*, and *Zugehörigkeit* come to mind, that is, tradition or what has been handed over to us, customary mores, and our belonging-to tradition and customary mores (Gadamer, 1986, pp. 266–68). Rather than a fallen world. or *kosmos*, to which an individual self has forfeited its authentic self, what we together find ourselves "thrown" into, and what provides the basis for our own genuine projections of meaning in conversation with each other, are the traditions within which we always already find ourselves underway and to which we belong.[5]

We see here Gadamer's decisive move from the "am" of "I am," which is so central to Heidegger's investigations, to the "are" of "we are." Consequently, Heidegger's self-understanding of *a* self that relates itself to itself has changed in Gadamer to how we understand *ourselves* in relation to *our* collective past, present and future:

> that *we* can do history, to the extent *we ourselves* are historical, means that only the historicity of human existence in the entirety of its movement between bringing to mind and forgetting makes it possible that *we* can make what is past present to mind at all. (Ibid., p. 266, emphasis added)

To be sure, Gadamer can adapt Heidegger's own critique of Cartesian subjectivity in seeking an idea of what *we are*. For Heidegger, says Gadamer:

> At the origin being-there is being-with [others], and being with [others] does not mean two 'subjects' being together with each other. Rather it refers to an original way that *we are*. Here an 'I' is not merely complemented by a 'you.' Instead, the relationship consists in our having something in common in the first place. (Gadamer, 1987, p. 184)

Nevertheless, this passage sounds far more like Gadamer than Heidegger. For Gadamer what we have in common, this *Gemeinsamkeit*, is the language we share, in which we reach an understanding with each other, *die Mitte der Sprache*, the language from time out of mind that exists in *our* midst, among *us*. For Heidegger, however, this language that exists in our midst is the fallen mere talk of the public world, for which *Dasein* itself has fallen. And so we read in *Ontology (the Hermeneutics of Facticity)* about the meaningless talk of "today" (*heute*) that governs the public realm:

> The way it [*Dasein*] is there at any given time is co-determined by the "today" [*das Heute*] of any given time. *One* way in which the "today" presents itself, in which, accordingly, one sees something like *Dasein* exemplified, is *Dasein's* public realm [*Öffentlichkeit*]. The public realm is carried out in various kinds of talk [*in bestimmten Reden*] about something, having opinions of something, handing out orders, conversing. . . . Thus . . . it becomes necessary to explore such prattling [*Gerede*] in its [*Dasein's*] public realm. (Heidegger, 1988, p. 48)

We have here a foreshadowing of *Being and Time* in which *Rede*, or talk, is exposited primarily in its deficient form of *Gerede* or idle talk, which is to say, the talk of the world into which *Dasein* has fallen (Heidegger, 1960, § 35). Here the possibility of valid speech in the public realm, speech that brings things into the open as what they are for us, is neglected or even denied.

To be sure, we must always keep in mind Heidegger's overall purpose of clarifying not-being by starting from the deficient ways things are, for example, the tool's *not* being ready at hand or *Dasein's not* being itself. Nevertheless we cannot fail to recognize in his denigration of public talk as *not* saying anything, a Johannine tendency of withdrawal from the *kosmos* or "world," which in the end thwarts any recovery of a valid *Öffentlichkeit*, a valid public realm of speech, a valid community. It is significant that for Gadamer, in whom there is none of this Johannine tendency, genuine understanding is reached, not in the *Destruktion* of a false world and the self's coming to its genuine self by itself, but in the *Konstruktion* of the world we share in *Gespräch*, in conversation, with others "there," in this world. For it is precisely in the world "at any given time" and even in the world "today" that we experience our community in the language among us and in the midst of us, our community in the *Mitte der Sprache*.

Surely there is something to be said for Gadamer's shift in emphasis away from the anxiously existing individual to the community. After all, the language in which any understanding takes place was never mine, privately, but ours. I did not find it in myself by myself; I heard it and learned it from another. It is Gadamer, then, and not Heidegger, who most successfully breaks with Cartesianism's isolated ego: for him it is not *cogito ergo sum*: I think therefore I am; instead it is *loquimur ergo sum*: we talk therefore I am.

Gadamer on Heidegger

For a final clarification of the differences between Gadamer and Heidegger, it is useful to turn to what Gadamer has to say about his relationship to the early Heidegger. On the occasion of the rediscovery and publication of Heidegger's

1921 proposal of his Aristotle project to Paul Natorp, Gadamer composed an introductory essay, "Heidegger's youthful 'theological study,'" in which he outlines most sympathetically and incisively where Heidegger was headed at that time and makes clear how he diverged from Heidegger even as he took Heidegger as his inspiration. He finds Heidegger pursuing two distinct tasks. The first was to develop "a critique of Aristotle's concept of being and the concept of the divine as the [paradigmatic] being that maintains itself entirely in the present time carrying out the perpetual action [of thought thinking itself thinking, *noêsis noêseôs*]" (Gadamer, 1989b, p. 232). The second task was to summon the existing individual to genuine self-understanding by showing that the desire to "know more" in Aristotle (*mallon eidenai*) was at its ground precisely a desire of human existence to shed light on clouded and dark regions of itself.

In pursuit of the first task Heidegger sought to counter Aristotle's idea of divine being with human being that *ek-sists*, or always already stands outside of itself in action carried out (*vollzogen*) over time. Here, past time, *Geworfenheit*, having already been thrust, conditions existing individuals' continual projection of themselves into an indeterminate future. As opposed to Aristotle's divine being that looks on from nowhere at no time, human being is *Dasein*, existing "there," at a place and for a time, while taking care (*Besorgen*) of what needs to be done. Consequently, it is here where understanding, *Verstehen*, as opposed to divine intellection of the intelligible, comes into play. Understanding is seeing and knowing what to do from within the finite horizons of a given situation while under way "there" in the world. And with no overview of the whole, understanding, as opposed to divine knowledge, is always limited.

Precisely this contrast of divine, infinite thought and *Dasein*'s finite understanding provides Gadamer with his own starting point, and, following Heidegger, he too finds a prefiguration of human understanding as opposed to divine intellection in Aristotle's *phronêsis* or practical discernment. In reference to a Heidegger seminar on Aristotle from around this time (1922?) Gadamer comments that

> for me personally this Aristotle seminar, the first in which I took part, became above all an introduction to the fundamental meaning of *phronêsis*, of practical knowledge. As is well known, I moved this idea later into the foreground in order to distinguish practical knowledge from the concept of method in the modern sciences and thus to show the limits of the latter. (Gadamer, 1989b, p. 231)

The second task that Heidegger set for himself, says Gadamer, was to summon the existing individual to authenticity. In a highly productive projection of his own purposes back onto Aristotle, Heidegger finds that Aristotle shows how authenticity could be recovered within the facticity of human existence as a consequence of *Dasein*'s desire to "know more" (*mallon eidenai*), which is to say, of *Dasein*'s being "out after elucidation (*aus sein auf Erhellung*)." "The elucidation that human existence seeks," writes Gadamer in elaboration of Heidegger's point, "consists above all in one's becoming transparent to oneself, and in this way elucidation allows one to take hold of one's own potentials despite all of one's own limitations" (ibid., p. 233). In other words, what we have here will become in *Being and Time* the instant of clarity, the "blink of an eye" (*Augenblick*) when *Dasein* hears the silent call of conscience, recovers, and owns the self it had hidden from itself in its "plunge" into the everyday world (see Heidegger, 1960, §§ 56–57).

The translation of *mallon eidenai* that Heidegger gives is significant: "*das mehr an Hinsehen*" (see Heidegger, 1989, p. 262). This higher degree of *Hinsehen*, this "looking on more at" something, is linked to being *sophôteron*, more wise (ibid.) and, thereby, to *sophia*, theoretical wisdom, or as Heidegger calls it, "unconcerned pure apprehension, that has leisure time [*scholê*] to spend with the *archai*, [first principles] of what always is" (ibid., p. 261). This unconcerned *Hinsehen* is thus to be thought of in contrast to concerned and even fretted *Umsicht* and *Sich-umsehen*, "looking around" "seeing about" how to take care of practical matters at a place and time. This last is guided by *phronêsis* or practical discernment, which becomes, by implication, *im*pure understanding as opposed to the "pure understanding" of *Hinsehen* (see ibid., pp. 260–61). Gadamer does not find any contradiction in this line of thought with the first task he finds Heidegger pursuing, namely "a critique of Aristotle's concept of being and the concept of the divine as the [paradigmatic] being that maintains itself entirely in the present time carrying out the perpetual action [of thought thinking itself thinking, *noêsis noêseôs*]" (Gadamer, 1989b, p. 232). Still, he does not himself make the move Heidegger does from *Sich-umsehen* and *phronêsis* to *Hinsehen* and *sophia*, which is to say, from hermeneutics to "philosophy" in Heidegger's sense of the word.

Though Gadamer explains Heidegger in a genuinely appreciative way here, his own very different aims keep him from following Heidegger in this "striving for the elucidation of life," as Gadamer calls it (ibid., p. 232). For Heidegger, however, this second task eventually overrides the task of expositing human being-there in the world and subordinates the later to itself. For him the hermeneutics of facticity becomes an attempt to penetrate the disguises and diversions with which *Dasein* obscures itself from itself. The preponderance of this search for self-elucidation forces a shift in Heidegger's concerns from *Dasein*'s circumspective "looking around" and "seeing about" "taking care of things," (*Umsicht, Umsehen, Besorgen*) to *looking on at* oneself and one's world (*Hinsehen, theôria*). This is why, in other words, in Heidegger Aristotle's *sophia* eventually displaces *phronêsis*.

In keeping with this shift of focus from the "hermeneutics of facticity" to self-elucidation, Gadamer finds that in the "Phenomenological interpretations of Aristotle" Heidegger is already reading Aristotle's account of *phronêsis* in the *Nicomachean Ethics*, book VI, with an eye toward moving past the *Ethics* altogether and moving on to Aristotle's *Physics* and *Metaphysics*. The "hermeneu-tics of facticity" had become the platform from which the question of being can be pursued: "[T]he fretful concern [*Bekummerung*] of human existence for itself and its being," says Gadamer, "generates the question about the concept of being that received its comprehensive ontological answer in Aristotle's *Metaphysics*" (ibid., p. 232). In rereading Heidegger's proposal after a 50-year hiatus, Gadamer relates that in Heidegger's understanding even *phronêsis* itself had been aligned with the project of a self-elucidation sought through the revival of the question about being, and this at the cost of deleting one of *phronêsis*'s essential components in the deliberations it guides:

> What struck me most of all was the preponderant interest in ontology that shows up even in the analysis of *phronêsis*. As a consequence the concept of *êthos* is scarcely mentioned *per se* in the program proposed. For *êthos* is precisely not elucidation but habituation. In his analysis of life's facticity Heidegger recognized habituation as constitutive but characterized it as the tendency of life to fall [into inauthenticity]. Thus habituation occurs less in the elucidation of existence than in the distortion and obscuring of it, against which the efforts of existence must be concentrated in order that existence become transparent to itself. (Ibid., p. 233)

What is Gadamer getting at? There are, I think, two issues in play here. First, we can say that, for Aristotle, habituation shows up as essential to *prohairesis*, to the choice, that is, which one makes after deliberation guided by *phronêsis*. For one makes the right choices only if one has been properly habituated to make them by having already made them *under the guidance of others* "there," in precisely that quotidian world of the "today," to which Heidegger claims that the self has forfeited itself. Second, this habituated predisposition lies outside the purview of conscious deliberation even as it codetermines it, and as such it resists elucidation; consciousness is unable to shed light on it, to get clear about it. For exactly these two reasons habituation is for Heidegger an impediment to the self's recovery of its authentic self from its loss of itself to the anonymous "everybody," *das Man*. In contrast, Gadamer's guiding idea of cultivation (Hegel: *Bildung*) leads him in the opposite direction of this retrieval of oneself from the everyday world. It leads him to restore the individual to a traditional community, which in its historical effects always exceeds the horizons of any finite individual consciousness. Since Gadamer is not seeking self-elucidation, there is no reason for him to move beyond Aristotle's *Ethics* to the *Metaphysics*, no reason, that is, to move to *sophia* and beyond *phronêsis* with its embeddedness in entire dimensions of our being that withhold themselves from our awareness, such as habituation, custom, and tradition.

Despite his differences from Heidegger, however, Gadamer gives us remark-able insights into what Heidegger is after in his treatment of *phronêsis*. There is Gadamer's now famous account of an Aristotle seminar, perhaps the same one alluded to in "Heidegger's youthful 'Theological Study,'" in which Heidegger jolts his students, Gadamer among them, by exclaiming in response to their struggle to make sense of *phronêsis*, "*Das ist das Gewissen!* [That's conscience!]" (Gadamer, 1987, p. 200).[6] "What Heidegger found in Aristotle's analysis of *phronêsis*," Gadamer relates,

> and what so fascinated him about Aristotle's critique of Plato's idea of the good and Aristotle's concept of practical knowing was this: here a kind of knowing (an *eidos gnôseôs*) was described that simply could no longer be reduced in the end to objectification in the sense of "science," a kind of knowing, that is, in the concrete situation of the existing individual. (Ibid.)

Here, then, we have the crux of Gadamer's own use of *phronêsis*. But there is something more at stake in Heidegger, as Gadamer acknowledges: "One is reminded by this violent appropriation of Aristotle for his own purposes," he continues,

> of [Heidegger's] own questions in *Being and Time* regarding how the call of conscience makes visible for the first time, in its onto-chronological event structure [*in seiner sein-zeitlichen Geschehensstruktur*], that special "being-there" of human existence. (Ibid.)

In this concern of Heidegger's for the elucidation of human being-there Gadamer recognizes something, however brilliant and compelling, that tends nonetheless in a quite different direction from his own work.

Community, Affect, and Paul Ricoeur

We have seen that Gadamer's hermeneutics reopens a path abandoned by Heidegger, the path, namely, to an exploration of our *Zugehörigkeit*, our "belonging-to" a community. But we have also seen that in one respect, at least, Heidegger probes an underlying dimension of understanding, communication, and speech that Gadamer neglects: namely their ineradicable affective ground. We want to ask now what contribution Ricoeur might have made in regard to the discussion of these two issues—first, of community and, second, of affect—and if he might have remedied the deficiencies we found in Heidegger on the one hand and Gadamer on the other. To this end we turn to Ricoeur's *Oneself as Another*.[7]

With regard to community, it is significant that Ricoeur takes up where Heidegger seems to have left off in *Being and Time*, namely with Heidegger's initial and tentative explorations of our authentic being together with another person and our "solicitude" for her or him (Heidegger: *Fürsorge, Sorgen für den anderen*) (Heidegger, 1960, p. 26). To further develop Heidegger's inchoate idea of solicitude Ricoeur turns to Aristotle's account of *philia*, or friendship, in the *Nicomachean Ethics*, books VIII and IX (Ricoeur, 1992, pp. 180ff.). We note that *philia*, though not in the forefront of Gadamer's hermeneutical theory, is certainly present in his accounts of *euboulia*, being well advised (see Gadamer, 1986, p. 326). Aristotle uses *euboulia* in regard to the *bouleuesthai* or deliberation in which the individual engages prior to *prohairesis* or taking up one action in preference to another. It is clear, though, that just as the origins of *bouleuesthai*, literally, taking counsel with oneself, are in *sumbouleuesthai*, taking counsel with others, so too being well advised as an individual has its origins in the advice we receive from another and, as Gadamer points out, only a friend can give advice: "Those who ask for advice just as much as those who give it, presuppose that the other is bound to them in friendship" (ibid., p. 328). Friendship is present, too, in Gadamer's treatment of *sunesis*, which, in Gadamer's quite original account, is the understanding shown for someone else (*Verständnis*). As such it is a modification of, and adjunct to, *phronêsis* (practical discernment) that is applied not with regard to choices I am about to make but in passing judgment with regard to the choices someone else has made (ibid.). *Sunesis* so conceived fits nicely with *gnôme* and *sungnômê*, considerateness and forbearance (ibid., pp. 328–29), both of which are grounded in *epieikeia*, which Gadamer glosses as *Nachlassen*, or "letting up," in what otherwise would be a rigidly strict application of the law to another; in short, clemency (ibid., p. 323).[8] All of these take single individuals outside of themselves and involve them with others who are dear (*philos*) to them in some way, others with whom they share some sense of kinship or *philia*. In contrast, it is clear, given Heidegger's focus on self-elucidation and the recovery of oneself from the "world"—the Johannine *kosmos* into which one has fallen—that he has been diverted from further exploration of just such matters as these.

What is more, when Ricoeur appropriates Levinas's inversion of "no-other-than-self without a self" into "no self without another who summons it to responsibility" (Ricoeur, 1992, p. 187), he seems to move in the same direction as our own Gadamerian reconstruction of *cogito ergo sum* (I think therefore I am) as *loquimur ergo sum* (we speak to each other, therefore I am). "[E]very participant is affected by the speech addressed to him or to her," writes Ricoeur, and "[l]istening to speech then becomes an integral part of discourse inasmuch as it itself is addressed to another" (ibid., p. 329). Thus, both Gadamer and Ricoeur shift the starting point for a hermeneutics of human existence away from a self's relationship to itself and to a source of one's being other than oneself.[9] Consequently, there is good reason to believe that Ricoeur's elaboration of *philia* in Aristotle, and in particular, his thesis that I can be who I am only in relation to an other, coincides nicely with Gadamer's advances beyond Heidegger in this regard, and might even extend them.

In fact, however, Gadamer and Ricoeur move in quite different directions. Under the influence of Anglo-American scholars—Charles Taylor, in particular (see ibid., p. 181)—Ricoeur pursues friendship as the relationship of one individual self to another, and neither as a sense of kinship with a group of others nor as the bond of community. Ricoeur's turn to two individual selves in relationship to each other, which is to say, to the "I-thou" relationship, is reinforced by Levinas's biblical emphasis on the responsibility of one self for an other insofar as the other as the "master of justice" demands my response (see Ricoeur, 1992, pp. 189–90). Restricting the discussion of friendship to one-on-one, personal interactions is surely in keeping with Aristotle's intent in his chapters on friendship. However, insofar as it stays with individual selves apart from the world in which they first encounter each other, this way of addressing the matter does not help in reversing Heidegger's withdrawal of the self from the fallen "world" in the way that Gadamer achieves this reversal: namely by cultural education beyond individual idiosyncrasy and the conse-quent movement from the "abstract" I to the "concrete" We—if we may adopt the Hegelian, not Kierkegaardian, use of these expressions.

To be sure, Gadamer does have something to say about the I-thou relation-ship in his hermeneutical theory, but only insofar as it models for us the right and wrong relationships of an interpreter to a text (Gadamer, 1986, pp. 364–67) and "the openness to the tradition possessed by historically effected/effec-tive consciousness" (ibid., p. 367). Certainly, if measured against Levinas, Gadamer's account would seem gravely deficient, but this would be to apply a misplaced standard. For when Gadamer speaks of a *Gespräch*, or conversation, his focus is not on the selves engaging in the conversation and their responsibil-ity to each other, but on *die Sache*, the subject matter about which they seek to get clear. The model here is Plato's *pathos tôn logôn*, the experience (Gadamer: *Widerfahrnis, Erfahrung*) undergone in conversations by the participants in them that leads either to a good outcome (*euporia*) or impasse (*aporia*) or, as usually happens, a mixture of both.[10] (see *Philebus*, 15d) For Gadamer reaching an understanding, *Sich-verständigen*, has primarily to do with the subject matter and not with the understanding (*Verständnis*) the interlocutors show for each other. And as in play, so too in a conversation, the key to a valid experience is not so much self-respect and respect of the other as the self-forgetting that comes with losing oneself in the experience of where the conversation takes us. One might think of this as the vanishing of self-consciousness in musical performance when one forgets about the impression one is making on the audience and other players and yields to the flow of the music being performed. Good conversations are like that. For Gadamer, then, the more appropriate English translation of *philia* would be kinship rather than friendship, for *philia* for him is the sense of belonging, *Zugehörigkeit*, shared among participants in a community, be this an orchestra, a household (*oikos*), a neighborhood, a team, an army, or a philosophical symposium:

> The language or speech in which something comes to be spoken of is not a possession at the disposal of one or the other of the partners in the conversa-tion. . . . Something is there, set down in the middle, as the Greeks would say,

in which the partners in the conversation participate, and about which they exchange what they have to say with each other. . . . In the successful conversation both fall under the spell of the truth of the subject matter that binds them in a new community. Reaching an understanding in conversation is not at all playing one's trump cards and forcing one's own standpoint through, rather it is transformation into a community, in which one no longer remains what one was. (Gadamer, 1986, p. 384)

Hence we may say that, even if Gadamer and Ricoeur are concerned to situate the solitary self in relationships with others, ultimately they have very different things in mind. For Ricoeur the emphasis is on the relationship of two individuals to each other. For Gadamer, on the other hand, the relationship is tripartite: individuals do not so much relate to each other as, in their discursive interaction with each other, they are related to each other by a third in which they participate, the music, the game, the conversation, in which they are joined. And this event is not something they do and for which they are responsible but something that happens to them and with them. They are not moral agents here, that is, not the subjects of active verbs, rather they are in the dative case as in the King James English, "For *unto us* a child is given."

This difference between Gadamer and Ricoeur is only reinforced when Ricoeur extends his exploration of solicitude by turning from Aristotle on friendship to Kant's moral imperatives (see Ricoeur, 1992, pp. 222–27, 262–73). And here Gadamer's often overlooked reliance on Hegel comes into play. The problem with Kant that Hegel identifies, and that Ricoeur seems to recognize (see ibid., pp. 342 n.48 and 344 n.51), is that specific content cannot be generated from Kant's universal, formal imperatives. For example, it is clear that I should always treat the other as an end in himself or herself and never as a means, but while this serves as an external check, it does not tell us, for instance, just how one spouse in a particular culture should act on a particular occasion in regard to another. Like it or not, and generally we children of the Enlightenment do not, autonomous individuals cannot generate what Hegel calls ethical substance, or *sittliche Substanz*, out of themselves any more than they can generate a private language. Though they are free to use ethical traditions to modify ethical traditions or to use extant languages to modify a language, they are unable to create a completely new morality *ex nihilo* any more than they are able to generate a new language from some sheerly speechless "original position." However reluctant we may be to admit it and however much it irks us, we are dependent on what Gadamer calls the "authority of tradition."

Now Gadamer surely does not accept Hegel's claim in the end to have raised all "ethical substance" to the level of full, infinite comprehension by absolute intellect. On the contrary, anything we can know of ethical substance always recedes beyond the horizons of our limited comprehension. Still, what we do know of it we do not know as individuals but as participants in it with others, and this means that we must rise above privacy to community.[11]

In short, Ricoeur, following Levinas, has concerns that are Hebrew whereas Gadamer, following Hegel, has concerns that are Greek. Ricoeur comes closest to Gadamer when he insists that "the good life with and for others" must be lived in "just institutions" (ibid., p. 180) and defines an institution as the "structure of living together as this belongs to a historical community—people, nation, region, and so forth," and adds that "what fundamentally characterizes the idea of institution is the bond of common mores" (ibid., p. 194), and here we might think of *Sitten* and *Sittlichkeit*, ethical mores and the patterns of behavior they determine. These are words Gadamer takes over from Hegel and that figure prominently in Gadamer's thought. These traditions provide the setting for the exchange of an "I" and a "thou" in Ricoeur, but they are not the concern in this exchange. Rather, the issue for him is the responsibility of one self to the other, where I take a stand—as in Moses's "Here I am"—in response to the face of the other and, if human, to his or her suffering. For Gadamer, in contrast, "I" become who "I" am precisely in participating with others in "our" customs and mores (*Sitten*) and in getting clear about them in "our" conversations.

With regard to the second of our questions concerning the affective ground of discourse, Ricoeur seems to come much closer to Heidegger's insights than Gadamer does. For one thing, Ricoeur introduces *eleos* and *phobos*, the ground feelings in Aristotle's account of tragedy, as a necessary supplement to his exploration of Aristotle on friendship. He does not go so far as Heidegger to say that Aristotle's exploration of the *pathê* or affects in Aristotle's *Rhetoric* (II, 2–11) are of singular importance to any account of human understanding and communication (see Heidegger, 1960, §§ 29–30), but the opening for an exploration the basic affective dimension of discourse is certainly there when Ricoeur speaks of "the role played by feelings—which, in the last analysis, are affects—in solicitude," as well as the "feelings that are revealed in the self by the other's suffering," and the "union between the ethical aim of solicitude and the affective flesh of feelings" (Ricoeur, 1992, pp. 191–92), and this we certainly cannot say of Gadamer. Moreover, Ricoeur refers, albeit in passing, to the "Song of Songs," and here he could have surpassed Gadamer completely and come close to Plato's insights in the *Symposium* about the fundamental role of *Erôs* in human existence. But in Ricoeur the stringent Kant wins out over the erotic Plato.

In fact, Gadamer and Ricoeur seem equally oblivious to Nietzsche's cogent demonstration that the self and its "small reason" (*die kleine Vernünft*) is but an epiphenomenon of the body and the feelings that it undergoes.[12] Neither seems to acknowledge that *die Mitte der Sprache*, the medium of speech that exists in between us, is at its origin song and dance in which we are joined physically. They fail to see that original speech is neither discourse that makes things clear, as in Gadamer, nor the appeal of the other for justice, as in Ricoeur, however much for Ricoeur there is in any such appeal a real physical presence in the suffering of the other. As we know from early Greek history and Pindar in particular, "communities" are established and maintained in *chorein* and chore-ography. Festivals of song and dance precede, and then continue to sustain "rational" discourse. And even if it is lost in the later Heidegger, there is in his account of the fundamental role of *Stimmung*, of mood, voicing, corporeal disposition, an opening to the ideas Nietzsche was pursuing.[13]

In contrast, the communion of individuals seems ultimately to be understood by both Gadamer and Ricoeur as the encounter of desexualized beings with each other, be this in Gadamer's *Gespräch* about a "subject matter" in which they reach an understanding, or even in Ricoeur's "thou" commanding justice from an "I." Either way this remains the intercourse of eviscerated shades. In the end, Gadamer's and Ricoeur's understandings of our human being remind me of the weightless ethereal figures with which Virgil populates his underworld:

> *Corripit hic subita trepidus formidine ferrum*
> *Aeneas strictamque aciem venientibus offert,*
> *et ni docta comes tenuis sine corpore vitas*
> *admoneat volitare cava sub imagine formae,*
> *inruat et frustra ferro diverberet umbras.*

And now, filled with dread and sudden fear, Aeneas waves the edge of his drawn sword at these oncoming shapes. And did his wise companion not warn him that these tenuous, disembodied souls were hovering about, less than the empty image of a form, he would have rushed at shades, and sought in vain with his sword to slash them in half. (*Aeneid* VI, 290–94)

Notes

[1] The discussion in this chapter concerns only Heidegger's work up through *Being and Time* (*Sein und Zeit*). To be sure Heidegger's later work after the *Kehre*, the "turn" or "switch-back," figures prominently in *Truth and Method*. However, we will need to limit ourselves here to the influences of the early Heidegger on Gadamer, influences, which, I would argue, are decisive. Given both Heidegger's and Gadamer's conviction that the original language, in this case German, determines the content of what is said, I will work from the German texts and translations will be free and my own.

[2] See Heidegger, 1960, §§ 35–38 on inauthenticity, or one's failure to own oneself, and § 16 on the deficient ways in which a tool *is not* ready at hand.

[3] With the exception of a note captioned "*Zur Destruktion Plotins*" Plotinus is not mentioned in Heidegger's 1921 Augustine lectures, but even if in the end they dealt exclusively with Augustine, their title was *Augustinus und der Neoplatonismus*. See Heidegger, 1995b, p. 269. Theodore Kisiel cites a 1921 letter from Heidegger to Karl Löwith in which Heidegger speaks of his decision not to teach Plotinus, as he had considered doing, but to turn instead to Aristotle. See Kisiel, 1995, p. 227.

Thus Heidegger's familiarity with Plotinus is beyond question. I would even suggest that Plotinus prepares the soil for Heidegger's later reception of Hölderlin. See Heidegger, 1995a, pp. 60–65.

4 See Heidegger, 1988, p. 16 and Heidegger, 1960, p. 32. The violence done in Heidegger's radical treatment of these three, *Vorhabe*, *Vorsicht*, and *Vorgriff* in his 1924 lectures on the "Basic Concepts of Aristotelian Philosophy" provides a clear indication of an underlying difference in attitude between Heidegger and Gadamer. In Heidegger's text these words are stripped of their original meanings and assigned what Heidegger himself calls specific "terminological" senses: *Vor-habe* becomes the way I "have" my world to begin with; *Vor-sicht* becomes the given, guiding understanding of being; *Vor-griff* becomes the prevailing preunderstanding behind my own expression and articulation of my world. See Heidegger, 2002, pp. 274–75. Heidegger thus wrenches these words around to make them serve his project: namely, *Destruktion* of these falsifications that *Dasein* must get free of to reach genuine self-knowledge. There is, of course, none of this in Gadamer, who patiently sounds out these words to hear what they disclose about the circular structure of understanding.

5 I am indebted to William Koch, who points out in his dissertation for the University of South Florida, "Heidegger's realist historicist answer to the problem of meaning" (2009), that in Heidegger, 1960, pp. 383–85, Heidegger's talk of taking over a heritage (*Erbe*) of authentic possibilities handed down from the past seems to draw close to Gadamer's emphasis on our belonging to a tradition. For better or worse, I find a good deal in this passage that is singularly Heideggerian. First, there is the fusion of "inherited" (*ererbt*) with "chosen" (*gewählt*) in reference to a "possibility" that exists only for a *Dasein* that has owned his or her death and that lives unto death (ibid., p. 384). Death, of course, is radically individualizing and the appropriation or choice of a heritage in living towards it would seem, therefore, to presuppose a separation of the individual self from the community such that he or she might freely select or not select a particular heritage in an act of resolve (*Entschlossenheit*)—as in those placards they used to have in New York subways 50 years ago that urged you to "attend the church of your choice." In Gadamer, however, we do not select or choose a tradition from outside it any more than we choose our native language this way. Rather, we find ourselves always already underway within it, albeit with some level of obliviousness to it. And then there is Heidegger's unsavory vocabulary here that is quite foreign to Gadamer: *Schicksal*, *Volk*, *Kampf*. The entire passage seems, to me at least, to be an infelicitous blend of Nietzsche's *amor fati* with Leni Riefenstahl's *Triumph des Willens*.

6 Ricoeur, too, alludes to this account of Gadamer's about Heidegger on *phronêsis*. See Ricoeur, 1992, p. 342.

7 We will focus on the parallel second sections of chapters 7, 8, and 9, respectively, "With and for Others," 180–94, "Solicitude and the Norm," 218–27, and "Respect and Conflict," 262–73.

8 To be sure, Gadamer is exploring these Greek words not as a contribution to social theory but as examples of understanding that differ, as does *phronêsis* itself, from *technê* and *epistêmê*, knowing how to make something and science. It is significant, however, that they figure prominently in his account of Aristotle's EN, but are largely bypassed by Heidegger. For a more complete account of them and their role in Gadamer's hermeneutics, see Smith, 2003, pp. 180–81.

⁹ Of course Heidegger after the *Kehre* or "switchback" makes precisely the same move, except that the other from which we must begin is not another person and not the community to which we belong, but *Sein* or Being.

¹⁰ For Gadamer's treatment of this passage see Gadamer, 1985, Griechische Philosophie 1, *Gesammelte Werke* 6, and Gadamer, 1991, Griechische Philosophie 2, *Gesammelte Werke* 7, pp, 182–83, 328.

¹¹ I submit, accordingly, that in some matters Hegel influences Gadamer more than Heidegger. True, Heidegger and Gadamer following him are beyond thinking of human existence in terms of consciousness and self-consciousness, let alone absolute, infinite *Geist* in Hegel's sense. Nevertheless—and notwithstanding his indebtedness to Heidegger in getting around Hegel's spirit/mind to an earlier, original sense of "we"—Gadamer pursues Hegel's idea of enculturation, *Bildung*, the education of the individual consciousness to participation in the cultural traditions, and this even if he shares Hegel's abiding sense that these traditions are in decline and that it is in the twilight of their day that the owl of Minerva, philosophy, takes flight.

¹² See Nietzsche, 1960, p. 34:

> *Der Leib ist eine große Vernunft, eine Vielheit mit Einem Sinn, ein Krieg und ein Frieden, eine Herde und ein Hirt.*
>
> *Werkzeug deines Leibes ist auch deine kleine Vernunft, mein Bruder, die du 'Geist' nennst, ein kleines Werk- and Spielzeug deiner großen Vernunft.*
>
> *(The body is a grand reason, a multiplicity with One sense, a war and a peace, a herd and a shepherd.*
>
> *Your small reason is a tool of your body too, my brother, what you call "mind," a small tool and plaything of your grand reason.)*

¹³ Heidegger's *Grundbegriffe der aristotelischen Philosophie* has quite extraordinary passages on the fundamentality of affect and the body. See, for example, "*Das Pathos als Mitgenommenwerden des menschlichen Daseins in seinem vollen leiblichen In-der-Welt-sein* [Affect as human existence's being carried along in its full bodily being in the world.]" Heidegger, 2002, pp. 197–203.

Part II

Engagements

Chapter 2

The Dialectic of Belonging and Distanciation in Gadamer and Ricoeur

Merold Westphal

Paul Ricoeur and Hans-Georg Gadamer are often described as opposite poles of hermeneutic thought, with Gadamer elaborating our belonging and Ricoeur our distanciation. In this chapter I will challenge this misleading characterization and contend that Gadamer and Ricoeur, together, expose the dialectic of belonging and distanciation. Ricoeur suggests that for hermeneutical phenomenology interpretation seeks its goal not so much through a direct path "to the things themselves," but rather through detours that follow the paths of earlier, not necessarily philosophical, interpretations. Thus, in *The Symbolism of Evil* he approaches his topic indirectly through various symbols and myths in which evil has already been interpreted.[1] Similarly, we might approach our theme indirectly via a detour, this one through Merleau-Ponty and Derrida.

In terms of distanciation, Merleau-Ponty says phenomenology is reflection, a deliberate distancing from immediate experience and, moreover, that such experience "is accessible only through a phenomenological method" (Merleau-Ponty, 1962, p. viii). In a genuinely Husserlian voice, he says that in this reflection "I am the absolute source, my existence does not stem from my antecedents, from my physical and social environment" and that this applies to the traditions I "elect" and the horizons I "abolish" (ibid., p. ix). In other words, distanciation—he does not use the term—is understood as methodological reflection in service of the objectivity available to an unconditioned subject.

But then he qualifies this claim in three ways that seem to emphasize a belonging from which distanciation can never fully distance itself. First, the goal of this reflection is to see clearly our "facticity," our "direct and primitive contact with the world" and the world as it is "always 'already there' before reflection," the world that "precedes knowledge" (ibid., pp. vii, ix). The goal, unlike that of the sciences, is not to replace prereflective and prerational experience and its world with something somehow superior; it is rather to notice our immediate belonging, from which the sciences and even common sense arise, and to which they belong.

Second, we belong in terms of interest as well as immersion. So the goal of reflection is in some sense practical.

> Reflection does not withdraw from the world toward the unity of conscious-
> ness as the world's basis; it steps back to watch the forms of transcendence fly
> up like sparks from a fire; it slackens the intentional threads which attach us
> to the world and thus brings them to our notice. . . . The need to proceed by
> way of essences does not mean that philosophy takes them as its object, but
> on the contrary, that our existence is too tightly held in the world to be able
> to know itself as such at the moment of its involvement, and that it requires
> the field of ideality in order to become acquainted with and *to prevail over its*
> *facticity.* (Ibid., pp. xiii, xv, emphasis added)

Reflection is not some pure theory unconditioned by our purposes. Our projects, in this case becoming more nearly autonomous, precede and guide our reflection as much as they result from it.

Third, although the method of phenomenological reduction—the slacken-ing of the intentional threads, the move to ideality—suspends the natural standpoint, "the most important lesson which the reduction teaches us is the impossibility of a complete reduction[;] radical reflection amounts to a consciousness of its own dependence on an unreflective life which is its initial situation . . . phenomenological reduction belongs to existential philosophy" (ibid., p. xiv).[2] In other words, although the goal of the process is to become the absolute source,[3] to be the sovereign choice of the traditions and horizons that guide interpretation, this is a goal that is never reached but is, at best, approxi-mated. Phenomenology takes the existential and hermeneutical turn when it acknowledges that distanciation always belongs to belonging, that reflection always presupposes the immediacy from which it seeks to free itself.

In relation to texts, Jacques Derrida speaks of an interpretation as a signifying structure that critical reading should *produce.* . . .

> To produce this signifying structure obviously cannot consist of reproducing,
> by the effaced and respectful doubling of commentary, the conscious, volun-
> tary, intentional relationship that the writer institutes in his exchanges with the
> history to which he belongs thanks to the element of language. This moment
> of doubling commentary should no doubt have its place in a critical reading.
> To recognize and respect all its classical exigencies is not easy and requires all
> the instruments of traditional criticism. Without this recognition and this
> respect, critical production would risk developing in any direction at all and
> authorize itself to say almost anything. But this indispensable guardrail has
> always only *protected*, it has never *opened*, a reading. (Derrida, 1974, p. 158)[4]

Once again we have distanciation insofar as the goal is to reproduce what the author said, or was trying to say, without our subjectivity influencing the result.

That is the task of "doubling commentary." The interpreter must neutralize, so far as possible, the contingency and particularity of the perspectives from which the text is read, so as simply to reproduce or mirror what the author meant. So much for the widespread view that deconstruction is a nihilism in which "anything goes." And once again we have method as the key to this distanciation from the interpreter's self and situation in order to let the author's self and situation shine through. The "instruments of traditional criticism"—grammatical, historical, psychological, and so forth—are the methods with which objectivity is sought in interpretation as reproduction of authorial intent.

But language, history, and psychology are double-edged swords. They signify forces that already inhabit the interpreter, worlds to which the interpreter always already belongs. Thus, for example, "Language has started without us, in us and before us. This is what theology calls God" (Derrida, 1992, p. 99). In other words, both author and interpreter belong to language before it belongs to them.

The theological reference is important, and not just because it is typical of the way in which, for Derrida, "God" is always the name for something else. God, according to a long tradition, created the world *ex nihilo*. We, by contrast, are finite, and neither the author nor the reader creates meaning; neither is an absolute source with absolute power over meaning.[5] This is why reproducing the authorial meaning, however close it comes to perfect mirroring (a regulative ideal to be sure), does not complete the task of interpretation.[6] By means of methodological distanciation, it provides a guardrail against the arbitrariness of an "anything goes" hermeneutic.[7] But since the author has always said both more and less than (s)he intended to say, distanciated mirroring, so far as it is possible, can only be a necessary condition of a good interpretation, not a sufficient one.. Reproduction is in the service of production.[8] The author and the interpreter are coproducers of the meaning of the text, just as the rule book and the umpire are coproducers of the strike zone in baseball.

I

Turning now to Gadamer, we find the concept of belonging has two distinct but interrelated meanings. The first is perhaps the more familiar. "In fact, history does not belong to us; we belong to it" (Gadamer, 1989, p. 276; cf. ibid., pp. 290, 295). Many of the most familiar concepts of Gadamer's hermeneutics cluster around this claim: prejudice, the hermeneutical circle, tradition, *wirkungsgeschichtliches Bewusstsein*, and application.

Prejudice. Immediately after the passage just cited, Gadamer says, "*That is why the prejudices of the individual, far more than his judgments, constitute the historical reality of his being*" (ibid., pp. 276–77). He understands the term in its etymological sense as prejudgment. It signifies the a priori element in our experience of/as interpretation, except that, in distinction from Kant, this element is not conceived to be ahistorically universal and necessary, but rather historically particular and contingent. Different individuals and different cultures have different prejudices, or prejudgments. The meaning is very close to what Husserl means by *horizon* and by *life-world,* "the pregiven basis of all experience . . . the whole in which we live as historical creatures" (ibid., pp. 245–47).[9]

Of course, "prejudice" can have its ordinary meaning; we must "break the spell of our own fore-meanings" so that the text can "present itself in all its otherness and thus assert its own truth against one's own fore-meanings" (ibid., pp. 268–69). But there are "legitimate" and "enabling" prejudices, those that are "true" insofar as they are the conditions of possible understanding, as well as those that are "false" insofar as they lead to misunderstanding (ibid., pp. 277, 295, 298–99).

Hermeneutical circle. The process by which we try to distinguish the "true" prejudices from the "false" ones is the hermeneutical circle. Every interpretation is guided by a preunderstanding, a projection of the whole in terms of which the parts are read. But the circle is not a vicious one because our presuppositions are not permanent but provisional. We can be "pulled up short by the text." Our fore-projections are "constantly *revised,*" and "every *revision* of the fore-projection is capable of projecting before itself a new projection of meaning[;] . . . interpretation begins with fore-conceptions that are *replaced* by more suitable ones" (ibid., pp. 267–68, emphasis added). Revise, revise, replace. The process is circular in the following sense. We can think of the movement from twelve o'clock to six o'clock as the process by which interpretations are guided by a priori projections of meaning, while the movement from six o'clock to twelve o'clock is the process by which those a priori projections, coming up against the alterity of the text, are revised or even replaced. Presupposition and interpretation are determined by one another. In Kantian language, the a priori conditions the empirical, but then the empirical in turn conditions the a priori, which (against Kant) thereby manifests its particularity and contingency.

Tradition. Gadamer sees the demand to escape this hermeneutical circle by breaking free from all prejudices as itself the "prejudice against prejudice itself" that on the one hand defines the Enlightenment and on the other hand "denies tradition its power" (ibid., pp. 270, 276). Gadamer does not hesitate to call the power of tradition its authority. The language is descriptive. Romanticism sees, as Enlightenment does not, that "that which has been sanctioned by tradition and custom *has* an authority that is nameless, and our finite historical being is marked by the *fact* that the authority of what has been handed down to us—and not just what is clearly grounded—always *has* power over our attitudes and behavior" (ibid., p. 280, emphasis added). This is why Gadamer's concern is "not what we do or what we ought to do, but what happens to us over and above our wanting and doing" (ibid., p. xxviii).

Reason itself is finite. It is because we are "situated within traditions" that "the idea of an absolute reason is not a possibility for historical humanity. Reason exists for us only in concrete, historical terms" (ibid., p. 276). There is something of Greek tragedy in this "insight into the limitations of humanity, into the absoluteness of the barrier that separates man from the divine. . . . Real experience is that whereby man becomes aware of his finiteness. In it are discovered the limits of the power and self-knowledge of his planning reason" (ibid., p. 357). The desire for absolute autonomy is not only hubris; it is a misunderstanding of what it means to be human.

Wirkungsgeschichtliches Bewusstsein. This last citation comes from Gadamer's analysis of consciousness, not as a transparent and unconditioned source of meaning, but as historically effected by virtue of its being situated in and saturated by the historical traditions without which it would be only an abstract possibility and not a concrete reality. Here, the root verb, *wirken*, points not only to the passivity of having been produced but also to the process of becoming actual or real in the only way human beings can be more than figments of their own imagination. By the concept of historically effected consciousness, Gadamer means "at once the consciousness effected in the course of history and determined by history, and the very consciousness of being thus effected and determined" (ibid., p. xxxiv). But the consciousness of being inescapably such a consciousness is the end of the Enlightenment Project, the existential and hermeneutical turn, the transition from modernity to postmodernity.[10]

Gadamer seems to understate his position when he writes, "At any rate, our usual relationship to the past is not characterized by distancing and freeing ourselves from tradition." Usual? As if sometimes we do so free ourselves? Gadamer immediately countermands any such reading: "Rather, we are *always* situated within traditions, and this is no objectifying process—i.e., we do not conceive of what tradition says as something other, something alien. It is *always* part of us" (ibid., p. 282, emphasis added). This obviously means that any methodological distanciation we might undertake will itself always be situated and tradition laden.

Application. Gadamer regularly insists that application is an essential part of interpretation and not a subsequent and different activity. Application does not consist "in relating some pregiven universal to the particular situation. The interpreter dealing with a traditionary text tries to apply it to himself. But this does not mean the text is given for him as something universal, that he first understands it per se, and then afterward uses it for particular applications. . . . Application is the very understanding of the universal" (ibid., pp. 324, 341).[11] In the case of law, for example, it is not a matter of subsuming the particular under the universal that can be fully understood without it, but of rendering the law determinate by concretizing it (ibid., pp. 329–30).

Another way of making the same point is to say the task is to relate the past to the present, to show what a text *means*, not simply what it *meant* once upon a time. In that light, interpretation must be faithful to the past, to be sure,[12] but also to the present (ibid., pp. 310, 326–28). This means, of course, that "a person reading a text is himself part of the meaning he apprehends. He belongs to the text he is reading" (ibid., p. 340).[13] It is addressed to the reader and makes claims on the reader,[14] and it cannot do this if the reader's present is neutralized in a reproduction that distances the reader from the present world and makes the reader contemporary with the past world of the author and the original audience for the text. In short, "temporal distance is not something that must be overcome" (ibid., p. 297). Whether we are reading the Bible, or Shakespeare, or the Constitution of the United States, we are situated in, and conditioned by, a different world from the one in which the text emerged.[15] The "fusion of horizons" (ibid., pp. 305–07, 373–75) is not the collapsing of the difference between the two, through empathy perhaps, but the attempt to enlarge both so that they overlap significantly. The past is enlarged as it is concretized in relation to the present, and the present is enlarged by taking the past to heart, or at least into account as addressed to the present.

Thus, it is in terms of application that we can most easily understand why, for Gadamer, distanciation is always in the service of belonging. "The real meaning of a text, as it speaks to the interpreter, does not depend on the contingencies of the author and his original audience. It is not identical with them, for it is also always codetermined by the historical situation of the interpreter." The consequence of this is clear. "Not just occasionally but always, the meaning of a text goes beyond its author. That is why understanding is not merely a reproductive, but always a productive, activity as well."[16] To guard against misunderstanding, Gadamer adds, "Understanding is not, in fact, understanding better. . . . It is enough to say that we understand in a *different* way if we understand at all" (ibid., pp. 296–97).

II

I have tried to show how central themes of Gadamer's hermeneutics cluster around the notion of the interpreter as belonging to a world, a horizon of meaning and expectation that functions as the a priori conditions of the possibility of experience as interpretation. In the process we have come across a second meaning of belonging, expressed in a passage just cited: the reader "belongs to the text he is reading" (ibid., p. 340), not just to the traditions that condition interpretation (and make it possible). The text is incomplete without the reader; because it is a mixture of determinacy and indeterminacy, the author and reader will have to be codeterminers of the meaning. The author gives a certain determinacy, which is why we are not talking about an "anything goes" hermeneutics in which the text "means whatever we take it to mean."[17] But the incomplete determinacy of the text calls upon the interpreter to render it more fully determinate, to concretize it in new and different contexts.

That the interpreter *belongs to history* (traditions, horizons, life-worlds, language-games, cultural self-evidences, etc.) means that fully distanciated (objective, unsituated, presuppositionless, unprejudiced) interpretation is simply not possible. We are too finite, too concrete for that. Vis-à-vis the Enlightenment's aspiration for that kind of neutral (or neutered?), unconditioned objectivity, that conclusion is bad news.[18] For Gadamer, however, this limitation is not a fate to be outwitted and escaped, but the simple fact that we are human and not divine. Accepting the finitude of our historicality is like accepting the finitude of our embodiment. Moreover, at least for Gadamer, the fact the reader "*belongs to the text* that he is reading" (our second sense of belonging) is good news. It means the text is not a lifeless artifact but a living voice that has its own history. It belongs not in our museums or mausoleums but in our churches (Bible), our schools (Shakespeare), our law courts (Constitution), and wherever people read. Let those who have ears to hear listen carefully! As we interpret, these texts address us and make truth claims on us.

What kind of truth? The negative part of Gadamer's argument is to distance hermeneutics from the distanciated, methodological objectivism of the natural sciences (*Naturwissenschaften*). The positive part of his argument is to turn to the human sciences (*Geisteswissenschaften*) to find domains in which the truth that belongs to belonging (in both senses) is found. One might say that *Truth and Method* reinforces the duality of explanation (*Erklären*), as found especially in the natural sciences, and understanding (*Verstehen*) as found in the human sciences.[19]

It might seem that, by contrast with Heidegger, for whom hermeneutics is "radicalized" (Ricoeur, 1981, p. 44) by being extended to every aspect of human cognition, Gadamer gives us a narrower theory of interpreting just texts. But for two reasons this not quite right. He will argue, as we will see, that methodological, distanciated, explanatory science is itself a mode of interpretation and subject to the basic structures thereof; and his focus on the human sciences includes not just texts but "works" that in a broader sense especially include nonverbal works of art such as music, pictures, and sculpture. The scope is roughly that of the cultural deposits and works referred to by Ricoeur.[20]

In answering the question regarding what kind of truth is to be found in the *Geisteswissenschaften*, Gadamer presents two models that help us understand an important consequence of the notion that interpretation is productive and not just reproductive, namely that there can be numerous interpretations of the same work, interpretations that differ from one another without any of them being false. Different understandings do not necessarily involve misunderstanding. The first paradigm is performance. Musicians interpret sonatas and symphonies by playing them, and actors interpret plays by performing them. In both cases there are performances that are just plain wrong, violations of the letter and/or spirit of the score or script. But there is no such thing, in spite of marketing propaganda, as THE DEFINITIVE interpretation of the Appassionata Sonata or *King Lear*. There will be numerous performances, live and recorded or filmed, that the most discriminating experts will describe in superlatives. Although I might prefer Schnabel's Beethoven to Brendel's, I do not for a moment think the former makes the latter a misinterpretation.

The same logic applies to translations, whether we speak of Homer, of the Bible, of Dante, or of Kant. It is far from being the case that "anything goes," and some translations will be judged to be too mistake-ridden, or too clunky, to be acceptable. However, there will be variety of translations that, while different from each other, will be judged to be excellent from both a linguistic and literary point of view. Distinguishing good from bad interpretations, or perhaps better from worse, will be more complex than determining that 54 is a good answer and 56 is a bad answer to the question, "How much is 9 x 6?" This is as it should be, for (as Aristotle reminds us) our level of precision should correspond to the nature of our subject matter.

But that which especially concerns us in Gadamer's answer to the question, "What kind of truth?" is the way in which he argues that interpretation, and thus the interpreter *belongs* to the work. Gadamer makes an ontological claim: "understanding belongs to the being of that which is understood" (Gadamer, 1989, p. xxxi). He expresses the same claim in these rhetorical questions: "Is the meaning of all texts *actualized* only when they are understood? In other words, does being understood *belong* [*gehört*] to the meaning of a text just as being heard [*Zu-Gehör-Bringen*] *belongs* to the meaning of music?" (ibid., p. 164, emphasis added). Or again, "*all encounter with the language of art is an encounter with an unfinished event and is itself part of this event. . . .* There is no absolute progress and no final exhaustion of what lies in a work of art" (ibid., pp. 99–100).

Gadamer asks us to consider the experience of dramatic art in a play under four headings: absorption, correctness, identity in difference, and truth. We might add the movie or the television drama, insofar as these are art and not merely entertainment.[21]

Absorption. "Play," Gadamer tells us, "fulfills its purpose only if the player loses himself in play" (ibid., p. 102).[22] The play "absorbs the player into itself, and thus frees him from the burden of taking the initiative" (ibid., p. 105). The experience is one of "being outside oneself[,] . . . of being wholly with something else. This kind of being present is a self-forgetfulness" (ibid., p. 126).[23]

Of course this absorption is not automatic. I remember seeing Richard Burton in *Equus* years ago. At least for that night he was not "on"; he was just reciting his lines. Of course, hearing Richard Burton recite his lines is worth the price of admission, but it was, by Gadamerian criteria, bad acting. A "dramatic" contrast for me occurred when I saw Frank Langella in *Frost/Nixon*. In the drunken rant in which he explained to Frost how "they" would never respect "us" no matter how high we get, I had a sense of meeting the real Nixon more fully than when in 1960 I shook his hand in real life after a campaign rally. Nor was this an accident. Langella had immersed himself in the study of Nixon's whole life, the better to become him before the cameras.

The difference between that Burton and that Langella was not the difference between fact and fiction. Nixon's rant was doubtless a piece of historical fiction, not derived from a White House taping system; and when I had seen Langella, years earlier, in *Long Day's Journey Into Night,* his absorption into Edmund made a fictional character into the *ens realissimum* while the lights were down and for a good while thereafter.

Correctness. In these three encounters I met three people: Richard Burton, Richard Nixon, and Edmund. In other words, when (and only when) absorption culminates in self-forgetfulness, acting is not the presentation of the actor but of someone else. In a different context, Hegel describes "scientific" philosophy in similar terms.

> Instead of *entering into* the immanent content of the thing, [mere Understanding] is forever surveying the whole and *standing above* the particular existence of which it is speaking [distanciation], i.e., it does not see it at all. Scientific cognition, on the contrary, demands *surrender* to the life of the object, or, what amounts to the same thing, confronting and expressing its inner necessity. Thus, *absorbed* in its object, scientific cognition forgets about that general survey, which is merely the reflection of the cognitive process away from the content and back into itself [interpretation as self-projection]. Yet, *immersed* in the material, and advancing with its movement, scientific cognition does come back to itself. (Hegel, 1977, p. 32, emphasis added, cf. p. 3)

Ironically, Hegel sees this surrender/absorption/immersion as the means of the self returning to itself, while Gadamer sees it in the service of the voice of another that addresses claims to the interpreter, in the present case to the actor and the audience. What these two accounts share, however, is a repudiation of a subjectivism in which the interpreter projects himself or herself onto the subject matter as described, perhaps, by Feuerbach or Freud.

Thus it is precisely this surrender/absorption/immersion that prevents interpretation from lapsing into subjectivism.

> Thus it is not at all a question of a mere subjective variety of conceptions, but of the work's own possibilities of being that emerge as the work explicates itself, as it were, in the variety of its aspects . . . one fails to appreciate the obligatoriness of the work of art if one regards the variations possible in the presentation as free and arbitrary. In fact they are all subject to the supreme criterion of "right" representation. (Ibid., p. 118)

Gadamer acknowledges the criterion of a " 'correct' presentation" is

> a highly flexible and relative one. But the fact that the representation is bound to the work is not lessened by the fact that this bond can have no fixed criterion. Thus we don't allow the interpretation of a piece of music or a drama the freedom to take the fixed "text" as a basis for arbitrary, ad-lib effects, and yet we would regard the canonization of a particular interpretation . . . as a failure to appreciate the real task of interpretation. . . . In view

of the finitude of our historical existence, it would seem that there is something absurd about the whole idea of a unique, correct interpretation. (Ibid., p. 119)

Identity in Difference. We have just heard Gadamer speak of the play explicating itself "in the variety of its aspects" and repudiating the notion of a particular, "canonized" interpretation, the one "unique, correct interpretation." He asks "what this identity is that presents itself so differently in the changing course of ages and circumstances. It does not disintegrate into the changing aspects of itself so that it would lose all identity, but it is there in them all. They belong to it" (ibid., pp. 120–21). Speaking of the festival, a kind of play in which all participants are on stage, so to speak, he says that "its own original essence is always to be something different. . . . An entity that exists only by always being something different is temporal in a more radical sense than everything that belongs to history. It has its being only in becoming and return" (ibid., p. 123).

This identity in difference is the *raison d'être* of the text or the work, of that which gives itself to be interpreted. It is abstract and incomplete apart from the series of "readings" that history gives to it, and it retains its identity "however much it is transformed and distorted in being presented" (ibid., p. 122). I remember hearing a concert in which an East German pianist made Chopin sound like music to goose-step to. But painful as it was to listen, the "music" was unmistakably Chopin.

But Gadamer is doing hermeneutics and, only incidentally, aesthetics. What is the denouement of this drama about the dramatic arts that Gadamer is staging? We can recall that the underlying, motivating question was about the kind of truth that belongs to belonging, in its double sense. The text, or the work, creates a world that is not "the world in which we live as our own." The question is not whether it is real or even realistic "because a superior truth speaks from it. . . . In being presented in play, what is emerges" (ibid., p. 112).[24] This world is "a wholly transformed world. In and through it everyone recognizes that that is how things are" (ibid., p. 113). Here, we hear echoes of Walter Cronkite's famous sign-off, "And that's the way it is." Gadamer, in effect, assimilates the task of the interpreter of text and work to that of the most trusted reporter. "From this viewpoint 'reality' is defined as what is untransformed, and art is the raising up [*Aufhebung*] of this reality into its truth" (ibid., p. 113). Like Plato's sensible world and Hegel's empirical world not yet *aufgehoben* into the Idea, Gadamer's text, or work, is not quite real. It becomes actual only in the historical diversity of interpretations that belong to its very being. That is what Langella did with the historical Nixon and the fictional Edmund. His portrayals brought human life to life so powerfully and vividly that, to this day, I get chills thinking about it. I learned more from him about reality than from scores of nightly newscasts.

The event in which texts and works are produced and then, no doubt with the help of scholarly reproduction (Derrida's doubling commentary), produced again (not reproduced in the sense of mirroring) in interpretations that bring the original seed toward its completion (without ever arriving there) is the event in which being and truth happen as two sides of the same coin.

Gadamer will develop his account of truth in art with respect to the plastic arts and to literature, where every reading is at once performance and translation. But we have enough before us to summarize, at least provisionally, Gadamer's deep commitment to belonging. Because the *interpreter belongs to history and its traditions*, the objectivity of unsituated, presuppositionless "interpretation," if it could still be called that, is not a human possibility. But in light of the fact that interpretation and thus, *the interpreter, belong to the very being of what is to be interpreted*, that is just as well. For the text, or work, is not the kind of "thing" that is well suited to the univocal construal that is so often the goal, the promise, and even the claim of various methods of distanciation. In its determinacy it is indeterminate, and in its actuality it remains a possibility. It needs to be actualized, or concretized, through the many, inevitably different and yet faithful, interpretations that can be given to it.

III

Distanciation does not get much respect in Gadamer's hermeneutics, which is overwhelmingly devoted to belonging. In his polemic against methodological objectivism—which he finds to be neither possible nor desirable—he seems to have people like Dilthey in mind. Based on his studies of Schleiermacher and Hegel, and on his own research as a cultural historian, Dilthey was keenly aware of the hermeneutical circle and the historical relativity of human culture. He was smitten with a bad case of the "vertigo of relativity."[25] He writes:

> The finitude of every historical phenomenon . . . the relativity of every kind of human apprehension of the totality of things is the last word of the historical world-view. . . . And over against this both the demand of thought and the striving of philosophy for universally valid knowledge assert themselves. . . . But where are the means to overcome the anarchy of opinions that then threatens to befall us?

It is to answer this last question that he devotes his life project, "a critique of historical reason." Just as Kant responded to what he understood to be Hume's skepticism with a critique of pure, and then practical, reason, so Dilthey sought to respond to the historical relativity of human culture with a critique of historical reason.

In the first two paragraphs of an important essay on hermeneutics, he states as his goals "*scientific* knowledge," "objectivity," and "universal validity." Then he gives two crucial definitions. Understanding is to be rule-guided. "Such *rule-guided understanding of fixed and relatively permanent objectifications of life is what we call exegesis of interpretation*," and "Hermeneutics is the theory of the rules of interpreting written monuments" (Dilthey, 1996, pp. 235–38). These rules will be the method of distanciation by means of which objective and universally valid knowledge of historically relative cultures will be obtained. Cultures may be tradition-relative, but scientific knowledge need not be.[26]

Ricoeur sees Gadamer and himself as engaged in a critique (in the Kantian sense) of the human sciences. But, unlike Dilthey, these two are post-Enlightenment, postmodern thinkers who, on the inescapability of belonging, are closer to each other than to Dilthey. Ricoeur insists that his own work is "not neutral, in the sense of being free from presuppositions. Indeed, hermeneutics itself puts us on guard against the illusion or pretension of neutrality" (Ricoeur, 1981, p. 43). But he thinks Gadamer has tipped the scales too far in the direction of belonging and, thereby, slighted distanciation.

It can be left as an exercise for the reader to work out the deep agreements between Ricoeur and Gadamer on this point.[27] We can turn our attention immediately to the former's claim that the opposition between explanation and understanding, the classical way of speaking about distanciation and belonging, is "disastrous" (ibid., p. 43; cf. pp. 90, 92). Gadamer's work revolves around the "scandal" of alienating distanciation in modernity's understanding of the human sciences. "The methodology of these sciences ineluctably implies, in Gadamer's eyes, a distancing, which in turn expresses the destruction of the primordial relation of belonging [*Zugehörigkeit*] without which there would be no relation to the historical as such" (ibid., p. 60).

So we have a debate between Ricoeur's claim of disaster and Gadamer's claim of scandal. Ricoeur's proposal comes in the form of a question and an answer: "*how is it possible to introduce a critical instance into a consciousness of belonging which is expressly defined by the rejection of distanciation?* It is possible, in my view, only insofar as historical consciousness seeks not simply to repudiate distanciation but to assume it" (ibid., p. 61. The "rejection of distanciation" in question here is a rejection of the all-out objectivism envisioned by the likes of Dilthey, Hirsch, and Betti.[28] To "assume" distanciation, nevertheless, into historical consciousness (belonging, *wirkungsgeschichtliches Bewusstsein*) means to find a qualified place for objectification and explanation greater than Gadamer seems ready to permit.

Instead of "dichotomy" and "opposition," Ricoeur wants to see the "tension" between the two preserved in a "dialectic" in which they are "complementary," "interpenetrating," and "mediated by" each other (ibid., pp. 92, 43, 62, 212, 150–51, 95, 220). Explanation is a "stage" of understanding that takes place "within" or "at the very heart of belonging" (ibid., pp. 218, 62, 116). To see more clearly just what this relation is that Ricoeur describes in so many different ways, we need to pose two questions: How does he see distanciation (explanation, reflection) as possible? Why does he think it is necessary?

Explanation (methodological distanciation, reflective objectification) is possible because of the autonomy of the text. When discourse—in which someone says something about something to someone—moves from speech to writing, the author (the first someone of discourse) is absent from the reader (the second someone). This involves two changes from everyday oral discourse. First, the something about something of discourse, its content, becomes an "object" that escapes the control of the author. Second, the author becomes not so much the speaker as the producer of this object. Such an object is open to explanation, especially with respect to the conditions of its production (ibid., pp. 139–41, 146–49).

The text becomes an object in two ways. On one hand, in writing, the subject matter of discourse is given a structure than can be studied (ibid., pp. 92, 145, 161, 209–10, 216–20). Structuralism is always in the back of Ricoeur's mind, not least because it is an objectifying, distanciating *Geisteswissenschaft* that does not presuppose the psychologism that led Dilthey so sharply to separate explanation from understanding (ibid., pp. 145, 216).

But unless the point of structuralism is to point us to the "referent" of the text it is "reduced to a sterile game" at which no one would want to stop (ibid., p. 217). Like certain modes of biblical criticism, it would turn the text into "a cadaver handed over for autopsy" and "give the funeral eulogy of someone yet alive" (Ricoeur and LaCocque, 1998, p. xii). In other words, a certain rigor produces rigor mortis when the text is reduced to nothing but an object. Structuralism compromises the discourse character of the text by abstracting entirely from the two someones, the someone who says something and the someone to whom it is said. So while it can serve, it cannot replace the hermeneutics of belonging.

But it need not. The autonomy of the text does not mean the abolition of the author and thereby the subjectivity of the textual "object."

> Not that we can conceive of a text without an author. . . . But the text's career escapes the finite horizon lived by its author. What the text says now matters more than what the author meant to say, and every exegesis unfolds its procedures within the circumference of a meaning that has broken its moorings to the psychology of its author. (Ricoeur, 1981, p. 201)

In short, the text must signify a referent other than the author, but in such a way as to preserve its own subjectivity, its power to address us, or, as Gadamer would put it, make a claim on us. For this reason Ricoeur agrees with Gadamer that application and appropriation are essential to hermeneutics (ibid., p. 143). Thus, "the intended meaning of the text is not essentially the presumed intention of the author . . . but rather what the text means for whoever complies with its injunction" (ibid., p. 161).

What is that referent, and how does it address us? The referent is not the inner life of the author, hidden behind the text, but the world presented by the text, or, as Ricoeur likes to put it, the world opened up in front of the text. This world is a possible mode of being-in-the-world that is proposed to own being-in-the-world (ibid., pp. 47, 53, 93, 111, 141–42, 218). Insofar as a method such as structuralism can illumine this world as the text's reference, it is a valuable *stage* in the process of interpretation. Texts are like purposive actions or psychic symptoms. We understand *what* is happening when we can explain *why* it is happening (ibid., pp. 85, 213). This means that explanation need not be the imposition of an external method on a text, but more nearly an act *of* the text itself rather than an act *on* it (ibid., pp. 139, 162). "The distanciation in which [Gadamer's] hermeneutics tends to see a sort of ontological fall from grace appears as a positive *component of being* for the text; it characteristically *belongs* to interpretation, not as its contrary but as its condition" (ibid., p. 91, emphasis added; cf. p. 131). In other words, the text invites explanation. Just as for Gadamer performance *belongs* to the score or script, so for Ricoeur explanation *belongs* to the text. It is meant to be explained *so as to be understood.*

This belonging of distanciation and explanation to belonging and understanding is the first answer to our second question: assuming that it is somehow possible, why is the moment of explanation necessary? It is necessary because the ontology of the text as object requires that we treat it as an object precisely to preserve its subjectivity, the alterity of its voice. But Ricoeur gives at least two other reasons, one concerning validity and one concerning critique.

As an object the text is like an object of visual perception. It is perceived from a variety of perspectives, which is why there is a multiplicity and indeed a conflict of interpretations. But they are not all equal, as if "anything goes." Hirsch's question about validity in interpretation is as legitimate as Gadamer's concern to distinguish the "true" prejudices—or perspectives that give rise to understanding—from the "false" ones that give rise to misunderstanding. Distanciated explanation of how and why a text has come into being (that is, an examination of the conditions of its production) introduces a moment of objectivity into the attempt to avoid both dogmatism and skepticism in working within the hermeneutical circle (ibid., pp. 211–13). It serves a function, like Derrida's "doubling commentary," that is a methodological guardrail against arbitrary readings, a necessary but not sufficient condition of interpretation.

After the ontology of the text and the need for validity, a third reason for seeing explanation as a necessary moment in interpretation is Ricoeur's desire to find "an orientation of thought which is less subordinated [than Gadamer's] to the problematic of tradition and more receptive to the critique of ideology" (ibid., p. 66). This is the point at which Ricoeur turns our attention to the Gadamer-Habermas debate.[29] Actually, more is at issue than this particular debate. Ideology critique in the tradition of Marx and western Marxism is for Ricoeur one dimension of the hermeneutics of suspicion, whose masters he identifies as Marx, Nietzsche, and Freud (Ricoeur, 1970, p. 32).[30] Here, critique signifies the exposure of the false-consciousness in which individuals and groups hide the deepest motivations for their beliefs and practices and the critique, prophetic in nature, of the traditions and institutions that embody and support such self-deception.[31] Here, explanation serves understanding by helping us to see *what* is going on as we find out *why* it occurs. In his work as a whole, Ricoeur devotes far more attention to critique in this sense than to the explanation that methodologies like structuralism make possible.[32] To understand by means of this kind of explanation is to discredit, if not the beliefs and practices in question directly, at least the way in which they function in the lives of some believers and practitioners.

This is, no doubt, Ricoeur's most serious complaint about Gadamer's hermeneutics. In rehabilitating tradition and its authority, Gadamer mentions the need to distinguish "true" from "false" presuppositions, but leaves this dimension of the hermeneutical task underdeveloped. We need the moment of distanciation as a guardrail against simply projecting ourselves into the text. But even more, we need it as a prophylactic against the traditions and institutions that support such suppression of the text's alterity. If we are rightly to hear tradition's claims on us as a voice other than our own, we need to treat it as an object accessible through distanciated reflection.

How can Gadamer respond to this criticism that his hermeneutics is insufficiently critical? To begin, he will remind us of why he claims universal scope for hermeneutics. He quotes Dilthey's reference to a certain Wilhelm Scherer. "He was a modern man, and the world of our forebears was no longer the *home* of his spirit and his heart, but his historical *object*." Gadamer comments: "The antithesis shows that for Dilthey scientific knowledge obliges one to sever one's bond with *life*, to attain distance from one's own *history*, which alone makes it possible for that history to become an *object*" (Gadamer, 1989, p. 7, emphasis added). In other words, just as Merleau-Ponty argues that we can never completely neutralize the natural attitude and become pure, transcendental thought, Gadamer argues that we can never leave home completely. We can move to another home, a new perspective, which, in turn, will be conditioned by the homes that preceded it on our journey and will provide new prejudgments.

Distanciation as the move to a new home, a new belonging? Yes. "For Helmholtz," Gadamer writes, "the methodological ideal of the natural sciences needed neither to be historically derived nor epistemologically restricted" (ibid., p. 6). For Gadamer, the appeal to a distanciated objectivity is always both. "Historically derived?" Yes, it emerges out of traditions to which it is indebted; it does not create itself *ex nihilo*. Moreover, it becomes a tradition itself, which is to say that it is "epistemologically restricted." It is, itself, one possible perspective; like other perspectives it enables us to see some things and keeps us from seeing others. In other words, it is not just the case that there are paradigms within science; science itself, as the project of methodologically desituating knowledge, is itself a paradigm—and not the only one. "Is not the fact that consciousness is historically conditioned inevitably an insuperable barrier to its reaching perfect fulfillment in historical knowledge?" This rhetorical question is directed not only against the Hegelian claim to absolute knowledge but also against Dilthey's claim to objectivity (ibid., p. 231).

This is not an unqualified repudiation of distanciation. In the *Geisteswissen-schaften* our historical tradition in all its forms is certainly made the *object* of investigation, but at the same time *truth comes to speech in it* . . . the experience of historical tradition reaches far beyond those aspects of it than can be objectively investigated. It is true or untrue not only in the sense concerning which historical criticism decides, but always mediates truth in which one must *try to share*. (Ibid., p. xxiii)

In the foreword to the second edition of *Truth and Method*, Gadamer repeats, "Therefore I did not remotely intend to deny the necessity of methodical work within the human sciences" (ibid., p. xxix). But this might seem to apply only to the first two of the three necessities identified by Ricoeur: the need to treat the textual object as an object and the need to do so in the service of validity, as a guardrail against arbitrary readings. What about ideology critique? Is hermeneutics politically passive to a fault? Gadamer replies to the charge that his hermeneutic universalism "lacks a critical principle in relation to tradition and, as it were, espouses a universal optimism. . . . Understanding certainly does not mean merely appropriating customary opinions or acknowledging what tradition has sanctified." But he admits, "I have emphasized the assimilation of what is past and of tradition" (ibid., p. xxxvii).

These last responses come in 1965, before the debate with Habermas. But after that debate, without denying that Habermas seeks to ground ideology critique on a more sophisticated objectivism than Dilthey's,[33] Gadamer repeats his basic point. Hermeneutics remains fundamental, because "the work of ideology critique has a dialectical structure. It is related to determinate social conditions upon which it has corrective and dismantling effects. It belongs itself, then, to the social process that it criticizes. That is the ineluctable presupposition that cannot be replaced by any scientific pretension" (Gadamer, 1981, p. 79).

So it is not just a matter of emphasis with reference to social critique, no trivial matter to be sure.[34] There remains a fundamental onto-epistemic disagreement. Hegel's conception of *Aufhebung* can be helpful here, according to which X is *aufgehoben* in Y if X is denied the autonomy and primacy sometimes given to it and is recontextualized as a subordinate moment in Y, whose fundamental principle it is not. So we might say that for Habermas, belonging is to be acknowledged, but it is, as it were, *aufgehoben* as a surpassable moment in a reconceived strategy of distanciation. For Gadamer, by contrast, there is a legitimate place for distanciation, but it is *aufgehoben* in a historical belonging that it cannot and need not escape.

Ricoeur expresses the same thought in different words. Gadamerian hermeneutics "claims to set itself up as a critique of [Habermasian] critique, or meta-critique" (Ricoeur, 1981, p. 76). Habermas, using psychoanalysis as a model for ideology critique, sees it as a "depth hermeneutics" that invokes theoretical explanations and is thus a "meta-hermeneutics" (ibid., pp. 84–85, 95). Ricoeur, ever the mediator, sides first with Habermas, and then with Gadamer. With Habermas he sees a need, overlooked by Gadamer, for critique, for a hermeneutics of suspicion, of which ideology critique in the Marxist tradition is an instance. But he sides with Gadamer on the onto-epistemic question, rejecting Habermas's attempt to salvage modernity's objectivism by a switch from method to conversation. After all, he says, "a depth hermeneutics is still a hermeneutics, even if it is called meta-hermeneutical" (ibid., p. 97).

In light of the conversation between Gadamer and Ricoeur we can conclude that hermeneutics is incurably dialectical. Not, of course, in the sense where dialectic is a method that leads to systematic synthesis and organic harmony. No, it is dialectical in the sense that it is a *lived tension* that it does not try to eliminate. The tension is between inside and outside, between (a) interpreting from within horizons of expectation inherited as presuppositions from language, culture, and tradition, and (b) trying to stand back from this immersed belonging with the help of various methods, Derrida's "instruments of traditional criticism," so as to guard against subjectivism, ideology in the Marxist sense, and fundamentalism in its present usage. Dialectical tensions are not comfortable, and the temptation is to privilege one pole to the virtual exclusion of the other. The French—Ricoeur and Derrida—call Gadamer back from such a danger, without lapsing into equal but opposite danger, the spurious objectivism of Dilthey, Betti, and Hirsch. Gadamer welcomes their warning and insists he does not mean to exclude distanciation and critique. But he reminds us that the methods of distanciation are themselves instances of belonging. And yet, they function to challenge that self-enclosed mentality locked in by its horizons. Understanding the lived tension between belonging and distanciation is important. But more important is learning to live it, to do it in our ongoing tasks of interpreting texts and all the text-like things that make up the world.

Notes

[1] Thus he speaks of "the detour through the contingency of cultures, though an incurably equivocal language, and through the conflict of interpretations" (Ricoeur, 1970, p. 494). There is also "the long detour of the signs of humanity deposited in cultural works" and of "the detour of understanding the cultural signs in which the self documents and forms itself [so that] reflection is nothing without the mediation of signs and works. . . . " (Ricoeur, 1981, pp. 143, 158–59).

[2] Ricoeur traces "the existential turn of transcendental phenomenology" in (Ricoeur, 1967, pp. 202–12).

[3] Not a bad summary of the Enlightenment Project. For Emmanuel Levinas's attempt to give an ethical twist to the existential turn, see (Levinas, 1998).

[4] This statement comes immediately after Derrida agrees with Gadamer and Ricoeur that the author does not unilaterally determine meaning. "The reading must always aim at a certain relationship, unperceived by the writer, between

what he commands and what he does not command of the patterns of the language that he uses."

[5]   On the importance of this theological language in the "death of the author" discourse in Foucault and Barthes as well as Derrida, see (Westphal, 2002).

[6]   Richard Rorty uses the mirror metaphor to express modernity's aspirations toward pure, presuppositionless objectivity; and he sees the abandonment of this ideal as the movement "from epistemology to hermeneutics" (Rorty, 1979, ch. VII). But, of course, hermeneutics is epistemology as a theory of the nature and limits of human knowledge. See (Westphal, 1999).

[7]   So far as I can see, such a hermeneutic exists only in the fantasy of those who think they can establish the triumph of distanciating objectivity over belonging by refuting it. But not even Nietzsche, as radical a perspectivist as one might hope to find, thinks that "anything goes," that, for example, Christianity and Platonism are just as good as the will to power and the overman.

[8]   Very possibly Derrida has Gadamer in mind in using the language of production, reproduction, and belonging here. For the "more than" and "less than" theme in Gadamerian context, see (Weberman, 2002, pp. 45–78).

[9]   Gadamer also links the idea to Heidegger's notion of a "hermeneutics of facticity" (Gadamer, 1989, p. 254; cf. Heidegger, 1999).

[10] Big tent postmodernism includes not just French poststructuralism but all those who decisively abandon the Enlightenment's prejudice against prejudice and the corresponding tradition that seeks to free itself from tradition. The existentialist connection is perhaps best seen in Kierkegaard's *Concluding Unscientific Postscript*, where Johannes Climacus satirizes the Hegelians who, in their demand for absolute knowing, forget who they actually are and see themselves as an abstraction that has no reality, or as an absoluteness that exists only in God.

[11] In his attempt to preserve an objectivism in which distanciation triumphs over belonging, E. D. Hirsch, Jr. insists on sharply separating interpretation and meaning from application, which he calls significance, the "value or present relevance" of a text (Hirsch, 1967, p. 8). To allow application to be intrinsic to interpretation would be to allow the interpreter to be a coproducer of a text's meaning, and Hirsch holds the weird view that unless the author is the sole and unilateral giver of source of a text's meaning the author becomes completely irrelevant and the interpreter need not be in the least concerned with what the author was saying or trying to say.

[12] This is what Derrida referred to above as doubling commentary that functions as a guardrail to keep interpretation from being subjective in the sense of arbitrary.

[13] This last sentence signifies the second sense of belonging in Gadamer, to which we shall shortly turn.

[14] This theme of the text not merely as an object to be mastered but as a subject, a voice by which we are addressed and which makes claims on us, is far more important to Gadamer's argument than this essay has indicated.

[15] Schleiermacher's attempt to develop a general or "deregionalized" (Ricoeur, 1981, p. 44) hermeneutics was the attempt to show what is common to three disciplines where interpretation is central: theology, literary criticism, and law. Hence the three texts cited. On Schleiermacher as a "founding father" of philosophical hermeneutics, see (Westphal, 2001).

[16] So desperate is he to discredit Gadamer that Hirsch makes hash of this text by omitting both the "merely" and the "as well." His version reads, "Understanding is not a reproductive but always a productive activity" (Hirsch, 1967, p. 249). But this is very different from what Gadamer says. The German text reads, "*Daher ist Verstehen kein nur reproductives, sondern stets auch ein productives Verhalten.*" Hirsch conveniently omits the *nur* and the *auch*. He objects that for Gadamer the text "means whatever we take it to mean," but such interpretation is found not in Gadamer's theory, but in Hirsch's practice.

[17] See previous note.

[18] One can find that yearning for "scientific" objectivity not only in Hirsch (see note 11) but also in (Dilthey, 1996, pp. 235–58) and (Betti, 1980, pp. 51–94). The goal is to make the human sciences as "scientific" as the natural sciences. It also lies at the heart of the Gadamer-Habermas debate, of which more in due course.

[19] See (Dilthey, 1989) and the discussions in (Ermarth, 1978, especially ch. 5).

[20] See note 1 above.

[21] What Gadamer says about the play provides suggestive criteria for distinguishing the two, which is not to suggest that art cannot *also* be entertaining, providing ephemeral enjoyment and distraction from the numbing routines and debilitating traumas of daily life.

[22] Gadamer is speaking of play in an extended sense that includes games as well as dramas. Just as in the theater the "real" world fades into (near) oblivion, so for the athlete the game becomes the only reality for its duration.

[23] Gadamer says that this applies to the audience as well (Gadamer, 1989, pp. 110, 126, 128). Aristotle rightly notes "that the spectator belongs essentially to the playing of the play" (ibid., p. 130). So we have two levels of interpretation, that of the actors and that of the audience.

[24] This is a special case of Heidegger's view that the being of beings is their unconcealment, their presencing or coming to presence. Truth is to be found in presentation, not representation.

[25] This phrase is central to the discipline known as the sociology of knowledge (Berger and Luckmann, 1966; Berger, 1970, p. 32). Hirsch's almost pathological obsession with objectivity is an extreme case of this vertigo.

[26] For a similar statement of the problem and its solution, see (Mannheim, 1936). This way of thinking seems to presuppose a sharp fact/value dichotomy. The values of a culture will remain historically relative, while its factual knowledge of itself and other cultures will be objective. Thus Max Weber's claim to a value-neutral sociology. As Raymond Aron summarizes it, "One of the fundamental themes in Weberian thought is the antithesis between *Werturteil*, or value judgment, and *Wertbeziehung*, or value reference. Men make value judgments; they create values; historical existence is essentially a creation and affirmation of values. And the science of culture is a comprehension, through value-reference, of existences that are defined by the creation of values" (Aron, 1970, II, p. 249).

[27] See, for example, Ricoeur's account of the finitude of human understanding (Ricoeur, 1981, pp. 105–09).

[28] See notes 11 and 18 above.

[29] For our theme of belonging and distanciation, the key texts of this debate deserve a detailed analysis that cannot be given here (Gadamer, 1976a; Gadamer, 1976b;

Habermas, 1977, pp. 335–63; Habermas, 1980, pp. 181–211). For other perspectives on the issues involved see (Habermas et al., 1971).

[30] For Ricoeur's assessment of Freud, see also (Ricoeur, 1974, Part II). For Ricoeur's assessment of Marx, Althusser, and Habermas, see also (Ricoeur, 1986, ch. 2–8, 13–14).

[31] I have defined the hermeneutics of suspicion as "the deliberate attempt to expose the self-deceptions involved in hiding our actual operative motives from ourselves, individually or collectively, in order not to notice how and how much our behavior and our beliefs are shaped by values we profess to disown" (Westphal, 1998, p. 13). I argue that the origins of this kind of critique are biblical, especially in the Hebrew prophets, including Jesus.

[32] See, for example, the previous note.

[33] For Habermas, objectivity is achieved dialogically rather than monologically. In an interesting affinity with Gadamer, it is a matter of conversation rather than method.

[34] The difference of political import between the two theories can hardly be reduced to a difference of emphasis. In that connection there is a delightful irony in the personal relations between the two men. Back during the cold war, when Habermas was seen as a kind of Marxist rather than the liberal he later became, Horkheimer, of all people, blocked his *Habilitation* for being too leftist. But Gadamer gave him an extraordinary professorship in Heidelberg (roughly an associate professorship) on the basis of that dissertation even before he defended it in Marburg rather than Frankfurt (Grondin, 2003, p. 305).

Chapter 3

Hermeneutics as Project of Liberation: The Concept of Tradition in Paul Ricoeur and Hans-Georg Gadamer

Andreea Deciu Ritivoi

Although in the history of hermeneutics the exact identification of its origins and the tracing of its subsequent developments are still cause for debate, the traditional objects of study have been the law, scriptural writing, or philological (Greco-Latin) documents. What they all have in common is a pious attitude toward another region, or another era, whose positive role for the interpreter's own time and universe is recognized and actively probed for its formative lessons. In seeking to explain and provide an understanding of legal, scriptural, or philological texts, hermeneutics represents a concerted effort to create meaning-making rules and principles needed in understanding a way of being that is not (or is no longer) ours, yet remains salient. One can say, then, that hermeneutical reflection springs from a desire to understand a way of being other than one's own—whether this different order is the past or another culture—and the derived need to develop a procedure for gaining access to it. At the crux of the intellectual project of hermeneutics lies the task of understanding texts as messengers of another world, a world that is alien, but also relevant, indeed a source of enlightenment to the interpreter's own realm of reference.

It would seem, then, that hermeneutics should occupy a distinguished place in a global world that, increasingly, both values cultural difference, yet also must try harder than ever to accommodate it through mutual respect and understanding. Hermeneutic theorists, likewise, should be stars among other scholars. But in 1967, when Paul Ricoeur and Michel Foucault were both considered for the College de France chair, the appointment went to the latter. More than a contest between two individuals, this was in all likelihood also a competition between schools of thought. The victor was, at the time, Foucault's archeology of knowledge, rather than Ricoeur's phenomenological hermeneutics. It is probably not mere coincidence that in his inaugural address Foucault made some (only) slightly veiled remarks against hermeneutics (Foucault, 1972). Accused of foraying for meaning into nonexistent depths of language, hermeneutics appears on this account unable to account for the ideological forces that create meaning through discourse and, thus, incapable of explaining language use in its more ubiquitous and insidious manifestations. The charge, whether formulated in Foucault's elegant terms, or later in Jürgen Habermas's blunter terms (see below for a fuller discussion), defines the difficult position occupied by hermeneutics in the post-structuralist era.

In this chapter I propose a "defense" of hermeneutics, one based on a careful reevaluation of one of its core concepts, that of tradition. I focus on Hans-Georg Gadamer's conception of tradition, and then offer a modified understanding grounded in Ricoeur's concept of distanciation, a key contribution of his hermeneutical theory. Through such a revision, my goal is to present a hermeneutical project anchored in concepts that make it less vulnerable to the sort of criticisms adduced by Foucault and Habermas. I argue that Ricoeur's own hermeneutical theory can be described, to use his terms, as a "project of liberation" grounded in historical experience. Further, I discuss the fundamentals of such a project, focusing on its relationship to other hermeneutical theories, especially Gadamer's, and on Ricoeur's work on ideology and philosophy of language. The concept of tradition, as I use it in this paper, represents both—in Gadamerian terms—a "horizon," and—in Ricoeur's terms—a symbolic system that functions as the basis for self-understanding and self-transformation in a particular community. The latter definition is made available through Ricoeur's reflections on ideology and utopia.

I seek to incorporate these reflections into hermeneutical theory in order to address especially the criticism made by Habermas: that tradition, as defined by hermeneutics, can also systematically distort, and not only inform, understanding.

Hermeneutics in the Post-Structuralist Era

The rather controversial status of hermeneutics in the intellectual climate of the twentieth century has been indelibly shaped by its encounter with critical theory, through the confrontation between Jurgen Habermas and Hans-Georg Gadamer. The focus of their debate was the epistemological and moral implications and consequences of hermeneutics (especially in its Gadamerian design). Habermas's remarks reveal important questions that still need to be asked, especially when we approach hermeneutics as an analytical framework (rather than a strictly theoretical project). Habermas was especially concerned with the epistemological status of hermeneutics, specifically its role as a method of inquiry for the social sciences. Habermas saw Gadamer as trying to situate hermeneutics between the ideal of objective rationality espoused by positivism, and the rejection of such rationality, captured in the latter's rehabilitation of the concept of tradition. Habermas charged that without a firm grounding in a concept of rationality, hermeneutics lacks the critical distance it would need to reflect on its own methods and ideas. He was especially skeptical of Gadamer's notion of a fusion of horizons, not because he did not think we can understand another culture through a "fusing" of traditions, but because he was worried that such "fusion" might render us incapable of critiquing other cultures. Thus, Habermas charged, Gadamer had created a hermeneutical theory that had inadvertently "ontologized moral relativism" (Cameron, 1996, p.162).

Finally, Habermas also reproached Gadamer for his idealism, as revealed especially in the latter's claims that "linguistically articulated consciousness determines the material practice of life" (Habermas, 1997, p. 361). By ignoring the contingent nature of experience, shaped by power and wealth distribution, and through an overstated optimism regarding the possibility of understanding and accepting cultures and traditions other than our own, Gadamer created, in Habermas's view, a theory "apt to foster political conservatism." What hermeneutics lacked most sorely, according to Habermas, was a clearly articulated role for critique.

Ricoeur's position vis-à-vis this controversy was, characteristic of him, a carefully moderate one. In *Lectures on Ideology and Utopia*, he presents the debate between Habermas and Gadamer as not only the result of a clash in philosophical systems vying for epistemic superiority, but also the reflection of different political agendas. "For Habermas," Ricoeur claims,

> Gadamer is an old gentleman who must vote on the right, and so hermeneutics represents the conservation of the past in a kind of museum. Gadamer, on the other hand, sees Habermas as the radical who made concessions to the students and was punished for it. I no longer find interesting this opposition between the two figures, because I do not see how we can have a critique without also having an experience of communication. And this experience is provided by the understanding of texts. We learn to communicate by understanding texts. Hermeneutics without a project of liberation is blind, but a project of emancipation without historical experience is empty. (Ricoeur, 1986, pp. 236–37)

Ricoeur recognized this limitation, but unlike Habermas, who sought to replace hermeneutics with his own theory of ideology as communicative practice, he tried to reform the hermeneutical project upon the foundation set by Gadamer. The result was "critical hermeneutics," an original system of thought based on a rehabilitation of the epistemological question: how is it possible to interpret other texts and thus to understand other worlds and cultures? In his debate with Gadamer, Habermas complained that hermeneutics is solely committed to addressing this question in abstract terms, paying little attention to the concrete conditions of communication (material, ideological, cultural, political). As a way to defend hermeneutics against this charge, a logical move would be to point to the conceptual role played by tradition in hermeneutical theory—which would suggest that hermeneutics implicitly recognizes the significance of specific, contingent constraints on communication. Ironically, however, it is precisely this concept that, in Gadamer's work, remains rather vaguely defined.

Further, Gadamer's hermeneutics, which stays heavily grounded in his notion of "fusion of horizons," reveals a potentially naive optimism regarding the possibility of understanding, since it makes no proviso for situations wherein such fusion is hard to achieve, or where it altogether fails to take place. Thus, hermeneutics appears both too abstract and too idealistic to function as a method of analysis for the study of specific social and political phenomena.

Against this indictment, Georgia Warnke has tried to rehabilitate hermeneutical theory by showcasing, and then capitalizing on, precisely its analytic potential. In her study of current public debates over social issues in the United States—abortion, surrogate motherhood, affirmative action, and pornography—Warnke relies on hermeneutics as a way of avoiding an approach that would assume that one position in a debate must be illegitimate. Moreover, her recourse to hermeneutics is intended as a way of responding to the more common way in which the debates are approached, which, in her view, removes the debates from the domain of conflict of principle. She contends that "in contrast to this interpretive approach [one focused on conflict, ADR], our present debates over these issues can be characterized as mighty attempts by each side to ignore, dismiss, or find arguments against the view promoted by its opponents" (Warnke, 1999, p. 29).

For Warnke, taking a hermeneutic approach amounts to finding a way to see the validity in an opposing viewpoint, rather than dismissing it as illegitimate. Hermeneutics, for her, offers an analytic alternative to traditional agonistic approaches that view debates as confrontations that need to end with a clear winner and loser. Her goal in choosing this approach is to offer a modified intellectual foundation for policy making and decision making, one that no longer seeks to rule out invalid positions but, instead, is more content to look for potential points of compromise and accommodation. If hermeneutics can deliver on this front, the advantages are clearly major. Instead of perpetuating irreconcilable positions on key social issues, we can move toward a shared space of understanding in which different actors can appreciate each other's beliefs and arguments, and even accept some while still resisting others. As Warnke tries to refashion it, "a hermeneutic conception of our public debates might lead us . . . to appreciate the possibility of different legitimate compromises and accommodations arrived at in different states and communities with the salutary result that all can learn from the solutions or partial solutions each state and community has found to the understanding of principles we continue to share" (ibid., p. 192). This approach, Warnke admits, offers no normative gain, because it does not tell us which standpoint is valid, or should be accepted. Rather, hermeneutics can offer awareness of more than one option at a time, an important desideratum, Warnke believes, in a multicultural society such as ours.

Promising as it seems, Warnke's approach has been criticized for its lack of attention to the material constraints on communication and interpretation.

For instance, critics have charged that, even though concerned with debates that are squarely focused on the female body, her work pays no attention to how the body is conceptualized in these arguments (Laden, 2001). But the reproach can be generalized: while dealing with public policy and the very concrete aspects of life such policy impacts, Warnke promotes a rather abstract and idealistic approach that has little room for concrete details. Her frequent reliance on literary examples, while compelling on a conceptual plane, tidies up and glosses over precisely the more complicated and unruly aspects of experience. More importantly, although Warnke recognizes that different positions in the debates she discusses are grounded in their own traditions of values and beliefs, she remains overly optimistic, a priori, about the possibility of overcoming or avoiding the clash of traditions. In real (rather than fictional) situations, differences in tradition are more likely to become exacerbated rather than abrogated. Furthermore, Warnke is concerned with the legitimacy of a particular interpretation, and the grounds on which such legitimacy can be established. Her hope is that, once an interpretation can be reliably deemed legitimate, policy makers and decision makers can, and should, uphold it. For instance, once a particular interpretation of surrogate motherhood is considered legitimate—whether it is one that sees the surrogate as performing a contractual service, or by contrast, as abandoning her child—policies and even laws can be passed on the basis of that interpretation. In other words, the legitimacy of an interpretation serves as the foundation for normative interventions.

Warnke's main criterion for establishing the legitimacy of an interpretation is Gadamer's unity between part and whole: if all the details and aspects of an interpretation are coherent, and one particular dimension fits with all the other ones, then the interpretation can be deemed valid. But this criterion leaves out the issue of perspective: who decides whether the interpretation is coherent? What might seem coherent to one, will be grossly incoherent to another. Another criterion she uses for determining the legitimacy of an interpretation is confidence in one's interpretation. Says Warnke:

> Our textual interpretations are not ones about which we can have conviction as long as the concept of conviction implies an absolute trust in the correctness of our own views; nor are our interpretations ones that we think others could reject only on pain of irrationality. Rather, our textual interpretations are ones in which we appropriately have confidence as adequate, revealing, and illuminating interpretations insofar as they can tell us something about a text and, perhaps, even about ourselves. (Ibid., pp. 176–77)

The point in stressing the difference between confidence in one's interpretations and conviction that they are correct is to allow for the possibility that other interpretations might also be legitimate in their own way. As Warnke puts it, recognizing that the pro-choice and pro-life advocates have different

conceptions of motherhood does not mean that we should have to choose one
between them. She continues:

> Rather, each set of interpretations is one in which proponents can have
> confidence as a legitimate understanding that illuminates some part of what
> abortion, respect for the sanctity of life, sex, reproduction, and motherhood
> mean even if it cannot illuminate all of what any mean and, indeed, even if
> no interpretation can illuminate all of what any mean. But if each set of inter-
> pretations is one in which its advocates can have confidence as opposed to
> conviction, then might we not look for legislative solutions to the controversy
> abortion than try to accommodate both? (Ibid., p. 179)

If the answer to the above question is affirmative—as Warnke wants it to be—
we still have to pay attention to what could preclude, conceptually, a legislative
solution that accommodates different, indeed sometimes radically different,
interpretations. Thus, having confidence in one's interpretation might not be
sufficient for accepting the possibility that other interpretations are, in a different way, also enlightening for the issue at hand. What might also be needed
is a willingness or ability to recognize one's values and principles—and thus
oneself—in the world that is part of another interpretation. Such willingness
might come at a price: confidence in one's own interpretation can be considerably weakened when other interpretations are deemed potentially legitimate.
The new self-understanding made possible through another interpretation
might be more than one has bargained for, in the sense that it might require
additional changes in values and beliefs that would end up marking too much
of a departure from the original self. Finally, and perhaps most importantly,
the ability and willingness to accept that other interpretations might also be
valid is kept in check by one's tradition. If a member of a pro-life group sees
abortion as murder because she subscribes to a tradition of religious thought
that emphasizes the sanctity of life, then to see abortion as reflecting an
individual's personal procreative decision is difficult. It would entail the ability
to see oneself as not *bound* to respect the sanctity of life by having a baby, but
rather *free* to decide when and whether to have a baby. Even if we only have
confidence in our interpretations and do not insist on their correctness, the
traditions to which we subscribe might limit what else we can accept as potentially legitimate.

Still, one must applaud Warnke's efforts to offer an approach that recognizes
the importance of tradition, yet also sees ways of moving beyond it, in debates
about current affairs. In social and political matters, the focus on change is
important. How can one break off a traditional way of thinking and accept a
new, alternative way? As I try to show in the following sections, a response to this
question is what a "hermeneutic of liberation" can offer. I begin by investigating
the role historically played by tradition in hermeneutical theory, then present
the conceptual and methodological disadvantages associated with this role and,
finally, offer a revised conception of tradition that can reshape hermeneutics

into an intellectual framework systematically focused on understanding what makes change and transformation possible.

In the next section I discuss the emergence and role of the concept of tradition in hermeneutical theory, drawing especially on Gadamer's work, but also presenting the broader disciplinary context of his ideas.

The Concept of Tradition in Hermeneutical Theory

In its historical course from Friedrich Schleiermacher to Wilhelm Dilthey, hermeneutics has consistently viewed language, in Ricoeur's terms, as "an instrument at the service of individuality" (Ricoeur, 1991, 57). But what kind of individuality is this? For Gadamer, individuals are fundamentally historical beings, immersed in specific traditions and linguistic communities, who bring their experience and knowledge to the encounter with the text they are interpreting, and make sense of it in light of how they have been shaped by their own tradition and language. Gadamer writes:

> We are always situated in history[,] I mean that our consciousness is determined by real historical becoming in such a way that it does not have the freedom to situate itself over against the past. In addition, I mean that for us it is always a matter of becoming conscious once again of the action exerted upon us in this way, so that every past that we have just experienced obliges us to take complete charge of it, to assume in a way its truth. (Gadamer, 1967, p. 158, quoted and translated in Ricoeur, 1991, p. 72)

Understanding occurs, in Gadamer's account, as a result of a fusion of horizons (*Horizontverschmelzung*) that involves a double adjustment: of the interpreter's assumptions and expectations to those recognizable in the object of interpretation, and of the object's perceived nature and structure to the background of the interpreter. According to Gadamer, a horizon is "the range of vision that includes everything that can be seen from a particular vantage point" (ibid., p. 302). This definition might suggest that a horizon is what limits a person's perception— that is, what cannot be seen from that particular vantage point does not exist for the person in question. But Gadamer adds that

> "to have a horizon" means not being limited to what is nearest but being able to see beyond it. A person who has an horizon knows the relative significance of everything within this horizon, whether it is near or far, great or small. Similarly, working out the hermeneutical situation means acquiring the right horizon of inquiry for the questions evoked by the encounter with tradition. (Ibid.)

But what does Gadamer mean by "tradition"? The term is used rather vaguely in *Truth and Method*, without a precise or even a working definition. Clarification comes through an important distinction made by Gadamer when he differentiates tradition from merely a set of beliefs and customs inherited from the past:

> A written tradition is not a fragment of a past world, but has always raised itself beyond this into the sphere of the meaning that it expresses. The ideality of the word is what raises everything linguistic beyond the finiteness and transience that characterize other remnants of past existence. It is not this document, as a piece of the past, that is the bearer of tradition but the continuity of memory. Through it tradition becomes part of our own world, and thus what it communicates can be stated immediately. Where we have a written tradition, we are not just told a particular thing; a past humanity itself becomes present to us in its general relation to the world. (Ibid., p. 390)

Thus defined, tradition becomes a way of experiencing life rather than a particular set of objects or artifacts. Tradition, then, is a filter that allows new experiences to take place, but only after they have been validated and assessed through the lens of previous ones. This particular conception of tradition is based on the rehabilitation of the notion of prejudice, which no longer amounts merely to preconceived ideas, as in the negative sense inherited from the Enlightenment. Where, previously, the authority of one's tradition was understood as a source of prejudice because it was seen as limiting the ability to understand texts belonging to another tradition, Gadamer argued for the inescapable, and indeed formative, nature of prejudice. For him, prejudice becomes the condition for understanding texts, and thus the term loses entirely its negative connotations. In Gadamer's words,

> Hermeneutics must start from the position that a person seeking to understand something has a bond to the subject matter that comes into language through the traditionary text and has, or acquires, a connection with the tradition from which the text speaks. On the other hand, hermeneutical consciousness is aware that its bond to this subject matter does not consist in some self-evident, unquestioned unanimity, as is the case with the unbroken stream of tradition. Hermeneutic work is based on a polarity of familiarity and strangeness. . . . It is in the play between the traditionary text's strangeness and familiarity to us, between being a historically intended, distanciated object and belonging to a tradition. The true locus of hermeneutics is this in-between. (Ibid., p. 295)

The "in-between" envisioned by Gadamer is what results through the fusion of horizons made possible by our ability to place ourselves in another "world," that is, realm of reference. To stress his departure from Dilthey's psychologism, Gadamer insisted that

> [t]ransposing ourselves consists neither in the empathy of one individual for another, nor in subordinating another person to our own standards; rather,

it always involves rising to a higher universality that overcomes not only our own particularity but also that of the other. (Ibid., p. 305)

Ricoeur relies on Gadamer's notion of historical consciousness to pose, and reflect on, his own hermeneutical question: "[H]ow is it possible to introduce a critical distance into a consciousness of belonging that is expressly defined by the rejection of distanciation?" (Ricoeur, 1991, p. 73). In other words, if we are always situated in a particular tradition, how at the same time is it possible to escape the prejudice triggered by this belonging, in order to understand other traditions? Ricoeur answers: "It is possible, in my view, only insofar as historical consciousness seeks not simply to repudiate distanciation but to assume it. Gadamer's hermeneutics contains, in this respect, a series of decisive suggestions that will become the point of departure for my own reflection" (ibid.).

The main departure from Gadamer's hermeneutic theory consists in how Ricoeur conceptualizes distanciation. Gadamer viewed distanciation as the consequence of a more general alienation that occurs in the human sciences insofar as their "object" of study is the human experience itself, and hence not something "detachable" from the investigator. For Ricoeur, however, distanciation is a more concrete, as well as deliberately paradoxical, notion. He defines distanciation as a consequence of being already immersed in a tradition before one can attempt to understand the tradition to which a text belongs. Understanding another tradition is possible, as Ricoeur contends, because "we live neither within closed horizons nor within one unique horizon" (ibid.), which implies there is a constant tension "between what is one's own and what is alien, between the near and the far" (ibid.). Distanciation, thus defined, lies "within the near, [as well as] the far" (ibid.).

For Ricoeur, the main task for hermeneutics is to formulate a set of principles that can articulate how distanciation works. At stake in this effort is the very status of hermeneutics as a method of analysis rather than merely an abstract set of concepts. How can we explain what makes possible a dialectic between the near and the far enacted in the interpretation of a text? In addressing this question, his theory draws on previous efforts (once again especially Gadamer's), but makes significant departures. In the next section I identify these departures, focusing on Ricoeur's efforts to avoid the reduction of hermeneutics to a psychological project that seeks to uncover intention in order to identify meaning.

Hermeneutics as a Theory of Understanding: From Intention to Text

As Ricoeur explains, in the history of hermeneutics Friedrich Schleiermacher was the first to show a special interest in bridging scriptural and philological interpretive principles. He marked a new era in the history of the field with his decision that hermeneutics "requires that the interpreter rise above the particular applications and discern the operations that are common to the two branches" (ibid., p. 55). The interpretation of biblical texts relied primarily on so-called "divinatory" processes, later renamed (somewhat deceptively) "technical," whose goal was to identify the meaning of a message based on ascertaining the intentions of the author. The divinatory approach viewed the nature of the message as unique—such uniqueness a direct consequence of the divine persona of the author. Conversely, philological interpretation relied on "grammatical" techniques focused on uncovering characteristics common to a culture and reflected in semantic and syntactic patterns. In one instance of interpretation, language was viewed as the expression of irreducible individuality, while in the other as a medium of shared experience. How, then, to reconcile such seemingly opposed approaches?

In Schleiermacher's dilemma, Ricoeur sees a longstanding source of conceptual tension underlying most efforts to clarify the hermeneutical enterprise. Schleiermacher's own response to this impasse, though decidedly not Ricoeur's, played a major role in subsequent developments. By conceptualizing the fundamental task of hermeneutics as one of understanding texts when one does not have the luxury of consulting their author as one of reconstruction, Schleiermacher posited that to understand is to re-create the authorial intention. As Ricoeur describes his work, it was inspired by the ideal of becoming a *Kunstlehre* (methodology) in which "what must be reached is the subjectivity of the one who speaks, the language being forgotten" (ibid., p. 57). Schleiermacher tried to incorporate, or subordinate, "grammatical" principles to "technical" ones, but he was also forced to leave room for interpretive divination as unavoidable, which makes the ideal of a *Kunstlehre* rather unattainable. On such an approach, language as a shared medium of experience can no longer be the focus of investigation, and becomes instead "an instrument at the service of individuality" (ibid.). According to Ricoeur, the grammatical and technical principles cannot be applied concurrently, since focusing on what is common to a culture requires one to gloss over what is uniquely characteristic to the writer.

Ricoeur does not mention that Schleiermacher never published his reflections on hermeneutics, which are available to us from the notes of one of his students. Other scholars have pondered this issue and suggested that it reflects the author's dissatisfaction with his own conclusions, awareness of the impasse at which he had arrived, and inability to see a way out of it (Grodin, 1994, p. 72). For Ricoeur, the dilemma that eventually became a stopping point for Schleiermacher was a false one. His objections to Schleiermacher's account focuses on a misconception in the latter's thought with regard to the notion of technical interpretation, which "is never restricted to establishing an affinity with the author [and] implies critical motifs in the activity of comparison: an individuality can be grasped only by comparison and contrast. . . . We never directly grasp an individuality but grasp only its difference from others and from ourselves" (Ricoeur, 1991, p. 57). Schleiermacher, then, mistakenly aligned language solely with individuality. For this reason, even though he had the necessary theoretical elements, he failed to develop a *Kunstlehre* that would include both technical and grammatical elements.

Schleiermacher's dilemma, and his unsuccessful effort to avoid it by focusing on language as individual expression, shaped in a fundamental way subsequent attempts at clarification. In Dilthey's work, the individual as the locus of intention became the paramount element guiding the understanding of texts, as well as of history in general. At the same time, Dilthey's attempt to explore the intelligibility of history was influenced by his ambition to do so from a methodological and epistemological basis that would measure up to the standards of research in the sciences, dominated at the time by the rise of positivism as a cultural model. He was, however, careful not to collapse the two domains together and make historical knowledge accountable to the standards of scientific knowledge. To keep them separate, yet compatible, Dilthey stipulated a distinction between explanation and understanding: the former can only be achieved in a scientific demonstration and relies on general principles that have both descriptive and prescriptive power, while the latter operates in the field of humanistic endeavors and involves an empathic access into the mental lives of others.

In Dilthey's hermeneutical vision, explanation and understanding were fundamentally opposed as they each spoke to different epistemologies and, thus, to different models of intelligibility. When we consider a historical event, read poetry, contemplate art, or observe another human being's behavior, the epistemological processes involved in such activities are radically different from those at work when we study natural phenomena—the reflection of light, the motion of stars, or the growth of plants. We try to explain natural phenomena by discovering an underlining general principle, law, or rule based on which we can also predict new, similar phenomena. We understand poetry, history, or art by understanding the "mental universe" these domains capture.

As a historian, Dilthey believed that lived experience holds together in coherent patterns (*das Zusammenhang des Lebens*), as we do not understand the events of our own life in separation from other events that preceded or followed them. This universal interconnectedness of experience makes historical knowledge possible and it also serves, Ricoeur points out, as "a primordial capacity to transpose oneself into the mental life of others. . . . Man is not radically alien to man, because he offers signs of his own existence. To understand these signs is to understand man" (Ricoeur, 1991, p. 59). In Ricoeur's view, Dilthey posited this unproblematic inner-outer, thought-expression relationship as a way to discard the divinatory residue left by Schleiermacher's hermeneutical theory. Reconstructing an authorial intention becomes possible, not through Romantic intuition or empathy, but "because life produces forms, externalizes itself in stable configurations; feelings, [and] evaluations, and volitions tend to sediment themselves in a structured acquisition that is offered to others for deciphering" (Ricoeur, 1991, p. 60). Thus, Dilthey was, perhaps inadvertently, exploiting the very cultural-etymological root of the term "hermeneutics": for the Greeks, *hermeneia* (utterance) was "a translation of inner thoughts in externalized language" (Grodin, 1994, p. 21). But Ricoeur blames Dilthey for axiomatically privileging and reifying the notion of the individual mind as an abstract and universal topos of mental life, instead of offering an analytical and more precise account of individuality. In Dilthey's conception, hermeneutics saw "the rise of the individual to the knowledge of universal history, the universalization of the individual" (Ricoeur, 1991, p. 60).

Ricoeur is not the only critic disappointed in Dilthey's radical psychologization of hermeneutics, and in its reduction to a question of how the individual mind processes meaning. But while reverent in expression, his criticism of Dilthey is perhaps more severe in substance than that of others. Ricoeur deems the psychological emphasis propounded by Dilthey as the first act in a long process of radicalizing hermeneutics by shifting the attention away from an epistemological concern with understanding to a broad ontological perspective that defines human beings as capable, a priori, of crossing cultural distance. He sees Heidegger's philosophy as having marked the heyday of such a radicalized hermeneutics. Heidegger dismissed the epistemological question of understanding by claiming "it is part of its structure as being to have an ontological preunderstanding of being" (ibid., p. 64). If, for Dilthey to understand was to decipher the intentions of another mind based on following the externalized expression to the internal intention, for Heidegger such a dichotomy between inner and outer no longer exists, as "[t]he question of the world takes the place of the question of the other. In thereby making understanding worldly, Heidegger depsychologizes it" (ibid., p. 66).

Despite his criticism of Dilthey, this is not the kind of depsychologizing Ricoeur favors, because it comes at a price he is not willing to pay. His own hermeneutical project seeks to restore, and then address, the initial epistemological question: how do we understand the meaning of texts belonging to a different time or tradition? A similar goal motivates Gadamer's *Truth and Method*, a book that confronts boldly, in Ricoeur's opinion, a new version of Schleiermacher's dilemma, now intensified under Heidegger's influence: is knowledge of the past possible as the result of some methodological exploration, or is it "truth coming to light not simply as the result of a technique—of something that the subject does—but as a result of a something that happens to us over and above our wanting and doing?" (Howard, 1982, p. 123).

Ricoeur does not believe Gadamer had an actual answer to this question. "Knowledge of others is possible," Ricoeur notes,

> because life produces forms, externalizes itself in stable configurations; feelings, evaluations, and volitions tend to sediment themselves in a structured acquisition that is offered to others for deciphering. The organized systems that culture produces in the form of literature constitute a secondary layer, built upon this primary phenomenon of the productions of life. . . . If I can understand vanished worlds, it is because each society has created its own

medium of understanding by creating the social and cultural worlds in which it understands itself. Universal history thus becomes the field of hermeneutics. To understand myself is to make the greatest detour, via the memory that retains what has become meaningful for all mankind. (Ricoeur, 1991, pp. 60, 62)

In the next section I discuss Ricoeur's effort to establish hermeneutics as a theory that sees texts as not only the linguistic encoding of meaning, but also as a vehicle for self-understanding.

Interpretation as Self-Understanding

The stark contrast, posited by Dilthey, between understanding and explanation is a historically-situated phenomenon. In the early nineteenth century, the influence of positivism led to an increased effort to develop and use explanatory frameworks in the study of history and other humanistic disciplines. Dilthey opposed attempts at importing a scientific method into a humanistic domain, and argued that no such trafficking was philosophically viable. By insisting that natural sciences and the humanistic fields were radically different in goals, methods, and concepts, Dilthey was operating under the assumptions of a body-mind dualism—a distinction he inherited from the Enlightenment. Ricoeur rejects such dualism in several contexts. With respect to hermeneutics, the main disadvantage of positing a rift between science and the humanities—between, respectively, explanation and understanding—is that it leads to inconsistency. On the one hand, by defining understanding as "transference into another mental life," Dilthey placed hermeneutics at a particularistic level, making it into knowledge of individuals, concerned with comprehending the singular, since mental life is assumed to vary from one person to another. On the other hand, by aspiring to give hermeneutics the status of a human science, he was also committed to a discipline capable of universal validity.

For Ricoeur, the need for an interpretive process that includes both understanding and explanation is the result of our ontological condition, as beings immersed in language, facing interpretive challenges "at the most elementary and banal level of conversation" (Ricoeur, 1991, p. 54). Polysemy—the multiple meanings a lexical item can have—makes it necessary to select an appropriate context in which to place the message in order to understand it. Sometimes, such a selection is possible with the help of the speaker, as "the use of contexts involves, in its turn, an activity of discernment that is exercised in the concrete exchange of messages between interlocutors, and that is modeled on the interplay of questions and answers" (ibid., p. 55). Interpretation, then, requires the ability to recognize "which relatively univocal message the speaker has constructed on the polysemic basis of the common lexicon." But if interpretation is a matter of reconstructing the speaker's intention, the less available that intention is via the "interplay of questions and answers," the more problematic become the premises of interpretive activity. When language is realized in writing, interpretation can no longer rely on asking questions, because the author is not present to answer them. The interpretation of texts, then, demands techniques based on which meaning can be disambiguated. Such techniques are all the more necessary when the texts in question are already assumed important, as in the case of sacred texts or documents that belong to a valued cultural tradition.

Ricoeur insists on the importance of separating the internal mechanisms of a text, its syntactic and semantic structures, from both their origin of production—the author—and the point of reception—the reader. The text, for him, has its own "matter," which constrains the reception, is distinguishable from the intentions of the author, and guides the interpretive process. Ricoeur's strong background in structuralism accounts for such emphasis on the materiality of texts and their life outside the intersubjective chain of communication. His notion of text is tied up with the concept of distanciation. Indeed, the text, as Ricoeur defines it, is symbol of the historicity of human experience. Texts capture past eras and make communication at a distance possible. Their transmission is the survival of human civilization.

Ricoeur's notion of text is influenced by structuralism in an additional way. He defines texts as part of a bipartite relation between language, as an abstract system of rules (Ferdinand Saussure's *langue*), and discourse (as language in use, or Saussure's *parole*). Language is "realized" in discourse, in the sense that abstract principles (from syntactic patterns to lexical entries) become concrete in use. In its turn, discourse can be both spoken and written. Speech, for Ricoeur, is "the fugitive manifestation of language" (ibid., p. 130), and it precedes writing, "sociologically and psychologically." But precisely because he subscribes to the two Saussurean levels, Ricoeur maintains that even in the most transient spoken intervention, there is something lingering, wanting to endure beyond the moment of its utterance. For him, this lingering element is meaning, which can be comprehended and then immediately forgotten in an oral encounter, but which can also be captured and "fixed," or "inscribed," in writing. On a theoretical level, writing does not come after speech, but takes its place,

> occurring at the very site where speech could have emerged. . . . [W]hat comes to writing is discourse as intention-to-say and . . . writing is a direct inscription of this intention, even if, historically and psychologically, writing began with the transcription of the signs of the speech. This emancipation of writing, which places the latter at the site of speech, is the birth of the text. (Ibid., pp. 106–07)

Following Emile Benveniste's insights, Ricoeur maintains that a theory of language for hermeneutics should differentiate language from language-in-use, or discourse. Says Ricoeur: "If the 'sign' (phonological and lexical) is the basic unit of language, the 'sentence' is the basic unit of discourse. The linguistics of the sentence underlies the dialectic of event and meaning, which forms the starting point for our theory of the text" (ibid., p. 77). The event, in Ricoeur's view, is "the advent of a world in language by means of discourse" (ibid., p. 78). Since events have a temporal structure—marked by a beginning and an end—discourse, too, is anchored in the temporality of exchange, in a dialogue that unfolds between a speaker and a listener. Discourse also rises above its own temporality through meaning: "What we wish to understand is not the fleeting event but rather the meaning that endures" (ibid.). If language comes into use in time, in a given situation and among actual participants or speakers, then meaning is realized as an event, something that punctures an existing order and draws attention to "a world that it claims to describe, express, or represent." The task of hermeneutics is to develop an explanatory procedure on the basis of which alien worlds (or eras) can become meaningful and accessible.

Ricoeur's conception of what constitutes an explanatory framework is, again, indebted to structuralism: an explanation uncovers "stable correlations between discrete units," and its task is "to carry out the segmentation of the work (horizontal aspect), then to establish the various levels of integration of the parts in the whole (hierarchical level)" (ibid., p. 116). Such an explanatory protocol is particularly necessary when understanding is rendered problematic by the fact that we have no way of guiding or verifying it. A verbal message can be understood on the basis of situational clues, through additional questions and answers, and with further clarification required from and offered by the author. "Understanding calls for explanation when the dialogical situation ceases to exist, when the play of questions and answers no longer permits our interpretation as the dialogue unfolds" (ibid., p. 129).

The interconnectedness of explanation and understanding in the process of interpretation, then, is a consequence of the historical, noncontingent nature of texts (by contrast with spoken communication). By defining texts as "dislocated" speech, Ricoeur wants to emphasize an important transformation that accompanies the emancipation involved in writing: the suspension of reference. Face-to-face communication is referential in the sense that the interlocutors are anchored in a reality the understanding of which they share via the same circumstantial clues, and the deictic use of language (through words like "here," "now," or "today"). In Ricoeur's view, at its limit this referential function would merge into ostensive designation, speech becoming gesture as "[s]ense fades into reference and the latter into the act of showing" (ibid., p. 108). But in a text, reference is suspended, no longer obvious or in any way directly available:

> The suspense that defers the reference merely leaves the text, as it were, "in the air," outside or without a world. In virtue of this obliteration of the relation to the world, each text is free to enter into relation with all the other texts that come to take the place of the circumstantial reality referred to by

living speech. This relation of text to text, within the effacement of the world
about which we speak, engenders the quasi world of texts or literature. (Ibid.,
p. 109)

By explaining a text, Ricoeur claims, we become aware of its internal mechanisms and structural features, but the explanatory stage alone does not resolve
the suspense of reference or restore the circumstantial world of the text. For
that we need interpretation, which will return the text to living communication
by incorporating it in the circumstantial world of the interpreter. The interpretation of a text is possible insofar as a cultural heritage does not become reified
in that text (or historical artifact) that offers itself to analysis, revealing patterns
and meanings once probed and interrogated. Understanding that cultural heritage is not a task in itself but also a way of self-elucidation. Ricoeur writes:

> [T]o understand is to understand oneself in front of the text. It is not a ques-
> tion of imposing upon the text our finite capacity for understanding, but of
> exposing ourselves to the text and receiving from it an enlarged self, which
> would be the proposed existence corresponding to the most suitable way to
> the world proposed. (Ibid., p. 88)

If texts have this elucidating potential, the traditions that contain them serve as
repositories of meaning for more than individual subjectivities, because traditions are shared by communities of actors. But for Ricoeur, traditions can also
be transformed. As he insists, "It is undoubtedly necessary to go still further:
just as the world of the text is real only insofar as it is imaginary, so too it must
be said that the subjectivity of the reader comes to itself only insofar as it is
placed in suspense, unrealized, potentialized" (ibid.). By acquiring a "new" subjectivity made available through the world of a text, the interpreter achieves
what Ricoeur calls "distanciation," which is also what allows the escape from the
tyranny of a given tradition.

What is the mechanism through which distanciation becomes possible? This
is a question that did not receive, I believe, an explicit answer in Ricoeur's
hermeneutical theory. But an answer is, nevertheless, available, in other parts of
his work. In the following section, I discuss how his work on ideology and utopia allow us to explain the relation between tradition and distanciation.

Tradition and Ideology, Distanciation and Utopia

What makes traditions both useful—as a space of belonging—and potentially
oppressive—as a space of captivity—is their marriage to particular ideologies.
A tradition in which immigrants are deemed dangerous is steeped in a nation-
alistic and xenophobic ideology. A tradition in which women are deemed in
control of their bodies is likely to promote a pro-choice ideology. Traditions

coalesce around ideologies, while ideologies draw their justification from being connected to a tradition.

By some accounts, tradition and ideology could be even deemed synonymous. To distinguish between them is important, however, because it allows us to see precisely what makes a tradition so powerful and also what might be required to change it. Ricoeur's definition of ideology is shaped by several other major theories, but its main objective is to present an alternative to the more common, Marxist approach to the topic. In contradistinction to Marx's emphasis on the dissimulative dimensions of ideology, Ricoeur emphasizes its interpretive dimension. Thus, he offers a concept of ideology defined as a framework that holds together ideas and beliefs that are the foundation of a community. As he puts it, his is an

> attempt . . . not to deny the legitimacy of the Marxist concept of ideology. We must integrate the concept of ideology as distortion into a framework that recognizes the symbolic structure of social life. . . . I am seeking a function of ideology more radical than the distorting, dissimulating function. (Ricoeur, 1986, p. 8)

In the following section I will try to show that this "more radical" function lies in the connection Ricoeur allows us to establish between the two axes that, since Gadamer, define hermeneutical theory: one being ideology and utopia (coupling them in the same way Karl Mannheim did) and the other being tradition and distanciation.

For Ricoeur, ideology is a symbolic system predicated on "an interpretation, in images and representations, of the social bond itself" (Ricoeur, 1991, p. 255). Although influenced by several philosophical approaches to ideology, his own remains fundamentally a Weberian one. Like Max Weber, Ricoeur makes ideology part of a theory of social actions and relations (ibid., p. 184). Weber argued that social action results from the belief that general human behavior is meaningful to individual agents, and from the coordination of an individual's behavior with others' responses and own conduct. Ideology, on such an account, is what turns potentially meaningless, or arbitrary, encounters between individuals or groups into lasting social relations.

For Ricoeur, ideology is an overarching concept that includes the "simplification, schematization, stereotyping, and ritualization" (ibid., p. 182) that render life comprehensible. Ricoeur distinguishes three functions of ideology, adding integration and legitimation to the more familiar Marxist conception, which only saw ideology as distortion or dissimulation (ibid., pp. 182–83). In his view, all three functions, including the negative or pathological one, play the role of "reinforcing and repeating the social tie in situations that are after-the-fact" (ibid., p. 182). Using the example of the Declaration of Independence as an ideological document, Ricoeur argues that the ideas inscribed there express the shared beliefs that symbolically frame the life of a historically situated community, that of the founding fathers. For Ricoeur, ideology is deeply anchored in history. Ideology becomes necessary, partially as a result of temporal distance, its presence all the more important given the irreducible gap between the levels of experience and that of interpretation. The role of ideology and of a document like the Declaration of Independence "is not only to diffuse the conviction beyond the circle of founding fathers, so as to make it the creed of [a completely different] group, but also to perpetuate the initial energy beyond the period of effervescence" (ibid., p. 249).

Ideology works by creating and reinforcing social bonds, and thus by offering concretions of identity (ibid., p. 250). Ideology, as defined by Ricoeur, is what grounds a tradition and, when needed, also is what justifies it. Ideology becomes domination when it legitimizes "above all, the relation to the system of authority." Says Ricoeur, "[I]t is when the mediating role of ideology encounters the phenomenon of domination that the distorting and dissimulating character of ideology comes to the fore" (ibid., p. 252). This is what makes utopia necessary.

Ricoeur's notion of utopia capitalizes on the idea of extraterritoriality the term carries with it. The literal meaning of the term "utopia," consecrated in 1516 by its creator, Sir Thomas More, is that of a nonexistent idyllic world. More used the term in his rendition of a heavenly land, described in vivid contrast to a decayed and corrupt England. The word comes from the Greek term for "nowhere," a strategy of signaling that the heavenly realm described in the book was nonexistent, rather than not part of the contemporary social order. Ricoeur writes: "It is indeed starting from this strange spatial extraterritoriality—from this nonplace, in the literal sense of the word—that we are able to take a fresh look at our reality; hereafter, nothing about it can continue to be taken for granted" (ibid., p. 184).

The function of utopias is to create a breach in our everyday world, to bring the "far" into the "near" and thus to allow us to look with a critical eye at what is familiar to us, our customs, beliefs, values; in other words, our tradition. Says Ricoeur, "Utopia is the mode in which we radically rethink the nature of family, consumption, government, religion, and so on. From 'nowhere' emerges the most formidable challenge to what-is" (ibid.). Most importantly, utopia does not mean "never": the utopian mode projects one outside one's familiar universe of reference, that is, tradition, but it does not signify purely a fantasy world. Utopias identify the realm of what may be possible—in contradistinction to "what-is"—in order to signal the need to attain new possibilities, and thus to change an existing order.

Insofar as utopias distance us from our practices, they offer a counterpoint to ideology: while the latter integrates individuals into a tradition, the former provides the possibility of changing that tradition by offering a vantage point from which the seemingly "given" can be questioned and a replacement considered. When the ideology that defines a tradition becomes oppressive, and that tradition works as domination and prejudice in the original, nonenlightened sense of the term, utopia functions as a way of exposing the domination through reflection upon alternative possibilities. To understand texts that belong to another tradition not only amounts to projecting oneself into a "proposed existence," but also uses that "proposed existence" in order to change one's given existence. Significantly, utopia is not merely an arbitrary imagining of a nonexistent world. Rather, it is the carefully chosen projection of an imaginary world, the role of which is to model actions and behaviors in the real, existing one. Thus, utopia creates the very rapprochement between the "near and the far" that defines Ricoeur's concept of distanciation.

Missing in Gadamer's hermeneutics is a discussion of how, exactly, tradition becomes enabling rather than merely staying limiting. As a strategy for challenging a dominating ideology, utopia also plays a key role in the "fusion of horizons" by making sure that one horizon—the tradition—does not become limiting. At the same time, utopia can act as a mechanism of rapprochement in a different sense: different ideologies might come together via the same utopian projection. Consider, again, Warnke's example of the abortion debate and the competing interpretations of abortion that accompany the pro-life and pro-choice ideologies. A utopian projection that might bring the two camps together would envision women as free agents who exercise control over their bodies, while at the same respecting the sanctity of life because they live in environments that allow them never to violate this principle. For Warnke, a rapprochement between the two competing ideologies and the attendant ideologies would amount to "finding ways to reduce the incidence of abortion while creating the social and economic conditions under which families can make autonomous and responsible choices" (Warnke, 1999, p. 180). She ignores, however, the fundamental utopian projection upon which such an approach would need to rely. One must first be willing to entertain the vision of a world in which families benefit from social and economic conditions that allow them to make autonomous and responsible choices. Such a vision requires a utopian projection, not in the sense of an imaginative leap into an ideal, unattainable universe, but as a corrective vision that allows one to think beyond one's given realm of reference. Arguably, pro-life supporters insist on making abortion illegal precisely because they do not believe that free agents will always decide to respect the sanctity of life when provided with the option of terminating an undesired pregnancy. Likewise, pro-choice supporters insist on the legality of abortion precisely because they do not believe that free agents will always afford respect to others' decisions about control of their bodies. Both camps need to envision a world in which one principle—the sanctity of life—can coexist with another—the right of free and autonomous individuals to make their own decisions. It is only then that legislative solutions that accommodate competing interpretations can be sought.

Conclusion

In the 1981 encounter between Jacques Derrida and Gadamer, another famous debate that forced hermeneutics to defend itself, it became clear that one of the most important dimensions of hermeneutics is the ethical one. A hermeneutics focused solely on defining meaning as a static phenomenon that results from the understanding of culturally distant objects, without paying attention to what hinders understanding, is also one that remains indifferent to the concrete conditions of communication and the great potential for miscommunication and misunderstanding involved in them. Derrida reproached Gadamer's failure to consider the possibility that the commonality of language and experience that lie at the core of the concept of "fusion of horizons" is a dangerous illusion (Derrida, 1989, pp. 52–54). It is this illusion Ricoeur sought to problematize, and then to remedy, through his own hermeneutical theory. In this theory, the text is a place where different universes come together, and at the same time it is a space for trying on different self-identities as a way of continuously enriching the identity we have. Ricoeur's hermeneutics is one that recognizes the epistemic dimension of tradition, while also connecting it to distanciation for its emancipatory function. But, unlike the emancipatory projects of critical theory, a hermeneutics defined in Ricoeur's terms remains grounded in history, because it relies on tradition and ideology as a historically transmitted symbolic system. Thus, its liberating potential is also a realistic one: for each given tradition and its attendant ideology, one must seek the appropriate utopia and the emancipation thus made possible.

Chapter 4

Gadamer's Rhetorical Conception of Hermeneutics as the Key to Developing a Critical Hermeneutics

Francis J. Mootz III

The rhetorical dimensions of Hans-Georg Gadamer's philosophical hermeneutics have not been fully appreciated and developed by his commentators,
leading to a skewed understanding of the critical potential of his work. In the
last years of his life Gadamer expressed what had been largely implicit during
his long career: the ancient tradition of rhetoric is an important touchstone
for philosophical hermeneutics and all humanistic inquiry. Recovering and
elucidating the rhetorical basis of Gadamer's philosophy reveals his understanding of interpretation as a rhetorical accomplishment, which in turn gives
rise to a rich conception of critical hermeneutics that should finally put to rest
the canard that philosophical hermeneutics is politically naive and quiescent.
This rhetorical dimension of Gadamer's work proves superior to Paul Ricoeur's
more philosophically-oriented project, but I acknowledge and draw from
Ricoeur's rhetorically inclined approach in his *Lectures on Ideology and Utopia* to
provide critical support for my reading of Gadamer.

Gadamer's Rhetorical Conception of Hermeneutics

Gadamer signals the tremendous importance of the rhetorical tradition by
positioning, at the center of his philosophy, a phenomenological account of the
experience of conversation. However, Gadamer's explicit references to rhetoric
appear to be minimal and peripheral, even if they do occur at critical points in
his philosophy. Gadamer begins *Truth and Method* by recalling Vico's development of the humanist concept of *sensus communis* as a means of preserving
the independent validity of moral-practical wisdom, as distinguished from the
logical-empirical truths of science (Gadamer, 1989, pp. 19–24). Aligning Vico
with the substantive rhetorical goal of saying the right thing well, Gadamer
applauds the development of the "positive ambiguity of the rhetorical ideal"

(ibid., p. 20). Vico's importance for the modern era rests on his prescient critique of the unitary Cartesian paradigm of knowledge by reasserting "the independent rights of rhetoric [—] the art of finding arguments[, which] serves to develop the sense of what is convincing, which works instinctively and ex tempore, and for that very reason cannot be replaced by science" (ibid., p. 21).

Gadamer emphasizes the breadth of rhetoric in the ancient world, given the need for argumentation without recourse to compelling proofs in most areas of human inquiry (Gadamer, 2006b, p. 89). Rhetoric is dialogical because one's interlocutor can never be abstracted as a "rational person" who must accept your rigorously logical position, but rather is a conversation partner whom one seeks to persuade. This situation, Gadamer concludes,

> corresponds exactly to what Aristotle in the *Rhetoric* calls the *enthymeme*. In it is expressed a paying attention to the other person that characterizes true rhetoric. Using an enthymeme does not mean that one reaches a com-pelling conclusion, but it is not for this reason without meaning nor without persuasive power and claim to truth. All discourse is such that the thing meant can be shown from various sides and thus allows of being repeated in various ways. This is the sense of a kind of conclusiveness which expresses itself in a powerfully persuasive way without being a compelling proof. (Gadamer, 2006b, p. 90)

In the modern era, spellbound by the awesome technological power unleashed by the scientific method, we have lost our appreciation of the rhetorical tradition that resided at the center of Greek life.

Gadamer recalls his opening reference to Vico at a key juncture of his conclusion to *Truth and Method*, suggesting his book has been concerned principally with recovering and rehabilitating what I would term a rhetorical model of knowledge. Acknowledging that his guiding focus on the "event" of understanding is drawn from "an ancient truth that has been able to assert itself against modern scientific methodology," Gadamer concludes that the "*eikos*, the verisimilar, the 'probable[,]' . . . the 'evident,' belong in a series of things that defend their rightness against the truth and certainty of what is proved and known. Let us recall that we assigned a special importance to [Vico's development of] the *sensus communis*" (ibid., p. 485; Gadamer, 2006b, p. 95). This framing of *Truth and Method* presents the book as an extended meditation on the implications of Vico's defense of the rhetorical tradition in response to the nascent methodologism that ultimately dominated academic inquiry.[1]

Gadamer never expounded on Vico's "special importance" in a systematic way, but in various essays and interviews he repeatedly emphasizes the signifi-cance of rhetoric, asserting it "is the universal form of human communication, which even today determines our social life in an incomparably more profound fashion than does science" (Gadamer, 1986, p. 17). Rejecting the sophistic abasement of rhetoric, Gadamer champions a genuine rhetoric that concerns the "discovery and transmission of insight and knowledge," an event exemplified in the "art of leading a conversation" (Gadamer, 1992a, p. 348). Gadamer invokes Plato's account of rhetoric in the *Phaedrus*, but he steadfastly argues against an attempt to constrain rhetoric by linking it to certainty and unchanging truth. He looks to Plato's activity of writing the Socratic dialogues rather than Plato's philosophical self-understanding, insisting that what we learn from the Platonic dialogues is that it "is more important to find the words which convince the other than those which can be demonstrated in their truth, once and for all" (Gadamer, 1992b, p. 71).

Gadamer does not refer to rhetoric only out of historical interest, nor as a casual gesture. He argues that rhetoric and hermeneutics are joined by their attention to the activity of overcoming localized disruptions in shared understandings, going so far as to emphasize that "the rhetorical and hermeneutical aspects of human linguisticality completely interpenetrate each other" (Gadamer, 1976, p. 25), and concluding that "there is a deep inner convergence with rhetoric and hermeneutics" (Gadamer, 1984, pp. 54–55). He explains:

> Clearly the ability to speak has the same breadth and universality as the ability to understand and interpret . . . . Hermeneutics may be precisely defined as the art of bringing what is said or written to speech again. What kind of art this is, then, we can learn from rhetoric. . . . (Gadamer 1981a, p. 119)
>
> [Because] the being of the interpreter pertains intrinsically to the being of what is to be interpreted . . . the orator always has to link up with something like [a prior, sustaining agreement] if his persuading and convincing in disputed questions is to succeed. So, too, any understanding of another's meaning, or that of a text, is encompassed by a context of mutual agreement, despite all possible miscomprehensions; and so too does any understanding strive for mutual agreement in and through all dissent. (Gadamer, 1981b, p. 136)

There should be no doubt, then, that Gadamer's principal works were informed by the rhetorical tradition, even if this influence was never elaborated in detail.

In a late interview Gadamer acknowledged the significance, in his formative years, of Heidegger's inventive reading of Aristotle's *Rhetoric* during the 1924 lectures, and he explained that his own lack of formal attention to rhetoric was simply a matter of not being "able to do everything" (Gadamer, 2005, p. 64). Looking back over his long and productive career, Gadamer unequivocally registers his appreciation of the vital importance of the rhetorical tradition. "Rhetoric is the starting point. The whole of ethics is rhetoric, and the idea that *phronesis* is rhetoric already occurs in Aristotle. *Phronesis* cannot be gauged with a scientific concept like mathematics: It's something quite different—it's rhetoric" (ibid., p. 53).[2]

Gadamer's late self-assessment should promote a reconceptualization of philosophical hermeneutics, but few scholars have recognized that Gadamer's philosophical hermeneutics propounds a sophisticated rhetorical theory. This general inattention is unfortunate, because it is precisely this rhetorical character of philosophical hermeneutics that preserves the critical element of understanding and provides guidance for those seeking to articulate a critical hermeneutics.

Rhetoric as the Key to Critical Hermeneutics

It is telling that Gadamer expressly emphasizes his alignment with the rhetorical model of truth as part of his vehement response to Habermas's insistence on the need to develop a critical theory to serve the emancipatory interest in human progress. The afterword of *Truth and Method* defends rhetorical reason against Habermas's intellectual hubris:

> I would like to see more recognition of the fact that this is the realm herme-neutics shares with rhetoric: the realm of arguments that are convincing (which is not the same as logically compelling). It is the realm of practice and humanity in general, and its province is not where the power of "ironclad conclusions" must be accepted without discussion, nor where emancipatory reflection is certain of its "contrafactual agreements," but rather where controversial issues are decided by reasonable consideration. . . . Vico rightly assigns [rhetoric] a special value: copia, the abundance of viewpoints. I find it frighteningly unreal when people like Habermas ascribe to rhetoric a compulsory quality that one must reject in favor of unconstrained, rational dialogue. This is to underestimate not only the danger of the glib manipula-tion and incapacitation of reason but also the possibility of coming to an understanding through persuasion, on which social life depends. . . . Only a narrow view of rhetoric sees it as mere technique or even a mere instrument for social manipulation. It is in truth an essential aspect of all reasonable behavior. (Gadamer, 1989, p. 568)

In the face of Habermas's challenge Gadamer insists the rhetorical dimension of knowledge provides both the motivation and the resources for social critique, and he criticizes the urge to develop philosophical constructs that purport to exert critical leverage from outside the arena of rhetorical engagement.[3]

Although Gadamer relies heavily, even if often indirectly, on the classical rhetorical tradition to develop his hermeneutical phenomenology of under-standing, it is a profound mistake to conclude he is motivated by idealist con-ceptions of the bygone era of the polis.[4] Gadamer regards the hermeneutical task as markedly different from the rhetorical task in ancient Greece. Social meanings are reproduced and disseminated today through texts (all manner of media) rather than by persuasive speeches made in the assembly or law courts. Ancient rhetoric was transformed irreversibly by the movement from an oral culture to one founded on writing and reading; rhetorical performances now require a hermeneutical recovery by later readers who might be removed from the original event by hundreds of years and wide cultural differences (Gadamer, 1992a, p. 348; Gadamer, 1984, pp. 56–57; Gadamer 1981, pp. 123–24). Despite these fundamental changes, Gadamer argues that the rhetorical tradition is a vital resource for textual interpreters in our hyperliterate and culturally fragmented global village.

The transition from ancient oral traditions to modern written traditions is decisive for Gadamer because the temporal gulf between text and interpreter magnifies the critical distanciation inherent in every interpretive event (Gadamer 1989, pp. 291–300). The participatory immediacy of a rhetorical exchange between two persons permits room for critical inventiveness, but textual interpretation invites a critical appraisal to an even greater degree. Gadamer writes:

> Rhetoric as such, however, is tied to the immediacy of its effect. . . . While under the persuasive spell of speech, the listener for the moment cannot and ought not to indulge in critical examination. On the other hand, the reading and interpreting of what is written is so distanced and detached from its author—from his mood, intentions, and unexpressed tendencies—that the grasping of the meaning of the text takes on something of the character of an independent productive act, one that resembles more the art of the orator than the process of mere listening. Thus it is easy to understand why the theoretical tools of the art of interpretation (hermeneutics) have been to a large extent borrowed from rhetoric.[5] (Gadamer, 1976, pp. 23–24)

This analysis holds great significance. By expressly equating the textual interpreter with the rhetorical actor rather than with the receptive audience, Gadamer emphasizes the dynamic character of interpretation and the space for critical reappraisal of the tradition that is opened by, not despite, the decentering dialogic structure of understanding. Eschewing a superficial account of the rhetor speaking and the hermeneut listening, Gadamer establishes that the interpreter is engaged in a rhetorical-hermeneutical activity structured by the logic of question and answer and is conversational in nature.

Perhaps the most important feature of Gadamer's model of conversation is that it clarifies his rhetorical focus and reaffirms the interpenetration of rhetoric and hermeneutics. An interpreter understands a text when she falls into conversation with it and allows it to speak to the question posed by the case at hand. Rather than adopting a subjective attitude of dominance over the text by charting in advance the lines of inquiry, the interpreter suppresses her subjective aims and attends to "the saying" of the historically effective text as it is revealed in a particular context. But this attitude is not one of passivity or obeisance. The hermeneutic experience of the reader parallels the need for a rhetor to conceive a speech only in connection with the particular audience that will be addressed on a given occasion, in recognition that persuasive speeches do not exist in the abstract, ready to be used indiscriminately at some point in the future. Gadamer drives this point home in his discussion of understanding and interpretation *as* application, rather than construing them as distinct activities that precede application.[6] Understanding a text is as much a rhetorical activity as a hermeneutical accomplishment.

The conversational nature of interpretation explains the source of critical distanciation. Gadamer distinguishes the dialogical activity of two participants fully engaged in conversation from mere superficial banter or social pleasantries, and for this reason he equates conversation with rhetorical exchange. By choosing as his guiding metaphor an image of the interpreter enmeshed in an inventive discourse with another person in real time, Gadamer reaffirms his opposition to the exegetical model of a reader prostrate before a classical text that must be honored with reverent deference or the critical model of the all-knowing reader "decoding" the text as a fixed object. This is most clearly expressed in his consideration of the "classical" in literature (Gadamer, 1989, pp. 285–90).

In *Truth and Method*, Gadamer rejects the simplistic prejudice that only methodological thinking is capable of revealing truth, but it is notoriously unclear what role Gadamer believes truth can play in philosophical hermeneutics. It is the rhetorical dimension of Gadamer's work that preserves the role of truth as a criterion with critical bite, even if it is not equivalent to the truth we obtain in mathematics. In a late interview, Gadamer explained:

> Science, which is power and which claims to be able to control things, is only one form of knowledge. There is another form of knowing, however, and it is this that I would like to defend: [it is the capacity] to come up with the right word at the right moment, this kind of exactness itself. This was the ancient, honorable concept of rhetoric.
>
> Thus, this misunderstanding is actually something that misleads us. I mean, it is completely self-evident when I say: everyplace where the procedure of measuring and logic gives rise to blindness, the true blindness does not reside in this knowledge itself but in the fact that one regards it as the whole of knowledge. It is this viewpoint that I would like to defend against. (Gadamer, 2006b, p. 96)

I have expanded this suggestion (drawing from Gadamer, Chaïm Perelman, and Nietzsche) by defending the reality and significance of "rhetorical knowledge" that is dynamic, historical, and productive of critical insight (Mootz, 2006).

Gadamer emphasizes that the orientation to *die Sache*—the subject matter in dispute (Gadamer, 2006b, pp. 89–90)— avoids, in a genuine dialogue, the twin perils of asserting one's own prejudices as a pregiven truth (which Gadamer terms "sophistic"; ibid., p. 90), or remaining content to artfully understand the other's opinion (which would be a mere exegesis; ibid., 2006a, p. 51). Rhetorical knowledge is an achievement that arises from a "fusion of horizons" (in Gadamer's famously misleading, and misunderstood, term) that takes place when both dialogic partners surrender to the play of *die Sache*.[7] Gadamer's account of the hermeneutical event as an active and critical appropriation of meaning is the core of his philosophy, although he fails to develop fully the rhetorical dimension of this experience.[8]

Comparing the Critical Hermeneutics of Gadamer and Ricoeur

The rhetorical dimension of Gadamer's philosophical hermeneutics provides the basis for the development of critical hermeneutics. We can elaborate a Gadamerian model of critical hermeneutics by contrasting it with the position developed by Paul Ricoeur in response to the Gadamer-Habermas debate. Ricoeur famously rejects a strict bifurcation of explanation and understanding, refusing to grant authority to one disposition over the other.[9] Ricoeur's effort to maintain the tensive relationship between explanation and understanding in order to develop a critical hermeneutics is appealing, but he purchases his ameliorative position at too high a cost. Although he insists explanation must continually be located within the narrative world of understanding, his effort to give explanation its due as a separate moment emerges from an overly generous response to the structuralist philosophy of his day. Gadamerian critical hermeneutics—rooted in the decentering, rhetorical experience of dialogue—presents a more radical (in the full sense of the word) approach than Ricoeur's effort to mediate explanatory methods with interpretation.

Ricoeur contends Gadamer's resolute plea to acknowledge the finitude and historicity of all understanding has precluded effective critical theory, and so he sets as his task the investigation of the distance created by the "matter of the text" that leaves behind the immediacy of conversational understanding (Ricoeur, 1981a, pp. 61–62; Ricoeur, 1981b, p. 92; Ricoeur, 1976, pp. 71–75). Ricoeur explores the dialectic between belonging and distanciation to overcome Gadamer's inadequate account, under which "the hermeneutical experience itself discourages the recognition of any critical distance" (Ricoeur, 1981b, p. 90). The "emancipation of the text" by writing creates a distance that is productive of understanding, but Ricoeur acknowledges critique is not a subjective accomplishment, but rather a product of the critic's attentiveness to the autonomous world of the text (Ricoeur, 1981b, pp. 94–95; Ricoeur, 1976, p. 94). Structuralism provides an analytic method that is a "necessary stage" in the development of a sophisticated comprehension that bridges understanding and explanation by temporarily "repressing" the mythic character of the text without ever purporting to wholly "suppress" it (Ricoeur, 1976, p. 87).

Francisco Gonzalez recently has argued that, by placing too much reliance on a text-centered structuralist hermeneutics to engender the distanciation necessary to permit critical explanation, Ricoeur underestimates the critical element of Gadamer's dialogue-centered hermeneutics (Gonzalez, 2006). Gonzalez emphasizes that Ricoeur's overlay[10] of critical explanation has the perverse effect of suppressing the inherently critical character of dialogic experience revealed through Gadamer's phenomenological accounts of understanding, thereby obscuring Gadamer's fundamental teaching that to "experience is to suffer critique" (ibid., p. 333). Gonzalez accurately describes Gadamer's insistence on the priority of understanding and the derivative character of all explanation. Writing about Ricoeur's efforts to define a critical hermeneutics, Gadamer emphasizes that the radical suspicion evidenced in explanatory approaches to texts cannot be reconciled with the hermeneutical event of understanding: "I think even Paul Ricoeur must in the end give up attempts to bring them together, because we have here a basic difference involving the whole philosophical role of hermeneutics" (Gadamer 1984, p. 58). Indeed, Ricoeur appears to acknowledge the unavoidable conflict between explanation and understanding, conceding that each disposition claims universality from a different "place"[11] (Ricoeur, 1981b, p. 64). Gonzalez's illuminating article suggests Ricoeur's mediation fails for this reason, leaving us with Gadamer's assertion of the ontological priority of understanding as the seat of critique.

Unfortunately, Gonzalez does not move from Gadamer's ontological commitment to the dynamics of dialogue to a satisfactory account of critical hermeneutics. He properly emphasizes that, in a later edition of *Truth and Method*, Gadamer changed a key sentence from the claim that "it is only temporal distance" that can illuminate unproductive prejudices, to the more ambiguous suggestion that historical distance "*often*" can foster critical insight (Gonzalez, 2006, p. 329). Gadamer makes two important points with this change: first, historical perspective does not *inevitably* lead to critical insight; second, historical perspective is not the *only* stimulant for such insight. With regard to the second point, Gonzalez suggests Gadamer is signaling that the "experience of dialogue" provides critical distance no less than historical distance (ibid., p. 330), but this contention misunderstands Gadamer's detailed claim that all understanding, including historical understanding, is dialogic in character. Gadamer's change is significant because it indicates that historical distance is not the only stimulus for a critique of unproductive prejudices, which is to say there are other hermeneutical experiences that can initiate a "genuine" dialogue capable of realizing the critical potential of all dialogue. Gonzalez ends his analysis where he should begin, eliding the important question that follows from Gadamer's clarification of his thesis: *how* can we invite and promote a genuine decentering dialogue other than by reading texts that time has shown can fulfill this function?[12] This is just to rephrase the question that asks how hermeneutics can be critical.

My thesis is that, by embracing the rhetorical dimensions of Gadamer's approach, the critical element of dialogue can be drawn out of Gadamer's philosophical hermeneutics. Ricoeur's mediation failed because he sought a philosophical answer to the role of explanation rather than seeking a rhetorical account of the distanciating features of dialogue. If we are to make good on Ricoeur's project and extend Gadamer's insights we must reorient the project of critical hermeneutics to the rhetorical realm and continually attend to the rhetorical limits of philosophy.[13] A genuine dialogue that can expose unproductive prejudices is possible only when our own preunderstanding is confronted by an "other." Gadamer fully agrees with Ricoeur that historical distance renders a text foreign to us and thereby provokes us to pose new questions to the text—questions that can illuminate our prejudices—but historical distance is not the only distanciating "otherness" we can seek out. The confrontation with other contemporary cultures can also expose one's unproductive prejudices, as Gadamer often argued.[14] Idle chatter does not generate critique, nor does discussion among those who are locked within the same prevailing ideologies. Understanding is enriched by sustained confrontation with the other in a rhetorical exchange oriented to *die Sache* rather than to victory in debate. When the other seeks to persuade one of something one does not already accept, this is an experience in which one is brought up short and subjected to the risk of discovering that one's limited horizon is unproductive.

Ricoeur emphasizes the "world of the text" because it provides the basis for an explanatory intervention that is not lodged in ordinary dialogue, and he then extends this model to social interaction by construing social action as a "text." In sharp contrast, Gadamer begins with dialogue and looks to the experience of textual interpretation in order to highlight the distanciating features of dialogic engagement. Ricoeur interjects philosophical critique into hermeneutics, whereas Gadamer philosophically recovers the critical features of understanding. I contend that Gadamer's path is more productive because the goal of a critical hermeneutics is to foster *rhetorical experience*, not to deliver *philosophical truths*.

Theory and Practice in Critical Hermeneutics

How can a critical theorist foster the rhetorical experience in which critique occurs? Construing critical hermeneutics as a rhetorical achievement rather than the product of an explanatory methodology might suggest that theoretical guidance is unavailing; it is precisely this implication that motivated Ricoeur to embrace the philosophy of structuralism even while attempting to hew closely to Gadamer's ontological insights. Paradoxically, it is possible to appreciate the role of theory only by reading Gadamer's philosophy rhetorically. Drawing from the rhetorical tradition commenced by Isocrates, Aristotle, Quintilian, and Cicero we find the resources for understanding the relationship between theory and practice. Gadamer's rhetorically grounded antimethodologism has been misconstrued as an attack on theory, rather than properly understood as a celebration of the limited role of theory in fostering rhetorical-hermeneutical practices.

Gadamer's careful rehabilitation of Aristotelian practical philosophy in response to the overbearing claims of modern science does not subordinate theory to practice; instead, it restores the essential equilibrium of theory and practice that has been disturbed in modern life. Gadamer insists "theory is just as primordial an anthropological datum as is practical and political power. So everything depends on constantly renewing the balance between these two human forces. And I am convinced that human society exists only because and as long as there is a balance of this kind" (Gadamer, 1998, p. 68). Gadamer credits Aristotle for recognizing that theory is a relinquishment of immediate and pressing questions within a practice by holding oneself open in dialogue to different understandings that can reveal the unproductive nature of one's prevailing prejudices. This underscores why Gadamer places primary significance on *phronesis*: it is social reason, rooted in experience within a dialogic tradition, rather than the cognitive mastery of data or the technical mastery of materials. The sociality of reason and the practical dimensions of theory arise from their entwined dialogic character. As Robert Dostal explains, it is Gadamer's productive development of Heidegger's early philosophy that delivers this insight.

> Tarrying, as the way of attending to art or to the world, is to be understood as a mode of comportment (to speak anglicized Heideggerian) or as a habit (to speak anglicized Aristotelian). "Tarrying" takes time, and in tarrying we lose ourselves in the thing and, thereby, lose track of time. Where Heidegger would have us await the sudden flash of insight, Gadamer would have us develop the habit of tarrying with things.
>
> This tarrying is also a conversation—a conversation with one-self, with the thing at hand, and with others about whatever is at stake. . . . Although Heidegger, both in *Being and Time* with its concept of Being-with (*Mitsein*) and in his later work, provides a framework for the social and the dialogical, he never makes good on this aspect of the conversation that he says we are. . . . Gadamer, however, explicitly characterizes the conversation with the other as providing a "bridge." (Dostal, 2002, p. 257)

Gadamer's emphasis on dialogue relates theory, practice and truth to the rhetorical event, without collapsing these elements into an undifferentiated practice.

Gadamer claims Aristotle, by his very activity of writing the *Nicomachean Ethics*, provides substantial guidance regarding the interactions of theory and practice. Aristotle quite obviously is not engaged in ethical decision making in this work, but instead is theorizing about that activity. Gadamer's praise of theory should come as no surprise because his philosophical hermeneutics is a theoretical treatment of the practical activity of interpretation in much the same way as Aristotle's work. Gadamer justifies his theoretical bent by insisting that philosophical hermeneutics "must arise from practice itself and, with all the typical generalizations that it brings to explicit consciousness, be related back to practice" (Gadamer, 1981a, p. 92; *see* Gadamer, 1981b, p. 113). Theory is a distinctive part of dealing with the paradoxical social demands for action that are placed on individuals, but it remains intimately related to practice and cannot be separated entirely. As Gadamer insists, the "myth of the ivory tower where theoretical people live is an unreal fantasy. We all stand in the middle of the social system" (Gadamer, 1992c, p. 221).

We can clarify the role of critical theory by returning to the primary example in the Gadamer-Habermas debate: the claim that psychoanalysis is an emancipatory reconstructive science that cannot be reduced to the realm of empirical-logical science, nor to the realm of ordinary hermeneutical understanding. Habermas recognized the theoretical "know-that" generated by psychoanalytic theory must be woven into the "know-how" of the client's social life in order to become effective, and precisely this aspect of his theory has vexed his efforts to extend the model to social critique. Gadamer properly rejected the suggestion that the social critic could bring expert knowledge to bear in the manner a Freudian psychoanalyst might diagnose a patient and then bring the patient to self-awareness.[15] However, many contemporary psychotherapists have abandoned the explanatory focus of Freudian theory and embraced an approach that regards therapy as the cultivation of a critical dialogue in which the therapist does not presume to hold the (theoretical) answer to the client's problem (Mootz, 2000, pp. 349–72). Under this view, the therapist employs theories, but they are theories about how to facilitate a rhetorical exchange that can augment the client's capacities rather than theories that direct a treatment. We might characterize this practice as a reciprocal relationship of explanatory theories and hermeneutic understanding, but it is more accurate and productive to characterize it as a rhetorical event that provides critical insight.

Regarding psychotherapeutic dialogue as a site of theoretical intervention reveals the role and limits of theory in a rhetorical realm. The "talking cure" is theoretically informed, if we regard theory as a "tarrying" with the presencing of the world rather than as mastering the world through a methodological discipline. The therapist does not direct the client to divulge information according to methodological rules; rather, she opens herself to the client and, by refusing to adopt the posture of the all-knowing expert, attends to what the client says. The therapist is an expert, but she is an expert in "suspending" her urge to diagnose quickly in accordance with a template. Her expertise lies in *not* "establishing understandings, explanations, and interpretations based on prior experiences, formed truths, and knowledge," but rather in facilitating a genuine dialogue that is a collaborative discovery (Anderson, 1997, p. 107). Psychotherapy is a theoretically informed practice because it draws on general insights into the nature of dialogue, but these insights are rhetorically deployed rather than discovered methodologically and then imposed as a technical intervention.

Ricoeur regards Gadamer's approach to be overly conventional because he detects in the analysis of "coming to understanding" a flattening of difference that all too easily falls prey to ideology. Ricoeur's solution is to posit the distanciation of textual interpretation as a paradigm and to insist on the possibility and necessity of a critical moment modeled on structuralist philosophy; but this tack depends on the subject-centered expertise of the critic, despite Ricoeur's express efforts to avoid this result. Gadamer's analysis of dialogue as a confrontation of one's horizon remains true to the phenomenology of understanding as a critical event without surrendering the possibility of critical theory. Gadamer's rhetorical conception of understanding provides an account of how theory can guide practice, but only to the extent that theory arises from practice and does not purport to stand apart as a guarantor of practice. The long tradition of rhetorical theory, when brought to bear within Gadamer's ontology of understanding, provides the key to developing an effective critical hermeneutics.

Ricoeur's lectures on ideology and utopia, less ponderously philosophical than his many books,[16] provide more fertile ground than his analysis of explanation for developing a critical hermeneutics grounded in the intersection of rhetoric and hermeneutics that builds on Gadamer's ontological insights.[17] Working from Geertz's anthropology, Ricoeur argues that ideology is rhetorically secured and therefore can serve an integrative function (Ricoeur, 1986, pp. 257–58). He specifically answers Habermas, arguing that "ideology is not the distortion of communication but the rhetoric of basic communication" (ibid., p. 259). Thus, ideology in the pejorative sense really just means that rhetoric, in the pejorative sense, has occurred. (ibid., p. 266) Utopia displays the same ambivalence, because it too is rhetorically deployed in social discourse: "Because the concept of utopia is a polemical tool, it belongs to the field of rhetoric" (ibid., p. 310). Ricoeur's lectures emphasize that the interplay of ideology and utopia is grounded in the rhetorical-hermeneutical realm of social practice and cannot be directed by the philosopher standing outside the social arena. This activity embodies the polarity of imagination, and calls on us to make practical judgments, through the exercise of prudence, to ensure the potentially vicious circle of ideology and utopia can be a liberating spiral of social progress. (ibid., p. 314) In these lectures Ricoeur appears open to the possibility that the dialectic of belonging and distanciation is not a dialectic between hermeneutical experience and philosophical explanation, but rather is the dialectical character of hermeneutical experience as rhetorical event.

The Exemplary Significance of Legal Hermeneutics

We can explore the critical hermeneutics implied by reading Gadamer's hermeneutics rhetorically by turning to the practical example of law, a practice Gadamer argues has "exemplary significance" for his philosophical hermeneutics (Gadamer, 1989, pp. 324–41). Legal practice provides a model of an interpreter who must be hermeneutically attuned and rhetorically adept to ensure a successful event of understanding through application. William Eskridge's Gadamerian approach to statutory interpretation explains how the interpreter must utilize various perspectives on the statute (including intent, purpose, consequences, and coherence) to build a persuasive account of the meaning the law holds for the present case, although he worries that the critical bite of Gadamer's philosophy may be limited because Gadamer disavows our ability to transcend tradition[18] (Eskridge, 1990). Eskridge analyzes a Supreme Court opinion from the 1960s that interpreted an immigration statute to bar the admission of gay men and lesbians, showing how Gadamer's account reveals the simultaneous flexibility and conservatism of statutory interpretation. He concludes that philosophical hermeneutics breaks the tenacious grip of various ideological approaches to statutory interpretation, but argues it does not lay the groundwork for revolutionary insights into the homophobic structure of law through a comprehensive theoretical intervention such as Habermas's discourse theory (Eskridge, 1990, pp. 673–76).

Eskridge reads Gadamer too narrowly because he does not appreciate the rhetorical dimension of Gadamer's hermeneutics. If Eskridge had developed the patently rhetorical features of Gadamer's account of law, he would have more accurately revealed the critical potential inherent in every application of a statute to a current dispute. The conservative overtones of "applying traditionary understandings" evaporate when this activity is construed as formulating a question for the purpose of initiating a dynamic give-and-take that never simply reproduces a "given" meaning. Understood to be a rhetorical accomplishment, statutory interpretation could never be misconstrued as necessarily beholden to preexisting meanings and immune to critical reconsideration. Additionally, Eskridge errs by conflating the critical potential of legal interpretation with the social acceptance of a particular interpretation at a given point in history. Rhetorical theory distinguishes sophism, in which victory is the sole criterion of success, from genuine rhetoric, which is the art of finding the available means of persuasion in a particular case. Gadamer's philosophy does not provide a method to ensure that a lawyer could have secured victory and undermined deep-seated antigay biases in the case before the court, but this is a necessary consequence of his antimethodologism rather than a symptom of an insufficiently critical approach. The critical dimension of Gadamer's hermeneutics is demonstrated by the fact that *we can imagine how a lawyer or judge at that time could have utilized the available textual resources to make such arguments.* Eskridge's work in the 1990s did much to bring Gadamer's philosophy to bear on important questions of statutory interpretation, but had he developed the rhetorical dimensions of Gadamer's philosophy he would have been in a position to accentuate the critical depth of this application.[19]

Read rhetorically, Gadamer illuminates the practice of legal interpretation in a manner that underscores the critical dimensions of his hermeneutics. Critique is not achieved by rising above a practice; it is a comportment within the practice. The same holds true for legal practice, whether it is extensions of the common law or interpretation of the Constitution, statutes, or other regulations. The ongoing conversation of legal doctrine and commentary is indelibly shaped by the prejudiced contexts in which judgments are demanded, but the rhetorical activity of lawyering and judging generates the resources for criticizing existing doctrine. By declaring that legal practice is exemplary for philosophical hermeneutics, Gadamer emphasizes that legal interpretation can never be a matter of subsuming the individual case under the applicable rule because the interpretation of the law is a (rhetorical) act that "creates" the law. (Gadamer, 1989, pp. 517–18). This, in turn, provides the space for critique and rhetorical development.

> Legal positivism, which would like to limit legal reality entirely to the established law and its correct application, probably has no supporters today. The distance between the universality of the law and the concrete legal situation in a particular case is obviously essentially indissoluble. . . . What is remarkable about the situation is this: that the hermeneutical task of bridging the distance between the law and the particular case still obtains, even if no change in social conditions or other historical variations cause the current law to appear old-fashioned or inappropriate. The distance between the law and the individual case seems to be absolutely indissoluble. . . . It is no mere unavoidable imperfection in the process of legal codification when it leaves free play for its application to concrete instances, as if this free play could, in principle, be reduced at will. To be "elastic" enough to leave this kind of free play seems rather to be in the nature of legal regulation as such, indeed of legal order generally. (Gadamer, 1989, pp. 518–19)

In the free play of legal interpretation we find the rhetorical space for critique that is ubiquitous in hermeneutical encounters. There can be no methodology that ensures an appropriate level of critical assessment, but neither can ideology absolutely preclude such assessment.

Eskridge's concern that a Gadamerian understanding of statutory interpretation means courts may err in their judgments leads him to seek a theoretical safety net that is unavailable. The theoretical urge to protect rhetorical discourse from error is the modern project of attempting to overcome rhetoric. Because every case can be differently argued and differently decided, a critical element is present in every act of judgment, even when it purports to reaffirm status quo understandings; a lack of critical insight would simply make the act of judgment unnecessary. The inventiveness of lawyers in bringing cases, and of judges in deciding them, makes it possible for accepted understandings to be challenged continually. That, in every interpretive act, some preunderstand-ings remain unchallenged is not cause for regret over a lack of radicality, but is instead an inevitable consequence of the hermeneutical and rhetorical requi-sites for understanding.

Eskridge's characterization of the modes of statutory interpretation provides a theoretical intervention, in Gadamer's sense of the term, even if Eskridge ultimately desires a more revolutionary theoretical approach. In developing his theory of "dynamic statutory interpretation," Eskridge does not purport to direct the practice of interpreting statutes; rather, he reveals the nature of the practice and clears away conceptual confusions that inhibit rhetorical inventive-ness (Eskridge, 1994; Eskridge, 1987). Eskridge opposes the various theories of interpretation developed to constrain judicial interpretation—intentionalist, purposive, and textualist—and argues that the practice of statutory interpreta-tion is pragmatic and eclectic, and as such is not subject to a methodologically driven form of dialectical reasoning.[20] Had Eskridge read Gadamer's philoso-phy rhetorically, he would have proceeded from the understanding that the nonmethodological development of arguments invoking these different per-spectives (on statutory meaning) amount to an inventive use of topics. Seen in this light, there is no basis for lamenting the lack of a critical theory that can direct ingenuous developments of the practice; there is only the dialogic prac-tice itself. And that is enough.

Conclusion

Gadamer's hermeneutical philosophy does not advocate reverence for traditional understandings; instead, it acknowledges that tradition is a linguisti-cally structured and contested medium through which understanding takes place in a conversational manner structured by the humanistic logic of ques-tion and answer. Seen in this way, Gadamer propounds a rhetorical theory of human understanding. By recovering Gadamer's rhetorical conception of hermeneutics, we obtain guidance on how to develop the work of contempo-rary critics who seek to enact cultural criticism as a rhetorical-hermeneutical activity that, in securing the rhetorical knowledge upon which social life depends, navigates between the Charybdis of Habermasian rationalism and the Scylla of postmodern irrationalism.

Ricoeur's intervention in the Gadamer-Habermas debate accentuated, rather than mediated, the tension between understanding and explanation in

Gadamer's philosophical hermeneutics. Turning to his lectures in *Ideology and Utopia*, however, we find Ricoeur's hermeneutical philosophy is more attentive to the dialectical character of hermeneutical experience as rhetorical event. As is true of Gadamer, by accentuating the rhetorical dimension of his hermeneutical philosophy we can better appreciate and develop its critical element in a manner that respects the fundamental hermeneutical themes he and Gadamer have so persuasively established as guideposts for contemporary thinking.

Notes

[1] Several commentators have emphasized that rhetoric is central to the argument developed in *Truth and Method*. For example, in his review of *Truth and Method* Klaus Dockhorn suggests Gadamer underestimates the extent to which the rhetorical tradition underwrites his project; nevertheless, Dockhorn declares the "widespread depreciation or dismissal of rhetoric . . . should be effectively brought to an end by this book" (Dockhorn, 1980, p. 160).

[2] There are additional points, late in his career, when Gadamer acknowledged the rhetorical dimension of his philosophical hermeneutics (Gadamer, 1997a, p. 30; Gadamer, 1997b, pp. 154–55). In an interview with Jean Grondin, Gadamer makes clear he embraces rhetoric in its broadest possible sense:

> One would really honor the realm of the *Geisteswissenschaften* [human sciences] much more adequately, I think, if we brought them back under the older concept of rhetoric, where one deals with believable statements and not compelling proofs. This also applies for historical research, as well as for the sciences of law and theology, and as a matter of fact it also applies to the experience of art. (Gadamer 2006b, p. 89)

John Arthos notes similarly broad readings of the rhetorical tradition in other interviews and concludes that Gadamer's "reflective summary has a liberating effect. Instead of orienting ancient rhetoric from the text that history has canonized as its point of orientation, Gadamer steps back and looks at rhetoric as the achievement that the tradition itself has discovered" (Arthos, 2007, pp. 71).

[3] Susan Shapiro contends rhetoric provides the "place for both the recognition and correction" of systematically distorted communication and also avoids Habermas's return to "enlightenment ideology" (Shapiro, 1994, p. 132). She emphasizes that "it is just its participation within the problem of the ideological formation of discourse that peculiarly qualifies the art of rhetoric for the critique of ideology" (ibid., p. 133), and that only "when rhetoric is released from the rule of logic can it, then, become critical itself. Rhetoric may then offer a mode of ideology critique that is more properly post-Enlightenment for being more thoroughly grounded in praxis" (ibid., p. 147).

[4] In the course of detailing Gadamer's contributions to rhetorical theory, John Arthos asserts in a note that "Gadamer's promotion of rhetoric shares in the dangerously utopian vision of civic community that pervades all his work," but suggests we can avoid this deficiency by following "Gadamer in locating rhetoric

in the basic claim of speech" (Arthos, 2007, p. 79 n.17). My purpose in this chapter is to demonstrate that Gadamer does not need to be saved from naiveté by his rhetorical leanings, but rather that the thoroughly rhetorical character of his philosophy demonstrates he is not beholden to the ideal of a flattening consensus.

5   For example, Gadamer argues that Melancthon's Protestant hermeneutics was "epoch-making" because it directed the "basic concepts" of rhetoric to "the right reading of books . . . which was the prevailing pattern and theme in rhetoric during late antiquity. . . . Indeed, the basic demand to understand the individual part from the whole goes back to the relationship of *caput* (head) and *membra* (members of the body), which ancient rhetoric took as the pattern to follow." (Gadamer, 2006a, pp. 32–33)

6   Gadamer famously insists that "understanding always involves something like applying the text to be understood to the interpreter's present situation," and thus understanding, interpretation and application comprise "one unified process" (Gadamer, 1989, p. 308).

7   Gadamer expresses this most clearly in his discussion of "The Logic of Question and Answer" as the essence of our linguisticality.

> When we try to examine the hermeneutical phenomenon through the model of conversation between two persons, the chief thing that these apparently so different situations—understanding a text and reaching an understanding in conversation—have in common is that both are concerned with a subject matter that is placed before them. Just as each interlocutor is trying to reach agreement on some subject with his partner, so also the interpreter is trying to understand what the text is saying. This understanding of the subject matter must take the form of language. It is not that the understanding is subsequently put into words; rather, the way understanding occurs—whether in the case of a text or a dialogue with another person who raises an issue with us—is the coming-into-language of the thing itself. Thus we will first consider the structure of dialogue proper, in order to specify the character of that other form of dialogue that is the understanding of texts. Whereas up to now we have framed the constitutive significance of the *question* for the hermeneutical phenomenon in terms of conversation, we must now demonstrate the linguisticality of dialogue, which is the basis of the question, as an element of hermeneutics.
>
> Our first point is that the language in which something comes to speak is not a possession at the disposal of one or the other of the interlocutors. Every conversation presupposes a common language, or better, creates a common language. Something is placed in the center, as the Greeks say, which the partners in dialogue both share, and concerning which they can exchange ideas with one another. Hence reaching an understanding on the subject matter of a conversation necessarily means that a common language must first be worked out in the conversation. This is not an external matter of simply adjusting our tools; nor is it even right to say that the partners adapt themselves to one another but, rather, in a successful conversation they both come under the influence of the truth of the object and are thus bound to one another in a new community. To reach understanding in a dialogue is not

> merely a matter of putting oneself forward and successfully asserting one's
> own point of view, but being transformed into a communion in which we do
> not remain what we were. (Gadamer, 1989, p. 378)

[8] John Arthos identifies the rhetorical elements in Gadamer's philosophy as
anticipated, and perhaps surpassed, in Heidegger's 1924 lectures, and concludes
that Gadamer,

> in spite of the obliqueness of his attention to rhetoric, made extraordinary
> contributions to many facets of the canon that are somewhat camouflaged by
> the tack he took toward civic humanism. He advances with inestimable depth
> and originality a number of rhetoric cruces—to name a few, the structure of
> deliberative judgment (*phronesis, krisis*), the nature of issues (*res, Sache*), the
> function of starting points (*topoi, loci, sensus communis*), the role of audience,
> the definition of praxis, the location of agency. The lacuna for which he felt
> some responsibility was less a deficit of attention as a question of framing, and
> it remains a task for us to describe hermeneutics as the depth dimension of
> rhetoric. (Arthos, 2007, p. 15)

Arthos argues that Gadamer's creative reading of Aristotle reveals the originality
of his contribution to contemporary rhetorical philosophy: "Gadamer placed
rhetoric first in his understanding of Aristotle, against Aristotle's manifest
intention, because Gadamer understood the key insight of ancient rhetoric to be
that reason is embodied, that logos is thinking and speaking, that rhetoric is the
locus of social discursivity, and that this principle was deep at work in Aristotle's
exercise of thought" (ibid., pp. 7–8).

[9] Ricoeur's summary of this point is oft-quoted, but still underappreciated.

> My own interrogation proceeds from this observation. Would it not be appro-
> priate to shift the initial locus of the hermeneutical question, to reformulate
> the question in such a way that a certain dialectic between the experience of
> belonging and alienating distanciation becomes the mainspring, the key to
> the inner life, of hermeneutics? (Ricoeur, 1981b, p. 90).

In Habermas's terminology, Ricoeur insists that we need not—and indeed cannot—choose to elevate "know-that" or "know-how" over the other.

[10] Keith D'Souza correctly reads Ricoeur as endorsing Gadamer's hermeneutic
ontology and then adding structuralist explanation as the basis for critique,
rather than as offering a different account altogether (D'Souza, 2006). I will
interpret Gonzalez's argument in light of this characterization of Ricoeur's
project.

[11] Ricoeur readily accepts Gadamer's insistence that critique must be reintegrated
into the hermeneutical form of life from which it arises (Ricoeur, 1982, p. 311).
In a late work, Ricoeur agrees that we have surpassed the false antagonism of
explanation and understanding, a situation that he graphically acknowledges by
using the term, "Explanation/Understanding" (Ricoeur 2004, 185). But this
retreat from an overly schematic and analytical approach to the critical moment

of interpretation is not complete. He analyzes historiography in terms of three related phases: gathering documents, explanation/understanding of the documentary evidence, and representation of explanation/understanding in historical writing. Interestingly, he wishes to retain a broad meaning of "interpretation" to include all phases. "In this sense there is interpretation at all levels of the historiographical operation; for example, at the documentary level with the selection of sources, at the explanation/understanding level with the choice among competing explanatory models, and, in a more spectacular fashion, with variations in scale" (ibid., 235). He regards the hermeneutical experience of interpretation as multifaceted and ill-suited to chronological or analytical exposition. "The three phases of the historiographical operation, let us recall, do not constitute successive phases, but rather intermingled levels where only our didactic concern gives them the appearance of chronological succession" (ibid., 234–35). The very format of the book evidences his desire to minimize the didactic nature of the work (ibid., xvii), but it is my contention that this concession is insufficient to overcome the philosophical bent that tends to occlude the organic rhetorical-hermeneutical event that served as Gadamer's lifelong focus.

[12] Gadamer's analysis of the "classic" in *Truth and Method* addresses this issue. The "classic" is recognized precisely because it persistently poses questions, not because it provides timeless answers (Gadamer, 1989, pp. 285–90).

[13] Habermas steadfastly refused to accept this thesis in his debate with Gadamer. Habermas's political claims rooted in his discourse theory are "motivationally impotent" precisely because they attempt to avoid the rhetorical reality in which politics is constituted and sustained (Abizadeh, 2007, p. 446).

[14] Gadamer traveled the world and learned a variety of languages after the worldwide success of *Truth and Method*. It was undoubtedly this personal experience that led him to emphasize the importance of multicultural experience in his later philosophy.

[15] Gadamer insists this model of critical theory is fundamentally at odds with philosophical hermeneutics (Mootz, 2000, pp. 12–18). He explains:

> Both critique of ideology and psychoanalysis posit their own special knowledge in advance and hold it to be scientifically based. In contrast to this, hermeneutical reflection does not posit any scientific claim with specific content of this kind. Reflection in philosophical hermeneutics does not claim to know in advance that concrete social conditions only allow a distorted form of communication to take place. And included in the view of critique of ideology and psychoanalysis is that one already knows what will be the result of their undistorted, right kind of communication. Also, critique of ideology does not intend to operate like a therapist who through the reflection process will lead the patient to a higher insight into his or her life history and thereby enable them to find his or her true nature. In both critique of ideology and psychoanalysis the interpretation intends to be guided by a prior knowledge on the basis of which one will be freed of prior fixations and prejudices. In this sense, both are to be understood as experiences of "enlightenment." Hermeneutical experience, in opposition to this, regards with skepticism every conscious intention to employ a system of knowledge. . . . In the rich concreteness of this hermeneutical experience concepts like "enlightenment,"

"emancipation" and "compulsion-free dialogue" are revealed to be pale abstractions. Hermeneutical experience, in contrast, realizes how deeply rooted pre-judgments can be and how little even our becoming conscious of them is able to free one from their power. (Gadamer, 2006a, pp. 50–51)

In this short excerpt Gadamer not only distinguishes hermeneutical philosophy from the pretensions of the psychoanalytic model of critical theory; he also distinguishes the latter from therapeutic dialogue in a manner that supports the analysis in the text following this note.

[16] Even in an occasional address delivered in the presence of Chaïm Perelman, Ricoeur demarcates the boundaries among persuasion, poetics, and hermeneutics (Ricoeur, 1997). Claiming philosophical humility by not seeking to subsume different experiences under a single rubric, Ricoeur in fact maintains the philosophical nature of these demarcations and threatens to preclude an understanding of critique as a feature of an inextricably rhetorical hermeneutics (or, hermeneutical rhetorics).

[17] Andreea Ritivoi offers an imaginative reading of Ricoeur's work in terms of rhetorical theory, providing solid ground for the extension I undertake in this essay (Ritivoi, 2006). She acknowledges that Ricoeur does not explicitly deal with rhetorical concepts in his work, and so she proposes "a rational reconstruction of Ricoeur's contribution to rhetoric by carefully linking his ideas to basic tenets in the field" (ibid., p. 4). Ritivoi concludes that even though he does not seek to make a contribution to rhetoric, Ricoeur offers useful insights into its conceptual core by prompting fundamental questions [encouraging] us to consider the ways in which rhetorical discourse can successfully incorporate and modify public opinions" (ibid., pp. 157–58).

[18] Eskridge argues that Gadamer's dynamic approach to interpretation is liberating in an incrementalist manner, and that although this does not answer the criticisms of Habermas, Ricoeur, and others, it might be sufficient in the current political environment.

> This is the dilemma: Gadamer's desire to root his theory in tradition but to approach tradition critically will end up sacrificing either tradition or critique. Gadamer tends to err on the side of tradition, while his commentators Ricoeur and Warnke are more inclined to critique. Although this is a genuine tension inherent in Gadamer's theory, it does not seem a fatal tension, and in statutory interpretation concerns underlying the countermajoritarian difficulty might justify his intrinsic conservatism: Judges who are not elected and not directly accountable to the people are not in the best position to attempt radical critique of the nation's statutes.
>
> That is not to say that Gadamerian interpreters of statutes cannot engage in effective incremental critique. . . .
>
> [Critical scholars might object] that Gadamerian theory does not liberate interpreters enough from "oppressive" or "distorted" statutory texts. The hermeneutical therapy is not radical enough. I am open to this objection. . . .
>
> Because of the intrinsic conservatism of our democracy, and its traditional commitment to incremental change, it is my judgment that cautious Gadamerian hermeneutics may be as dynamic as statutory interpretation can legitimately be. For now. (Eskridge, 1990, pp. 675–76, 680–81)

[19] Eskridge offers a more balanced approach in his book published four years later. He discusses Gadamer's hermeneutics and the immigration case, but he recognizes the significance of the fact that there was a dissent at the court of appeals level and suggests that a "rupture" of the ideology sustaining the antigay holding that occurred within a few short years was presaged in this judicial dialogue (Eskridge, 1994, pp. 60–65). The "rupture" in attitudes and legal doctrine is best explained through a rhetorical-hermeneutical analysis of the legal developments (Mootz, 2006).

[20] With coauthor Phil Frickey, Eskridge argues that statutory interpretation is a form of practical reasoning in which the advocate and judge consider a variety of factors that point in different directions in difficult cases (Eskridge et al., 1990), and this appears to be the approach to statutory interpretation undertaken by most judges (Schneider, 2001). Eskridge has argued at length that statutory interpretation as practical reasoning is firmly rooted in judicial practices at the time of the founding, and that contemporary textualist theories represent a new, theory-driven approach (Eskridge, 2001). In a recent book review he succinctly challenges the reigning ideology of textualism (in terms of theoretical predilections of many judges and law professors, which is not to say in the actual practice of law) by arguing that judges are capable of exhibiting the practical wisdom necessary to effectively and reasonably interpret statutes (Eskridge, 2006).

Chapter 5

Understanding as Metaphoric, Not a Fusion of Horizons

George H. Taylor

The themes of this chapter are grounded in the following kinds of observations. The anti-imperialist scholar of world politics, Stanley Hoffman, argues: "The assumption that 'people everywhere are all alike' is something you have to get out of your system" (Quoted in Lambert, 2007, p. 34). Religion professor Jeffrey Stout asserts as "wishful thinking" the claim of some philosophers "that all human beings already share a common morality, *the* common morality, simply by virtue of being human" (Stout, 2004, p. 14). Linguists such as George Lakoff and Deborah Tannen note the limitations of communication between, respectively, liberals and conservatives, and men and women (Lakoff, 2002, p. 375; Tannen, 1990). Each group does not speak the same language as the other. How, then, in today's diverse world is it possible to engage in dialogue? The problem is often difficult enough when internal to any one culture, but we are now witnessing how much more problematic is conversation and understanding across cultures. The relationship between the West and the Islamic world is, of course, the most prominent current example, and an example that demonstrates in all too stark fashion the deadly consequences of dialogue's failure.

I agree with those quoted that the possibility of dialogue today will not be found in some underlying commonality across the divide. That is a contested proposition, of course. Opponents will argue that all humans share an underlying common linguistic or cognitive structure, genetics, morality, or ontology. I want to explore this opposition by comparison of Ricoeur and Gadamer. I thematize the discussion on the basis of the topic of dialogue itself as presented in Gadamer and as responded to by Ricoeur. In particular, I concentrate on Gadamer's development of the concept of the fusion of horizons, and on Ricoeur's own distinctive approach to that term. I agree with Jean Grondin that the concept of the fusion of horizons is emblematic of Gadamer's thought, even as the concept is not always justly understood (Grondin, 2005, p. 401). My argument is that Gadamer's notion of the fusion of horizon mistakenly claims the availability of an underlying commonality, while Ricoeur correctly emphasizes the notion of understanding as metaphoric—the creation of similarity across difference. In my view, then, the tensive relationship in metaphor between similarity and difference seems better to capture the possibilities of contemporary dialogue than does the fusion of horizons. I will further specify the differences between Gadamer and Ricoeur by contrasting their interpretations, both of metaphor and of translation.

The Hermeneutics that Ricoeur and Gadamer Share

Before exploring the differences between Ricoeur's and Gadamer's hermeneutics, let me begin by brief elaboration of the hermeneutic stance they share. Here we find, at a broad level, a common acceptance of hermeneutics's exemplification in the fusion of horizons, and this acceptance—which does not yet assess with any particularity the term "fusion"—is one I also endorse. As is well known, Ricoeur's and Gadamer's hermeneutics agree that we humans do not have the possibility of a viewpoint above the fray. Hegel's absolute knowledge is not available (Ricoeur, 1981b, pp. 61, 193).[1] We are individually located within situated and perspectival horizons, yet these conditions provide "the productive prejudices that enable understanding" (Gadamer, 1989, p. 295). The fusion of horizons is pertinent for understanding in at least three senses. First, our contemporary horizon is infused—a perhaps better term than fused— with horizons from the past. We are constituted in part by our past, by our traditions (ibid., p. 306).[2] Second, our understanding of the past (or of the other) is always infused with what we bring from our present horizon (ibid., p. 576; Ricoeur, 1988, p. 220).[3] Understanding is never merely a reproductive activity; what we bring to the text makes understanding ineluctably a productive action (Gadamer, 1989, pp. 296, 374). We always understand in a different way than the understanding in the original context (ibid., p. 297).[4] This hermeneutics rejects romanticist hermeneutics, which argued for the availability of "complete contemporaneity" (Ricoeur, 1988, p. 220) with the past, the reproduction of the original (Gadamer, 1989, p. 296).[5] We cannot annul our distance from the past (Ricoeur, 1988, p. 220).

Third, the fusion of horizons captures the claim that our individual stance is not enclosed within fixed boundaries. A horizon indicates only temporary limits; a horizon can expand. And the expansion occurs through the "fusion" with other horizons (Weinsheimer, 1991, p. 15).[6] The infusion of these other horizons allows us to test our horizons (Gadamer, 1989, p. 306; Ricoeur, 1988, p. 220). Ricoeur develops this aspect in some detail in his notion of appropriation (Ricoeur, 1981a), which he quite explicitly relates to the fusion of horizons (Ricoeur, 1978, pp. 90–91, 144). When faced with the horizon of the other, as in a text, appropriation is "quite the contrary of projecting oneself and one's own beliefs and prejudices; it is to let the work and its world enlarge the horizon of the understanding which I have of myself" (Ricoeur, 1981b, p. 178). Our original horizon is displaced (Taylor, 1994, p. 73). As Charles Taylor also emphasizes, part of the goal of fusion here is simply increased respectful understanding of the other (Taylor, 1990, p. 53). Taken at this level of generality, the fusion of horizons exemplifies the real promise of hermeneutics for contemporary conversation and dialogue. Toward the other it acts in a posture of attentiveness and openness rather than imposition or domination. Jean Grondin concludes his Gadamer biography by quoting Gadamer's similar hope for his hermeneutics:

> "[I]t may not be unjustified to conclude from our discussion a final political consequence. We may perhaps survive as humanity if we would be able to learn that we may not simply exploit our means of power and effective possibilities, but must learn to stop and respect the other as an other, whether it is nature or the grown cultures of peoples and nations; and if we would be able to learn to experience the other and the others, as the other of our self, in order to participate with one another." (Grondin, 2003, p. 329, quoting Gadamer, 1992, pp. 235–36)

As I turn to more detailed assessment of Gadamer's notion of the "fusion of horizons," my question is whether this concept and its framework that is representative of his hermeneutics allow hermeneutics to achieve its promise. My claim is that Ricoeur's hermeneutics takes us further.

The Challenge to Gadamer's Hermeneutics

As Ricoeur observes, Gadamer's hermeneutics wants to avoid either of two extremes. On the one hand, as we have already noted, Gadamer rejects the availability of a Hegelian absolute knowledge, under which all horizons would be ultimately subsumed. On the other hand, he also denies that each horizon is unique and incommensurable. The "fusion of horizons" represents the avoidance of these extremes: horizons are and remain plural, but they can interrelate; the distance between them is not uncrossable (Ricoeur, 1988, p. 220). In Gadamer's famous words:

> Hermeneutic work is based on a polarity of familiarity and strangeness . . . in the play between the traditionary text's strangeness and familiarity to us, between being a historically intended, distanciated object and belonging to a tradition. *The true locus of hermeneutics is this in-between.* (Gadamer, 1989, p. 295; emphasis in original)

My doubt lies in whether Gadamer's hermeneutics maintain this in-betweenness.

Joel Weinsheimer very aptly and precisely offers an elaboration and defense of Gadamer's hermeneutics that my thesis challenges. He argues:

> If not as subsumption[,] . . . then how should we understand understanding? The new model that Gadamer offers . . . is "the fusion of horizons." This

phrase is not very clear, and in one respect at least it is troubling, for fusion seems to imply precisely the same suppression of particularity and difference as does subsumption. Yet such homogenization, I think, is not at all what the fusion of horizons means for Gadamer. He regards understanding, instead, as the kind of fusion that occurs in metaphor, a fusion that respects plurality while not relinquishing the claims of unity. (Weinsheimer, 1991, p. 64)

Weinsheimer acknowledges what are my own hesitations about the term "fusion," which does seem to imply unification. Yet, consistent with language in Gadamer, such as hermeneutics's basis in a "polarity of familiarity and strangeness," Weinsheimer resists this simple reading of the term "fusion." We properly should not rest on an independent reading of the term, but on Gadamer's use of it. And at the latter level, my problem remains. I have great respect for Weinsheimer's depiction of understanding in Gadamer as metaphoric. Yet, while I agree and shall argue both that understanding represents the kind of activity that occurs in metaphor and that metaphor respects plurality, I want to build on Ricoeur to emphasize the abiding *tension* between sameness and difference found in metaphor. Gadamer, and to some degree Weinsheimer, himself, give too much weight to unity and commonality rather than maintain the tension between identity and difference that Ricoeur calls metaphoric *resemblance*. The difference between Ricoeur's and Weinsheimer's presentation of metaphor has some methodological interest, but more critical is the substantive difference. In the quest for dialogue across today's diverse cultures, I do not believe we can assume commonality; the relationship across these horizons remains much more tensive. These differences in presumptions may affect, significantly, both the approaches to dialogue and the possibilities of its fruition.

Gadamer's Presumption of a Preexisting Underlying Commonality

A hallmark of hermeneutics lies in its rejection of a notion of application whereby meaning is first known in its universal form and then rendered concrete in—applied to—a particular case (Gadamer, 1989, p. 341). For hermeneutics, the relationship between whole (existent meaning) and part (meaning as applied in a new context) is not one of subsumption; instead, part and whole determine the other (ibid., p. 291). Application involves "co-determining, supplementing, and correcting [a] principle" (ibid., p. 39). As Weinsheimer writes, a general knowledge of history is insufficient to understanding the course of a historical particular, such as the French Revolution. The latter is not simply a subsumable example of larger historical law. Our understanding of history (the whole) expands as we address and incorporate the specific stories of the French Revolution (the part) (Weinsheimer, 1991, pp. 42–43). Individuals, themselves, can be considered a part within a larger whole—part of a larger history, tradition, culture, or language—and a similar interplay between part and whole is at work. For our purposes, I want to attend Gadamer's apparent claim that understanding between individuals or cultures requires some whole—a common history, tradition, or language—a whole that either underlies, or is the product of, the dialogue. Again, my contention is that Gadamer's analysis grants too much weight to commonality, that such commonality is not available in contemporary dialogues across diverse cultures, and that Ricoeur's theory of metaphor as tensive shows how these dialogues can occur nonetheless.

In this subpart, I will present evidence of Gadamer's claim that a common history, tradition, or language is *presupposed* by understanding. In the next, I will turn to his claim—not always consistent with the present one—that dialogue can *create* such a commonality. Gadamer's most extended statement about the availability of an underlying commonality occurs in the following passage:

> When our historical consciousness transposes itself into historical horizons, this does not entail passing into alien worlds unconnected in any way with our own; instead, they together constitute the *one great horizon* that moves from within and that, beyond the frontiers of the present, embraces the historical depths of our self-consciousness. Everything contained in historical consciousness is in fact embraced by a *single historical horizon*. (Gadamer, 1989, p. 304; emphases added)

A few pages later Gadamer allows that the availability of a single horizon challenges the need for a fusion of horizons. The horizons "fused" seemed to be at bottom part of the one great horizon. He responds—fairly, in my view—that a tension persists between any historical text and the present. Past and present do project different horizons, and part of the hermeneutic task is to bring out this tension rather than engage in superficial assimilation. The need for expansion of horizons—for "fusion"—is predicated upon differences in horizons. Yet, Gadamer continues, present historical consciousness in its separation from the past is "only something superimposed upon continuing tradition, and hence it immediately recombines with what it has foregrounded itself from in order to become one with itself again in the *unity of the historical horizon* that it thus acquires" (ibid., p. 306; emphasis added).[7] This fusion of past and present obviously includes the *creation* of commonality—the subject of the next subpart— but here I want to emphasize the persisting availability of the single underlying horizon with which present historical consciousness recombines. The process is not one of subsumption of a part into simply an existing whole, an existing order, but the part does affect and recombine with an existing whole, a single historical horizon.

Gadamer returns to these themes elsewhere in *Truth and Method*. In another passage, describing the fusion of horizons between a historical text and an interpreter, Gadamer maintains that the interpreter's anticipation of an answer from the text "presupposes that the questioner is *part of the tradition* and regards himself as addressed by it" (ibid., pp. 377–78; emphasis added). Gadamer finds this unity not simply in tradition but also in language. "Every conversation obviously presupposes that the two speakers speak the same language" (ibid., p. 385).[8] For Gadamer, Weinsheimer writes, language is "the locus of belonging where subject and object, thought and world, meet—or, more precisely, where they are already at home together prior to their having been split asunder by conscious reflection" (ibid., p. 70).[9] Gadamer also argues that, in the conversation between individuals of two different languages, neither is imprisoned by his or her own language because of "the superior *universality* with which *reason* rises above the limitations of any given language" (ibid., p. 402; emphases added). Whether it be located in tradition, history, language, or reason, a universality or single horizon is available and grounds the fusion of horizons.[10]

Other elucidations in the secondary literature of Gadamer's fusion of horizons develop similar portrayals. Stanley Rosen writes that "the fusion of horizons is intrinsically the opening of a single horizon" (Rosen, 1997, p. 211). The fusion does not result in the disappearance of the self's or the other's horizon—this is the tension between present and past horizon that Gadamer discusses—but the two participate in a single underlying horizon (ibid., pp. 212–13). Philippe Eberhard argues that the fusion of horizons encompasses "a plurality of horizons in the process of fusing and . . . a single horizon that encompasses and makes up the fusion" (Eberhard, 2004, p. 80). The fusion of horizons entails "the elevation to a higher level of universality or commonality that encompasses the particularities of the other and of oneself" (ibid., p. 86). Jean Grondin contends that in Gadamer there is a fusion not only of thought and language but of the thing, thought, and language (Grondin, 2005, p. 416). That which makes possible the adequation of thought and thing is the capacity of language itself to uncover the things themselves (ibid., p. 417).[11]

Ricoeur is himself attentive to Gadamer's language about the availability of a single horizon. In his view, Gadamer's concern is to avoid a Nietzschean radical pluralism wherein horizons do not fuse but remain separate, incommunicable. Yet, Gadamer's insistence on a "horizon," Ricoeur argues, intends to avoid the other pole of a Hegelian absolute knowledge "wherein the fusion of horizons would itself be grasped" (Ricoeur, 1981b, p. 75). I certainly agree with Ricoeur that Gadamer wants to avoid the Nietzschean and Hegelian extremes, and I also agree that he does so, and his approach remains a hermeneutic project. Yet, Gadamer's success in avoidance of the two poles does not necessarily translate into the success of his approach on its own. Ricoeur may be too generous here in contextualizing Gadamer's negative aims but then in not assessing the adequacy of Gadamer's positive theory.

Gadamer's Presumption of the Commonality Established
by the Fusion of Horizons

At times, Gadamer's emphasis rests less on the commonality underlying the possibility of a fusion of horizons than on the commonality *achieved by* that fusion. We find such statements as: "Every conversation presupposes a common language, or better, creates a common language" (Gadamer, 1989, pp. 378, 388). Understanding creates "a common diction and a common dictum" (ibid., p. 387), "communion" (ibid., p. 379), "a higher universality" (ibid., p. 305).[12] It might be thought that the commonality created in the fusion of horizons is entirely dependent on the underlying commonality of tradition, history, or horizon in which conversationalists participate. But the creation of the common language in the fusion of horizons itself underscores the circular and dynamic relation between whole (underlying commonality) and part (the conversation); the relationship is not one simply of dependency by the part on the whole. Weinsheimer writes, "Understanding always projects the unity of a shared truth, even if the single horizon enabling understanding is not given in advance" (Weinsheimer, 1985, p. 183).[13] More generally, the dynamic evident in the fusion of horizons evidences what is for Gadamer "the basic movement of spirit." The movement is "[t]o recognize one's own in the alien, to become at home in it" (Gadamer, 1989, p. 14).[14] The ontological achievement of the fusion of horizons is belonging (Weinsheimer, 1985, p. 251).

Ricoeur's Hermeneutics

Ricoeur's Response to the Fusion of Horizons

As we begin to turn more directly to the contrast between Ricoeur's and Gadamer's hermeneutics, my hesitation remains that understanding does not create either "commonality" or a sense of being at home in what was originally alien. Let me enter the discussion of Ricoeur's hermeneutics by contrasting his approach on the latter point. As is well known, Ricoeur's hermeneutics is located more in a model of text interpretation rather than conversation. As we have also seen, Ricoeur characterizes interpretation as an act of appropriation. Ricoeur depicts this act as "making one's own what was initially alien" (Ricoeur, 1981b, p. 159).[15] This description has similarities to Gadamer's depiction of becoming at home in what was alien, but I am more struck by their differences. Both acts present a transfer of meaning and understanding, and this transfer is something I retain and endorse throughout. The transfer remains a power of the fusion of horizons in the large and general sense of that phrase. We are not simply caught in our own interpretive frames; transfer across frames does occur. But while Gadamer claims we become at home in the alien—the mark of commonality and belonging—Ricoeur speaks more modestly of making what was alien one's own. This is a transfer of meaning and understanding, not necessarily an identity of meaning and understanding.

Ricoeur's differences with Gadamer become more apparent in Ricoeur's own discussion of the fusion of horizons. Ricoeur sometimes describes appropriation as "close" to the fusion of horizons (Ricoeur, 1984, p. 77; Ricoeur, 1976, p. 93), but he does not describe this process as one of leading to commonality. Instead, his vocabulary is one of "convergence" (Ricoeur, 1981b, pp. 191–92; Ricoeur, 1988, p. 178), or "intersection" (Ricoeur, 1984, pp. 77, 79). This language might suggest an approximation to commonality, but while Ricoeur attends the possibility of transfer, he also repeatedly emphasizes the tension operative in the fusion of horizons. "This notion of a fusion of horizons leads to the theme that finally what is at stake in the hermeneutics of historical consciousness is the *tension* between the horizon of the past and that of the present" (ibid., p. 220; emphasis added). This tension exhibits not a singular sense of tradition but rather "the dialectizing of the idea of traditionality" (ibid., p. 221). The "convergence" of text and reader in the fusion of horizons establishes not commonality but "an analogizing relation" (ibid., p. 178). The fusion of horizons is not an achievement but "what we attempt to bring about" (ibid., p. 221). For Ricoeur the fusion of horizons remains an "ideal type of reading" (Ricoeur, 1988, p. 178). In his own close reading of Ricoeur and Gadamer, Daniel Frey underscores Ricoeur's attention to the ideal character of this fusion (Frey, 2008, p. 246). Behind general similarities between Ricoeur and Gadamer on the fusion of horizons, Frey urges, lie divergences that need to be raised (ibid., p. 240).

Ricoeur's reluctance to embrace the achievement of a fusion of horizons arises in his later work as well. In the section on forgetting in the third part of *Memory, History, Forgetting*, Ricoeur insists on the play of horizons. Whatever the fusion of horizons may be, it cannot be considered in isolation, for it exists in play with "the receding of horizons, incompletion" (Ricoeur, 2004, p. 413). The significance of this passage is heightened, as Domenico Jervolino reminds us that the final word of this volume is, in fact, "Incompletion" (ibid., p. 506, cited in Jervolino, 2008, p. 227). The fusion remains ideal; it is incomplete.[16]

Understanding as Translation

The tension at work in understanding is even more overt in Ricoeur's discussion of translation. Comparison with Gadamer's comments on translation will prove especially pertinent. In the posthumously published work, *On Translation* (Ricoeur, 2006), Ricoeur stresses that between two languages there is an "irreducibility" (ibid., p. 10), and "impassable difference" (ibid., pp. 9, 23). A translation attempts equivalence or correspondence but never attains adequacy (ibid., p. 10). Equivalence is something that can only be sought, because we have no basis for claiming in the translation an identity of

meaning (ibid., pp. 34–35). We cannot claim identity of meaning because
between the source and target texts there is *no third text* that could act as the
common source for each text's meaning (ibid., pp. 7, 22). This statement
is most significant: there is no third, underlying text; there is no one horizon,
one tradition, one history, one language. Between the original text and the
translation we have no independent, grounding measure of meaning or understanding. The nature of equivalence is "*produced* by translation rather than
presupposed by it" (ibid., p. 35; emphasis in original).

Ricoeur goes on to argue that the same problems found in translation
across languages are also at work within any linguistic community. In dialogue
internal to a language, identical meaning again cannot be found (ibid., p. 25).
We, in fact, do not finally hold in common language, meaning, history,
tradition, or horizon. "There is something foreign in every other" (ibid.). Our
human condition is one of "multiplicity at all the levels of existence" (ibid.,
p. 33). In contrast to Gadamer, understanding is not a product of commonality,
whether presupposed or supposedly created dialogically. Rather, *understanding
is translation* (ibid., pp. 24, 27–28). Translation becomes a model for hermeneutics (Kearney, 2006, p. xvii). Transfer across or within languages occurs, but it
does so without the presupposition or creation of commonality. Understanding
as translation elides both of the extremes Gadamer also wanted to avoid: we are
not left with incommunicability (no transfer) or absolute knowledge (transfer
subsumed to a common frame). I shall go on to argue that Ricoeur's theory
of metaphor renders more precise this possibility of tensive transfer, but
comparison first of Gadamer's versus Ricoeur's depictions of translation will
help further exemplify the differences between their hermeneutics.

For Gadamer, translation is an extreme example of the hermeneutic task,
and it highlights both the need to overcome alienness (Gadamer, 1989, p. 387)
and its necessary mediation by the interpreter's own horizon (ibid., p. 384).
Again, Gadamer rejects the availability either of absolute knowledge or of the
direct, unmediated reproduction of the other's thoughts claimed by romanticist hermeneutics. Yet, a "common world of understanding" (ibid.) remains the
model, even for translation. In both conversation within a culture and in translation the goal is to achieve "a common diction" (ibid., p. 387).[17] Gadamer
recognizes the achievement through translation of a common language may
fail. There may be an unbridgeable gap for which the translator seeks a best
solution, but the solution is merely a compromise (ibid., p. 386). Whereas for
Ricoeur these situations of translation are prototypical instances of the tasks of
understanding, for Gadamer they are atypical and circumstances where, due
to the lack of a common language, understanding does not occur (ibid.).[18]

Understanding as Metaphoric

Ricoeur's characterization of understanding as translation itself exemplifies an
even more refined portrayal of understanding in his work. Understanding is

ultimately metaphoric, and the most adequate representation of what is at issue in the fusion of horizons is captured in this light. We know from Gadamer that all understanding is application—such as an interrelation of a "whole" to a new part, or a historical text to a present circumstance (ibid., p. 291). The fusion of horizons overcomes the distance between elements to allow understanding to occur. My claim is that the moment of application is better described as metaphoric, and that appreciation of the character of metaphor in fact renders more intelligible and precise the operation of application. Application does not overcome distance, but establishes a metaphoric relationship, a "new pertinence . . . between the terms despite their 'distance' apart" (Ricoeur, 1977, p. 194). Metaphoric meaning, writes Ricoeur, has the character of *resemblance*:

> Metaphor reveals the logical structure of "the similar" because, in the metaphorical statement, "the similar" is perceived *despite* difference, *in spite of* contradiction. Resemblance, therefore, is the logical category corresponding to the predicative operation in which "approximation" (bringing close) meets the resistance of "being distant." In other words, metaphor displays the work of resemblance because the literal contradiction preserves difference within the metaphorical statement: "same" and "different" are not just mixed together, they also remain opposed. Through this specific trait, enigma lives on in the heart of metaphor. In metaphor, "the same" operates *in spite of* "the different." (ibid., p. 196; emphases in original)[19]

In metaphor, Ricoeur continues, "the identity and the difference do not melt together but confront each other" (ibid., p. 199). Metaphor does not create a fusion, a unity, a single horizon. François Dosse writes that while metaphor might appear to be a fusion of meaning (*fusion de sens*), it is, in fact, the place of conflict between the new meaning and the old (Dosse, 2008, p. 358). Sameness is inextricably intermixed with difference; sameness cannot be distilled out of the mixture of sameness and difference. No common language either underlies the metaphor or is created by the metaphor, because difference is always retained. There is no third text, nothing literal that assures the commonality across the metaphoric relationship. Metaphoric resemblance, says Ricoeur, remains "the site of the clash between sameness and difference" (ibid., p. 196).

Joel Weinsheimer argues that, also for Gadamer, understanding is fundamentally metaphorical (Weinsheimer, 1991, p. 65), that understanding partakes of the same "irreducible tension of similarity and difference" found in metaphor (ibid., p. 78).[20] I close my comparison of Ricoeur and Gadamer by distinguishing Gadamer's (and Weinsheimer's) conception of metaphor from Ricoeur's. The differences here encapsulate the differences I have pursued throughout. In *Truth and Method*, Gadamer's overt references to metaphor are few, but weighty. For present purposes, one of these passages is particularly relevant[21] and worthy of quoting in detail:

[I]f a person transfers an expression from one thing to the other, he has in mind something that is *common* to both of them; but this in no way needs to be generic universality. Rather he is following his widening experience, which looks for *similarities*. . . . The genius of verbal consciousness consists in being able to express these *similarities*. This is its fundamental metaphorical nature. . . .

It is obvious that the particularity of an experience finds expression in metaphorical transference, and is not at all the fruit of a concept by means of abstraction. But it is equally obvious that knowledge of what is *common* is obtained in this way. (Gadamer, 1989, p. 429; emphases added)

There is much to admire in this passage. Metaphoric transfer is not reductive to a common concept, a generic universality. Difference exists across the elements in the metaphoric relationship. Different horizons need to be "fused." The process is not one of subsumption, either to an underlying common concept or of one horizon to the other (Weinsheimer, 1991, p. 84). Metaphor retains Gadamer's goal of a middle path between absolute knowledge and unsurpassable difference.

Yet, as the highlighted terms in the passage indicate, Gadamer's focus in metaphor remains persistently on similarity and commonality. Different horizons are *fused*. Similar emphases appear in Weinsheimer's elaboration, as he explicitly correlates metaphor with the operation of the fusion of horizons: "Metaphor consists in a *nondifferentiation* in which difference remains operative. Precisely this paradox is what Gadamer means by the fusion of horizons" (ibid., p. 85; emphasis added).[22] The priority is granted to nondifferentiation rather than to the abiding tension in metaphor between sameness and difference. Weinsheimer goes on to cite, in support, passages from Gadamer that we have already discussed to similar effect: historical consciousness is awareness of its otherness, its distance from the past, yet it " 'recombines' " with the past " 'to become *one with itself* again in the unity of the historical horizon that it thus acquires' " (ibid., pp. 85–86; emphasis added, quoting Gadamer, 1989, p. 306). Elsewhere Weinsheimer writes that metaphoric transference exiles the literal, yet ideally the result of the transference is the integration of the elements joined metaphorically into an expanded notion of the literal (Weinsheimer, 1991, p. 73).

Conclusion

Gadamer's emphasis on the commonality that understanding either presupposes or creates is insufficiently metaphorical. For Ricoeur, by contrast, understanding is more a product of a tension between sameness and difference, an attempt to find similarity across, and despite, difference. My claim is that Ricoeur's approach to understanding as metaphoric provides a more realistic depiction of understanding and a more creditable portrayal of its possible actualization in dialogues attempted in today's diverse world. As the following statement captures, while Gadamer well comprehends the significant tasks of conversation before us, he does not sufficiently appreciate both the limits and the potential of contemporary understanding:

> [T]oday what we are ultimately concerned with is a world civilization which in all its diversity of origins and history still must build a *common solidarity* if we are to survive at all. If we do not learn the spirit of reconciliation such as Leibniz represented, we may well not be able to master the crises that confront us. So it behooves us to honor exemplars of *universal integration* represented by such great figures as Leibniz, if we ever hope to perform the human tasks facing us today. (Gadamer, 1996, quoted and translated in Grondin, 2003, p. 250)

In contrast to Gadamer, Ricoeur's theory of understanding as metaphoric does not require commonality in order for it to succeed. Understanding does not leave as our only alternatives commonality and unmediable differences. Understanding as metaphoric allows for an understanding that is more limited and tentative, an understanding always in need of further dialogue, but still an understanding that helps mediate distance and difference even if it does not overcome them. This posture also requires great humility so that we do not impose upon the conversation our own presuppositions about commonality. This posture, then, seems to betoken a greater effort to fulfill the hermeneutic requirement of listening, a key characteristic of hermeneutics that is all the more precious in a contemporary world where it seems so evanescent.

My attempt, then, has been to speak across the divide between Ricoeur and Gadamer within a larger hermeneutics that they share. My attention here to Ricoeur and Gadamer on metaphor is part of a larger interest in their attention to the underlying metaphoricity of language, an attention that is cryptic in their works and that, as far as I know, scholarly commentary has not much explored.[23]

Notes

[1] "[A]ccording to Gadamer . . . the finite condition of historical knowledge excludes any overview, any final synthesis in the Hegelian manner. . . . " (ibid., p. 61). "It is because absolute knowledge is impossible that the conflict of interpretations is insurmountable and inescapable. Between absolute knowledge and hermeneutics, it is necessary to choose" (ibid., p. 193).

[2] "[T]he horizon of the present cannot be formed without the past. There is no more an isolated horizon of the present in itself than there are historical horizons which have to be acquired. *Rather, understanding is always the fusion of these horizons supposedly existing by themselves*" (ibid. at p. 306; emphasis in original).

3   "[T]he fusion of horizons . . . does not allow the interpreter to speak of an original meaning of the work without acknowledging that, in understanding it, the interpreter's own meaning enters in as well" (Gadamer, 1989, p. 576). "The past is revealed to us through the projection of a historical horizon that is both detached from the horizon of the present and taken up into and fused with it" (Ricoeur, 1988, p. 220).

4   See also (Ricoeur, 1988, p. 224) (quoting this passage).

5   See also (Ricoeur, 1988, p. 224) (quoting the passage).

6   "[T]he interpreter's world . . . horizon is not fixed and immutable. . . . [T]he horizon of understanding, no less than the visual horizon, can change. Gadamer images the process by which the interpreter's horizon is broadened as a dialectical fusion of horizons. . . ." (ibid., p. 15).

7   David Vessey explores well this paragraph of Gadamer's (Vessey, 2010, pp. 534-35).

8   By contrast, as the next subpart indicates, Gadamer will maintain at other points that conversation need not necessarily begin with the same language but can create it. Compare Weinsheimer's argument that a dialogue between author and interpreter is "always possible" because both "speak a language, whether or not they speak the same one" (Weinsheimer, 1991, p. 15).

9   In his argument for Gadamer's approach as metaphoric, Weinsheimer goes on to maintain that "being at home" represents only one side of metaphor. Metaphor also includes difference, "a divagation from the literal, or . . . an exodus from the homeland" (Weinsheimer, 1991, p. 71). Interesting here, as I shall pursue later, is the priority granted to the literal and the homeland; they are the "whole" from which the metaphoric "part" diverges and then reinforms.

10 This side of Gadamer's argument surfaces frequently in an important recent work by Jay Mootz (Mootz, 2006). Specifically referencing Gadamer, Jay writes, for instance, about the availability of "shared, accepted norms" (ibid., p. 8), "shared understandings" and "shared assumptions" (ibid., p. 9), "shared commonplaces" (ibid., p. 43), and "shared meanings"(ibid., p. 46). Prior extensive conversations with Jay on hermeneutics are a model and inspiration for the conversation to which this chapter aspires, and an implicit subtext of the chapter is that it is continues my conversations with Jay on topics long a source of our dialogue. As I argue in the main text, I am skeptical about the availability of the shared understandings Jay describes, and instead push on the side of his position that allows for the possibility of "reasoned argumentation in the absence of a substantially shared *nomos*" (ibid., p. 42).

11 In other work, Grondin expands on these points and argues that the concept of presentation (*Darstellung*) is key to understanding Gadamer's hermeneutics (Grondin, 2007). Another fruitful way to contrast Gadamer and Ricoeur would be to distinguish their evaluations of *Darstellung*. I have taken an initial step in this direction regarding Ricoeur (Taylor, 2010).

12 This vocabulary is found frequently in the secondary literature as well. "In dialogue," writes Weinsheimer, "a common language is formed that makes understanding possible" (Weinsheimer, 1991, p. 15). Elsewhere he comments that the fusion of horizons is "a fusion of languages into a common language" (Weinsheimer, 1985, p. 219). Georgia Warnke states that the fusion of horizons

creates a "consensus over meaning" (Warnke, 1987, p. 107). By comparison, Jay Mootz offers the more modest claim that understanding occurs when participants in a conversation "find common ground *sufficient* to develop a topic that informs [them] both" (Mootz, 2006, p. 5; emphasis added).

[13] Warnke cautions that there is an ambiguity in Gadamer whether the fusion creates substantive agreement or merely a formal one. In the latter case participants in a dialogue come to understand each other but do not necessarily agree (Warnke, 1987, pp. 107–8, 169–70). Because I am reluctant to conclude that understanding necessarily requires even formal consensus, I do not find substantive consensus either.

[14] The quote continues that spirit's "being consists only in returning to itself from what is other" (ibid, p. 14). The Hegelian nature of this process is drawn explicitly (ibid.). The extension of the quote highlights the ultimate "single horizon" of tradition, which I have previously criticized. My present emphasis focuses on whether understanding finds a "home" in the alien.

[15] Ricoeur's vocabulary here is careful and repeated elsewhere (ibid., p. 178).

[16] Ricoeur's hesitation about the achievement of fusion extends to descriptions in his personal life. On the occasion of the French publication of *Memory, History, Forgetting* (Ricoeur, 2004), Ricoeur invited those close to him (*"mes proches"*) to a celebration. In an address to those invited, Ricoeur reflected on what it meant that those in attendance were near (*proche*) to him. He noted that the term *proche* allows for a variable distance, but the distance is never zero. It lies between fusion and indifference (*"entre la fusion et l'indifférence"*) (Quoted in Dosse, 2008, pp. 657–58).

[17] Weinsheimer comments that, for Gadamer, "Interpreting, like translation, consists in finding within the resources of the interpreter's language, a common language. . . ." (Weinsheimer, 1991, p. 15).

[18] An even greater contrast to Ricoeur's conception can be found in Gerald Bruns's description of Husserl's theory of understanding:

> Understanding is like translating, which presupposes an ideality of meaning or an ideal object that can be transported without loss across historical, cultural, and linguistic boundaries. . . . The words and propositions of natural language are perhaps not so ideal as geometrical terms and expressions, but they are close. They have a univocality and universality about them; they can be handed down from past to present without (on the whole) leaving anything essential behind. Otherwise they would not be intelligible. The univocal and universal is what is understandable. . . . (Bruns, 1992, p. 2; characterizing Husserl)

[19] Imagination plays a significant role in the creation of metaphoric resemblance. "[I]t is . . . the imaginary that keeps otherness from slipping into the unsayable" (Ricoeur, 1988, p. 184). Elsewhere, I probe more of Ricoeur's work on imagination (Taylor, 2006).

[20] "For finite understanding, there is similarity, not identity; difference, not unrelatedness" (Weinsheimer, 1985, p. 187).

[21] In my conclusion I will briefly refer to two other passages.

22 In this context it is of particular interest that Weinsheimer appears to resist the notion that metaphor creates fusion (ibid., pp. 84–85), while allowing for the fusion of horizons.

23 In *Truth and Method*, Gadamer refers to metaphor in three basic passages (Gadamer, 1989, pp. 75, 429, and 431). The first and third are very brief. In the third, for example, Gadamer refers to "the fundamental metaphoricity of language," and Weinsheimer rightly notes that the phrase "gives us pause because it makes such a grand claim in proportion to the attention here accorded it" (Weinsheimer, 1991, p. 65). Weinsheimer builds on this passage to argue that for Gadamer understanding is metaphorical, and in the present chapter we have explored Weinsheimer's analysis of this theme. The larger chapter from which Weinsheimer's analysis is drawn is entitled "Metaphor as a Metaphor for Understanding" (ibid., pp. 64–86). As important as is this chapter—which I have tried to suggest—it does not engage in much assessment of the larger philosophical implications of language's "fundamental metaphoricity." I have quoted and analyzed in the text Gadamer's longest statement on metaphor. In passing I have seen two other brief Gadamer references to metaphor (Gadamer, 1980b, p. 111; Gadamer, 1980a, p. 13). The latter passage is quoted and translated by Weinsheimer (Weinsheimer, 1991, p. 74).

In Ricoeur's *The Rule of Metaphor*, he cites the passages on metaphor from *Truth and Method* in support of the thesis that there may be "a 'metaphoric' at work at the origin of logical thought, at the root of all classification" (Ricoeur, 1977, p. 22). His "most extreme hypothesis" is that "the 'metaphoric' that transgresses the categorical order also begets it" (ibid., p. 24). This thesis, however, appears very briefly in the book and appears more as the book's horizon than its specific subject (ibid., pp. 22–23, 24, 197–98).

As Weinsheimer appreciates, another topic to pursue in Gadamer's and Ricoeur's thinking on metaphor is their apparent difference on whether the underlying metaphoricity of language allows for a dialectical interchange between metaphorical and conceptual language. Gadamer says no; Ricoeur says yes (Weinsheimer, 1991, pp. 68–69).

Chapter 6

Where Is *Muthos* Hiding in Gadamer's Hermeneutics? Or, the Ontological Privilege of Emplotment

John Arthos

I was wondering what I should say further or what I should not say, and meanwhile, as is my custom, I was tapping the blank paper with my pen top. My action brought me a subject, for I reflected how in that brief interval time was flowing on, and I was flowing with it, slipping down, departing, or to use the right word, dying. We are continually dying; I while I am writing these words, you while you are reading them, others when they hear them or fail to hear them, we are all dying. I shall be dying when you read this, you die while I write, we both are dying, we all are dying, we are dying forever.

Francesco Petrarca (1966, pp. 202–03)

Why is there no explicit narrative theory in Gadamer anything like what came to occupy such a central role in Ricoeur's hermeneutics? As one looks deeper into the problem, this absence only becomes curiouser and curiouser. Gadamer devotes so much thought to the working of the poetic imagination—to the structure of play and dialogue, to the relationship of cognition and time, succession and presence, work and world—that the absence of a substantial consideration of narrative structure, like the prolonged absence of the groom at the wedding, grows genuinely perplexing. It was such a central building block for Dilthey in his conception of the human sciences, serving as the passageway between the lived experience of the individual and social history, that Gadamer would have had to come face to face with it, and indeed he describes Dilthey's commitment to narrative quite insightfully in *Truth and Method.* But the narrative aspect of the structural relationship of part to whole does not have a significant place in his account of hermeneutic understanding. Is it because he is so anxious to get away from the Diltheyan and Husserlian emphasis on "lived experience"? This clearly has something to do with it, but without any explicit justification, it is hard to know what to make of Gadamer's share in what Ricoeur calls the neglect of the constitutional role of narrative in the phenomenological tradition (Ricoeur, 1991a, p. 99).

To be sure, Gadamer travels right up to the edge of a narrative theory. His treatment of recognition (*Anerkennung*) is tied closely to Aristotle's theory of dramatic art. His location of metaphor in the productive economy of discourse is consonant with the structure of metaphor as miniature narrative in Ricoeur. And Gadamer regards the creative imagination as a fundamental mode of existential understanding, placing *poiesis* in an even more central role than Ricoeur in the economy of being. But Gadamer's work lacks a sustained consideration of mimesis as the temporal emplotment of human identity. Why? Keith D'Souza has a go at this question, but demonstrates mainly that certain Gadamerian categories can be superimposed on Ricoeur's three-stage mimesis (D'Souza, 2006). In constructing loose parallels between Ricoeur's schema of prefiguration/configuration/refiguration with the Gadamerian concepts of effective history, mimesis, and application—concepts that in Gadamer's hermeneutics have no strong structural relationship—D'Souza evokes the following question. Why does Gadamer relate hermeneutic understanding to the rules of play or dialogue rather than the order of emplotment? Why did Gadamer pass over what Ricoeur puts at the center of hermeneutic temporality? In one brief, tantalizing section, D'Souza contrasts Gadamer's and Ricoeur's frame of reference as, respectively, being-in-the-world and doing-in-the-world, but then abruptly concludes that what he calls Gadamer's Platonic essentialism "does not seem to take as seriously" the "practical and temporal concerns" that animate Ricoeur's Aristotelian approach (ibid., 152–53). This hardly begins to make sense of the privilege of being overacting in philosophical hermeneutics.

Sheila Ross takes on the question as well, but places in opposition what seems to me in some ways quite compatible, and in other ways quite unrelated— Gadamer's *Verweilen*, the "stretched" time of the world as text, with Ricoeur's narrative time, which is the third or hybrid time that weaves together cosmic and personal temporality: "It is important to see, for example, that the work of Paul Ricoeur on narrative is quite antithetical to Gadamer's basic orientation because Ricoeur is a thinker who couldn't be further from Gadamer in regard to this question of time" (Ross, 2006, pp. 114). Gadamer and Ricoeur both reject out of hand Hegel's faith in history's progress toward an eternal present, but both want to substitute a presence of some type ("*eine gewisse Gegenwärtigkeit und Gleichzeitigkeit*"), traceable in both cases to Augustine's search for a human approximation of the timeless (Gadamer, 1997, p. 176). Ricoeur looks for this in narrative temporality, and Gadamer in poetic experience, but there is overlap here as well as difference. Even working out the terms of the theoretical relationship is none too easy a task, but the character of hermeneutics depends, in a significant way, on doing so. To make a beginning, I will first lay out the advance in hermeneutics provided by Ricoeur's theoretical insight about emplotment.

Paul Ricoeur

i. The Syntax of an Ontology of Emplotment

In the late 1970s Ricoeur begins to elaborate on the central function of narrative in the constitution of human temporality. Ricoeur's epistemic claim for narrative is sweeping and fundamental, as "the modes of discourse appropriate to our experience of time" (Ricoeur, 1991a, p. 107). The way in which narrative resolves the insuperable speculative aporias of time is an original thesis in the hermeneutic context, and in making this case Ricoeur moves narrative closer and closer to the center of discursive understanding, and establishes mimetic emplotment as a deep existential competence.

Ricoeur is quite frank that his association of narrative emplotment with temporality is an innovation within phenomenology and hermeneutics. In his inaugural essay on the subject he notes that "the phenomenology of time-experience usually overlooks" the epistemic function of narrative emplotment (ibid., p. 99). When building a bridge between Heidegger's temporality of care and narrative structure, Ricoeur has to work hard to make the connection: "At first glance, the relation between his analysis of within-time-ness and narrative seems quite distant. Heidegger's text . . . seems to have no place for it" (Ricoeur, 1984, p. 63).

Why, in Ricoeur's mind, is it *narrative* in particular that establishes an existential order for human understanding? In the preface to *Time and Narrative*, he announces its role as "the privileged means by which" we make and remake the world "in the field of action." So, immediately, we have a clue about the difference in priority between Gadamer and Ricoeur. The idea of action denotes a willing agent intervening in the course of events. The thrust of Gadamer's hermeneutics is, unfailingly, to insist the event of meaning is something that happens *to* us. He would hardly deny the place of individual agency in unfolding history, but the focus of hermeneutic consciousness is what happens behind our willing and doing. Thus, the constructive role of narrative that lies in the telling rather than the hearing is off-message for him.

Ricoeur's project, by contrast, is to explore the invention of our own narrations to reconfigure "our confused, unformed, and, at the limit, mute temporal experience." Here[1] narrative emplotment would seem to be less a philosophical tool than what Kenneth Burke called equipment for living. The "referential function" of narrative works in what hermeneutics calls *Anwendung*, practical application, moving beyond "the aporias of philosophical speculation" (ibid., p. xi). Instead, the opening proper of the first part of *Time and Narrative* announces that "one presupposition commands all the others, namely, that what is ultimately at stake in the case of the structural identity of the narrative function as well as in that of the truth claim of every narrative work, is the temporal character of human experience" (Ricoeur, 1984, p. 3). This claim places the narrative function in service of temporal identity before anything else. What Ricoeur calls "narrative understanding" flows from the narrative capacity to bring some measure of constancy to a transient life, and as such it has functioned as "a prodigious workshop for . . . the expression of time" (Ricoeur, 1985, p. 8).

To this end, Ricoeur approaches the relationship between narrative and life by examining the repertoire of existential resources that emplot themselves discursively. Human time is constituted out of the configuring mediations of narrative discourse, and practical experience is permeated by this configuring activity, never outside the structures of emplotment that we associate with narrative art. The very notion of plot is "grounded in a pre-understanding of the world of action, its meaningful structures, its symbolic resources, and its temporal character" (Ricoeur, 1984, p. 54). Our ordinary dealings are expressed as conflicts, goals, complications, motives, blessings, and misfortunes, and they are embedded in signs, codes, symbolic systems, conventions, norms, and generic patterns. A symbolically mediated reality is set within a relay of interacting temporal modalities that ordinary language trades in. For example: "*Henceforth* that is, from now on, I commit myself to doing that *tomorrow*. . . . *Now* I intend to do that because I *just* realized that. . . . *Now* I am doing it, because now I can do it" (Ricoeur, 1984, p. 6). These shared discursive repertoires inaugurate "a community of meaning preliminary to any entering into fiction" (Ricoeur, 1991b, p. 141). Ricoeur maps this discursive activity of plotting on a threefold schema under the Heideggerian categories of within-timeness, historicity, and temporality through temporal adverbs ("'then,' 'earlier,' 'later,' 'until that . . . '[,] 'now that . . . '[,] in proverbial expressions such as one 'doesn't have time for' something, or time has been 'lost' or 'won,' etc.") (Ricoeur, 1991a, p. 108). Historicity refers to the configuring power of language to relate the succession of events, the grouping of these successions, the sense of ending, and the inversion of chronology that sees the beginning from the end. Temporality [*Zeitlichkeit*] is the dialectical gathering of what we normally refer to as past, present, future into a fragile unity (ibid., p. 112). Thus narrative discourse is integrated closely into the temporal analytic of Dasein. (This will be important when we get to the narrative implications of the analytic in the second part of *Truth and Method*.)

To be sure, the art of narrative does not just redeploy the resources of ordinary language in practical affairs. The syntax of storytelling has "its laws, its restrictions, its rigour, and its fecundity" (Ricoeur, 1991b, p. 145). It is by its very nature transformative. For one thing, the notion of *event* draws its meaning from narrative proper—its place in the progress of a narrative, charged by the energy of the motives, causes and outcomes that hold the tension of the plot. Emplotment orchestrates the effects of a story by calculated strategies of reversal, surprise, amplification, culmination, etc., as Ricoeur puts it, by "eliciting a pattern from a succession" (Ricoeur, 1991a, p. 106). Finally, it works out of a generic tradition that allows endless improvisations in the tension between expectation and innovation.

But if narrative proper creates its own boundaries—what Gadamer would refer to as the closed world of the text—it also redeposits its gifts back into the practical world, offering to our lives what François Dagognet refers to as "iconic augmentation" (Ricoeur, 1991b, p.150). The narrative sensibilities cultivated by storytelling inform our deepest understandings of the world as it happens to us, encourage us to read the symbolic resonance of historical events, allow us to anticipate complex results, construe hidden motives, and so forth. Narrative may constrain our view, but it can also impart an intelligibility more dense and layered than other discursive modes.

What I have enumerated here is only a bare sketch of the various permutations and levels of narrative that circulate amongst themselves, working as an ineliminable functioning of language and culture according to their own intuitive logic. It is mainly for explanatory purposes that Ricoeur develops a systematic progression of narrative production and application, since like language and culture, it is always already operating in the tension between chaos and order that constitutes our lives. The order it finds is of its own making.

ii. Narrative, Identity, and Agency

In Ricoeur's subsequent elaboration of narrative theory, storytelling is oriented toward an ethics of initiative. In *Oneself as Another*, he develops the manner in which narrative capacities are deployed in the constitution of character, identity, practical deliberation, communal ends, and so forth. Narrative is a medium, not in the reductive sense of a strategic, instrumentalist manipulation of attitudes and behaviors (although it can serve that function), but as a constituting principle of life.

What Ricoeur is positing in *Oneself as Another* (something he had only intimated in *Time and Narrative*) is a fundamental relationship between the act of emplotment and the enduring identity and character of a person, community, nation, or culture. Ricoeur stresses this breadth of application, but his theory is inescapably rooted in the pursuit of a subject identity, and this is certainly a major clue as to why Gadamer did not go down the same path. Ricoeur finds the initial resources for this constructive act in a semantics of action, that is to say, in the gift of speech. The first semantic act is of course the act of naming— "Adam." Once speech names a grammatical subject, Ricoeur proposes a semantic sequence of increasing complexity:

The power to designate oneself as the speaker of one's own words; the power to designate oneself as the agent of one's own actions; the power to designate oneself as the protagonist in one's own life story—here are so many uses of "I can" that can be considered coextensive with the notion of the self. (Ricoeur, 1996, p. 367)

The specific identity assigned to an individual or a community is a narrative identity. Someone speaks. Who speaks? In a family, in a community, a person is given a name, and this proper name comes to designate the person who speaks. But in the variety of its different states, what gives permanence to the subject to whom that name is attached? "The answer has to be narrative. To answer the question 'Who?' . . . is to tell the story of a life" (Ricoeur, 1988, p. 246). But this is only the beginning. The emerging subject can want, point, speak, declare, and judge, but beyond this it seeks at a broader level "the unifying principle of the operations among which it is dispersed and forgets itself as subject" (Ricoeur, 1991c, p. 12). The subject is grasped together out of the dispersion of mute and formless life by an act of configuration, a level operation that understands self within a temporal horizon of mistakes, achievements, expectations, and possibilities. On account of this capacity to grasp together, the emerging subject constructs a life in the manner of a story, as a history and a future of possibilities.

At the heart of this project of identity building is a problem. The self can never be transparent to itself, because self-understanding is always mediated by symbols, and symbols will always be subject to interpretation. That is, insofar as the dispersion of speech must be gathered together out of the flux into memory, the achievement of understanding oneself as a subject is by definition the insertion of oneself into a text, the gathering of traces. Thus, identity is hermeneutic: "To understand oneself is to understand oneself as one confronts the text and to receive from it the conditions for a self other than that which first undertakes the reading" (ibid., p. 17). And the tools by which we construct an identity are "the whole treasury of symbols transmitted by the cultures within which we have come" (ibid., p. 17). An identity in a life is created just as a story is constructed, already within the context of a being thrown into the world. Identity is possible for humans who have the ability to inculcate habits, to follow intentions, to observe their own behavior. Identity is possible for communities that look backward and forward, establish institutions, pass down cultural norms, and chart alternative futures. Biblical Israel created its identity out of the significance it gave to events in its history, and subsequently nourished its identity by responding to the narratives it created. The narrative analogy extends to the process of poetic creation, in which "the subject then appears both as a reader and the writer of its own life" (Ricoeur, 1988, p. 246). The moment is captured when reading moves to writing, for example, in the case of promise making and promise keeping. This moment of action grows out of a provocation to be and act differently, made possible not only through self-reflection, but also through the capacity to initiate. The human present of a narrative identity is something partly constructed, stitched together, constructed out of the interactions between the perception of time and the active interventions in time. Ricoeur proposes that communities overcome the determinism of the gaze by initiative, that is by intervening, or interrupting, with action the habits of tradition and institutional stagnation. By *starting*, which is the root meaning of initiative (Latin *initium*), communities intervene in, for, and against the flow of power that constitutes the space of experience. Therefore for Ricoeur, "to speak of initiative is to speak of responsibility," and to speak of responsibility is to speak of identity (Ricoeur, 1991c, p. 217).

It is impossible to escape the radically social nature of initiative and identity, whether at the personal or the community level. In all cases, the commitment to a perduring identity, the promise of initiative, and the integrity of the word is a social compact. Identity is a matter of self-constancy, and as such it touches other people in its very making by definition: "Self-constancy is for each person that manner of conducting himself or herself so that others can *count on* that person. Because someone is counting on me, I am *accountable for* my actions before another" (Ricoeur, 1992, p. 165). Initiative, by virtue of being an insertion and interference by a human agency into the present, proclaims an intention that is unavoidably either in good faith or deceptive: "I would say that every initiative is an intention to do something and, as such, a commitment to do that thing, hence a promise that I make silently to myself and tacitly to another, to the extent that the other is, if not its beneficiary, at least its witness" (Ricoeur, 1991c, p. 217). Here already at the heart of initiative is an implied promise. The language of commitment is already implicit in initiative and identity. Ricoeur conceives of the institution of speech as an ethical project that reaches backward to pre-understanding and forward to the construction and maintenance of social cohesion: "The properly ethical justification of the promise suffices of itself, a justification which can be derived from the obligation to safeguard the institution of language and to respond to the trust that the other places in my faithfulness" (Ricoeur, 1992, p. 124). The discursive function of promises is therefore a form of emplotment, for it self-consciously graphs time against identity ("true till death do us part").

Because it is with language that we understand ourselves, construct our personal and communal identities, and take responsibility for our acts, there is an ethical obligation "to safeguard the institution of language and to respond to the trust that the other places in my faithfulness" (ibid., p. 124). Identity is the triumph of constancy over time, over "diversity, variability, discontinuity, and instability," and insofar as human beings are social animals, the constancy of identity is necessary for properly ethical ends, that is, so that communities might survive and function through the practice of goodwill and accountability (ibid., p. 140).

What I have just sketched is a part of what I regard as the great advance Ricoeur made for the hermeneutic understanding of human temporality. The capacity for narrative structure is not just the skill of the storyteller to entrance an audience, but an existential competence. It is clear from my summary that the production of narrative identity in Ricoeur is heavy-laden with personal and communal agency. That this competence works more from the side of such agency may certainly have been a quiet critique of Gadamer's single-minded focus on the pathos of experience and understanding, as an event that happens to us. Both attributes of narrative temporality—that it occurs in the field of action, and that it grows from an intention to constitute identity—will be central to the confrontation with Gadamer's approach to human time.

Hans-Georg Gadamer

One rare place where Gadamer begins to affirm something like Ricoeur's grammar of narrative structure, if only *in nuce,* is in the essay, "The Western View of Time," in which he speaks of an "organic time" that emerges from the natural stages of life and from an awareness of them:

> For childhood, youth, maturity, old age and death mark out each individual's path through life, and these milestones of the individual life are reflected in the institutions and customs of society. The experience which man acquires as he passes through these different stages is a genuine form of experience of time itself. It is most closely connected with the historical sense, which is strictly speaking the awareness of epochs, of one's own epoch and, in an even more basic way, of the "pastness" of an epoch, a stopping-place in the constant flow of time, the establishment of a "block of time consisting of the simultaneous or contemporaneous. These . . . forms of time experience . . . have their basis in the organic unity of the living being." (Gadamer, 1977, pp. 42–43)

Present in this short space are elements of narrative that hearken back to Dilthey and forward to Ricoeur:

(1) Gadamer notes the parallel between the individual life and social history in the way that awareness of the stages of a life, or era, leads to a sense of articulated unity.
(2) What interrupts the constant flow of time is a time that separates itself off, and presents itself with, its own unique coherence.
(3) The accumulation of such "moments" of time presumably establishes a narrative history.
(4) And finally, the personal and the social-historical mirror each other through this common organizing dynamic.

To be sure, the milestones Gadamer recognizes are the conventional ones recognized by custom through ritual, so that they are not the unique events of a personal experience. Nevertheless, these structures that mark the passing of time are part of what Ricoeur would classify under the heading of mimesis.[1] Here, Gadamer does not go the next step to recognize the circulation of such experiences, taken up and reconfigured in the act of storytelling, to be then deposited back into the vast store of narrative preunderstanding. This is a sticking point we will have to come back to later on. But there is, at least, a unity that develops out of the awareness of interruptions.

Gadamer points out that organic time develops in its very nature out of the suffering flesh of human experience, the marks that history makes on the flesh. For instance, getting older is "a specific determination of that which has its own time" (Gadamer, 1970, p. 348). The historical epoch is "the temporal structure of that which endures as one and the same in every alteration and articulation of life's phases" (ibid., p. 349). The development of a unique life "in a being which is a self" set by the boundaries of birth and death is what creates a *Lebenszeit*:

> Thereby life-time is articulated in the course of a life. For that is the authentic temporal structure of such a life-time: the present is in formed phases which are constituted in periods of life, each of which has its own dimension as what it may be sooner and what it may be later. (Ibid., p. 348)

This "temporal structure" starts to sound like what Ricoeur means by the life experience that begs for narrative. It is a kind of incipient narrative material that structures itself before the recycling work of mimesis.[2]

But this caesura begins to point us toward the hermeneutic divergence. In developing his concept of organic time, Gadamer fuses together the life structures that constitute the building blocks of narrative and his own emphasis on the agency of culture. Old age is "that which has its own time" (ibid., p. 348). The time of an epoch is a mode of Being, "which radiates from life qua life" (ibid., p. 348). It is not we who establish an epoch-making event, but rather it that announces itself to us: "Many epoch-making events are simply announced on the radio. . . . An epoch-making event establishes a caesura. It establishes that which preceded as old, and everything which now comes, as new. The great insights of drama and ritual are handed down. Tragic downfall 'gives' existence to the old as it "is recollected in its dissolution" (ibid., p. 351). With the beginning of something new, "the will of 'maturing time' presents itself to the consciousness of the initiate" (ibid., p. 352). Absent from this formulation is the will that draws upon these periods, epochs, stages as threads to be woven into the fabric of a life; instead, there is only awareness. This proximity to and distance from Ricoeur's narrative theory will be repeated throughout Gadamer's corpus. There are suggestions of narrative structures in Gadamer's descriptions of human time, but they lie fallow, or sit next to other temporal forms such as ritual or poetic reverie. Gadamer never ties the knot with narrative as the organizing principle of lived experience.

In the face of Gadamer's oblique approach to narrative, Ricoeur's claim for emplotment as a central term of hermeneutic understanding raises the stakes significantly. Ricoeur, in fact, positions narrative as the dialectical twin of temporal experience caught up in the movement of the hermeneutic circle, a balance that is simply absent in Gadamer's philosophical hermeneutics:

"[T]ime becomes human time to the extent that it is organized after the manner of a narrative; narrative, in turn, is meaningful to the extent that it portrays the features of temporal experience . . . [T]he circle of narrativity and temporality is not a vicious but a healthy circle, whose two halves mutually reinforce one another" (Ricoeur, 1984, p. 3). In *Time and Narrative*, Ricoeur's magisterial confrontation of Augustinian time with Aristotelian emplotment is, consequently, an inaugural occasion for working out this basic dialectical interplay. He casts this theoretical juxtaposition in symmetrical terms as "the inverted interplay of concordance and discordance" (ibid., p. 4). The fact that narrative is set as an equal partner opposite temporality in a dialectical balance that nearly dissolves the aporias of human time, raises the profile of narrative in Ricoeur to the highest level of hermeneutic understanding. I am going to examine where Gadamer's hermeneutics impinges on this claim by tracking those places in *Truth and Method* where he navigates through the very same sources and themes Ricoeur draws upon for his narrative theory. This procedure will allow us to see with some specificity precisely how Gadamer's approach to human temporality embraces or shies away from a narrative understanding.

i. Art and Narrative in Gadamer: *Verweilen*

Art, ritual and language are preeminent among those human practices that work to make up for our temporal dispersion, mimicking the atemporal unity of the divine. They do this by securing or winning a space, a reprieve from the fragmentation of the quotidien: "[T]his is not a one-after-another sequence but the at-the-same-timeness that the temporal structure of tarrying [*Verweilen*] possesses. It is not a doing of this and that, first this and then that; it is a whole that is present in the seeing, and in the considering that one is immersed in" (Gadamer, 2007, p. 210). There is a danger in explication that has to be avoided here. To attribute to *Verweilen* the character of a personal experience—the tarrying that a person feels while experiencing a work—would make it an *Erlebnis*, not an *Erfahrung*, and this is not Gadamer's interest. *Verweilen* works not only, or even primarily, in individuals but with communities formed by their cultural heritage.

Gadamer draws his theme from Aristotle's concept of *energeia*, actualization (*Vollzug*), to describe the hybrid phenomenon of a time experience that hovers between extension and retention—"how it begins, ends, how long it lasts; how it remains in one's mind, and in the end how it fades away, and yet somehow remains with us and can surface again" (ibid., p. 217). Gadamer provides an example of such a dynamic in his exegesis of the concept of representation in the tradition of painterly portraits. The stretching in this instance is not simply a point of contact with another time, but a reciprocal transformation of audience and work that starts to get at the deep ontological basis of cultural continuity: "The picture points by causing us to linger over it, for as

I emphasized, its ontological valence consists in not being absolutely different from what it represents but sharing in its being. We saw that what is represented comes into its own in the picture" (Gadamer, 1993a, p. 153). The ontological structure Gadamer refers to in this schematism is not the identity structure of human initiatives and projects, but the merging lines that cross at these points of historical contact. In both cases, it is identity, but one is centered in the presence of spirit in history, and the other is centered in self-awareness, either as person or community. This difference of a centering point is fundamental to the distance between Gadamer and Ricoeur.

The temporality of *Verweilen*, which is a rebuke to the counting time of linear modernity, is grounded in the inextricable ontological bond between "work" as noun and verb—the work that comes about as a result of the working out of the thing, both in the act of creation and reception. This conceptual pairing draws inspiration from Aristotle's physics. His neologism *entelecheia* indicates a purposeful movement that is defining of its subject in such a way that the movement is itself an activation of the essence of the thing, movements of this kind being ends in themselves. Whereas building a house is not usually done for the sake of building, but for the sake of having a house, contemplation, speaking the truth, or living well is done for its own sake. This kind of defining movement expresses a peculiar relationship between the particular manifestation and the condition it announces. To use Kosman's example, "[S]peaking Greek is just the full manifestation of the ability to speak Greek" (Kosman, 1969, p. 58). The part *manifests* the whole, even as it remains only a particular manifestation.

Aristotle's use of the term *energeia* has a similar meaning, and is often used synonymously with *entelecheia*. Sachs explains the derivation:

> The root of *energeia* is *ergon*, deed, work, or act, from which comes the adjective *energon* used in ordinary speech to mean active, busy, or at work. *Energeia* is formed by the addition of a noun ending to the adjective *energon*; we might construct the word is-at-work-ness from Anglo-Saxon roots to translate *energeia* into English, or use the more euphonious periphrastic expression, being-at-work.[2]

Sachs uses a periphrasis "being-at-work-staying-itself" to capture the Aristotelian idea that a thing exists in a dynamic relation to its environment, and "can only exist as the outcome of a continuous expenditure of effort" to maintain itself in relation to its own purpose (Sachs, 1995, p. 31). This leads to the interesting temporal consequence that "an *energeia* is eternal, for its full actuality and realization is present in every instance of its occurrence" (ibid., p. 59). This kind of motion "is the mode in which the future belongs to the present, it is the present absence of just those particular absent things which are about to be" (ibid., p. 59).

In the famous *Verwandlung ins Gebilde*, Gadamer sets the *ergon* and *energeia* of the work of art in a productive tension. A *Gebilde* "has the character of the work, of *Ergon* and not only of *Energeia*" (Gadamer, 1990, p. 116).[3] The emphasis on *ergon* has to do with the repeatable aspect, and hence the durability over time, of a work. Gadamer will redefine repetition as recognition, but at the outset, he wants to say there is in fact something lasting and irreducible that serves as the inexhaustible source for the creative invention he calls *Spiel* (play). The yield of play, that is, what emerges between the poles of *Ergon* and *Energeia*, is a *Darstellung*, the creature of this hybridity. It has the permanence of a structure that is set down in place (*stellen*), and the contingent particularity of something that is there now (*da*), fulfilled only as it is actualized (*Vollzug*).

This qualified completeness is one of the trickier aspects of Gadamer's conception, because it incorporates the idea of autonomy, an Enlightenment virtue from which he is normally at pains to distance himself. But autonomy in this case is given to the work rather than to the person. The closedness of the world of play (*in sich geschlossene Welt*), or of *a* play, has to do with the standard that the work sets for itself (*sein Maß in sich selbst gefunden*). A *Gebilde* is a world that is closed in the sense that it never loses its context, or better, creates its own (expanding) context. Art would seem to give some access to the kind of wholeness that eludes human finitude, perhaps as a means of living within that finitude:

> Reality always stands in a horizon of desired or feared or, at any rate, still undecided future possibilities. Hence it is always the case that mutually exclusive expectations are aroused, not all of which can be fulfilled. The undecidedness of the future permits such a superfluity of expectations that reality necessarily lags behind them. Now if, in a particular case, a context of meaning closes and completes itself in reality, such that no lines of meaning scatter in the void, this reality is itself like a drama. Likewise, someone who can see the whole of reality as a closed circle of meaning in which everything is fulfilled will speak of the comedy and tragedy of life. In these cases, where reality is understood as a play, emerges the reality of play, which we call the play of art. . . . The world of the work of art, in which play expresses itself fully in the unity of its course, is in fact a wholly transformed world. In and through it everyone recognizes that that is how things are. (Ibid., pp. 112–13)

There is no denial of incompleteness in this *Vollzug*. Rather, it is a transcendence that takes its very meaning from the finite structure within which it lives. ("The event of the beautiful and the hermeneutical process both presuppose the finiteness of human life." [Gadamer, 1993, p. 486]). The enstructuring structure of a *Gebilde* thus anticipates many features of Ricoeur's narrative order, and even hints at the dramatic character of this structuration, without going that far.

Gadamer instead remains at a higher level of abstraction. He invokes Aristotle's *energeia* and *entelecheia* in order to mark a novel relationship between being and becoming and to overcome the reification of categorial epistemology. The temporal invasiveness and processivity of an *entelecheia* is carried over into *Verweilen* (the prefix ver- is activated in all its senses), but also its structural autonomy. Gadamer is at pains to say that it is not we who initiate and enact it; rather, it works inexhaustibly upon us. Its protean generativity stems, as Heidegger says, from "the fixing in place of a self-establishing truth in the figure," a figure that never yields up its full bounty any more than the springs into which the mountain streams return in the cycle of the seasons (Heidegger, 1971, p. 71). The attributes of art, literature, and culture that Gadamer most prizes are their endurance, their capacity to have meaning for new generations and communities, and their proof against linear progress in the Western sense, since the Odyssey and Santa Sophia are not superseded by what follows. The first attribute raises art above "the impotence of our subjective particularity," stretching being across temporal rupture; and the second attribute reconfigures the temporal modalities, undermining the disposition to place salvation in the future. *Verweilen* is thus the temporal constitution of art as culture being-at-work-staying-itself, a weakened version of the *imitatio Dei*. We can summarize by saying that the tarrying that art creates is across the history of its reception, and not primarily in the leisured contemplation of the spectator or reader. The shift of locus of what is meaningful from subjectivity to culture not only provides a greater constancy for life, but germinates the womb, provisions the nest that feeds our collective life. Seen from this perspective, narrative becomes one more rich cultural resource that spreads across time and constitutes cultures rather than a master-structure of understanding. Its character as *muthos* (emplotment) does not come forward as a key ontological attribute.

ii. *Erlebnis* as the Bridge Between the Romantic View of Art and History

Gadamer offers a history of the concept of *Erlebnis* and develops its meanings, both in the first and second parts of *Truth and Method*. This concept runs across his treatment of art and history as a kind of middle term between Romantic subjectivism and hermeneutic understanding. On one hand, it reflects the bias toward the inner experience of the individual, from which Gadamer wished to dissociate himself. On the other hand, it exemplifies the dialectical relationship between part and whole manifest in the hermeneutic coherence of experience. As he distances himself from romantic hermeneutics, Gadamer's signal polemical move is to discard the association of *Erlebnis* with hermeneutic experience in favor of the concept of *Erfahrung*, which he associates with the social understanding of the ancients (*phronesis*), and locates the coherence of identity in a dialogue of difference rather than in a uniqueness of personal experience. Gadamer locates continuity of identity in the deep, underlying accord of language as a common attribute, and difference as the basis of conversation: "[T]he immediacy of our worldview and view of ourselves, in which we persist, is preserved and altered within language because we finite beings always come from afar and stretch into the distance. In language the reality beyond every individual consciousness becomes visible" (Gadamer, 1993a, 440). This schematism disturbs the very principle that gives both Dilthey and Ricoeur a foothold in narrative theory. We have to work out exactly what is involved in this destabilizing substitution.

From Goethe on, the concept of *Erlebnis* was central to the doctrine of genius that underlay Romanticism, but its primary use for Dilthey lay in the development of his theory of history. It was either the principal analogy for, or the keystone of, the *Zusammenhang* of historical meaning. Because *Erlebnis* functions as a Diltheyan hinge between personal experience and social history, it takes us to the nexus of Gadamer's reinterpretation of hermeneutic temporality. In Gadamer's exegesis of aesthetic consciousness (*Truth and Method*, part I), *Erlebnis* has a negative polemical function in distancing hermeneutics from the aestheticist tendencies of nineteenth-century *Erlebniskult*. But Gadamer's close analysis shows in a positive way how the structure of life experience works from a chiasmatic energy between two contradictory dynamics (ibid., pp. 60–70; Gadamer, 1990, pp. 66–76). On the one hand, by its very nature an *Erlebnis* separates itself from the whole of a life as something unique and self-standing (a moment of being), and on the other hand, it is both charged with all the packed meanings of a life and illuminating *of* that life. This is the structure Simmel explains so memorably in his essay on the character of adventure (*Abenteuer*), and which Gadamer appropriates as the useful core of the concept. The important thing to see is that in this instance the circularity of part (*Erlebnis/ Abenteuer*) and whole (*das ganze Leben*) denominates what is essentially narrative structure, even though Gadamer does not make the point explicit:

> What can be called an experience constitutes itself in memory. By calling it such, we are referring to the lasting meaning that an experience has for the person who has it. . . . Everything that is experienced is experienced by oneself, and part of its meaning is that it belongs to the unity of this self and thus contains and unmistakable and irreplaceable relation to the whole of this one life. (Gadamer 1993a, pp. 65–66)

We need to fill out the narrative structure that is implicit in this statement, but manifestly present. The relationship between part and whole is not a pointillistic or timeless relationship, but an actively structuring insight of a history that builds from both ends. So here we have a crucial point of contact with narrative in philosophical hermeneutics that reverberates with countless variations of the part-whole relationship, but because it is tied in with Gadamer's dissociation from *Erlebniskunst*, and because Gadamer does not develop the positive residue in his later ontology, it simply lies fallow here.

Gadamer picks up on the *Erlebnis* theme again in the second part of *Truth and Method* in his exegesis of German historicism. This section contains some of the deepest connections to the principles of emplotment, because historicists such as Ranke, Droysen, and Dilthey had a strong tendency toward narrative understanding in the Ricoeurian sense, and the theoretical contributions that Gadamer highlights from them generally follow this line of significance. It is important to remember that Gadamer is not advocating what he describes in his historical exegesis; nevertheless, with care it is possible to determine what he wants to retain from it.

We can start from the basic fact that historical interpretation, like narrative emplotment, is a search for order. For Droysen, Gadamer points out, the reality of history "stands in the ever new capturing and forming that is being achieved by the mind of the 'restlessly changing finitude' which belongs to every human act."[4] In other words, the order of history is not given, but is the result of a creative act. Ranke, according to Gadamer, finds the continuity of history in the "constructive links of historical coherence"—*die konstruktiven Glieder des geschichtlichen Zusammenhang* (Gadamer, 1993a, pp. 207–08).[5] The coherence of history is no longer thought to grow out of an *a priori* telos, but somehow must establish a coherence within itself, a teleology without a telos. It accomplishes this end through what Gadamer calls a *Freiheit des Handelns*, which could almost be translated as the "free activity of emplotment." The dynamic is close to what Gadamer elsewhere calls iconic augmentation, a symbolic infusion backward (*Zurückwirken*), a phenomenon we can recognize is at the heart of narrative meaning-making. Gadamer explains the term *Zurückwirken*: "This expression means that in the infinite web of events there are particularly significant incidents [*bestimmte herausgehobene Auftritt*] in which historical decisions are, as it were, concentrated" (ibid., p. 204). In a universe without a telos, certain things that happen attain, in retrospect, their own deep significance because they suddenly make sense of all the rest. What is meaningful gets sorted out in the process, events come to be invested with symbolic weight in relation to everything else, and the fateful discovery confers an order on a sequence of events as a kind of delinquent insight. The revelations of these historical effects, *Wirkungsgeschichte*, "give to historical coherence its articulation"—*geben dem geschichtlichen Zusammenhang seine Artikulation* (ibid., p. 208). This is very close to Ricoeurian emplotment, so the question is, what does Gadamer affirm as genuinely hermeneutic? He would not be congenial to the centrality of "histori-cal decisions," since historical destiny is something that, for him, is revealed to us. But the articulation of historical coherence as an effect of history is perfectly amenable to hermeneutic understanding.

When the exegesis comes to Dilthey's place in the journey toward a herme-neutic perspective, Gadamer isolates Dilthey's proto-narrative theory of history. The first elements of this syntax are what evolve out of individual life experi-ence that create the possibility of coherence: "By elaborating the way an individual's life acquires continuity, Dilthey hopes to obtain constitutive concepts that will serve to ground both historical continuity and the knowledge of it" (ibid., p. 222). These "constitutive concepts" are remarkably similar to Ricoeur's structures of narrative coherence:

It is life itself that unfolds and forms itself in intelligible unities, and it is in terms of the single individual that these unities are understood. This is the self-evident starting point for Dilthey's analysis. The continuity of life as it appears to the individual (and is re-experienced and understood by others through biographical knowledge) is created through the significance of particular experiences (*Erlebnisse*). Around them, as around an organizing center, the unity of a life is created in the same way that a melody acquires its form—not from the mere succession of notes but from the musical motifs that determine its formal unity. (Ibid., p. 223)

It is so ironic that Gadamer uses a musical metaphor to clarify the biographical principles that Ricoeur will appropriate into a narrative vocabulary. It is almost as if Gadamer cannot or will not hear the patent connection to narrativity that Dilthey himself saw quite clearly. Gadamer does recognize what he calls "enduring units of significance" (*bleibenden Bedeutungseinheiten*), the *Erlebnisse* that serve as the pivot points of the story of a life. These components are the building blocks of the order established in history at the level of the individual as intelligible unities (*verständliche Einheiten*) that unfold and form (*ausfaltet und gestaltet*) in life itself as particular experiences (ibid., p. 226; Gadamer, 1990, p. 227). Gadamer emphasizes that Dilthey will, late in his career, place greater significance on the social and cultural structures of ritual, custom, mores, and so forth, but he stresses that Dilthey's prime imperative was to understand the coherence that developed out of a particular life, a "structure, which builds up its unity out of its own center" (Gadamer, 1993a, p. 230). In saying this, Gadamer identifies this dynamic as having a *hermeneutic* rather than a narrative structure, once again leaping past the rather obvious point: "Life itself, flowing temporality, is ordered toward the formation of enduring units of significance. Life interprets itself. Life itself has a hermeneutical structure" (ibid., p. 226). Thus the reflexive-recursive aspect of recounting (*narro, narrare*) is simply subsumed under the mantle of interpretation.

So this expository summary of Dilthey's link between biography and history walks right up to the heart of the narrative implications of Ricoeur's debt to Dilthey. What does Gadamer himself take from this proto-narrative theory for his own hermeneutics? Although he distances himself from Dilthey's commitment to "the individual's private world of experience as the starting point," Gadamer does repeatedly return throughout *Truth and Method* to the part-whole relationship of *Erlebnisse* and life-as-a-whole (ibid., p. 232). That connection is central to Dilthey's project, and congenial to hermeneutic understanding. Its dialectical interanimation is laid out most clearly in the first part (ibid., Part I.2.B.), but it reappears here and elsewhere as a hermeneutic principle. Gadamer is never quite clear about how one could abstract the meaning of personal experience to the individual from this particular dialectic. He is very clear why he rejects *Erlebnis* as the basic building block: "[I]t is still oriented to the interiority of self-consciousness" rather than to "the intersubjectivity of the communal world" (ibid., p. 250). Experience (*Erfahrung*) now becomes essentially dialogic, and its primary structures dialogue, play, and so forth.

It is from this distinction that the key question arises about the distance between Gadamer and Ricoeur on the question of emplotment: What is analogous in a Gadamerian perspective to the *Erlebnis*—experience that acts as the footing for the narrative structure of a life—that is, an event that both marks a juncture in the narrative progress and reflects the whole from which it prescinds? The title of Gadamer's essay, "The Continuity of History and the Existential Moment," would seem to suggest it confronts this question head-on (Gadamer, 1972). There he poses Dilthey's search for the continuity of history in the "inner self-confirmation" of experience "by reviewing that multitude of experiences, their sequence and their constellations, under which one's life has been lived" against "the completely different and larger-scaled criterion of historical continuity" (ibid., p. 231). Gadamer rejects precisely "our remembering and imagining consciousness" as the vehicle of continuity for this larger reality (ibid., p. 232). Instead, he turns to a concept of *historicity* that was apparently given a special meaning by Count Yorck von Wartenburg; historical epochs that are precisely "not simply reflections of our ordering, classifying, control-oriented desire for" order, but rather a recognition of an order that emerges out of the flows and interruptions of historical time. Gadamer goes to great lengths to demonstrate that the agency of the events lies in themselves, and also the passive role of consciousness in recognizing them, so that a narrative course of events is not imposed by us: "The historical constellation which marks an epochal time-span . . . determines the contents of time itself" (ibid., p. 233). At the end of this reflection, Gadamer says quite directly and explicitly what he believes stands in place of the inner self-confirmation of experience that gives unity and coherence:

> My own formulation of the answer is as follows: when something encounters us within the tradition in such a way that we understand it, then that itself is an event. And something happens when one, so to speak, accepts a word from the tradition, when one allows a word to speak to him. That is certainly not an understanding of history as a process, but rather an understanding of that which is given to us in history as addressing us [*ansprechend*] and engaging us [*angehend*]. (Ibid., p. 237)

The realization of historical time comes when we are confronted by the address of history, culture, or social change *to us*. The order is only realized in the exchange. By putting things this way, Gadamer thinks he has shifted the realization of order from inner experience to some middle place between ourselves and the course of events, or at least in the dialogue outside of "our remembering and imagining consciousness." The classic example would be the history of the word in the Jewish faith tradition, a history that is constructed not in the alembic of personal experience but in the shared history of a community as it is passed down. The order is not being created as an assurance of order—which is what a narrative accounting typically does (what Ricoeur calls a pledge of order)—but is simply revealed to us, whether of order or disorder, as something we must acknowledge.

This shift is the real crux of the matter, and is the chasm that opens up before anyone who chooses between Gadamer and Ricoeur on this issue. To choose Gadamer's side, one has to believe there actually is something substantially equivalent to the insight that an *Erlebnis* gives, that is, a meaning of the whole, crystallized in the existential moment (*dem erfüllten Blick des Augens*), or what Ricoeur calls "the epiphany of order" (Ricoeur, 1991a, p. 112). Dilthey is emphatic that the interpretive understanding of history writ large "is possible only on the basis of the subjective depth of lived experience," and it is indeed hard to imagine what is to replace the insight gained from one's own experience in facing the world, and "the reciprocal dependence of universal and singular knowledge," the chiasm of social history and self-knowledge (Dilthey, 2002, p. 174). And yet Gadamer expropriates precisely this phrase (*der Augenblick*), invoking the entire modernist aesthetic of epiphanic insight, for the sounding of fate (*Geschick*), which we only witness: "[T]he reality of history is not to be found in the cognitive imagining of history and controlling of events, but rather in the very experiencing of destiny" (Gadamer, 1972, p. 236). Presumably every one of us who recognizes our place in the eventfulness of history will hear its fatefulness differently, but can nevertheless hear it, like the porter the pounding at the gate, with a full sense of its significance. In any case, it is not important that we locate its place in the story of our lives, but rather that it is heard.

For myself I cannot diminish my constructive agency in this way. It seems to me the recognition and construction of one's location are not exchangeable experiences, and even if Dilthey is wrong that we should build from one to the other (from psychology to history), the kind of part-whole relationship that becomes manifest as the narrative order of a life is not incompatible with the understanding that emerges from dialogue. We have to do both. I want both and conclude that Gadamer's view is occluded by a thematic focus. He is most anxious to break away from subjective experience as an intersection because it places a limit on our ability to hear the voice of the other. He is afraid it leads only to assimilation rather than to a breaking open of one's own perspectives. That is a crucial warning, but an insufficient cause of omission.

Two Questions on the Possibility of Integration

Question 1. In the end I am left with two questions. The first is to Ricoeur: What accords emplotment the privilege of narrative as a form of temporal order over other hermeneutic forms (dialogue, play, ritual, *Gebilde*)? Ricoeur asks "[W]hat way is the ordinary experience of time, borne by daily acting and suffering, refashioned by its passage through the grid of narrative?" He answers that there is a privileged function for mimetic refiguration, "the power of revelation and transformation achieved by narrative configurations when they are 'applied' to actual acting and suffering" (Ricoeur, 1991d, pp. 338–39). I need to test the category claim here that allows refiguration to emerge for Ricoeur as a central hermeneutic phenomenon that distinguishes itself from the more generic concept of hermeneutic *Anwendung* (application).

There is an ambiguity in Ricoeur's writings on narrative that should be clarified in order to answer this question, and it has to do with the major claims he enunciates as he sets out his narrative project. I have already referenced these pivotal statements, but I need to return to them now to observe a subtle shift in register among them. In the inaugural paper (1978) on narrative and time, Ricoeur frames his approach as a consideration of the role narrative helps us in understanding time: "[N]arrative activity . . . provides a privileged access to the way we articulate our experience of time" (Ricoeur, 1991a, p. 99). Time is the subject matter in this formulation, and narrative is an aid to understanding. Ricoeur is primarily interested in the temporal structures of narrative insofar as they "constitute an answer to the ambiguities and paradoxes of our ordinary experience of time" (ibid.). He is consistent throughout about this epistemic function and, as a consequence, narrative would seem, insofar as it only addresses the questions we have *about* time, to yield a fairly narrow result. In the opening to the first part of *Time and Narrative*, Ricoeur seems to be constrained by the same delimitation. Narrative is enlisted to get at "the nature of time," since "the truth claim of every narrative work, is the temporal character of human experience" (Ricoeur, 1984, p. 4).

Ricoeur's ambitions, however, exceed this ostensible purpose, since a major claim later in the same study is that "time becomes human to the extent that it is articulated through a narrative mode, and narrative attains its full meaning when it becomes a condition of temporal existence" (ibid., p. 52). We are no longer talking simply about a mode of illumination, but about an ontological transformation. The preface to the whole of *Time and Narrative* confirms this more ambitious purpose: "I see in the plots we invent the privileged means by which we re-configure our confused, unformed, and at the limit mute temporal experience" (ibid., p. xi). "Temporal" in this claim is an attributive adjective that qualifies the particular character of experience, and the thrust of the claim is thus that because human experience is temporal, emplotment is the privileged discursive form of its intelligibility. Narrative no longer appears to be a cultural artifact that yields a meaning for philosophy, but is itself equipment for living.

This clarification of the claim for narrative would seem to render the integration with Gadamer impossible, since for Gadamer other discursive forms take precedence in the articulation of human experience, dialogue obviously having pride of place in his own frame of reference. But, immediately, such a conflict sounds unconvincing, because dialogue and narrative, even just from the standpoint of common sense, are hardly competitive with one another, but simply different modalities of communication—complementary, overlapping, but functioning differently and entering at different levels. What I am going to suggest is that Ricoeur needed to add a prepositional phrase to the above claim in order to make it fully accurate, and that this emendation makes integration more likely. The addition, borrowed from Ricoeur himself, would be something like "in the field of action," so that the claim would be: *I see in the plots we invent the privileged means by which we re-configure our confused, unformed, and at the limit mute temporal experience in the field of action.* This addition is in keeping with Ricoeur's approach, since he is at pains to stipulate everywhere that narrative emplotment governs, precisely, the field of action, as I have already shown. I think the qualification limits the ambition of Ricoeur's claim in a way that he would not object to, and allows without contradiction the privilege Gadamer accords to dialogue, since the privilege of the two discursive modalities now simply work at different levels.

Before leaving this question, it will be helpful to give greater specificity to the crucial phrase "field of action." Beyond the obvious element of intention that discriminates action from movement, what exactly is this *field* in which muthos operates? The key to this question lies in a summary phrase in the first volume of *Time and Narrative* that names the elements organized by narrative plot—"the miscellany constituted by the circumstances, ends and means, initiatives and interactions, the reversals of fortune, and all the unintended consequences issuing from human action" (ibid., p. x). This is a miscellaneous assortment indeed! In fact the resistance of this motley fabric to a more unified organizing principleiswhatwillyieldaproperunderstandingofthegeniusofnarrativemeaning—it is the irreducible complexity of the elements that interact in a human situation that grants it its own paradigmatic space, and action seems to be the nodal point around which all these elements interact. I would even go so far as to say there is no comparable irreducible complexity in the structure of dialogue, play, or work, and this is because none of them actualizes and connects, of necessity, the miscellany in play in the human situation occasioned by the need to act. This attribute, in fact, argues for the privilege Ricoeur accords to narrative understanding.

Question 2. The emendation I have made in Ricoeur's formulation removes an important barrier to an integration between Gadamer and Ricoeur, but it leads directly to another potential barrier, and this takes me to my second question. This question flows from the fact that action, the privileged concern of narrative, places agency squarely in the realm of human choice, something that distances it from the clear intent of Gadamerian hermeneutics. Gadamer is focused on locating agency in language and culture. This theme rings like a pedal point through the entirety of *Truth and Method* and in all of Gadamer's work. Understanding is neither subject to our will nor subservient to our calculations, but finds its own time and way. Creation "is not something that we can imagine being deliberately made by someone" (Gadamer, 1986, p. 33). In this thematic environment, it is easy to see why the constructive power of narrative ("I tell") hardly surfaces. Ricoeur says of historical events, "[W]e cannot say whether we produced them or they simply happened," and he seeks a balance between convention and invention (Ricoeur, 1988, p. 196). He has no difficulty in assigning primary agency to the self:

> Through the "I can," initiative indicates my power, through the "I do," it becomes my act; through interference or intervention, it inscribes my act in the course of things, thereby making the lived present coincide with the particular instant; through the kept promise, it gives the present the force of persevering, in short, of enduring. (Ibid., p. 233)

Partisans of Ricoeur find the reemergence of subjective agency less troubling, affirming an ethics of initiative, action, and choice.

For those still working at overcoming the privilege accorded to subjective agency, it is much harder to travel this distance. We can say Gadamer's polemic functions as a corrective, and, in any case, it is not the individual person but the apotheosis of the transcendental Ego that is his target. For this reason, we can hope the two hermeneutic projects are not ultimately irreconcilable. If interpretation and narration are both enlisted to address the fragmentariness of human identity, do they necessarily crowd each other out? What we know, of course, is that agency exists on a continuum, dispersed across culture, materiality, personal initiative, and communal deliberation. Certainly, we write, we inscribe our story, and we narrate ourselves as we live out our lives, and yet there are times when we know we are witnessing history, when each new incident takes on an iconic meaning, and events unfold with irresistible force.

Because Ricoeur would always ascribe to subjectivity the full dignity of the Augustinian drama of the inner life, he must find a way to connect hermeneutic experience with the vast experience of reflection, which he entitles the life of the soul. This task creates the very structure of the argument of *Time and Narrative*, where narrative acts as "a bridge set over the breach" between the time of the soul and the time of the world (ibid., p. 24).[6] This is the moment that forces a comparison with Gadamer's *Verweilen*, because, unlike the binary polarity of authentic and calculative time, Ricoeur's narrativity creates a "third-time" that mediates the otherwise insuperable gap between being-toward-death and the drama of the cosmos. This third-time is essentially a story of fate on the scale of history, a finitude too vast to imagine.

I do not want to reach this synthesis too quickly. After all this sorting and synthesizing, the oddity remains that Gadamer had all the elements of narrative enactment before him as he presented the *poietic* structures of temporality in the play art, theater, literature, and yet for him these contributions pointed toward the eventfulness of rites and ritual. It does seem as if the development that occurs in the plot through conflict, complication, crisis, and resolution—the wisdom that comes through trial, the change that is effected through suffering—that all the processive elements of dramatic incident and occasion are set aside, and we are left with, on the one side the calculative agency of human making and doing, and on the other side the rising to the timeless that we only witness. The most transcendent experience of art moves beyond our making and doing and "shows what we cannot achieve" (Gadamer, 1986, pp. 104, 153). Is it possible that the "self-fulfilling moment" of art, theater, and ritual—and Gadamer's entire interest—is in the "transformed state of being" that occurs in the moment of recognition? How does this square with the hermeneutics of human finitude? (Ibid., p. 59).

But just before we accuse Gadamer of a contradiction, he draws us back, reminding us of the hermeneutic structure of which art is exemplary. Art is always in fact the most particular, the "unique and irreplaceable" (ibid., p. 107). It initiates that endless movement, back and forth, between the contingent and the permanent. The extremes of this polarity are only ever virtual, and human beings emerge out of this in-between. A notable thing about Gadamer's aesthetics is the reference to self-tension ("*in sich Verspannten*"): "But art is present whenever a work succeeds in elevating what it is or represents to a new configuration, a new world of its own in miniature, a new order of unity in tension" (ibid., p. 103; Gadamer, 1993, p. 36). This world in miniature is a recognition that there is a dialectic in play, that something is added, augmented, increased, but that the contingent is never left behind. We can lose sight of that in Gadamer's epideictic. There are times when we can even see in art's function as a "presentation of order" something at work between order and its construction:

> The work of art provides a perfect example of that universal characteristic of human existence—the never-ending process of building a world . . . . Perhaps our capacity to preserve and maintain, the capacity that supports human culture rests in turn upon the fact that we must always order anew what threatens to dissolve before us. (Gadamer, 1986, p. 103)

Here, we might read in Gadamer's formula something consonant with Ricoeur's appropriation of narrative as making.

Or not. We are every so often transfixed, and held captive by, the realization that a certain gesture, phrase, action, or object suddenly summarizes, encapsulates, or epitomizes the significance of an event, the character of a person, or a period of a life. Such recognitions, as unwilled as they are, so vulnerable to the inscrutable laws of experience, are nevertheless built on, and serve as the basis of, the constructing work that we set about in order to make a place for ourselves. This seems to me to be incontrovertible. I would like to affirm, then, that Gadamer did not sufficiently bring out this feature or dynamic, but that it is a necessary adjunct to the description of hermeneutic experience.

Notes

1 I address an ambiguity in this aspect of Ricoeur's theory below.
2 Sachs, J. "Aristotle: motion and its place in nature," *The Internet Encyclopedia of Philosophy*, available at http://philo.ruc.edu.cn/po104/mirror/www.iep.utm.edu/a/aris-mot.htm.

[3] Gadamer sets up a conceptual valence here that his last great summary statement on art, "Wort und Bild," inverts. There, the emergence of truth in the work of art is analogous to Aristotle's *energeia*:

> The Aristotelian terms that inquire into the being of movement—like dynamis, energeia, and entelecheia—point to the side of the action in the process of being carried out and not to the "ergon"—the completed action. . . . What is being moved is still underway, has not yet arrived. It is still becoming.

[4] "[B]esteht in einer immer neu vom Geist zu leistenden Erfassung und Gestaltung der 'rastlos wechselnden Endlichkeiten,' denen jeder Handelnde angehört" (Gadamer, 1990, p. 217)

[5] *Zusammenhang* means not merely context or connection, but the coherence of associations.

[6] The concept of time really acts for Ricoeur as a placeholder for subjective experience on the one hand and objective events on the other.

Chapter 7

Paul Ricoeur's and Hans-Georg Gadamer's Diverging Reflections on Recognition

David Vessey

As the story goes, Hans-Georg Gadamer was furious at Paul Ricoeur for not backing him in his debate with Jürgen Habermas. Gadamer thought everyone sympathetic to hermeneutics would see Habermas was confused in thinking hermeneutic understanding was insufficiently critical. Yet instead of joining Gadamer against Habermas, Ricoeur sought a middle ground that satisfied neither. Although siding primarily with Gadamer, Ricoeur took Habermas's criticisms more seriously than Gadamer and argued for a dialectic of engagement and distanciation, a dialectic toggling between the hermeneutics of meaning and the hermeneutics of suspicion. Gadamer thought all that was required was a historically informed, careful phenomenology of the essential place of reason in linguistic understanding. He thought that once reason and linguistic understanding are separated and isolated, they would never be properly united again, not even dialectically.

Their difference with respect to Habermas is indicative of much of their philosophical approaches. Ricoeur is nothing if not synoptic. He takes in all views from any tradition he can understand, and he works hard to assign them their proper place. In Ricoeur's hands, seemingly intractable differences often turn out to be only differences in emphasis. Personal identity: is it the identity of a person over time, or is the way a person identifies him or herself—*idem* or *ipse*? Both are correct, but each is only half the story. Meaning—is it about the continuity of tradition or the critical overcoming of tradition? Both; we need a hermeneutics of meaning and a hermeneutics of suspicion. Gadamer is a reader, not a synthesizer. He certainly holds expansive views about language, rationality, art, and morality, though they tend to arise only in the process of reading other's views. That is why it can be so difficult to detangle Gadamer's views from those views upon which he is commenting, and why it is so difficult to excerpt a selection of Gadamer's views for collections in Continental philosophy. Ricoeur reads to find a thinker's place in the overall picture; Gadamer reads to find out what questions he can learn to ask. Gadamer is also more thematically focused—he is concerned above all with understanding fully what happens when we understand. What happens when we engage a text, another person, or a work of art in dialogue? Gadamer is concerned with understanding the place of language in human understanding, and with understanding the place of the humanities in contemporary life. However, his reflections have neither the scope nor the breadth of Ricoeur's ambitious program. Ricoeur seeks to incorporate all reasonable positions into a synthetic dialectical whole; Gadamer shows little interest in philosophical positions or traditions he thinks have gone astray. In this respect, Gadamer is a student of Heidegger's approach to the history of philosophy, Ricoeur a student of Hegel's. Even though, philosophically, Ricoeur is the closest hermeneut to Gadamer, comparisons between them are never as fruitful as one might expect. It should be that they share so much that focusing on their differences highlights the nuanced ways one might approach a philosophical problem. But it rarely works that way, in part because they are such different thinkers.

As a synoptic philosopher committed to dialectic, Ricoeur's rival is Hegel. It should come as no surprise that he has written comparatively little on Hegel nor has he drawn extensively on Hegelian concepts. In the third volume of *Time and Narrative*, Ricoeur even hints that Hegel should be "renounced," but in the end he could not ignore the important impact Hegel's account of recognition, *Anerkennung*, has had on twentieth-century European thought, first in France through Alexandre Kojève's *Introduction to the Reading of Hegel* (Kojève, 1969), and more recently in Germany through Axel Honneth's work on the *Struggle for Recognition* (Honneth, 2003). Comparing Ricoeur's and Gadamer's discussions of recognition provides an ideal place for comparing their different philosophical approaches. Ricoeur works to present all the various meanings of *reconnaissance* and then uses that taxonomy to situate the contemporary debate. He eventually shows how a core understanding of recognition, in terms of *agape* love, escapes some of the concerns raised against accounts of recognition. It is a synoptic understanding—a conceptual mapping that grants everyone his or her piece of conceptual soil to till, but no one, except Ricoeur himself, a claim to the whole.

Gadamer says virtually nothing about recognition—*Anerkennung*—in its technical philosophical sense. I say "virtually" nothing because the concept played a fairly significant role in *Truth and Method* (Gadamer, 2004), making an appearance in two key sections. (Coincidently or not, it appears in the two sections most relevant for his debates with Habermas.) But after *Truth and Method* it vanishes from his technical, conceptual vocabulary. It seems he decided that recognition, as it functioned technically in *Truth and Method*, had no important role to play in an adequately articulated phenomenology of linguistic understanding as exemplified by dialogue. Where Ricoeur seeks to preserve as much as possible the legitimacy of the various philosophical meanings of recognition, Gadamer abandons the term. To bring Ricoeur and Gadamer into dialogue, then, will require us to understand why Gadamer thinks a phenomenology of recognition is not the path to understanding dialogue. We will find the differences revolve around the two competing ancient meanings of love—*agape* and *philia*.

Ricoeur on Recognition

Ricoeur's *The Course of Recognition* (Ricoeur, 2005) explores the range of possible philosophical meanings of *reconnaissance*. He starts with 23 different meanings in the *Dictionnaire de la langue francaise* and moves to three general categories in *Grand Robert de la langue francaise*. The three are, roughly, recognition as grasping with the mind, recognition as accepting as true, and recognition as acknowledging a debt by showing gratitude. He distills these down to three interconnected philosophical motifs, moving from the more active to the more passive. There is the recognition of something as something, in coming to know it; there is self-recognition; and there is being recognized. "Recognition as Identification," "Recognizing Oneself," and "Mutual Recognition," are the titles of the three chapters of the book. The discussions are richly detailed and draw on a wealth of material and a lifetime of reflection that few, other than Ricoeur, could sustain.

For bringing Gadamer and Ricoeur into conversation, the most important part is his third chapter, where he takes up the Hegelian concept of *Anerkennung*, especially as it is explicated in Alex Honneth's writings. Ricoeur reads Hegel as providing a response to Hobbes, for whom all recognition is the recognition of struggle and the threat of death. Hegel's account of recognition shows how we are connected to others at a more basic level than the level of the social contract and, if there is going to be any sort of contract, it can only be sustained on the back of values we must always already share. A contract can neither be the original nor the sole source of social norms. Likewise, our relationship to the other cannot solely be one of struggle. In Hegel's writings in the Jena period (as opposed to, for example, Hegel's later *Philosophy of Right*), Ricoeur finds more promise, for Hegel's early account links recognition and self-reflection, moves from injustice to respect, and makes explicit the levels of institutionalization involved in mutual recognition, from the interpersonal to the political.

Ricoeur seeks an account of mutual recognition that still takes seriously the "original dissymmetry that widens the gap between the one and the other" (ibid., p. 152). If we start with the original dissymmetry, as he claims phenomenology does, then we have the problem of explaining how mutuality and reciprocity are possible. Edmund Husserl and Emmanuel Levinas are Ricoeur's models for mistaken starting points. Starting from the Ego pole (Husserl) or the absolute Other (Levinas), each must find a way to "account for a reciprocity between unequal partners" (ibid., p. 160), something they accomplish only with difficulty, if at all. One way to see what Ricoeur is doing is to see him as Hegel to Levinas and Husserl's Hobbes. Levinas and Husserl focus on the originary asymmetry between self and other. Ricoeur helps us see how this asymmetry can only presuppose a deeper affinity modeled on recognition.

After discussing Honneth's views and ways that the struggle for recognition could open up possibilities for self-confidence, self-respect, and self-esteem, Ricoeur raises the question of whether all forms of recognition are best understood as struggles. His concern is that the account of a struggle without end amounts to a version of Hegel's "Bad Infinity." He writes,

> To ward off this worry about a new "unhappy consciousness" and the consequences that follow from it, I propose to take into consideration our actual experience of what I shall call states of peace. . . . [Such] experiences of peaceful recognition cannot take the place of a resolution of the very perplexities raised by the concept of struggle, still less of a resolution of the conflicts in question. The certitude that accompanies states of peace offers instead a confirmation that the moral motivation for struggles is not illusory. . . . The thesis I want to argue for can be summed up as follows: The alternative to the idea of struggle in the process of mutual recognition is to be sought in peaceful experiences of mutual recognition, based on symbolic mediations as exempt from the juridical as from the commercial order of exchange. (Ibid. pp. 218–19)

Ricoeur's focus is on *agape*, which is different from Aristotelian *philia* and Platonic *eros*, and is a suspicious category for recognition since it seems to lack the mutuality Ricoeur claims is the focus of the chapter. *Agape* is a gift of love. It is not in any way connected to justice, as is Aristotle's account of *philia*, nor is it an expression of a kind of lacking, as is Plato's account of *eros*. *Agape* is pure generosity, pure gift, freed from any expectation of recompense, "without any regard for the obligation thereby engendered to give something in return" (ibid., p. 232). The gift of *agape* inaugurates gratitude, which, in French, is often expressed by *reconnaissance*, recognition. So by focusing on *agape* as that which escapes the logic of the gift, Ricoeur connects his discussion of mutual recognition with the third meaning derived from the dictionaries: recognition as an expression of thanks.

Gadamer's Abandonment of *Anerkennen*

In the course of his *Course of Recognition*, Ricoeur mentions Gadamer's discussion of the recognition of the authority of a tradition. Ricoeur calls this "the recognition of superiority," and admits that such an account of authority "constitutes a thorn in the flesh of an enterprise like my own, deliberately limited to *reciprocal* forms of mutual recognition" (ibid., p. 212). It is true, as we shall see, that in *Truth and Method* Gadamer speaks of recognition in nonreciprocal terms, but we should not conclude that he lacks an account of mutuality that is analogous to Ricoeur's account, one that neither denies an "originary dissymmetry" nor reduces relations to struggles, and does not succumb to the logic of the gift. Rather, we just should not seek in Gadamer's account an account of mutual *recognition*. In fact, I will argue, Gadamer sees what relying on talk of recognition misses and rightly turns to other conceptual resources, ultimately to *philia* as the proper model of the mutual relations between persons.[1]

Throughout his writings Gadamer uses versions of *anerkennen* in its everyday sense of acknowledgement or recognition, and, of course, in its philosophical sense when discussing Hegel and Jean-Paul Sartre. However, the term plays a distinctive technical, philosophical role in his writings on philosophical hermeneutics up to and including *Truth and Method*. Gadamer gets from Karl Löwith the idea that *Anerkennung* is the proper way to characterize "I-Thou" social ontologies. His 1929 review of Löwith's *Das Individuum in der Rolle des Mitmenschen* contains the densest set of references to *Anerkennung* outside his essay on Hegel's account of self-consciousness (Gadamer, 1987). Gadamer cites this book for its influence on his pivotal discussion in *Truth and Method* of three ways of treating others as "Thous." Yet, despite his life-long friendship with Löwith, Gadamer moves away from adopting an I-Thou account of inter-subjectivity and, at the same time, abandons the terminology of *anerkennen* as a technical term. We will want to see why he rejects such I-Thou accounts of inter-subjectivity, and why these arguments apply equally well against the usefulness of speaking of recognition.

There are two notable places in *Truth and Method* where Gadamer speaks of recognition, *Anerkennung*, and both are significant for his interaction with Ricoeur. They are seldom read together, but need to be. The first comes in his "rehabilitation of authority and tradition" from the Enlightenment's "prejudice against prejudice."[2] He wants to argue that granting a text the authority to teach us something is not an abdication of reason, even though it is a kind of acceptance, on authority, of the legitimacy of the text. Gadamer would never deny there is a difference between accepting something on authority and accepting something on the basis of reason—"[t]he Enlightenment's distinc-tion between faith in authority and using one's own reason is, in itself, legiti-mate" (Gadamer, 2004, p. 280)—his concern is that when learning something new we cannot solely rely on reason. After all, in such cases our reason is itself being informed. He suggests the Enlightenment failed to understand that authority could be "a source of truth." He writes:

> [T]he authority of persons is ultimately based not on the subjection and abdication of reason but on an act of acknowledgment [*Anerkennung*] and knowledge [*Erkenntnis*]—the knowledge, namely, that the other is superior to oneself in judgment and insight and that for this reason his judgment takes precedence—i.e., it has priority over one's own. This is connected with the fact that authority cannot actually be bestowed but is earned, and must be earned if someone is to lay claim to it. It rests on acknowledgment [*Anerkennung*] and

hence on an act of reason itself which, aware of its own limitations, trusts to the better insight of others. Authority in this sense, properly understood, has nothing to do with blind obedience to commands. . . . Thus, acknowledging [*Anerkennung*] authority is always connected with the idea that what the authority says is not irrational and arbitrary but can, in principle, be discovered to be true. (Ibid., p. 281)

An authority becomes an authority by virtue of his or her superior rationality, and it is this rationality we recognize when we accept as true what an authority tells us. Because being and authority are connected to rationality, what the authority teaches is in principle confirmable by us. Not only is the authority's rationality what we recognize, but the recognition itself is an act of reason. It is always rational to take the word of someone more knowledgeable and rational than oneself. Importantly for the topic at hand, *Anerkennung*, according to Gadamer, is essentially and exclusively rational, both in what justifies it and what it acknowledges.

The second place Gadamer speaks of *Anerkennung* is in his discussion of the analogy among the three ways in which we might engage a text, and the three ways we might treat an other as a Thou. At this juncture of *Truth and Method*, Gadamer has just completed a discussion of Hegel's theory of experience in order to stress that all experiences are also self-experiences—we experience the world self-consciously. Gadamer concludes that the more experienced we are the more open we are to the possibility of finding truth elsewhere. Openness to others comes in the form of putting ourselves in the position to learn from them. Here, his discussion of tradition converges with his discussion of experience. Openness to the truth of others and tradition is the rational response to the self-awareness that accompanies all experience.

Since all experience has the form of revealing finitude, so must hermeneutic experience, the experience of an interpretive understanding of a text. Gadamer considers three ways of being open to texts and others as Thous. The preliminary significance of speaking of texts or others as Thous is to highlight that we stand in relation to them. We belong to them in the sense that an address, to be successful, requires an addressee. We could talk about someone without engaging him or her, but we could not address someone without succeeding to engage him or her. An address is not something that can be achieved by only one person. It invites a relation and succeeds only through that relation.

The first way of treating someone as a Thou lies in understanding them as manifesting scientifically predictable behavior. We see them as experimental subjects. Citing Kant's maxim against treating humanity solely as a means, Gadamer claims this way of treating others is immoral. It is simply using their responses for our purposes, with no concern for the truth in what they say. The analogue to textual interpretation would be a kind of strong methodologism, such as trying to understand a poem by focusing on the quantifiable features of the poem. It is only the second way of treating another as a Thou that includes genuine recognition.

"A second way in which the Thou is experienced and understood is that the Thou is acknowledged as a person [*als Person anerkannt wird*]" (ibid., p. 353). Here, Gadamer uses *Anerkennung* as a technical term. The interlocutor is recognized as someone who has a view on the world that should be taken seriously. The problem occurs when we seek to reduce the other person's views to placeholders in a larger, and previously articulated, conceptual framework, rather than recognizing the authority of what the other person has to teach us. The result is a struggle for genuine recognition as the participants each claim authority and try to "reflectively to outdo the other" (ibid.). The analogous situation to texts is to read a text as an example of a historical or philosophical standpoint. He writes,

> The text that is understood historically is forced to abandon its claim to be saying something true. We think we understand when we see the past from a historical standpoint—i.e., transpose ourselves into the historical situation and try to reconstruct the historical horizon. In fact, however, we have given up the claim to find in the past any truth that is valid and intelligible for ourselves. Acknowledging [*Anerkennung*] the otherness of the other in this way, making him the object of objective knowledge, involves the fundamental suspension of his claim to truth. (Ibid., pp. 302–03)

Two points should be made here. First, Gadamer is not treating recognition, *anerkennung*, as taking only one form. People can be recognized in different ways, and some forms of recognition are more open to the otherness of the other than to other forms of recognition. Or, perhaps better put, there are various aspects of the rationality of a person that could be the object of recognition. In this case, it is the way in which their views exemplify a different point of view. Second, it is clear from Gadamer's references that he considered Hegel's account of recognition to fall into this second category of ways of engaging another as a Thou. Gadamer takes it as significant that the outcome of the Hegelian struggle for recognition is not a greater appreciation of our finitude and the importance of dialogue, but is instead an always increasing self-consciousness and individuation—a masking of our essential finitude. According to Gadamer, the transition to the "highest" form of relating to others comes with the recognition that finitude is not a hindrance to understanding, but is what makes understanding possible. The highest form of understanding others comes not from locating their views in a broader conceptual context, but from recognizing they have something to teach us.

With regard to the highest form of relatedness to others, Gadamer writes:

> In human relations the important thing is, as we have seen, to experience the Thou truly as a Thou—i.e., not to overlook his claim but to let him really say

something to us. Here is where openness belongs. . . . Openness to the other, then, involves recognizing [*Anerkennung*] that I myself must accept some things that are against me, even though no one else forces me to.

This is the parallel to the hermeneutical experience. I must allow tradition's claim to validity, not in these sense of simply acknowledging [*Anerkennung*] the past in its otherness, but in such a way that it has something to say to me. (Ibid., p. 355)

The question is not simply one of recognition, but of recognizing something in a specific way, in this case that the tradition, or the other person, "has something to say to me." Gadamer says the same thing with regard to the reasoned acknowledgement of an authority based on our awareness of our own finitude. The two discussions converge at this point, and bringing to bear the insights from his earlier "rehabilitation of authority and tradition" helps stem misunderstandings that might arise concerning his discussion of a Thou. The crucial point of the first discussion is to recognize the authority of a text, or another person, to teach us something as a judgment of reason rooted in the self-knowledge of our own finitude. We recognize that we do not know everything and that others may have an expertise we lack. By engaging them as having something true to say, we need to listen in a way that allows the truth of their views to show itself. Above all, according to Gadamer, it means understanding their views as an answer to a question—a question we must take seriously enough to ask ourselves. There is nothing passive about such listening, nor is there anything irrational about it.[3] On one hand, the recognition that occurs in the highest form of I-Thou relationships is a kind of rational acceptance of authority, and so Ricoeur is right about its asymmetry. On the other hand, the realization of an I-Thou relationship also serves as a model for the highest way of being together, what Gadamer calls *miteinandersein*.

After *Truth and Method* Gadamer never returns to using *Anerkennung* as a technical term to mean the reasoned acceptance of an authority, though he retains the idea that we always need to grant another person authority as a condition of dialogue. The motivation for dialogue remains the awareness of our own finitude, the awareness of the need for language for any understanding, and the awareness that the meanings in language always go beyond our control. Certainly, it is the case that others might understand a subject matter better than we can. More than that, others might understand our own views better than we do. Even if it turns out the other person does not live up to his or her granted role as an authority on the subject matter, simply the act of reformulating what we think for an interlocutor forces us to be attentive to our own beliefs in a new and constructive way. Thinking, for Gadamer, simply is finding the right word for something. Therefore, finding new words for something as a result of a conversation with someone is thinking anew. The essential connection Gadamer finds between reasoning and using language should immediately cast doubt on any criticism of Gadamer that suggests his account of dialogue marginalizes the role of reason.

Consider one of the few relevant places where *Anerkennung* appears as a technical term after *Truth and Method.*

> We seek conversation not only to understand the other person better. Rather we need it because our own concepts threaten to become rigid; and also because when we say something we want the other person to understand what we are thinking. My own efforts at thinking are led by yet another evident fact: the problem is not that we do not understand the other person, but that we don't understand ourselves! For precisely when we seek to understand the other person, we have the hermeneutical experience that we must break down resistance in ourselves if we wish to hear the other as other. This is really a basic determinant of all human existence and also still governs the success of our "self-understanding." . . . Life is easier if everything goes according to one's own wishes, but the dialectic of recognition [*Anerkennung*] requires that there can be no easy laurels. We learn this from the resistance we feel in ourselves when we let the other person be right. To make ourselves aware of this, the best help may be for us may be to get as fully as possible in the matter itself, overcome our own biases, and in the end to see ourselves as put in question—and where does this happen best if not in standing before the other person, a person who exists in himself or herself? So I would like to close with a short saying of Kierkegaard that makes this point especially clear and may even suggest a deeper meaning in my insistence on conversation, for conversation is the medium alone in which language is alive. The saying of Kierkegaard is the title of a talk he once wrote. It is "On what is edifying in the thought that against God one is always wrong." (Gadamer, 2007, p. 371)

The dialectic of recognition Gadamer refers to is what he finds in Hegel and what he refers to in *Truth and Method* as the second way of treating others as Thous. It is the struggle for recognition. The struggle arises from the resistance to granting the other person authority; Gadamer thinks we must overcome this dialectic (or avoid falling into it in the first place) and embrace the fact that "I must accept some things that are against me, even though no one else forces me to" (Gadamer, 2004, p. 355). In *Truth and Method* the highest form of *miteinandersein* was still an expression of recognition; in his later writings the "dialectic of recognition" needs to be overcome to realize the proper mode of being with others.

By looking at his criticisms of I-Thou accounts of intersubjectivity, we can understand Gadamer's decision to abandon the vocabulary of recognition. Although he seemed open to the I-Thou terminology in *Truth and Method,* later he will write that "[t]o say 'the I' and 'the Thou,' seems to us, at least since Wittgenstein, no longer quite allowable" (Gadamer, 2000b, p. 282). He clarifies it somewhat in one of his contributions to the Habermas-Gadamer debate.

We say, for instance, that understanding and misunderstanding take place between an I and a Thou. But this formulation "I and Thou" already betrays an enormous alienation. There is nothing like an "I and Thou" at all—there is neither the I nor the Thou as isolated, substantial realities. I may say "Thou," and I may refer to myself as over against a Thou, but a common understanding always precedes these situations. We all know that to say "Thou" to someone presupposes a deep common accord. Something enduring is already present when this word is spoken. (Gadamer, 1976, p. 7)

Over the course of his writings, Gadamer makes four arguments against I-Thou accounts of intersubjectivity. All return to the same basic point: seeing I-Thou relations as the primary intersubjective relation fails to appreciate the shared, especially linguistic, background that shapes persons so as to make dialogue possible in the first place. Dialogues take place in language and, thus, intersubjective elements are already in place as a condition of the dialogue. First, Gadamer argues that I-Thou relations are asymmetrical, and speaking of an "other" rather than a Thou can help make clear that the one is the other's other. His second argument is that in I-Thou accounts of intersubjectivity there is a "mystifying substantialization" of the "between," as if a new subject were introduced, the between, which in principle escapes all phenomenological investigation (Gadamer, 200b, p. 282). Third, he argues that understanding relations as I-Thou fails to appreciate the way our relations to others are always mediated through language, culture and tradition. Finally, he thinks those who emphasize I-Thou relations do so in recognition of the limitations of Cartesian accounts of autonomous subjects, but in doing so they preserve the notion of an autonomous subject (which must be qualified dialogically) because the meaning of the encounter depends too heavily on the agency of a person saying "Thou." As I mentioned above, an address establishes a relationship between the parties only if it is accepted, but with regard to the most fundamental relationship it ends its analysis on the accepted agency of a person rather than spelling out the already established relationship that provides the condition for the possibility of the address.

Here, then, we get a glimpse of the problem Gadamer has with speaking of recognition. No matter how much one emphasizes, as Ricoeur does, the passivity of being recognized as a condition for mutual recognition, the description of the relation still relies too much on the agency of individual subjects. Hegel and Ricoeur may have found a level of collaboration beneath the Hobbsean account of struggle between autonomous subjects that undermines the idea that the relation between two subjects is fundamentally one of struggle, but the account of recognition they embrace still preserves a mistaken sense of the independence of subjects. If you like, the "originary dissymmetry" that Ricoeur wants to acknowledge, but not start from, can only arise, Gadamer argues, against a background of shared agreement, of a shared *miteinandersein*.

Play as the Form of Irreducibly Social Actions

Recall that in *Truth and Method* Gadamer insists there is a close connection between being open to the meaning of texts, tradition, and others, such that for all three *Anerkennung* initiates a proper encounter. But a reasoned acknowledgement of authority is not a consummation of a dialogue, as if the outcome of the dialogue were accepted on authority; rather it initiates the dialogue in the sense of establishing the necessary attitude someone must take in order to engage in a genuine dialogue with another person, text, or work of art. What occurs in the dialogue is not a mode of recognition, but a mode of play.

Gadamer says about play that it "fulfills its purpose only if the player loses himself in play" (Gadamer, 2004, p. 103). We give ourselves over to the game as we recognize its potential value for us above and beyond what we could accomplish alone. This is not pure resignation, because "a person playing is, even in his play, still someone who comports himself" (ibid., p. 107)—in other words, we choose to engage in dialogue with particular people at particular times for particular reasons on particular topics—but we take for granted that the proper playing of the play will guarantee the successful outcome of the game. The engagement of another in play—for it is essential to play that it involve someone or something else—generates an irreducibly social action. Play is irreducible in two senses. First, it cannot be done alone. Gadamer writes, "The movement to-and-fro obviously belongs so essentially to the game that there is an ultimate sense in which you cannot have a game by yourself" (ibid., p. 106). Ricoeur agrees: "This 'in-itself' of play is such that, even in solitary play, there must be something with which or against which one plays" (Ricoeur, 1981, p. 186). Tennis is an example of an irreducibly social activity. As much as we might practice alone we cannot play a game of tennis by ourselves. We need a partner; even practicing alone is only intelligible against the shared social background of playing tennis. Play is irreducibly social in a second sense: what occurs in the playing, the outcome of the play, cannot be explained by reference to the subjective intentions of the participants. The event of the game is irreducible to a description in terms of the actors, not even in terms of the back and forth of the actors. Admittedly, the two players in tennis take turns hitting the tennis ball, but what occurs in the game itself cannot be explained as the sum of alternating agencies. The play has an agency of its own, to which the players give themselves.

In the case of dialogue, the participants are engaged in the collaborative attempt to arrive at an articulate understanding of a subject matter. They give themselves over to the play by granting the other person authority over the subject matter such that the obligation of each player shifts to charity—to take what the interlocutor says as true, even if the truth is not apparent—and to collaboration—to express what one believes in terms that could be convincing to the interlocutor. The dialogue is guided by the subject matter of the dialogue and what it takes to make the subject matter clear to the interlocutors. It "is not so much one's being toward the object (taking that as something to be communicated) as the sharing of this being toward the object" (Gadamer, 1991, p. 33). The subjectivity of the interlocutors is displaced—there is a "primacy of play over the consciousness of the players" (Gadamer, 2004, p. 105)—so much so that Gadamer will say an understanding that arises from the dialogue is not an accomplishment of the participants, but an accomplishment of language itself.

The participants give themselves over to the play of the dialogue. In what sense is there a giving here, and does it fall under the logic of the gift? First, it is a kind of renunciation, or suspension, of intervention in order to open up the possibility of being led by language. It is not a one-sided offering, though. Rather it is an invitation, or more accurately a promise as an invitation. It is a commitment to refrain from withdrawing from the game and to listen to what the text, work of art, or other person has to reveal about the subject matter. It is a willingness to let the truth of the subject matter show itself in the dialogue with the understanding that the dialogue itself is the necessary occasion for the event of truth.

Is this gift reducible to the logic of exchange? It would appear not to be. An offer of an opportunity to collaborate, and a promise to honor the terms of that collaboration, are not things that incur a debt. Gadamer says that promises occur only through their acceptance.[4] Instead of the standard model of a gift whereby we do something *to* or *for* someone, dialogue is essentially a doing *with* someone only on the condition of the other person's mutual contribution. It does not incur an obligation on another's part, as it is up to the other person to accept or reject the offer of friendship. The address of a Thou, and play, can only be realized if they are accepted, joined. It is impossible to understand the address if it is understood as the activity of one person for another. It can only be understood as a joint activity.

Friendship in Place of Recognition

I am suggesting Gadamer moves away from the use of the term recognition as a technical term to characterize the actualized relations between persons because it shares the same flaw as I-Thou accounts of intersubjectivity: it overemphasizes the activity of one or the other subject and misses the fundamental character of a genuinely social action. What occurs in a genuinely social action—dialogue is Gadamer's most obvious example—cannot be explained in terms of the participants taking turns. The agency of the participants is irreducibly social. To get at this essentially social *miteinandersein* Gadamer appropriates the ancient concept of friendship as *philia*. Gadamer writes,

It seems to me an important modification that now one does not only avoid speaking of "the Thou," nor does one (like Fichte) simply speak of the "Not-I," which sounds like an opposition or a reduction against which one must struggle, or which one must overcome. Rather, one speaks of the Other. It changes the perspective to say here "the Other." Immediately, there is brought in a change in the state of the I and Thou. Every Other is at the same time the Other of an Other, as one may learn from Michael Theunissen's book. I myself have taken the measure of the ancient teaching on friendship in this regard. (Gadamer, 2000b, p. 282 [referring to Theunissen, 1984])

In his later writings, friendship, *philia*, is the term Gadamer uses in place of the I-Thou. Drawing on Aristotle's account of friendship, Gadamer argues that it is the highest form of *miteinandersein*—being-with-one-another—and that it is an essentially linguistic relation. It is a mutual bond that preserves the asymmetry between persons as it realizes the recognition of authority a friend should have over oneself; as Gadamer says, "only friends can advise" (Gadamer, 1985, p. 239). For the ancients, the test of friendship was the willingness of the person to speak the truth to you when you least wanted to hear it (e.g., Plutarch, 1992). *Philia* is a kind of shared life, a shared perception, just as "[t]he true conversation is a lived with-one-another, in which the one and the other unite themselves." (Gadamer, 2000a, p. 45)

Conclusion

Let us return at this point to Ricoeur's views. Ricoeur wrote in *Course of Recognition* that Gadamer's account of recognition was a "thorn in his side" as it involved the recognition of superiority rather than mutual recognition. We now know that Gadamer has an account of mutual recognition that amounts to a mutual recognition of superiority; he simply does not present it in the conceptual vocabulary of *anerkennung*. After *Truth and Method* Gadamer abandons the term recognition as a technical term because it cannot fully capture what occurs in irreducibly social actions. The version of mutuality he develops is characterized by play, is exemplified best in dialogue, and is reflected in relations of friendship (*philia*). We are rationally motivated to engage in dialogue through recognizing that others may understand matters, including ourselves, better than we understand them. In this way, the point of his earlier discussion of the recognition of authority is continued in his discussions of dialogue and of friendship, as a motivation for both and a condition of the success of both. *Philia*, as an irreducibly social action, does not give rise to concerns about "the logic of the gift" that arise with Ricoeur's conception of recognition. It also avoids the theological overtones that persist in the concept of *agape* and that may be required to make sense of a love "free from the rules of equivalence governing justice" (Ricoeur, 2005, p. 232). Granted, *philia* cannot track the French sense of *reconnaissance* connected to expressing gratitude, but perhaps this indicates Ricoeur should not give the philosophical weight he gives to the distinctively French connotation of recognition. Finally, and perhaps most importantly, talking about mutual reciprocity in terms of *philia*—which Ricoeur himself says is "closest" to *agape* (ibid., p. 220)—reintroduces justice to matters of mutual recognition. Ricoeur was concerned that speaking of justice requires us to enter into the logic of the gift, but the irreducibly social character of *philia* puts off that concern. It preserves our intuitions that acting from the recognition of the essential rationality of others is acting morally.

Notes

[1] It is beyond the scope of this paper, but certainly not incidental, that agape is a religious term appropriate for Ricoeur, a committed Christian, and for that reason is less likely to be embraced by the agnostic Gadamer.

[2] The important pages are (Gadamer, 2004, pp. 277–84).

[3] Axel Honneth makes this mistaken criticism of Gadamer's views in (Honneth, 2003).

[4] He emphasizes this in (Gadamer, 1980).

Chapter 8

Is *Phronēsis Deinon?* Ricoeur on Tragedy and *Phronēsis*

David H. Fisher

Sharing the pain of suffering is not symmetrically opposite to sharing pleasure. In this regard, philosophy must continue to allow itself to be instructed by tragedy. The trilogy "purification" (catharsis), "terror" (phobos), and "pity" (eleos) cannot be classified under the subcategory of friendship for the sake of pleasure. . . . From tragic phronein to practical phronēsis: this will be the maxim that can shelter moral conviction from the ruinous alternatives of univocity or arbitrariness.

Paul Ricoeur (1992, pp. 191, 249)

Introduction: Shopping at Borders

A visit to Borders (or similar mass market bookstores) reveals an interesting fact: in many outlets, sections designated under headings such as "metaphysical studies" have crowded out philosophy, while more and more space is given over to texts offering assistance with aspects of technology. Shelves once filled with philosophical literature from Plato to Derrida are now filled with intellectual cream cheese for the brainless, offering a bogus form of "wisdom" on matters such as "pyramid power" or "secret" meditation techniques said to produce total tranquility with 15 minutes a day of practice. This expansion of the vacuous feeds consumer desires for something—anything—to escape the tedium of the everyday or to allay media-incited terror of death in varied forms (biological, ecological, or explosive). In *Liquid Life,* Zygmunt Bauman provides a snapshot view of the persons who seek such anodynes:

Andrzej Stasiuk . . . develops a typology of the "spiritual lumpenproletariat" and suggests that its ranks swell fast. . . . Those affected by the "spiritual lumpenproletariat" virus live in the present and for the present. They live to survive (as long as possible) and to get satisfaction (as much of it as possible). . . . Flattened into a perpetual present and filled to the brim with survival-and-gratification concerns . . . the world inhabited by "spiritual lumpenproletarians" leaves no room for worries about anything other than what can be, at least in principle, consumed and relished on the sport, here and now. (Bauman, 2005, p. 7)

Bauman has more to say about "liquid life." It is a life of consumption, feeding on the self's dissatisfaction with *itself*, a life of constantly new beginnings in which getting rid of old things takes precedence over the acquisition of new ones. The "heroes" of the contemporary narrative described in *Liquid Life* are not concerned with the state of the world; they resent the thought of ever stopping or staying put and are "on the move because *move* they must" (ibid., pp. 127–34). The one thing not sought or valued in liquid life is wisdom—*phronēsis*—a complex way of seeing, thinking and responding to choice.

This may, in part, be a consequence of contemporary *forms of reading*. Kevin Kelly, in "From Print to Pixel," notes that while

[b]ooks were good at developing a contemplative mind, screens encourage more utilitarian thinking. A new idea or unfamiliar fact will provoke reflexes to do something: to research the term, to query your screen "friends" for their opinions . . . or tweet the thing rather than contemplate it. Book reading strengthened our analytical skills, encouraging us to pursue an observation all the way down to the footnote. Screen reading encourages rapid pattern-making, associating this idea with another, equipping us to deal with thousands of new thoughts every day. . . . A screen can reveal the inner nature of things. (Kelly, 2010, pp. 122–28)

The possibility that the "inner nature of things" may elude the power of computer linkages with multiple data bases, or that "problems"[1] are figures that can only be seen as such against backgrounds—backgrounds of beliefs, assumptions, and values embedded in cultural history or traditions; backgrounds as resistant to comprehension as to change—none of this occurs to those who live on screens, or to consumers of self-help manuals, life-planning exercises or (when these fail to materialize on schedule) of release sought via immersion in some new, "deep," preferably foreign, "transcendental wisdom."

The present chapter considers an understanding of *deinon phronēsis* instructed by tragedy, as developed in the work of Paul Ricoeur. In a world of "all consuming images" (Ewen, 1990), *deinon phronēsis* can provide a way toward being grasped by the question of ethics.

No unique English translation exists for the Greek word *deinon* (δεινον). As Martha Nussbaum observes,

Most generally, it is used of that which inspires awe or wonder. But in different contexts it can be used of the dazzling brilliance of the human intellect, of the monstrousness of evil, of the terrifying power of fate. That which is *deinon* is somehow strange, out of place. . . . (Nussbaum, 1986, p. 52)

Charles Segal observes that the term "means not only 'wonderful,' but also 'terrible,' 'fearful'" (Segal, 1964, p. 53). George Steiner indicates that if there is in the term "the concept of 'terror' and of 'excess', there is also . . . the notion of 'sagacity', of 'practical wisdom' and 'canniness'. Our own 'uncanny', in fact, points to a similar congruence of associations" (Steiner, 1984, p. 89).[2]

By contrast, *phronēsis* is often translated as "practical reason," that which is concerned more with the quotidian, the everyday, the cumulative rather than the unique or strange.

Yet, as Charles Scott suggests:

> The question of ethics is constituted by a disruption of the control of axioms and values that structure and govern the lives of those who live in a given discourse. . . . When I undergo the impact of the question of ethics, I find that . . . the cry of the other—as other—seems to be audible in the passing interruption of my values. Not the value of the other or the dignity of the other or the autonomy of the other or the right of the *other*. But the cry of the other. (Scott, 1991, p. 262)

Phronēsis, in the senses discussed by Ricoeur, disrupts familiar ways of seeing; it disrupts the narcissism of liquid life, inviting a different kind of movement than the restless search for the new, the gratifying, the linked. A conversational movement between figure and ground—figure as the immediate focus of perception, ground as tradition (Gadamer), ground as the polysemic voices of the Other (Ricoeur)—becomes a basis for expanded possibilities of judgment and action in the present, responding to the claims of the other. "One enters into conversation in order to become an other for the other" (Lingis, 1994, p. 88).

Ricoeur on *Phronēsis*

In *Oneself as Another*, Paul Ricoeur develops an account of the importance of tragedy for an ethics of *phronēsis*, one that parallels Hans-Georg Gadamer's discussion of tragedy and *phronēsis* in *Truth and Method* (Gadamer, 1992, esp. pp. 129–34 and 312–24). Ricoeur's discussion of *phronēsis* is found primarily in "The Self and Ethical Aim" (Ricoeur, 1992, pp. 171–80) and "The Self and Practical Wisdom: *Conviction*" (ibid., pp. 240–49). Ricoeur writes: "From tragic *phronein* [thinking] to practical *phronēsis*: this will be the maxim that can shelter moral conviction from the ruinous alternatives of univocity or arbitrariness" (ibid., p. 249).[3]

This observation occurs at the end of a section in *Oneself as Another* entitled "Interlude: Tragic Action" (ibid., pp. 241–49), which serves as an introduction to the chapter on "The Self and Practical Wisdom: *Conviction*" (ibid., pp. 240–96). "Interlude" combines three senses of "tragedy," as work of art, real-life event or worldview (Eagleton, 2003, p. 9).[4] Ricoeur's response to Hegel's "realization" of the truth of tragedy in the "Interlude" explores dimensions of "the tragic" as a worldview. The "Interlude" also includes a dimension of personal tragedy. It is dedicated to Ricoeur's son, Olivier, who committed suicide a few weeks after Ricoeur's return from delivering the Gifford Lectures in Edinburgh, lectures later to be reworked as *Oneself as Another* (Ricoeur, 1998a, p. 91).[5] Finally, the "Interlude" aims to "restore to conflict the place that all the analyses [in *Oneself as Another*] up to now have avoided" (Ricoeur, 1992, p. 241). Using for that purpose the Greek tragedy discussed by Hegel—*Antigone*—Ricoeur emphasizes that "tragedy resists a complete 'repetition' in the discourse of ethics or morality" and that tragedy is "comparable to . . . the aporia-producing limit experiences" (ibid., pp. 241, 243).

By recovering a sense of aporia-producing limit experiences within ethics and morality,[6] Ricoeur is insisting that "one of the functions of tragedy in relation to ethics is to create a gap between tragic wisdom and practical wisdom" (ibid., p. 247). This approach to ethics challenges a widely shared conviction of modern ethical theory summarized by Charles Larmore:

> Modern moral theory in its two principal forms, Kantianism and utilitarianism, has urged that what is morally right can be specified by rules. Indeed, this demand for a fully explicit decision-procedure was a reaction to what modern moralists perceived as the intolerable vagueness of Aristotle's appeals to φρόνησις [*phronēsis*]. . . . Modern moral philosophy . . . has stubbornly assumed that moral conflicts must only be apparent, that there must be some single higher-order principle that captures our most basic intuitions. (Larmore, 1987, pp. 4, 10)[7]

A basic question for ethicists who reject these assumptions is whether "it is possible to combine a phenomenology of moral judgment, based upon an Aristotelian conception of action, with a Kantian model of intersubjective validity" (Benhabib, 2001, p. 195).[8] Ricoeur responds to this question affirmatively, insisting the aim of his reflection on ethics is to reconcile "Aristotle's *phronēsis* by way of Kant's *Moralität*, with Hegel's *Sittlichkeit*." Of *phronēsis*, Ricoeur states he will "retain the fact that its horizon is the 'good life,' its mediation deliberation, its actor the *phronimos*, and its place of application singular situations" (Ricoeur, 1992, p. 290).[9]

In his analysis of the *phronēsis* embodied in Aristotle's "ethical aim," Ricoeur joins Aristotle with tragedy:

> Sharing the pain of suffering is not symmetrically opposite to sharing pleasure. In this regard, philosophy must continue to allow itself to be instructed by tragedy. The trilogy "purification" (*catharsis*), "terror" (*phobos*), and "pity" (*eleos*) cannot be classified under the subcategory of friendship for the sake of pleasure. (Ibid., p. 191)

He returns to the question of suffering in the final chapter of *Oneself as Another*:

Undergoing and enduring are . . . revealed in their complete passive dimension when they become suffering. . . . With the decrease of the power of *acting*, experienced as a decrease of the effort of *existing*, the reign of suffering, properly speaking, commences. (Ibid., p. 320)

Dennis J. Schmidt claims,

What is essential in Greek tragedy, what it poses as a question to philosophizing today, is that it awakens in us a renewed sense that we do indeed live in a world that is larger than we can either control or define and that we are held in the grip of that which we cannot comprehend. (Schmidt, 2001, p. 280)

From this perspective, an ethics instructed by tragedy in all its meanings will attempt to characterize that which exceeds or eludes the grasp of thought: inexplicable, unmerited suffering,[10] and human life as uncanny, *unheimlich, deinon.*

Ricoeur was informed by Heidegger's approach to *phronēsis*, if indirectly. Is something of Heidegger's understanding of *Dasein* and of the *deinon* of *Dasein*'s "throwness" present in his work? Consider Heidegger's claims that "[u]ncanniness is the basic kind of Being-in-the-world, even though in an everyday way it has been covered up" (Heidegger, 1962, p. 322).[11] Before turning to these questions, it is first necessary to specify the way *phronēsis* will be understood in this chapter. I then turn to further development of Ricoeur's understanding of tragedy. The final section analyses the influence on Ricoeur of Heidegger's Aristotelian-inspired version of the "call of conscience," of *phronēsis*, and of the meaning of *deinon* in Greek tragedy. In addition to exploring influence and connections among Aristotle, Heidegger, and Ricoeur, the broader issue for this chapter is to trace the movement in Ricoeur "from tragic *phronein* to practical *phronēsis*" in order to ask in what ways *phronēsis*, as a moral virtue instructed by tragic wisdom, can or should be understood as *deinon*? This question—introduced but not fully answered here—is intended to open a conversation between those who, such as Ricoeur, find neo-Aristotelian versions of *phronēsis* a valuable resource for addressing *aporia* within contemporary ethical theory, and those who do not.

Phronēsis

Phronēsis (φρόνησις) is usually translated as "prudence" or "practical wisdom." However, a case can be made for "sound judgment" as a better translation of the Greek. That term avoids contemporary idiomatic shadings of the word "prudence,"[12] as in parodies of former President George H. W. Bush's phrase, "it wouldn't be prudent." In modern English usage, "prudence" has become linked with fussy timidity or cautiousness, a calculated reluctance to take risks, which, while remaining a virtue in the case of *unnecessary* risks, becomes the vice of cowardice when extended to avoidance of *all* risks. These contemporary associations of prudence with timidity and extreme risk avoidance stand in marked contrast with notions of *phronēsis* as the ability to respond to unique circumstances, involving choice, against a background awareness of the strange, the uncanny, or monstrous, all of which play a role in tragic wisdom.

Phronēsis is the habitual, learned ability to perceive and attend to relevant, contrasting aspects in a presenting issue, dilemma, or aporia seen against a background of complex circumstances.[13] Allen emphasizes the context-specific character of *phronēsis* when he argues that "phronesis is the historically implicated, communally nurtured ability to make good sense of relatively singular contexts in ways appropriate to their singularity" (Allen, 1989, p. 363). In Gestalt terminology, the relevant aspects discerned are the figure of attention and the "circumstances," the tacit background (Polanyi, 1983). In reaching judgment about the fitting (*kalon*) action in a situation,[14] the practically wise individual (*phronimos*) remains mindful of the circumstances as well as the focus of attention. As Gadamer observes,

> Even perception conceived as an adequate response to a stimulus would never be a mere mirroring of what is there. For it would always remain an understanding of something as something. All understanding-as is an articulation of what is there, in that it looks-away-from, looks at, sees-together-as. All of this can occupy the center of an observation or can merely "accompany" seeing, at its edge or in the background. (Gadamer, 1992, pp. 90–91)

For a poetic example of what "background awareness" implies, consider Robert Penn Warren's "The Corner of the Eye." The poem begins: "The poem is just beyond the corner of the eye" (Warren, 1985, pp. 103–04).

One reason for this Gestalt awareness on the part of the *phronimos* is that his or her aim, beyond acting fittingly in the present moment, is to live well (*eu zēn*) throughout the course of an entire life. Ricoeur, responding to Alasdair MacIntyre's emphasis on the ideal of a "narrative unity of a life," notes:

> The term "life" that figures three times in the expressions "life plan," "narrative unity of a life," and "good life" denotes both the biologic rootedness of life and the unity of the person as a whole, as that person casts upon himself or herself the gaze of appraisal. . . . The idea of the narrative unity of a life serves to assure us that the subject of ethics is none other than the one to whom the narrative assigns a narrative identity. . . . The person appears here from the outset as suffering as well as acting, subject to the whims of life which have prompted . . . Martha Nussbaum to speak of the "fragility of goodness." (Ricoeur, 1992, p. 178)

In addition to serving as a basis for perception, judgment, and action in situation, the aim to live well requires character based on acquired excellences (*aretai*).[15] Character includes achieving a fitting balance between a *range* of excellences, just as performing a fitting action requires a balance between perceived choices and awareness of background circumstances. A hermeneutical circle is "traced, by virtue of the back-and-forth motion between the idea of the 'good life' and the most important decisions of our existence (career, loves, leisure, etc.)." This action is likened by Ricoeur to interpreting a text: "For the agent, interpreting the text of an action is interpreting himself or herself" (Ricoeur, 1992, p. 179).

Finally, *phronēsis* is an intellectual excellence linked with *praxis*:

> *Praxis* . . . has to do with the conduct of one's life and affairs primarily as a citizen . . . [I]t is activity which may leave no separately identifiable outcome behind it and whose end, therefore, is realized in the very doing of the activity itself. . . . The absence of disposable materials and of a substantial end product . . . has as its other side the presence of the agent, who is vested in his action more completely than the producer in his product. . . . *[P]hronēsis* arises within the whole striving that a person *is*. . . . (Dunne, 1993, pp. 244, 264)

A way of seeing, thinking, and acting constitutes the character of the *phronimos*.

One difference between Aristotelian *phronēsis* and Ricoeur's version is that Aristotle's depiction is primarily self-regarding, and only secondarily or derivatively, other-regarding. Others are a means, rather than an end. to achieving one's goals. "The just man needs people towards whom and with whom he shall act justly, and the temperate man, the brave man, and each of the others are in the same case" (Aristotle, 1984, 10.7.1177a, pp. 30–34, cited in Dunne, 1993, p. 263). Others serve as a means for expression of right desires, leading to the development of excellence. "*Phronēsis* is . . . a type of knowledge that emerges within a person's striving or desire: 'of the part [of the soul] which is practical and intellectual, the good state is truth in agreement with right desire (*orthē orexis*)'" (Dunne, 1993, pp. 263–64).

David Depew summarizes Aristotle's perspective on *phronēsis*:

> *Phronēsis* is a cognitive act [that is] supposed to be intellectual insight (and not mere opinion [*doxa*], a la Isocrates) into what course of action should be chosen in a particular, usually vexing, situation if the best interests of the self and those who are extensions of the self (family, friends, fellow citizens) are to be preserved. (It differs from *sunesis*, which is insight into what others should do; advising is not deliberating.) *The best interests of the self are made evident* in the practically wise person's emotional reactions to situations that call for decision (*prohairesis*). . . . (Depew, 2004, pp. 167–75; emphasis added).[16]

By contrast, Ricoeur's interpretation of *phronēsis* balances a self-regarding aim (the desire to live well) with two coordinate, other-regarding aims: *solicitude* for and with others, and an understanding of just institutions as a necessary background condition for living well with others:

> One will readily grant that there is no place for a straightforward concept of otherness in Aristotle. . . . To self-esteem, understood as a reflexive moment of the wish for the "good life," solicitude adds essentially the dimension of *lack*, the fact that we *need* friends; as a reaction to the effect of solicitude on self-esteem, the self perceives itself as another among others. . . . The very definition of ethics that we have proposed—living well with and for others in just institutions—cannot be conceived without the project of living well being affected by solicitude, both that which is exerted and that which is received. (Ricoeur, 1992, pp. 187, 192, 330)[17]

Ricoeur on Tragedy and the Tragic

Beyond explicit references to tragedy in *Oneself as Another* (Ricoeur, 1992, pp. 241–49) and *Time and Narrative* (Ricoeur, 1984), there are instances as early as 1967, in *The Symbolism of Evil* (Ricoeur, 1967), of Ricoeur's engagement with the tragic as a mythic structure. The primary focus of interest in the present chapter, however, is on the role played by his later understanding of tragedy and the tragic in *Oneself as Another*. There, building on Martha Nussbaum's account of relationships between tragedy and ethics in Aristotle (Nussbaum, 1986), and Michelle Gellrich's comparison of Hegel and Aristotle on tragedy (Gellrich, 1988), together with his close reading of *Antigone*, Ricoeur emphasizes the nonphilosophical character of tragedy: "adverse mythical powers echoing the identifiable conflicts of the roles; an unanalyzable mixture of constraints of fate and deliberate choices; [and] the purgative effect of the spectacle itself at the center of the passions it produces" (Ricoeur, 1992, p. 242). He concludes, as noted above: "Tragedy is comparable . . . to the aporia-producing limit experiences. . . . The instruction of ethics by tragedy comes out of the recognition of this limit" (ibid., pp. 243, 245).

For Ricoeur, the point of divergence with Hegel is not "where it has too often been situated, as if Hegel had imposed a *theoretical* solution to the conflict, and as though the conflict were to be hailed as a subversive factor with respect to the tyranny of totalitarian reason" (ibid., pp. 248–49). Ricoeur's views on tragedy are similar to Gellrich's:

> [T]ragedy[,] . . . by making conflict a structuring unit in a dialectical process moving to resolution[,] finds its principle of order in the experience that first threatens to dissolve it. Both philosophical history and dramatic art are rational not because they dispose of conflict, but because they mediate it in the interests of a higher unity. . . . Purged of its associations with dissolution and irrationality, conflict can be identified as the *logos* of drama, as a structural

element that gives unity to the shape of dramatic events. (Gellrich, 1988, pp. 41–42)

The issue is not Hegel's attempt to *understand* tragic conflict. It is rather how to think about the nature and cultural location of the conflicts represented in tragedy:

> For us, after beginning with an Aristotelian-style ethics and then assuming the rigors of a Kantian-style morality, the question is to identify the conflicts that morality produces on *the very level of spiritual powers* that Hegel seems to take to be uncontaminated by the conflict. . . . Tragedy . . . is not to be sought only at the dawn of ethical life, but on the contrary at the *advanced stage of morality, in the conflicts that arise along the path leading from the rule to moral judgment in situation.* (Ricoeur, 1992, p. 249, emphasis added)

Conflict within tragedy mirrors conflict within ethical theory, among advocates of utilitarian teleology, Kantian deontology, and Aristotelian situational judgment based on perception (See Nussbaum, 1990, pp. 54–105; Blum, 1994; Kyte, 1996, pp. 97–113, and Ichheiser, 1966, pp. 546–60). Just as tragic characters must seek insight in the dark, finding themselves caught in circumstances they did not create, facing limits imposed by powers beyond their comprehension, so ethicists seek insight into the resolution of conflicts. Ricoeur writes:

> What makes ethical conflicts inevitable? And what solution is action capable of bringing to these conflicts? To the first question, the response proposed will be this: the source of conflict lies not only in the one-sidedness of the characters but also in the one-sidedness of the moral *principles*, which themselves are confronted with the complexity of life. To the second question, the response we shall sketch out is this: in the conflicts to which morality gives rise, only a recourse to the ethical ground against which morality stands out can give rise to the wisdom of judgment in situation. From tragic *phronein* to practical *phronēsis*. . . . (Ricoeur, 1992, p. 249)

An aspect of the "limit" is evoked in Ricoeur's discussion of the strangeness of tragedy: "One will note in this regard the strange tie between *eros* and the laws [thesmōn] of the world, which introduces the conflict at the very heart of the divine" (Ricoeur, 1992, p. 244 n.8). This strangeness is illustrated by consideration of the meanings of *deinon* in Sophocles's "Ode to Man" in *Antigone*:

> How is *deinon* to be translated? "strange"? "marvelous"? In fact, *deinon*, used many times in the play, has the sense the expression "formidable" sometimes has: oscillating between the admirable and the monstrous. In this

ambiguous sense of the word, the tragic hero is more *deinon* than any man. (Ibid., pp. 245–46)

In his discussion of movement in nineteenth- and twentieth-century German thought from a theory of tragedy as a genre to a theory of "the tragic" Dennis Schmidt claims that

> in [ancient] Greece, tragedy is not understood as a presentation of the conflict between good and evil, or right and wrong; rather it is one of the ways in which the horror that human beings can create for themselves is displayed and so reflected upon. . . . What is essential in Greek tragedy, what it poses as a question to philosophizing today, is that it awakens in us a renewed sense that we do indeed live in a world that is larger than we can either control or define and that we are held in the grip of that which we cannot comprehend. [Greek tragedy,] by virtue of its form[,] . . . does not permit itself to be taken up by the language of the concept. It does not . . . let itself be assimilated into the systematic concerns of philosophy. (Schmidt, 2001, p. 280)

In a 1963 lecture Ricoeur observed that "philosophy always has a relation to *non*-philosophy. . . . If the vital link between philosophy and non-philosophy were to be severed, philosophy would be in danger in degenerating into a mere word game, ultimately becoming a pure linguistic nihilism" (Ricoeur, 1998b, p. 22; see Ricoeur, 1963). In his early analysis of tragic mythic structure, Ricoeur had also noted that

> salvation, in the tragic vision, is not outside the tragic but within it. This is the meaning of the tragic fronein [*phronein*], of that "suffering for the sake of understanding" which is celebrated by the chorus in Aeschylus' *Agamemnon* . . . suffering for the sake of understanding—that is tragic wisdom, that is "tragic knowledge. . . . " (Ricoeur, 1967, p. 229)

Ricoeur's later understanding of tragic wisdom is found in the final pages of *Oneself as Another*. Having discussed Heidegger's depiction of *conscience* (*Gewissen*) as other, and Levinas's understanding of the face of the Other as the source of "[t]he injunction [that] comes from that which is prior to any beginning, any *arkhē*" (Ricoeur, 1992, p. 338), Ricoeur states:

> To find oneself called upon in the second person at the very core of the optative of living well, then of the prohibition to kill, then of the search for the choice appropriate to the situation, is to recognize oneself as being enjoined to *live well with and for others in just institutions and to esteem oneself as the bearer of this wish*. The otherness of the Other is then the counterpart . . . to this passivity specific to being-enjoined. (Ibid., p. 352)

Ricoeur insists—against both Heidegger and Levinas—on the *polysemic* character of otherness. Ricoeur proposes, as a working hypothesis

> the *triad of passivity and, hence, of otherness.* First[,] . . . the passivity represented by the experience of one's own body. . . . Next, . . . the passivity implied by the relation of the self to the *foreign*, . . . the otherness inherent in the relation of intersubjectivity. Finally, . . . the most deeply hidden passivity, that of the relation of self to itself, which is *conscience* in the sense of *Gewissen* rather than of *Bewusstein.* (Ibid., p. 318)

Philosophy instructed by tragic wisdom understands the otherness of the Other as replacing the otherness of *moira*, or the gods in Greek tragedy: human action takes place against a background that shapes the range of choices and limits, providing no certainty that *aporiae* will be capable of resolution, or that the judgment made and enacted by an agent was the product of human will rather than, or in addition to, the force of the Other.

> The ultimate equivocalness with respect to the status of the Other in the phenomenon of conscience is perhaps what needs to be preserved in the final analysis. . . . Perhaps the philosopher as philosopher has to admit that one does not know and cannot say whether this Other, the source of the injunction, is another person whom I can look in the face or who can stare at me, or my ancestors for whom there is no representation . . . or God—living God, absent God—or an empty place. (Ibid., pp. 353, 355)

What is ultimately *deinon* in Ricoeur is not a quality of humankind but the indeterminate nature of the Other, the source of the injunction to "*live well with and for others in just institutions and to esteem oneself as the bearer of this wish*" (Ricoeur, 1992, p. 352). Tragic wisdom recognizes the determination of action by powers and forces other than the intentions of agency—individual or communal.[18]

Ricoeur in Relation to Heidegger

Ricoeur does not respond directly to Heidegger's understanding of tragedy, which is found primarily in Heidegger's successive readings of the choral ode on "Man" in Sophocles's *Antigone* (Sophocles, lines 332–72), an ode that begins with the words "πολλὰ τὰ δεινὰ κοὐδὲν ἀνθρώπου δεινότερον πέλει" (ibid., line 332).[19] This is usually translated as: "Many things are strange, but none stranger than man." Heidegger, however, renders it as: "'The uncanny is many-sided; nothing, however, looms larger that the human in strangeness'" (Schmidt, 2001, p. 267, translating Heidegger, 1966).[20] Where Heidegger, early and late, privileged the notion of the "uncanny" origin of *Dasein* against the *Gestelle* of calculative, technological thinking, Ricoeur responds to Heidegger's equation of *phronēsis* with conscience (*Gewissen*) in *Being and Time* as a starting point for dealing with Nietzsche. Acknowledging his debt to Heidegger's "analysis . . . as this starting point of the entire discussion of the metaphor of the voice [of conscience]" (Ricoeur, 1992, p. 348), Ricoeur expresses reservations about the "subtle comparison . . . made between the strange(r)ness of the voice and the condition of fallenness," particularly the notion of "falling" as an "onto-logical trait prior to any ethics" (ibid., pp. 348–49). His disagreement is not about the "strange(r)ness" of the voice that calls, but with Heidegger's insistence on locating the "call" as prior to or beyond ethics, separating ontol-ogy from ethics without showing "how one could travel the opposite path— from ontology toward ethics" (ibid., p. 349). Ricoeur also argues against the solipsistic implications of Heidegger's claims that "[i]n conscience *Dasein* calls itself" (ibid., p. 348, quoting Heidegger, 1962, p. 320), and that a significant task of Dasein-analysis is "making the conscience intelligible as *an attestation of Dasein's ownmost potentiality-for-Being*—an attestation which lies in Dasein itself" (Heidegger, 1962, p. 324).

To the contrary, Ricoeur writes, "[t]o this demoralization of conscience, I would oppose a conception that closely associates the phenomenon of *injunc-tion* to that of *attestation*. Being-enjoined would then constitute the moment of otherness proper to conscience. . . ." (Ricoeur, 1992, p. 351). Conscience as attestation-injunction means human beings are "primordially structured by the optative mood of living well" and "the passivity of being so enjoined consists in the situation of listening in which the ethical subject is placed in relation to the voice addressed to it in the second person" (ibid., p. 352). As previously noted, what remains strange—indeterminate—is what Ricoeur calls the "triad of passivity and, hence of otherness" ("the experience of one's own body"—*flesh*; the relationship to the *foreign* in intersubjectivity; and the relation to oneself as *conscience*) (ibid., p. 318). The other is a polysemic aporia, stated but not resolved, by philosophical discourse (ibid., p. 355).

In *Oneself as Another*, Ricoeur, responding to Heidegger's understanding of being-in-the-world, notes that this is expressed in many ways, and that

> it is together that oneself, care, and being-in-the world are to be determined.
>
>   In an effort to articulate these three terms correctly, a certain reappropria-tion of Aristotle under the guidance of Heideggerian concepts can lead back in turn to a better apprehension of the leading concepts in *Being and Time*. (Ibid., p. 311)

Describing what Heidegger's analysis of conscience contributes to the potenti-ality-for-being, Ricoeur notes, "The novelty resides in the explication of the trait of strange[r]ness (following Martineau's *étrang[ér]eté*) by which conscience inscribes itself within the dialectic of Same and Other" (ibid., p. 348).

As Ricoeur observes, at the time he was working on *Oneself as Another*, "the most important text of Heidegger himself [on Aristotle], in the present state of publication of the *Gesamtausgabe*, [was] the interpretation of *Metaphysics 9. 1–3: Aristoteles Metaphysik Theta 1–3. Von Wesen und Wirklicheit der Kraft*" (ibid., p. 311 n.14, citing Heidegger, 1981). Unfortunately, neither Heidegger's lectures on basic concepts of Aristotelian philosophy (Heidegger, 2002) nor his commentary on Plato's *Sophist* (Heidegger, 1992) were available to Ricoeur, although, as his footnotes indicate (Ricoeur, 1992, p. 187 n.22, p. 307 n.10, p. 313 n.16), he was able to make use of Rémi Brague's work, *Aristote et la question du monde* (Brague, 1988), and Jacques Taminiaux's *Lectures de l'ontologie fundamental. Essais sur Heidegger* (Taminiaux, 1989). It becomes clear, in reading the two Heidegger texts developed prior to *Being and Time*, that Heidegger argued—against Aristotle—for the superiority of *phronēsis* over *sophia* as a way of knowing; *phronēsis* reveals or uncovers the truth of what is. By contrast, Ricoeur's understanding of phronēsis is less a revelatory moment than a way of responding to the aporias of alterity.

In the Aristotle text, Heidegger translates φρόνησις [*phronēsis*] as "looking around," in the context of a discussion of εθος (*ethos*—"the comportment of the speaker") as πίστις (*pistis*—belief, conviction). "The εῆθος must satisfy the definitions of ἀρετή [*aretē*], φρόνησις, and ενοια [good will]" (Heidegger, 2009, p. 114). In the *Sophist* commentary, Heidegger observes:

> Φρόνησις is nothing other than conscience set into motion, making an action transparent. Conscience cannot be forgotten. But it is quite possible that what is disclosed by conscience can be distorted and allowed to be ineffective through . . . the passions. Conscience always announces itself. (Heidegger, 1997, p. 39)

Further, "φρόνησις includes the possibility of a sheer grasp of αρχή [*arche*—beginning] as such, i.e. as a mode of disclosure transcending λόγος [word]. Insofar as φρόνησις is a mode of βελτίστέζις, [dear or precious disposition], it must be more than mere λόγος" (ibid., p. 100). The question being addressed, Heidegger states, is "whether there is in φρόνησις, too, something like a pure νοειν, a pure perceiving" (ibid.). In the *Sophist* commentary, Heidegger links *phronēsis* to *aesthesis* as a form of practical *nous*, which he "translates as the *Augenblick* of action, that moment of presence in which one's ownmost worldly being is held open for possible decision" (McNeil, 2001, p. 131).[21]

Gadamer recalls that when taking part in Heidegger's 1924/25 lecture course on Plato's *Sophist* seminar,[22]

> We were studying the analysis of *phronēsis* [in the *Nicomachean Ethics* when] Heidegger . . . as a topic for discussion, presented the distinction that separated all knowledge—especially that of mere *doxa*—from *phronēsis*: λήθη μὲν τῆς τοιαύτης ἕξεως ἔστι, φρονήσεως δ᾽οὐκ ἔστιν. (1140 b 29) [There is indeed a forgetting of states of this sort (i.e. of reasoned states concerning opinion) but not of practical wisdom.] As we groped for an interpretation, uncertain about the sentence and completely unfamiliar with the Greek

concepts, Heidegger explained curtly, "This is the conscience!" (Gadamer, 1994, p. 32)[23]

The implication was clear: "conscience"—in Heidegger's sense—is a *phronēsis* that gives insight into the (revealed/concealed) truth of an (historical) situation; a capacity which, once developed, cannot be forgotten, unlike *technē* which can be lost over time.

Michael Allen Gillespie argues that "Heidegger developed his vision of praxis and politics [based] on an Aristotelian foundation that he believed would reverse the domination of theory and technology in modern life and put in its place the rule of *phronēsis* rooted in an historical understanding of the world. . . ." (Gillespie, 2000, pp. 140, 153). At the center of this vision was Heidegger's re-reading of Aristotle, a re-reading that provided one of the bases for Heidegger's support of National Socialism:

> In his re-interpretation of *phronēsis*, however, Heidegger departs from Aristotle in a decisive way, converting practical reason and deliberation into a confrontation with nothingness and a revelation of destiny. Heidegger seeks to solve the problem of technology by establishing the rule of *phronēsis* but founds *phronēsis* on sheer insight. . . . The problem, as he saw it, was not technology per se but the hegemony that technology had come to exercise over human action. . . . Only if distinctively human action is placed at the center of our concern will technology serve our ends. We thus can become active (as opposed to productive) beings if we are guided by phronēsis. . . . It was this transformation of technology by *phronēsis* that Heidegger believed the Nazi movement might bring about. . . . Central to Heidegger's support of the Nazis was his belief that their radicalism made possible a courageous confrontation with the question of Being. (Ibid., p. 151)

Although *phronēsis* was necessary as a basis for overcoming the force of technology and technological thinking,

> *phronēsis* is not present in all human beings. Indeed, for the most part, human beings are lost in their everyday concerns. Only those rare individuals who are resolute in their questioning and courageous enough to face death and nothingness have *phronēsis*. It is these *phronimoi* who must lead the people. (Ibid., p. 158)

In his conclusion, Gillespie proposes an analogy relevant to the question of whether a *deinon phronēsis* is the result of movement from tragic *phronein* to *phronēsis*.

> The young Heidegger believed that a new Oedipus could solve the riddle of the technological Sphinx and establish a rule of *phronēsis*. The result was a monstrosity. In the aftermath of that failure, an older Heidegger concluded

that we must listen not to Oedipus but to Tiresias. Such blind wisdom, however, can provide no better ground for human praxis. What is surprising is that it never occurred to him to attend to the prayer of the ordinary people of Thebes that the hubristic adventurer who confronts the nothing in the search of world transformation never frequents their hearth. (Ibid., p. 151)

Heidegger's tragedy was, in part, a result of his belief that he could think the *deinon* of Dasein expressed in tragedy, without awareness of the dimensions of πάθος [*pathos*]—a suffering whose origin or meaning is unknown to the protagonists of tragedy, and endured by the community within which they function. It is telling that in his discussion of πάθος as πίστις, Heidegger lists three meanings of πάθος: "the *average, immediate* meaning of . . . *variable condition*; a *specifically ontological* meaning . . . one most often translates as 'suffering' and a *resulting* meaning" (Heidegger, 2009, 113). In the text, "suffering" disappears from view.[24]

Heidegger's silence, his refusal to acknowledge the extent of the horror his errancy had led him to embrace, or its origins in what Gadamer described as his "violent appropriation of the Aristotelian text for use with his own questions," is in many ways worse than his active participation in National Socialism as Rector of Freiburg. This "violent appropriation," Gadamer says, "reminds one of how the call of conscience in *Being and Time* is what first makes the 'Dasein in human beings' visible in its ontological and temporal event-structure" (Gadamer, 1994, p. 33).

In dealing with Heidegger on conscience in *Oneself as Another*, Ricoeur was responding to both Heidegger's insight and Heidegger's error, perhaps along lines suggested by Emmanuel Levinas:

It is impossible to be stinting in our admiration for the intellectual vigor of *Sein und Zeit*, particularly in light of the immense output this extraordinary book of 1927 inspired. Its supreme steadfastness will mark it forever. Can we be assured, however, that there was never any echo of Evil in it? The diabolical is not limited to the wickedness popular wisdom ascribes to it and whose malice, based on guile, is familiar and predictable in an adult culture. The diabolical is endowed with intelligence and enters where it will. To reject it, it is first necessary to refute it. Intellectual effort is needed to recognize it. (Levinas, 1989, pp. 487–88)

Gadamer responds differently to the disclosure of Heidegger's complicity with National Socialism, posing a question that remains relevant for anyone— Ricoeur, Gadamer, or any other thinker who has found in Heidegger a resource for thinking against the grain of technological culture:

I get asked whether, after these revelations (which for us are no such thing), one can "still even today" have anything at all to do with the philosophy of this man. "Still even today"? Whoever asks that has much ground to cover. What was received, in Germany and France and everywhere in the world, as a major spiritual renewal was Heidegger's lifelong altercation with the Greeks, with Hegel, and finally with Nietzsche. Did that all become fraudulent? Have we absorbed or gotten beyond it? Or is the real point, perhaps, that people should not think at all, but only follow a completed ideological-political recipe or apply a system of rules worked out by social science? (Gadamer and McCumber, 1989, pp. 427–30)

Conclusion

There is no simple way to respond to Levinas's challenge concerning evil, nor to the implications of Gadamer's remark about the "major spiritual renewal" many perceived in Heidegger's work, but there is a beginning sketched out in the previous discussion of *deinon phronēsis*. Greek tragedy's claim is that "we do indeed live in a world that is larger than we can either control or define and that we are held in the grip of that which we cannot comprehend," a claim that "by virtue of its form . . . does not permit itself to be taken up by the language of the concept" (Schmidt, 2001, p. 280). This claim should be heard as a caution for a philosophy that seeks to be open to the question of ethics: no matter how much *phronetic* wisdom may enable one to see, hear, and think, there always remains that which resists thinking, resists illusions of mastery and closure of the question.

Dennis Schmidt, whose words we have often cited in reference to Greek tragedy, concludes his work with this observation:

Philosophy, by virtue of the commitments of its own perspective will always bear the signature of hope no matter how deeply etched its qualifications about this matter are. . . . In tragedy we find the memento of the very real capacity of human life to call catastrophe down upon itself suddenly, whether by accident, design, or simple blindness. We learn from it that, knowingly or not, we can bring disaster into the world, even monstrous evil. . . . To philosophize is to index one's thought to some hope of healing. . . . The struggle of philosophers who address the great insight of tragedy is, in the end, to convert it into this hope and its language. (Ibid., p. 284)

Ricoeur illustrates this hope, both in *Oneself as Another* and even more explicitly in "Hope and the Structure of Philosophical Systems" (Ricoeur, 1995). There, he states:

To the problem of the "starting point" in philosophy we shall oppose the problem of the "closing point," or, better said, of the horizon of philosophical discourse. . . . [A] horizon of unfilled claims belongs to the most genuine experience of action. This reason relies on our experience of evil. (Ibid., pp. 207, 211)

Hope, for Ricoeur in this text, "is not a theme that comes after other themes, an idea that closes the system, but an impulse that opens the system, that breaks the closure of the system; it is a way of reopening what was unduly closed" (ibid., p. 211). Having been instructed in tragic *phronēsis*, Ricoeur is open to the ethical question and its horizon of hope.

A *deinon phronēsis* perceives from darkness, through darkness, toward light. The darkness *from* which *deinon phronēsis* perceives consists of experiences of loss, absence, grief and incomprehension in the face of these experiences. The darkness *through* which *deinon phronēsis* perceives is aporias—unresolved or unresolvable contrasts between opposing ideas or principles. The light *toward* which *deinon phronēsis* perceives is hope, neither imaginary nor irrational, but believed. "Hope means the 'superabundance' of meaning as opposed to the abundance of senselessness, of failure, of destruction. . . . I should say that freedom is the capacity to live according to the paradoxical law of superabundance. . . ." (Ricoeur, 1995, 206–7). Where the origins of *phronēsis* in its ordinary senses are relatively clear or at least open to clarification, *deinon phronēsis* never loses the trace of its obscure origins in the tragic. Where the horizon of *phronēsis* is closure in judgment and action reached through deliberation, the horizon of *deinon phronēsis* is credible hope in the light of justice and love.

The rehabilitation of *phronēsis* based on tragedy and its sense of the *deinon* offered in the work of Ricoeur will not produce, as Heidegger hoped, a group *phronimoi* capable of leading those immersed in "liquid life" out of the thoughtlessness into resoluteness. Nor does it offer, as contemporary neoconservative advocates of virtue ethics believe, the basis for a willed return to the virtues of ancient, agonistic, homogenous cultures, cultures where "difference" is relegated to the margins of discourse and social life. What the rehabilitation of *phronēsis* does offer is a way to reopen the "question of ethics," both at the theoretical and practical levels. At the theoretical level, a *deinon phronēsis* challenges the complacency of modern ethical theory, which "has stubbornly assumed that moral conflicts must only be apparent, that there must be some single higher-order principle that captures our most basic intuitions" (Larmore, 1987, p. 10). As John Caputo observes,

> On their best day, principles are the faded copies of the singularity of concrete situations, the scores of a music still under composition, the map of a territory that has not yet been explored. Principles fail before the demands of concretely situated responsibility. . . . (Caputo, 2003, p. 170)

At the practical level, a *deinon phronēsis* provides a means for developing a discourse—perhaps narrative, perhaps lyric, as well as critical—capable of challenging the flattened life, described by Bauman at the beginning of this chapter, by calling attention to the background of seeing, to what is glimpsed out of "The Corner of the Eye." As Ricoeur remarks, in the final words of *Oneself as Another*, "Only a discourse other than itself, I will say, plagiarizing the *Parmenides*, . . . is suited to the metacategory of otherness, under penalty of otherness suppressing itself in becoming the same as itself" (Ricoeur, 1992, p. 356). The development of such a discourse must combine the apprehension of what is *deinon* in the background that shapes human thinking and in the way thinking responds to aporias with the learning gained from phronetic *praxis*.

Notes

[1] Problems are experienced by the "spiritual lumpenproletariat" as annoying obstacles to instant gratification of desire.

[2] The central ambiguity of *deinon* is similar to the ambiguity of the sublime in Kant. For Kant, the sublime is that which exceeds the representational powers of the imagination. Whether the limit is produced by sheer physical extent, as in the case of the endless star field at night seen stretching into infinity, or the sheer power of the ocean's depths, the mind is incapable of grasping the whole into a coherent image. Kant writes:

> [T]he sublime, in the strict sense of the word, cannot be contained in any sensuous forms, but rather concerns ideas of reason which, although no adequate presentation of them is possible, may be excited and called into mind by that very inadequacy itself which does admit of sensuous presentation. (Kant, 1954, p. 92)

[3] The standard reference to the relationship between thinking and suffering is Aeschylus, *Agamemnon*, lines 176–78:

> τὸν φρονεῖν βροτοὺς ὁδώ-
> σαντα, τὸν πάθει μάθος
> θέντα κυρίως ἔχειν.
> Zeus, who guided men to think,
> Who has laid it down that wisdom
> Comes alone through suffering. (Green and Lattimore, 1942, p. 46)

[4] Eagleton adds:

> For most people today, tragedy means an actual occurrence, not a work of art. Indeed, some of those who nowadays use the word of actual events are probably unaware that it has an artistic sense at all; so that whereas some conservative critics claim that it is unintelligible to speak of real life as tragic, some of their fellow citizens who freely use the word of famines and drug overdoses might be puzzled to hear it used of a film of novel. (Ibid., p. 14)

[5] Ricoeur observes: "Even today, I am in the grip of two alternating reproaches: one is not to have been able to say no at the right time to certain tendencies, the other not to have perceived, or heard the call for help uttered from the depths of distress" (ibid.).

[6] Ricoeur notes that

> by convention . . . I reserve the term "ethics" for the *aim* of an accomplished life and the term "morality" for the articulation of this aim in *norms* characterized at once by the claim to universality and by an effect of constraint. . . . I propose to establish . . . (1) the primacy of ethics over morality, (2) the necessity for the ethical aim to pass through the sieve of the norm, and (3) the legitimacy of recourse by the norm to the aim whenever the norm leads to an impasse in practice . . . . [T]he ethical aim will correspond to what we shall call henceforth self-esteem, and to the deontological moment, self-respect. (Ibid., pp. 170–71)

[7] Annas (1995) discusses the difference between ancient and modern approaches to ethics.

[8] Benhabib argues, "The assessment of the maxim of one's intentions, as these embody moral practices, requires understanding the narrative history of the self who is the actor; this understanding discloses both self-knowledge and knowledge of oneself as viewed by others" (ibid.).

[9] In work following *Oneself as Another*, notably Ricoeur, 2000, and Ricoeur, 2007, Ricoeur expands his aim to include Rawls's and Habermas's respective understandings of justice applied to modern institutions.

[10] For recent accounts of the resistance of suffering to expression in words or images, see Sontag, 2003; Lingis, 1994; and Scarry, 1985.

[11] See also Heidegger, 1992a, p. 124: "Man stems from the district of the uncanny divine place of withdrawing concealment."

[12] In his review of a recent collection of essays on *Prudence: Classical Virtue, Postmodern Practice*, David Depew observes that the notion of *phronēsis*

> was diversely interpreted by fourth-century Greeks [and that] Cicero's assimilation of *phronēsis* to a Latin term [*prudentia*] already loaded with local emphasis . . . might not preserve the Greek notion intact; to the extent that Cicero does preserve aspects of Greek *phronēsis*, his version is probably closer to Isocrates' rhetoric-friendly conception of it than to Aristotle's. (Depew, 2004, p. 169)

Separately, David E. Tabachnik notes:

> There is disagreement on how to translate *phronēsis* into English. Terence H. Irwin, for example, presents the term as intelligence and, later, as prudence. However, intelligence puts too much emphasis on thought and not enough on action and, as Anthony J. Celano argues, the Latinized *prudentia* means something quite different from the Greek *phronēsis*. Practical wisdom, practical intelligence and practical deliberation are common translations. I think Rosen's "sound judgment" is closer to the mark, as is the similar "good judgment." Both [Celano and Rosen] suggest that *phronēsis* requires experience rather than just intelligence. Still, Ronald Beiner explains, "If I see what the situation requires, but am unable to bring myself to act in a manner befitting my understanding, I possess judgment but not *phronesis*." (Tabachnick, 2004, p. 999)

[13] The range of *phronēsis* extends beyond moral or ethical issues and dilemmas to
include aesthetic phenomena. The common characteristics of phenomena inviting *phronēsis* as well as *aesthesis* are (1) implications for human agents of conflicting
ways of seeing in situation, and (2) the difference in relevant backgrounds. As
Ricoeur observes, "at the end of book 6 of the *Nicomachean Ethics*" the exercise
of judgment "made *phronēsis* comparable to *aesthēsis*" (Ricoeur, 1992, p. 180).
Aesthetic phenomena appear against a background that includes elements such
as traditions of representation or composition, while moral phenomena, in
Ricoeur's sense, are grasped against a background that includes self-regarding
esteem, solicitude for the other, and understanding of the role of institutions and
ideologies in ways of seeing, or not seeing, oneself as another. *Oneself as Another*
in some ways fulfills Ricoeur's implied promise in his discussion of the "ambition
of the reflective method" (Ricoeur, 1969). There, he stated that "the ambition of
the reflective method is to get hold once again of pure acts, through signs in
which they reveal their signification, [aiming] at a reappropriation of the primary affirmation by a consciousness which discovers itself dispossessed of that
affirmation" (ibid., p. xxiv). In *Oneself as Another*, primary affirmation becomes
attestation, "by which I intend to characterize the alethic (or veritative) mode of
the style appropriate to the conjunction of analysis and reflection, to the recognition of the difference between selfhood and sameness, and to the unfolding of
the dialectic of the self and the other" (Ricoeur, 1992, p. 21). The present chapter is limited primarily to consideration of moral and ethical issues or dilemmas.

[14] This includes *whether* to act, *in what way, at what moment* (Cf. Blum, 1994,
pp. 30–61). Amélie O. Rorty summarizes the Aristotelian account of *phronetic*
action as follows:

> The virtuous person performs the right action in the right way at the right
> time on the right objects. Getting the timing, the tempo, and the manner
> right requires a well-formed character, the right desires and beliefs embodied
> in habits. ([*Nicomachean Ethics*,] 1106 b 36). It means, among other things
> really knowing what one is doing, being aware of the circumstances and con-
> sequences of one's action, with the right conception of the sort of action one
> is performing, of one's own intention as conforming to the normic descrip-
> tion of the action-type. Characteristically, such knowledge is manifest in
> a person consistently doing the right thing for the right reason, in view of
> general human ends. (Rorty, 1980, p. 380)

[15] Rorty observes that "it is his character rather than his purely theoretical capacities which assures the phronimos the right desires. Of course he must have good
judgment, keen perception, and a range of intellectual virtues in order to gauge
his situations well. But he must have developed habits of desire as well as action"
(Rorty, 1980, p. 384).

[16] Depew also notes,

> It is in and through the emotion-laden constructions of these situations (what
> Heidegger called "moods") that appropriate actions are found by way of
> deliberation. . . . These correct emotional reactions are implanted by early
> socialization (*paideia*), in large measure through inculcation of socially shared

narratives (*mythoi*). They are subsequently shaped by trial and error into good habits. Habits are good, or virtuous, if the emotions they evoke and the actions they help identify subordinate instrumental and external goods to noble values (*ta kala*). They are bad, or vicious, if instrumental and external goods, such as money or power or reputation, determine ends. (Ibid., p. 169)

[17] Ricoeur notes that "my thesis is that solicitude is not something added on to self-esteem from outside but that it unfolds the dialogic dimensions of self-esteem" (Ricoeur, 1992, p. 180). The notion of *solicitude* as a dimension of *phronēsis* accords well with Aristotle's distinction between a *deinotes* (clever or cunning) person and a *phronimos*. Robert Dostal observes, "'Cleverness' is the ability to find the means to achieve a goal, but cleverness does not set the goal. . . . *[P]hronēsis*, on the other hand, is the practical wisdom whereby we deliberate well concerning our ends and our happiness. It follows that a merely clever person does not make a good friend" (Dostal, 1992, p. 412).

[18] Translating *deinon* as *unheimlich* (strange or uncanny) in his *Introduction to Metaphysics*, Heidegger presents human life as "strange, powerful, dangerous, violent and engaged in multiple struggles" (Schmidt, 2001, p. 246). By asserting in his later reading of the choral ode, in a 1942 lecture course on Hölderlin's poem "*Der Ister*," "that the sway [of *phusis*] is overwhelming violence, Heidegger is saying that both *phusis* and being human are *deinon* because being human is derivative of *phusis*" (Schoenbohm, 2001, p. 157). While the standard English translation of *phusis* is "nature," this is disputed by Heidegger, among others, as a consequence of Latin rather than Greek usage. Nonet observes: "*Phusis* is the name for the action of the verb *fÊein*, 'to grow,' a cognate of our 'to be'" and of the Latin *fui, futurum* (Nonet, 2005). Groth, commenting on Guignon (2001), notes:

> Professor [Charles] Guignon's comments focus on Heidegger's understanding of the early Greek concept of phusis and "how such a notion is illuminating in trying to make sense of things that the substance ontology fails to make intelligible" (pp. 38, 41). He observes that history "provides a prime example of an entity whose Being is that of phusis" (p. 51). Such an interpretation of phusis is in striking contrast to the standard understanding of phusis as physical nature. (Groth, 2002, p. 452)

[19] Lines 332–72.
[20] Schmidt discusses in detail Heidegger's dependence on Hölderlin's several different translations of this line (ibid., pp. 245–66). Clare Pearson Geiman, 2001, compares and contrasts Heidegger's readings of the *Antigone* text in the 1932 *Introduction to Metaphysics* (Heidegger, 1968) with his 1942 lectures on Hölderlin's poem, "*Der Ister*" (Heidegger, 1984). In the first, *deinon* is understood as "the power of beings as a whole" and linked to *dikē*, as "fittingness" (*Fug*): "at once the using or actualizing of the collected force of beings as a whole and as doing violence in this use or actualization" (Geiman, 2001, p. 167). In the latter, the "violent confrontation between beings and Human being has dropped away, to be replaced by an emphasis on human dwelling in an open space of disclosure" (ibid., p. 167).

21 McNeil translates the *Sophist* text as follows:

> *Phronesis is a catching sight of the here-and-now*, of the concrete here-and-now character of the momentary situation. *As aesthesis it is the glance of the eye, the momentary glance* [der Blick des Auges, der Augenblick] *at what is concrete in each specific case and as such can always be otherwise.* (Ibid., p. 131, emphasis in original)

22 In Heidegger, 1963, Heidegger observes that

> a renewed study of the Aristotelian treatises (especially Book IX of the *Metaphysics, or Theta*, and Book VI of the *Nicomachean Ethics*) resulted in the insight into *aletheia* as a process of revealment, and in the characterization of truth as non-concealment, to which the self-manifestation of beings pertains. (Quoted in Taminiaux, 1991, p. 116)

23 Gadamer continues: "This is not the place to reduce the pedagogical exaggeration contained in this claim to its appropriate dimensions, and even less the place to point out the logical and ontological weight that Aristotle's analysis of *phronēsis* in fact carries" (ibid.).

24 Suffering is never absent from Ricoeur's consideration. In a discussion of whether we should renounce Hegel, Ricoeur opposes "a reconciliation without consolation," in which "the particularity that suffers, for a reason unknown to itself, receives no satisfaction" (Ricoeur, 1988, p. 198). In *Oneself as Another*, Ricoeur discusses the "cruel twentieth century" in his discussion of Hegel on conscience (Ricoeur, 1992, p. 345 n.51).

Part III

Extensions

Chapter 9

Ricoeur's Model of Translation and Responsible Political Practice

Bernard P. Dauenhauer

Paul Ricoeur proposes that we take the model of translation as our guide both to thinking about and to engaging in responsible political practice. This proposal has its roots in his overall hermeneutic anthropology. In this two-part chapter I want, on the one hand, to show the rich context out of which his proposal grows and, on the other hand, to offer reasons for endorsing it.

I will begin part I by (a) comparing Ricoeur's hermeneutics with that of Hans-Georg Gadamer. Since both Ricoeur and Gadamer owe much to Martin Heidegger's work, it is no surprise there is considerable agreement between their conceptions of hermeneutics. Nonetheless, there are some crucial differences that affect how one understands human action. Adjudicating between these differences is not part of my project, but taking note of them does serve to clarify several aspects of Ricoeur's political thought. With this background in hand, I will then recall (b) the basic features of Ricoeur's conception of action, (c) the persistence and pervasiveness, in the history of action, of man-made evil, and (d) the principal properties that characterize the distinctive domain of political action.

Part II consists (a) of a description of Ricoeur's model of translation, in the course of which I show that this model captures the salient features of political action, and (b) of support for the claim that this model serves to disclose at least two of the habitual attitudes, namely the attitudes of forgiveness and hope, that are conducive to sustained good political practice. Finally, in (c) I will illustrate the fruitfulness of applying his model to some practical political issues that regularly recur in either domestic or international politics.

I

(a) Ricoeurian and Gadamerian Hermeneutics

Common to both Ricoeurian and Gadamerian hermeneutics is the importance of the truism that to be human is to be born into some particular linguistic community. This natal community serves as the ever-present support for the lifelong endeavor to make sense of oneself, of other people, and of the physical and cultural milieus in which one finds himself or herself. But as we all know in some fashion, our experiences of both ourselves and our situation are not all of a piece. Some experiences strike us as familiar and largely unproblematic. We readily understand them and know how to respond more or less appropriately to them. Other experiences, though, strike us as strange and puzzling. To make sense of them we have to do some work. Taken together, this bifurcation of experience into the familiar and the strange lies at the root of the hermeneutic philosophy that both Ricoeur and Gadamer espouse. For both of them, to be human is to belong to some already established sense-making community. And for both of them, this sense-making is always a work in progress. Furthermore, in traditional terms, sense-making is a thoroughly practical enterprise. All theorizing is part of this practical effort of making sense of sense-making itself.

Both Ricoeur and Gadamer, as George Taylor points out, are in substantial agreement about a number of important features of sense-making (Taylor, 2011).[1] They agree, for example, about the following:

(1)   No one can arrive at a God's-eye view, a "view from nowhere." A person's sense-making is always indebted to his or her predecessors. The radical independence, or self-sufficiency, Descartes supposedly sought is simply unattainable. Similarly, Hegelian absolute knowledge is impossible.

(2)   Without the resources we receive from others, our own sense-making efforts could not get under way, much less succeed. Among these resources are the traditional understandings and prejudgments ("prejudices") our community makes available to us. That is, (a) these resources constitute us in part as the particular person each of us is, and (b) whatever understandings we ourselves achieve are always in some respects responses that we bring to these received resources.

(3)   Because we do not come empty-handed to the task of understanding our own experiences, our sense-making is always a productive, not a merely reproductive, activity. The sense we make, especially of the past and its artifacts, is always different from the sense that at least some of our predecessors made of them. For example, American legal scholars today do not understand the United States Constitution exactly as nineteenth-century legal scholars did. And physicists today, in the wake of Einstein's work, understand Newtonian physics in a quite different way than nineteenth-century physicists understood it.

(4)   Our own particular physical and cultural milieus do not radically isolate us from anyone, not even from our most distant predecessors or from our contemporaries who least resemble us. Every milieu is intrinsically permeable. For example, every natural language is translatable—albeit never perfectly translatable—into every other natural language. To learn of and

from others, properly to appropriate the sense they have made, requires "quite the contrary of projecting oneself and one's own beliefs and prejudices; it is to let the work [of others] and [their] worlds enlarge the horizon of the understanding which I have of myself" (Ricoeur, 1981, p. 178).

Thus, Ricoeur and Gadamer agree that the Enlightenment conception of ideal sense-making is mistaken. Following Heidegger's lead, they both recognize that, ontologically, "the interpreting subject belongs irreducibly to the world he or she interprets. This apparently vicious methodological circle (stated in terms of a subject-object relation) is in fact an unsurpassable ontological structure. The hermeneutical circle is constitutive of all understanding. We must not try to escape this circle but, on the contrary, correctly situate ourselves within it, for a 'presuppositionless' interpretation is impossible" (Abel, 2005, pp. 189–90). In short, "understanding is a way of *belonging* to the world" (ibid., p. 189, my emphasis).

Important as are these matters of agreement between Ricoeur and Gadamer, there is, nonetheless, a substantial difference in the ways they construe what counts as "correctly situating" ourselves within the hermeneutical circle. This difference goes hand in hand with the differences between their accounts of the fundamental finitude of everything human. Though both of them readily acknowledge this finitude, only Ricoeur reflects in detail on the fallibility that is ingredient in all sayings and doings. One helpful way to approach these differences is to attend to the analogies or models that each of them uses to clarify their respective conceptions of how we ought to construe our belonging to the world.

Consider first the two analogies Gadamer proposes. In one, he depicts the process of understanding or sense-making as a conversation. Conversations have both a multiplicity of participants and a topic. To be a genuine conversational partner, one has to submit to the discipline of focusing on the topic. Of course, since the participants themselves belong to the world, they too can be the topics of conversations. What is of utmost importance for a conversation is that the topic guide the back-and-forth exchanges among the participants. In and through these guided exchanges, understanding comes to pass (Linge, 1976, p. xxii).

Gadamer employs a second, and stronger, analogy to describe the process of gaining understanding: that of playing a game. Genuinely to play a game, a participant has to accept the game's constitutive rules and give himself or herself over to the game's flow. The movement involved in playing the game "has no goal in which it ceases but constantly renews itself. That is, what is essential to the phenomenon of play is not so much the particular goal it involves but the dynamic back-and-forth movement in which the players are caught up—the movement that itself specifies how the goal is reached" (ibid., p. xxiii).

As these two analogies suggest, Gadamer's hermeneutics emphasizes the success we can have in coming to understand the strange and the distant. In principle, there is nothing so strange or distant that it is forever impossible for us, or some other persons, to make any sense of it. Of course, like everything human, our understanding is always finite, always less than exhaustive. But, again, in principle, our understanding can always grow.

Gadamer of course is not blind to the fact that there are both failures to understand and misunderstandings. For example, he acknowledges that without constant self-reflection we would lapse into "ideological ossification" and thus block further growth in understanding. Nonetheless, such instances of ossification are, at least in principle, avoidable aberrations. Through historically situated hermeneutical reflection, I am "no longer unfree over against myself but rather can deem freely what in preunderstanding may be justified and what unjustifiable" (Gadamer, 1976, p. 38; see also Gadamer, 1989, p. 447).

David Linge nicely summarizes the conception of the human person that Gadamer reaches. On this conception, "man is not to be defined prior to or independently of the event of being which thinking essentially serves. Not only is man not primary in his relation to being; man *is* at all only insofar as he is addressed by being and, in his thinking, participates in the event of being" (Linge, 1976, liv; see also Gadamer, 1989, esp. pp. 460–64).

Ricoeur, for his part, does not deny that all our understanding depends upon our "belonging to the world." In this respect, Ricoeur's hermeneutics is, like Gadamer's, a hermeneutics of "belonging." But Ricoeur places considerably more emphasis on the tangled histories of human failures, failures that block or distort understanding, and failures that harm either ourselves or others. Whereas Gadamer, to the extent to which he attends to these failures, treats them as avoidable problems, Ricoeur emphasizes their persistence and frequency. Even though they are contingent, these failures are so pervasive that we cannot rightly deny they are constant features of all human life that we know anything about. Accordingly, thoroughgoing hermeneutical reflection requires detailed consideration of these flaws and their prevalence.

Ricoeur himself makes it explicit that we only come to recognize flaws as flaws by way of gaining some appreciation of them as defects that arise within the context of our fundamentally benign belonging to a world with other people. In that sense, it is belonging, with its successes, that holds ontological priority over the flaws (Ricoeur, 2002, p. 284).[2] But, even so, one cannot rightly minimize the flaws. Ricoeur therefore engages in a "critical hermeneutic" that serves as a crucial complement to his hermeneutics of belonging (Abel, 2005, p. 188; see also Ricoeur, 1991d).

The fruitfulness of Ricoeur's complementing his hermeneutics of belonging with a critical hermeneutics is evident in the rich context out of which his proposal of the model of translation grows. I turn now to describe that context.

(b) Ricoeur's Conception of Action

At the core of Ricoeur's mature philosophical anthropology is his expansive conception of action, a conception that corresponds to Heidegger's conception of Care as the fundamental way in which persons exist and inhabit the world they have been born into (Ricoeur, 1998, pp. 74–75). On this conception, action consists in a person's undertaking projects and joining them to the processes of the natural world. As such, action involves not only doing and making but also receiving and undergoing. In this expansive sense, every action is the exercise of some basic capability that is constitutive of a person as person. These basic capabilities are "the capacity to speak, to initiate a course of events by physically intervening in the course of things, to draw together the story of one's own life in a coherent and credible narrative" (Ricoeur, 1996, p. 20). A fourth constitutive capacity for action is the capacity to be the subject of a judgment of imputation, to be judged "the genuine author of an action that is subject to moral evaluation as good or bad, allowed or forbidden, just or unjust" (ibid.; see also Ricoeur, 2002, pp. 279–90). In and through these modes of action, a person fashions his or her personal identity (Ricoeur, 1996, p. 451, see also Ricoeur, 1992, pp. 165–68, and Dauenhauer, 1998, pp. 120–22), an identity properly construed as the narrative identity of one whom Ricoeur calls "l'homme capable," the Capable Person.

In exercising these capabilities, people purposely initiate changes in the world. That is, "acting is always doing something so that something else happens in the world" (Ricoeur, 1991b, p. 137). Nonetheless, as we all learn, there is often no perfect fit between what we aim to do and what our actions actually bring about. This familiar but strange situation calls for sustained hermeneutical reflection, reflection that brings to light the multiple aspects of the finitude both of our capabilities and of the particular actions we perform. Several aspects of this finitude are particularly relevant to our making sense of politics.

Consider first the fact that no action or set of actions can give complete expression to a person's capacity for action. Until death, there is always some unrealized capacity for action. Nonetheless, every action carries within itself the potential to interfere with further action. That is, agents always affect themselves by their own actions. Sometimes they do so in ways that improve themselves or their abilities. But sometimes they suffer from what they do, perhaps unintentionally. What they do can bring about fatigue or illness. This fact shows that persons, by reason of their bodyliness, belong to the world as entities in it. But, by acting they also show they are different from other worldly entities (Ricoeur, 1992, pp. 54–55).

Furthermore, all action is in some respects interaction. It is true that only individual persons are agents in the strict sense. There are no "higher order" agents (Ricoeur, 1991c, p. 204). Nonetheless, every action depends for its meaning on other actions that contextualize it. And every action impinges somehow on persons other than the agent. We are regularly either pleased, or at least not displeased, that what other people do affects us. For the most part, we experience no ill effects from what other people do. But every action unavoidably embodies the risk of adversely affecting someone else. And all too often actions do, in fact, hinder or thwart, at least temporarily, someone else's capacity to act. In these cases, those so affected suffer either physically or mentally. In severe cases, they may even feel that their very integrity has been violated. Thus we are compelled to admit that "the chance of doing violence lies within the very structure of human action—to act is to act upon another who undergoes my action" (Ricoeur, 1994, p. 15). In this sense one can rightly speak of the tragic potential inherent in all action.

Not only is all action interaction. Many particular actions are part of some practice, some previously established way in which a person does or should conduct himself or herself in some frequently recurring situation. These "practices are based on actions in which the agent takes into account, as a matter of principle, the actions of others" (Ricoeur, 1992, p. 115). Some practices are or ought to be relatively inconsequential, such as wearing clothing that custom makes appropriate for some occasions, for example, tuxedos. Other, more consequential practices are formally prescribed by some major social institution. Religious bodies prescribe ritual practices. Political societies promote a variety of practices, either through laws or through inducements of some sort. Indeed, as will become apparent below, political life consists in large part in the interaction at play in institutionalized practices. Politics deals in various ways not only with state institutions but also with the other institutions present in the society.

Before I discuss political action in greater detail, it is imperative that I say something more explicit about the pervasive presence of evil. Much political action is a response to the presence of evil in the society.

(c) Evil

Generally speaking, we are all aware that we are always at risk of suffering harm or evils of various sorts. Some harm, such as accidents or unavoidable illnesses, befall people through no one's fault. These are natural or physical evils. Other harm is the result of deliberate human action or omission. And among such omissions is the all too frequent neglect of opportunities to provide relief from remediable natural evils. All the harm that is the result of deliberate actions or omissions is moral evil. As such, all moral evils are contingent. None need to have happened. And yet, as we all know, human history is a history marked by the pervasiveness and persistence of moral evils. Apparently no normal adult is wholly without fault. As Ricoeur rightly says, "human action is forever submitted to the experience of fault.... Stripping guilt from our existence would, it seems, destroy that existence totally" (Ricoeur, 2004a, p. 466; see also Ricoeur, 1995b, p. 80).

Of particular relevance here are some evils that have come into being through the actions of political officials. These are political evils, of which there are two sorts. Some political evils come into being when political officials, acting in their official capacities, establish or enforce policies, rules, or procedures that wrongly favor or disfavor some citizens (Ricoeur, 2004a, pp. 474–78; see also Jaspers, 1947).[3] Citizens who benefit from these immoral actions bear some responsibility to remedy them "independently of their individual acts or degree of acquiescence in state policies. Whoever has taken advantage of the benefits of the public order must in some way answer for the evils created by the state to which he or she belongs" (Ricoeur, 2004a, p. 475, translation modified).

Political evils of a second sort can come into being even without any immoral action. They can come about as unintended consequences of some good action. Suppose, for example, that the United States invasion of Iraq was morally good, was a just war. Even so, the war did cause many Iraqis who had no responsibility for their government's activities to suffer the pains of having to migrate. As the late Senator Edward Kennedy has argued, the harms suffered by these refugees give rise to at least a prima facie responsibility of the United States and its citizens to alleviate this harm (Kennedy, 2006, pp. 74–75). Analogous cases are by no means rare in today's world.

Political evils of both sorts are resistant to ready remediation. Inertia, if nothing else, tends to perpetuate them. Responsible political practice requires constant vigilance, both to avoid perpetrating new political evils and to seek ways to remedy the damage done by past ones. It is, to be sure, unreasonable to think all evils can be eradicated or redressed. But, by recalling the past and imagining some possible alternative future, we can learn some things to avoid and some promising precedents to follow (See Dauenhauer, 2007).

(d) Political Action

Action, of course, whether political or otherwise, is not primarily corrective or remedial. As Aristotle rightly said, every action and pursuit aims at some good (Aristotle, 1962, pp. 1–2).

The goods at which our actions aim are of various sorts (ibid., pp. 1–9). Accordingly, there are different kinds of action. There is economic action, artistic action, pedagogical action, religious action, and, of focal interest here, political action. Many of these actions have well-defined institutions corresponding to them. Whatever the ranking of the specific goods at which each kind of action aims, political action in democratic societies is arguably the kind of action that has the greatest efficacy. As Ricoeur puts it, politics "takes on its meaning insofar as it is related to the basic structure of human action" (Ricoeur, 1987, p. 36).

The domain of political action is the domain in which the particular interests, aspirations, and goals of individual persons are related to the shared interests, aspirations, and goals, of the society to which they belong. It is the domain in which a historical society is organized as a state and thereby becomes capable of engaging in collective action. This state and its institutions establish and maintain a public space "for all those activities that we can designate in terms of different kinds of practices, including our crafts and professions, the arts, our sports, games, and leisure activities" (Ricoeur, 1987, p. 36). In short, the domain of politics is the fundamental domain of action inasmuch as it is directly and centrally focused on the basic human capabilities and their corresponding vulnerabilities.

More specifically, by virtue of its organization as a state, a community gives itself the capacity to make and execute decisions that preserve the unity of the community and that bring about the collective actions that give it a distinctive history. The overall aim of these decisions is "the survival, the lasting existence, of the historical community in the face of all threats, whether from inside or outside" (Ricoeur, 1991e, p. 331). In practice, in pursuit of this overall aim, the fundamental and perpetual task for the state is to reconcile (a) the demands of economic efficiency and (b) the aspirations for freedom and justice that animate individual citizens. Pronounced and prolonged economic distress threatens the durability of the state. Injustice and unwarranted legal restrictions on freedom undercut the loyalty of citizens to their state. For both ordinary citizens and their political officials, the defining political task is to satisfy sufficiently well their economic needs while at the same time upholding the norms and standards of "the living traditions that give the community the character of a living organism, whose aim is independence and longevity" (ibid.). Political action, then, is praiseworthy and responsible only insofar as it is a prudent—in the Latin sense of *prudentia*—contribution to this overall objective.

The responsible pursuit of this overall objective, though, is unavoidably complicated by two factors. On the one hand, political discourse is inherently rhetorical. It cannot reach ironclad certainties. Therefore, all political arguments are always open to reasonable contestation. On the other hand, democratic political life is inherently paradoxical. Though its citizens are, in all politically relevant senses, equal as persons, there are always some who rule and others who are ruled.

Consider, first, the rhetorical character of political discourse. Given that its defining task is the preservation of the community's independence and longevity, political action is fundamentally oriented to an open-ended future. Its institutions, practices, and policies may indeed reflect an effort to avoid the recurrence of past ills, but they are all basically oriented toward the community's present and future well-being. Since the future it will face is always in some measure uncertain, political discourse, with its proposals and criticisms, is always rhetorical discourse.

The objective of responsible rhetorical discourse is always to arrive at a shared practical wisdom, wisdom regarding matters about which no incontrovertibly established knowledge has been, or can be, attained. To be sure, some well established knowledge is always an ingredient in practical wisdom, and some new acquisitions of knowledge can decisively affect what can count as practical wisdom. For example, advances in the sciences of biology and chemistry have regularly changed what can count as wise applications of them to medical practice. Nonetheless, there is always a gap between such knowledge and its applicability to particular cases. Only practical wisdom can fill this gap.[4]

Furthermore, political discourse is always the discourse of some particular community that responds to issues of public concern. This discourse takes place at some particular time in a context of some array of limited resources. It is a discourse that weighs risks and likelihoods and aims at decisions that have a sufficiently high likelihood of success that they can gain widespread support. There may, of course, be some universal principles or some impossibilities, either theoretical or practical, that constrain all prudent political discourse, but these constraints, taken singly or collectively, are never sufficient to determine whether some particular political proposal or decision is wise. Indeed, even after decisions are reached, they remain open to review and revision in the light of new information or further discussion. Likewise, with the passage of time, any political issue may fade to the point of insignificance, but it cannot be rightly brought to definitive closure. There are no "final words" about any political matter the community is facing. There is always room for more talk about any of these matters.

There is one more feature of the rhetorical language appropriate to democratic political life that deserves mention here. In political discourse, consensus and conflict are intertwined. Indeed, in some sense, they are necessary for each other. As Ricoeur says, "a democracy is not a political regime without conflicts, but rather one in which the conflicts are open and subject to negotiation" (Ricoeur, 1987, p. 39). The objective of political language, then, is not to eliminate conflicts or disagreements, although it does have to seek a general consensus about the rules by which, and the forums in which, these conflicts are dealt with.

The fact that democratic politics embodies conflict as well as cooperation or consensus is itself a reflection of the irreducibly paradoxical nature of politics. There are multiple manifestations of its paradoxical nature, but arguably its most basic form can be put as follows. On the one hand, as the organization of a historical community, the state exists to promote the power of its members to work together to accomplish things they could not otherwise accomplish. Thus, responsible politics ought always to aim to preserve what Ricoeur calls power-in-common, the power of fundamentally equal citizens expressing, in concert, their equal freedom. On the other hand, every state we know of is marked by a distinction between the governors or rulers and those over whom they rule. The governors hold power over the governed and, within the state; there is always some struggle to gain or keep this domination or power-over (Ricoeur, 1992, pp. 194–97, 220).[5]

Though as a practical matter power-over, or domination, is, ineliminable from political life, it is defensible only insofar as it contributes to the power-in-common that is the raison d'être for the very existence of the state. The democratic project consists in "the set of measures that are taken . . . so that the horizontal bond of wanting to live together prevails over the irreducibly hierarchical bond of command and authority" Ricoeur, 1998, p. 99, translation modified).

Appreciation for the facts that (a) political discourse is always in some respects rhetorical, and (b) that political life is indelibly marked by a tension between conflict and cooperation, is of consummate importance for determining what counts as responsible political practice. To appreciate these facts and their implications, Ricoeur proposes that we think about political action in terms of his model of translation. In part II of this essay, I describe his model and offer reasons to adopt it. Of course, no model, as a proposal of a way of thinking or acting, is a candidate for definitive vindication or refutation. Rather, its value is properly gauged by the likelihood that adopting it will yield significant worthwhile fruit.

II

(a) Ricoeur's Model of Translation

So far as I know, it was in two essays published in the early 1990s that Ricoeur first proposed using a model of translation to guide reflection on political life in this era of globalization. One essay is "Quel éthos nouveau pour l'Europe ?" (Ricoeur, 1992, 107–16).[6] The other is "Fragilité et responsabilité" (Ricoeur, 1992a).[7] In these essays, Ricoeur's focus is on international politics, especially politics in Eastern Europe and the Balkans. But with the publication of three lectures he gave in the late 1990s and included in the volume titled *On Translation*, it became clear that his model of translation is no less applicable to domestic pluralistic democratic politics than it is to international politics (Ricoeur, 2006).[8]

Ricoeur's reflections on the process of translation start from the recognition that, so far as we know, there has always been a plurality and diversity of languages. If ever there were some "pre-Babel" era, it is now wholly opaque to us. So far as we know, people have always had and exercised the ability to translate, that is, to learn and use languages other than their natal language (Ricoeur, 2006, pp. 11–13). As Ricoeur uses it, the term "translation" has two senses. In its specific sense "translation" refers to the work of expressing the meanings of one particular language in some other language. In its generic sense the term refers to the entire process of making someone, oneself or someone else, intelligible to others (Kearney, 2006, p. xv). It is in the generic sense of the term that translation is an appropriate model for making sense of political thought and practice. The fundamental objective of all politics worthy of the name, as indeed of all important and worthwhile interaction, is the same as the fundamental "ethical intention" that Ricoeur has identified as "aiming at the 'good life' with and for others, in just institutions" (Ricoeur, 1992, p. 172). Each active participant in political life is somehow engaged in translating in the generic sense, because an ongoing process of translation is essential for establishing and preserving the capacity to cooperate.

To engage in the process of translation, in the generic sense, requires the activation of two distinct capacities, each of which needs ongoing cultivation. On the one hand, there is the cognitive capacity to learn something new about someone who, in some relevant sense, is a stranger. For genuine cooperation, the partners need a reasonably reliable understanding of one another's concerns. On the other hand, there is the volitional capacity that consists of a readiness to welcome the stranger, to adjust to his or her fears and aspirations, and to coordinate conduct with him or her. Taken together, these two capacities make possible what Ricoeur calls the "hospitality" that characterizes genuine cooperation among people who are strangers to one another (Ricoeur, 2006, p. 29).

Consider now how the process of translation can serve as a good model for responsible political action. At bottom, making and receiving translations are both unavoidably risky, for there is no fixed criterion for determining what counts as a good translation.

> [A] good translation can aim only at a *supposed* equivalence that is not founded on a demonstrable identity of meaning, An equivalence without identity. This equivalence can only be sought, worked at, supposed. And the only way of criticizing a translation—something we can always do—is to suggest another supposed, alleged, better or different one. (Ricoeur, 2006, p. 22, emphasis added)[9]

A large part of the reason the model of translation is so appropriate for making sense of politics consists precisely in the fact that there is no such thing as a perfect or definitive translation, and no such thing as an absolute criterion for assessing the merits of any particular translation. In any linguistic translation it is always possible "*to say the same thing in another way*" (Ricoeur, 2006, p. 25). And, of course, there is always the possibility of mistranslating, of misconstruing. Similarly, in political life there are always alternatives to any existing or proposed policies, laws, or practices, and always the risk of adopting or keeping destructive ones.

The primary objective of translation is not linguistic accuracy. Rather, it is communication. Thus, translation is a practical task one can perform more or less well. It is a task, not in the sense of an obligation to be either definitively discharged or definitively unfulfilled, but instead, is a practical task "in the sense of *the thing to be done* so that human action can simply continue" (ibid., p. 19). From this practical perspective, then, translations are matters of either faithfulness or betrayal. Like every other action, acts of translation always impinge on someone else. These impingements may be harmful, as in the case of either deliberate or accidental betrayals of what is to be translated. But to the extent that translations are faithful, they expand their recipients' understanding and thereby contribute to their capacity for cooperative interaction.

All too often, of course, the task of translating, in the generic sense, is so discomforting that we are sorely tempted to try to avoid it and its riskiness. At bottom, this riskiness is rooted in the gap between our own accustomed ways of talking and acting and the ways foreigners may have of doing so. We are tempted either (a) to insulate ourselves from anything that would suggest that our ways need improvement, or (b) to try to impose our ways on foreigners. Thus, the capacity to translate, with the vulnerability always inherent in it, confronts us in its own way with the ongoing ethical problem of figuring out how we ought to deal with foreigners.

For Ricoeur, our dealings with others ought always to be guided by what he calls "hospitality." Unless we cultivate a readiness to meet foreigners in their very foreignness, we run the risk of "shutting ourselves away in the sourness of a monologue" (ibid., p. 29). A linguistic hospitality is at the heart of the ethics of translating texts. Similarly, a cultural hospitality is at the heart of the ethics of learning to understand and cooperate with foreigners. The endless task of cultural hospitality is both to welcome others and to communicate with them. That this task is never wholly accomplished is not a sign of failure. It is, rather, a permanent occasion for hope, a hope that we can indeed find a " 'good life' with and for others, in just institutions." Thus the task of translation, in both senses of the term, is to establish and maintain an appropriate relationship with others, a relationship that "reconciles respect with intimacy" (Jervolino, 2008, p. 234; see also Ricoeur, 2001, p. 40).

Given these considerations, it is not hard to see the promise of applying Ricoeur's model of translation to political life. Developed as it is out of the ethical demand for a linguistic hospitality that does justice to the foreigner, this model emphasizes the political primacy of consensus and cooperation and, hence, of pursuing the primacy of power-in-common over domination.[10] Nonetheless, one has also to acknowledge that today, and for the foreseeable future, we live in a world riven by conflict and by efforts to subjugate, or even annihilate, some people. We live in a world fashioned in no small measure by a history of violence. What Ricoeur says of the history of Europe is no less true of global history. It is a history of "wars of religion, wars of extermination, subjugation of ethnic minorities, expulsion or reduction of ethnic minorities to slavery" (Ricoeur, 1995c, p. 9). It is a history that threatens to distort the political practice of even the most thoughtful and upright of us. These wars and the bitterness they have begotten continue to weigh upon large numbers of people. Given this sobering fact, we are prompted to ask how we might best prepare ourselves to search for wise or prudent ways to repair the effects of past violence and to ward off as well as we can future acts of violence. Are there any basic habitual attitudes or stances we can cultivate that are especially conducive to wise or prudent political practice? Ricoeur recommends, rightly in my view, two such attitudes, namely attitudes of forgiveness and hope.

(b) Forgiveness and Hope

As is well known, Ricoeur has spelled out, explicitly and in detail, the need for forgiveness in our dealings with one another. He has also, though with less elaboration, recognized the political importance of a properly conceived hope. Since all political action consists in drawing upon, in translating, outcomes of past actions to fashion projects directed toward bringing about a desirable future, there is always place for attitudes of both forgiveness and hope. Rightly conceived, forgiveness and hope are constituents of the kind of hospitality Ricoeur calls for.

Inasmuch as the work of translation is the work of making ourselves intelligible to one another, and inasmuch as the ethical intention that ought to animate this work is the "aim for the 'good life' with and for others, in just institutions," Ricoeur's model of translation serves to clarify just what kinds of forgiveness and hope are relevant to responsible politics. If they are to have this relevance, then both forgiveness and hope must be attitudes that are sustainable even in the face of the intractable constraints that make the task of translation, in the generic sense, interminable and risky and guarantee that its ethical intention can never be definitively satisfied.

Consider, first, the matter of forgiveness. Only victims can forgive, and only victimizers can rightly be forgiven. Everyday experience teaches us that properly offered and received forgiveness plays a major role in redressing harms we perpetrate on one another. Acts of forgiving or asking for forgiveness tend to transform hostility into peace. But even cursory reflection on the pervasiveness and persistence of the institutional evils that infect both domestic and international political life shows there is no neat division between sheep and goats, between the ranks of victims and those of victimizers. For example, how would one accurately apportion blame for narcotics problems and poverty problems in the United States? Or in Mexico? Or in Afghanistan? Most adults bear some responsibility for some nontrivial evils. At the same time, most adults are also in some respects victims. Nonetheless, there is no simple equality of innocence or guilt among them. Those who belong to the ranks of the dominant segments of the population bear the heavier burden of responsibility for redressing these evils.

Ricoeur's discussion of forgiveness arises from this tangled background of affliction. It builds upon Hannah Arendt's account of forgiveness (Ricoeur, 2004b).[11] Like Arendt, he does not require that the offender repent as a condition for being forgiven. But, unlike her (Arendt, 1958, p. 241), he denies that there are any unforgivable deeds, not even such heinous crimes as those that constitute the Holocaust. Ricoeurian forgiveness is radically unconditional.

This radical forgiveness, Ricoeur acknowledges, cannot be incorporated into a legal system (Ricoeur, 2000c, pp. 144–45). It is fundamentally different from such legal actions as pardons or amnesties. And whereas properly constituted legal systems deal directly only with specific actions and not with the personhood of those accused of legally actionable deeds, Ricoeur's radical forgiveness is addressed directly to the person who needs forgiveness.

Only individual victims can grant this forgiveness, but they are never morally obligated to do so. Victimizers, however repentant they may be, cannot rightly claim to have earned this forgiveness. Of course, repentance is never out of place. And, as I will say below, repentance does open the way for victimizers to join their victims in the kind of hope that makes for responsible political practice. But, because victimizers can never wholly expunge the wrong they have committed, no part of justice requires that the victim offer unconditional forgiveness.

Of course, a group of victims may join one another in giving explicit unconditional forgiveness to their victimizers. Doing so may be a practical necessity for the forgiveness to have public efficacy. But, Ricoeurian unconditional forgiveness is always a gift given by an individual person. It is not dependent upon what others do. Neither is it incompatible with any official legal action, including the action of legally punishing the guilty person (Ricoeur, 2004a, pp. 472–74).

Ricoeur applauds Arendt for grounding the forgiveness she advocates on the respect due to each person, regardless of his or her qualities or deeds. Because it concerns the person, as such, respect is "sufficient to prompt forgiving what a person did, for the sake of the person" (Arendt, 1958, p. 243). But, her claim that there are unforgivable deeds undercuts her distinction between the doer and the deed. Fidelity to this distinction requires one to admit that there is no one who cannot be unconditionally forgiven, for this forgiveness springs from an indefeasible prayer, or hope, that "you are worth more than whatever you do" (Ricoeur, 2004b, p. 493, translation modified). And because no one can forgive himself or herself, whatever forgiveness anyone needs can only be given by someone else. For Ricoeur, both to offer and to ask for unconditional forgiveness is a crucial element of the most fitting response we can make to the history of violence in which we have been, and remain, participants.[12]

There is much to admire about Ricoeur's advocacy of unconditional forgiveness, but its very difficulty gives one reason to fear that relatively few people will find themselves ready to grant it. The "rare souls" who do habitually offer it certainly are to be praised and prized. But their achievement ought not to lead us to underestimate the benefits of the amnesties, pardons, and so forth, that legal systems can grant. However subject to abuse these "forgivings" may be, they too are potent healers, as the recent history of "truth and reconciliation" programs have shown. Forgivings of this sort, if they are interpreted according to the Ricoeurian model of translation, make no pretense of being free of risk or of being perfectly calibrated to replace violence with peace. But, they do have the capacity to open the way for culprits to renounce hostility and rejoin a common search for a "'good life' with and for others, in just institutions."

However valuable a habitual attitude of forgiveness is for breaking with the hostility engendered by evils inflicted in the past, it nonetheless needs supplementation if it is to sustain the hard, lifelong work of practicing responsible politics. With the help of the model of translation, we see (as I have said above) that the work of making ourselves intelligible to others is not only interminable but is always subject to failure. No moment of this work is so perfect or successful that it is immune to either misunderstanding or reasonable criticism. To live with this realization is far from easy. The frustrations provoked by the finitude of all interaction, and of every effort to achieve a stable and fair political society, regularly tempt us to curtail, if not to abandon, the work of seeking mutual understanding and common purposes. Yielding to this sort of temptation would amount, in practice, to giving up on the hospitality needed to make power-in-common prevail, as far as possible, over domination.

Arguably the most effective way to fortify oneself against temptations of this sort is to cultivate a properly conceived habitual attitude of political hope.[13] Though this hope is inseparable from emotions or feelings of various sorts, they are not constitutive of it. Political hope, properly so called, is a basic attitude of the sort that Edmund Husserl identified as a "habitual fixed style of willing life comprising directions of the will or interests prescribed by this style" (Husserl, 1970, p. 280). This hope is, as I have said elsewhere, "the deliberately adopted and sustained attitude of respect and esteem both for oneself and for others based on our common capacity to initiate and carry out efficacious action" (Dauenhauer, 2005, p. 87). It is the attitude of trust that, whatever empirical evidence to the contrary notwithstanding, it is good for us to live with and depend upon one another. But, because the empirical evidence to the contrary is rarely in short supply, the cultivation of this attitude requires both patience and courage. In this respect, political hope is the counterpart—in the extrareligious domain of political life—to the Christian virtue of hope.

Unlike Christian hope, which refers to God, political hope has no superhuman referent. It is, rather, an attitude toward the bonds we share with others and without which we could not have a genuinely human life. Nonetheless, it resembles Christian hope inasmuch as it stands opposed to a Stoic resignation, or even despair, on the one hand, and to a presumptuous optimism, on the other. Hence, one can rightly say of political hope what has been said of Christian hope, namely: "Just as patience helps hope to continue and endure, so, in return, hope helps one to be patient, to resist, to struggle. There is a reciprocal influence. Courageous in its desire, serene in its courage, *hope is a principle of action*" (Harent, 1939, p. 611, emphasis added).

Though, like any other deliberately adopted attitude, political hope can be abandoned, no empirical evidence can either conclusively validate it or prove it to be futile. In this sense, it is indefeasible. It rests on the "primary affirmation" that "the goodness of man is more profound than the radicality of evil, a radicality that affects and infects a penchant [for evil] . . . without being able to equal the fundamental disposition toward the good" (Ricoeur, 1998, p. 148). According to this affirmation, people cannot radically vitiate their constitutive capabilities, no matter how badly they may misuse them. It would be a "performative contradiction" to claim that having these capabilities is worse than not having them. Political hope gives expression to the abiding respect and esteem these capabilities deserve.[14]

Adopting this attitude of political hope is fully consistent with understanding interaction according to the Ricoeurian model of translation. Because both interaction and translation are unavoidably pervasive, it makes sense to adopt some basic attitude toward them. But because both are inherently risky and can be abused, we have reason to refrain from adopting either an attitude of easy optimism or one of embittered frustration or pessimism. The attitude of hope, a "difficult hope," is the fitting counterpart to the "difficult forgiveness" that responds to the recognition that each of us, by virtue of our constitutive capabilities, deserves respect and esteem.

To be sure, as he himself would readily acknowledge, Ricoeur's model of translation, even if employed with appropriate attitudes of forgiveness and hope, does not prescribe specific "solutions" or "remedies" for particular political problems. Much less is this model part of some putatively comprehensive political philosophy that gives answers to all theoretical political questions. Instead, Ricoeur's model guides the search for political practical wisdom. That is, Ricoeur's reflections on political action, interpreted by way of his model of translation, yield a cluster of critical considerations concerning how one ought to take part in political life, whether as citizens or officeholders. These considerations bear upon the wisdom of particular political institutions, policies, or programs (Dauenhauer, 2002, p. 246; Dauenhauer, 1998, 287–88). In effect, these considerations serve to mark off the field within which political actions must fall if they are to deserve endorsement.

In my view, political thought that is fully attentive to the historicality of everything political ought not to aim to do more. In support of this proposition, let me point out two ways in which Ricoeur's model serves to clarify what we can reasonably expect of political life. His model warns us away from both excessively "high" and excessively "low" expectations. It keeps us aware that the work of fashioning responsible political practice is never done.

Some political theorists, such as Ronald Dworkin, have had the excessively high ambition to construct an "ideal theory" that would serve as a permanent norm both for assessing actual political practice and for determining what would count as an improvement in that practice (Dworkin, 2006, esp. pp. 1–24). Ricoeur's model warns us away from construing any political theory as definitive. It does, however, allow for regarding "ideal" theories as imaginative alternatives to prevailing norms or practices and, hence, as potentially constructive contributions to the ongoing critique to which everything political is rightly subject.[15] On the other hand, many people find themselves tempted to an uncritical acceptance of prevailing political practices. Whether by laziness or cynicism or despair, they are tempted to conclude that making significant improvements is a practical impossibility. Critique, for them, would be pointless. Ricoeur's model calls for resistance to such temptations to passivity.

Besides these general warnings, Ricoeur's model gives positive guidance for making decisions about, and discharging, important political responsibilities. Genuine translation, in the generic sense, requires that we acknowledge and embrace the consequences of the finitude and contingency of all political action. It requires both (a) that we truthfully express our convictions and commitments, and (b) that we stand ready to receive and appreciate reasonable criticism. Fulfilling these requirements will not remove or mitigate the riskiness of politics, but accepting this risk, with forgiveness and hope, is a necessary condition for making power-in-common prevail, as far as possible, over domination.

Nonetheless, in the end, the proof of the pudding is in the eating. To illustrate more clearly the utility of applying Ricoeur's model of translation to political practice, let me show how it bears on several substantial and perennial political issues. Some of these issues are domestic, others international.

(c) Applications of Ricoeur's Model of Translation

There is, as I said above, no firmly fixed criterion for determining what counts as a good translation. Nor is there any such thing as a perfect or definitive translation. Making a translation always involves risk. These factors underpin Ricoeur's proposal to use the model of translation to make sense of both the inherently rhetorical character of political discourse and of the action connected to this discourse. To see the fruitfulness of adopting Ricoeur's proposal, consider how his model applies to some perennially important components of political life.[16]

The relevance of Ricoeur's model of translation to the responsible handling of substantial and perennial political issues can be shown in the following examples. Consider, first, the process of collecting and managing a government's finances. Key components of this process are tax policies and practices, on the one hand, and budgeting, on the other. These complementary activities are essential to a government's functioning even passably well.

Crucial as these activities are, no one can rightly claim to have devised either the best tax regime or the best budget. Even with the best of wills and with abundant technical skills, there is no algorithm or set of premises that yield the best ranking of budgetary priorities, the best allocation of funds, or the best tax laws. Applied to these issues, Ricoeur's model guides the quest to deal with them sensibly. It emphasizes that arguments about these matters are always exercises, at least in part, in persuasive or deliberative rhetoric. Decisions about them are always prospective, awaiting future developments to determine their worth. Hence, all parties, citizens as well as elected officials, owe it to one another to recognize the fragility and fallibility of the rationales available to support any particular proposal or decision. They owe it to one another to express well-considered convictions and to be prepared to make and keep commitments. But, they also owe one another an unflagging readiness to receive timely criticism and newly available information.

In effect, Ricoeur's model of translation calls for both citizens and officials to display "hospitality" to one another's opinions, a hospitality that welcomes their differences even if it does not endorse them. It rejects hostility in favor of hope. It forgives whatever pains are caused by the disagreements. In short, this hospitality promotes the ethical aim of "living the 'good life' with and for one another, in just institutions." Mutatis mutandis, Ricoeur's model, has a comparable relevance for responsibly addressing legislation and policy decisions that deal with a wide range of issues, such as health and the environment, political campaigns and elections, and commerce.

Even if they have some "extramural" consequences, budgets and taxes are for the most part domestic political matters. The people who make them are all fellow citizens of some particular state. The next example I offer, namely immigration-emigration, has both international and domestic features that are, in some important respects, inseparable.

As we all know, people migrate from one state to another for a variety of reasons. There are economic migrants, political migrants, refugees from natural disasters and from warfare, and so forth. Besides the impact upon the migrants themselves, migration affects the "receiving" societies as well as the "sending" societies in multiple ways. To cope with the dislocations attendant upon migrations, there are bodies of both national and of international law.

Each of these bodies of migration law unavoidably gives expression to some interpretation of the respect and esteem the legislators accord or refuse to some, or all, would-be immigrants. Each of them translates into legal form attitudes about oneself and one's fellow citizens, on the one hand, and attitudes about "foreigners," on the other hand. Unsurprisingly, bodies of migration legislation not infrequently make discriminations of some sort among would-be immigrants. Regularly, at least in democratic societies, these discriminations reflect the opinions of the citizenry. The rationales citizens and their representatives have for these discriminations always reflect some reading of the history of migrations, That is, they take into account past migrations and seek to draw some lessons from them. In short, the legislation embodies the most salient features of the process of translation. Again, even assuming that the respect and esteem of the legislators for migrants is impeccable and that their legislative skills are of a very high order, it remains true that whatever text they produce, whatever body of law, will reflect all the marks of finitude and fallibility that characterize any text. There are no perfect texts, legal or otherwise.

Furthermore, migration legislation is necessarily, if only indirectly, addressed to foreigners as well as to one's own fellow citizens. Effective promulgation has to include a translation of both the text and its intent into the cultures of potential immigrants. Hospitality toward, and proper respect for, potential immigrants requires a willingness to listen to and address the reasonable criticisms of the legislation they or their governmental representatives make. For example, full promulgation of American immigration law requires its dissemination, as far as possible, to whatever portion of the Mexican populace is either itself prone to migrate to the United States or to be significantly affected by the migration. Respectful promulgation also calls for ongoing consultation with the Mexican government about the reasonableness of the legislation itself. Given the fluid circumstances in which migrations take place, the process of making and amending migration legislation is interminable. By construing this process and the enforcement of its results according to the Ricoeurian model of translation, one will have done as much as one can to insure that all relevant voices have been heard and responded to. One will, thereby, have honored the ethical aim of "living well with and for others, in just institutions."

Again, mutatis mutandis, the model of translation is relevant to other international political issues, such as negotiations for treatises and alliances. In these cases, the model calls for hearing and considering the voices, not only of the parties directly involved in the negotiations, but also of other parties likely to be affected by the outcome.

Furthermore, Ricoeur's model is pertinent to dealing with at least some important features of wars. Whatever else they are, wars are expressions, in words and deeds, of deep hostility. As such, they run counter to the ethical aim of living a good life with and for others. Paradoxically, the only reasonable justification for a war is that it is likely, somehow, to establish or reestablish peace. To have this likelihood, a war cannot be waged without some self-restraint. It must be waged with some respect and concern for the welfare of at least some of the enemy's citizens. Just-war theories and agreements, such as the Geneva conventions, give expression to such respect and concern. As Michael Walzer says: "The restraint of war is the beginning of peace" (Walzer, 1977, p. 335).[17] Like the work of translating, of making ourselves intelligible to others, the work of restraining war requires the participation of all parties involved. It is a work never definitively accomplished and, hence, a work that calls for forgiveness and hope.

A third example of Ricoeur's model of translation's relevance to the responsible handling of perennial political issues is the relationship between a modern democratic society and what Ricoeur has called "ecclesial" or "confessing" communities[18] (Ricoeur, 1968, pp. 242–54). This issue is at the core of the larger, more complex issue of church-state relations.

Some citizens of every modern democratic society are also members of some "ecclesial community," such as Judaism, Christianity, Islam, Buddhism, and so forth. As such, they adhere to some distinctive set of beliefs and have some extrapolitical commitments to the absolute norms or principles upheld by their respective communities. There are also some "secular" citizens who, for humanistic reasons, are similarly committed to some moral absolutes. For example, some citizens are, for humanistic reasons, committed to a set of absolute human rights. Both of these sorts of citizens believe they are conscience-bound to call upon their state to respect their commitments and allow them to act upon them. In this respect, these citizens are in deep disagreement with fellow citizens who do not have such extrapolitical absolute commitments.

This disagreement is, at least for the foreseeable future, ineliminable. At bottom, it manifests the tension between (a) an ethics of conviction, which makes absolute demands regardless of circumstances, and (b) an ethics of responsibility, which insists upon the decisiveness of consequences (Weber, 1978, pp. 212–25). This tension generates heartrending conflicts among even the best and most thoughtful of citizens (Ricoeur, 1991a, pp. 237–38; Ricoeur, 1992, pp. 194–95; Ricoeur, 1973, pp. 149–50). Indeed, this conflict not infrequently shows up within a conscientious person who holds a political office of some importance and, at the same time, is an adherent of some specific ethics of conviction.

Even though, as a practical matter, tensions of this sort are ineliminable, they must be managed if there is to be responsible political practice. Ricoeur's model of translation provides sound guidance for this difficult but crucial task. The Ricoeurian model does not call for curtailing disagreements concerning these two ethics. It preserves the "otherness" that this disagreement embodies, but it does so in the course of insisting upon unremitting hospitality toward all reasonably proffered positions. Roughly speaking, this hospitality requires proponents of an ethics of responsibility to refrain from blocking people who adhere to some ethics of conviction from access to opportunities to make public arguments for their beliefs. It likewise requires that these latter people foreswear attempts to write their own particular ethics of conviction into law or public policy. That is, they ought to rely upon the persuasiveness of their arguments in support of their convictions instead of seeking to coerce submission to them. This hospitality of forbearance, if lived out in a spirit of forgiveness and hope, promotes a shared commitment to live a "'good life' with and for others, in just institutions."[19]

As these examples display, Ricoeur's model of translation, when applied to the understanding and practice of politics, by no means endorses any sort of utopianism. Rather, it always acknowledges both the finitude and fragility of everything human and, at the same time, accords the full respect and esteem that all persons, by virtue of their constitutive capabilities, deserve. This model does not pretend to pick out exactly which policies, practices, or laws we ought to adopt. Rather, it shows how we ought to go about both formulating and implementing them and assuring their continued reasonableness. The Ricoeurian model, therefore, stands as a worthy model for responsible political practice. No more can rightly be asked.

Notes

1 Taylor goes on to differentiate the views of Gadamer and Ricoeur.

2 Ricoeur also speaks of the priority of the "absolutely primitive" affirmation, an "originary affirmation" that proclaims, problems notwithstanding, the "joyous affirmation of being-able-to-be, of the effort to be, of the conatus at the origin of ethics' very dynamic" (Ricoeur, 1978, p. 178).

3 In American legal practice, constitutional scholars recognize as "constitutional torts" some torts committed by officials acting in their official capacities. These torts call for a specific kind of redress. See, for example, Dauenhauer and Wells, 2001, pp. 903–29.

4 Ricoeur has explicitly called attention to four professions whose practice demands practical wisdom. These are the professions of physicians, historians, judges, and legislators; see Ricoeur, 2004a, pp. 269, 295; Ricoeur, 1996c; Ricoeur, 2000a, pp. 109–26; and Ricoeur, 2000b.

5 For an earlier version of his view of the relation between power-in-common and power-over, see Ricoeur, 1965, p. 225.

6 The English translation, to which I will hereafter refer, is Ricoeur, 1995c.

7 In the abbreviated version in English, Ricoeur, 1995d, there is no mention of the model of translation. In the French version Ricoeur proposes (as he also does in "Quel éthos nouveau pour l'Europe?") that we use in tandem three models for politics, namely the models of translation, the exchange of memories, and pardon. For present purposes it suffices to note that Ricoeur discusses in great detail in *Memory, History, Forgetting*, both the topic of the exchange of memories and that of pardon or forgiveness. I will take up the matter of forgiveness below.

8 Compare Ricoeur's account of translation with the account of James Boyd White (White, 1990, esp. Chapters 11 and 12). White does not accord sufficient weight to the fact that we always belong to a previously constituted language community. As a result, his account is excessively "individualistic." I thank George Taylor for having directed my attention to White's book.

9 Ricoeur's point is exemplified in G. Wills, 2009, in which Wills discusses some recent translations of parts of the *Oresteia*.

10 In practice, this pursuit always takes place in a specific historical context that reflects some substantive differences that have to be worked out. Whatever procedures are agreed upon to deal with these substantive differences cannot wholly prescind from this context.

11 For a brief earlier treatment of forgiveness that focuses directly on politics, see Ricoeur, 1995a. For Hannah Arendt's treatment of forgiveness, see Arendt, 1958, pp. 236–48.

12 Regrettably, Ricoeur's reflections on forgiveness have received little attention in Anglo-American philosophy. For example, though Margaret Urban Walker (2006) surveys a wide range of recent philosophical and psychological studies concerning forgiveness, she makes no mention of Ricoeur. And though Charles L. Griswold (2007) makes two brief references to Ricoeur, neither reference is relevant to the issue of forgiveness.

13 Ricoeur voiced support, with some qualifications, for this claim of mine (Ricoeur, 1986). I have defended this claim on several previous occasions; see, for example, Dauenhauer, 2007, esp. pp. 218–19.

[14] The poet Seamus Heaney, in discussing the Irish problems of the 1990s, refers to this kind of political hope. He says:

> Hope, according to [Vaclav] Havel, is different from optimism. It is a state of the soul rather than a response to evidence. It is not the expectation that things will turn out successfully but the conviction that something is worth working for, however it turns out. Its deepest roots are transcendental, beyond the horizon. The self-evident truth of all this is surely something upon which a peace process might reasonably be grounded (Heaney, 2005, p. 50).

I would not join Heaney in speaking of "self-evident truth."

[15] For a useful discussion of the evolution of John Rawls's theoretical ambitions, see Davion and Wolf, 2000, pp. 1–8.

[16] For present purposes, I will ignore malicious or manifestly foolish political conduct. I will discuss only discourse and actions that have some plausible claim to being constructive and responsible.

[17] See also Margalit and Walzer, 2009, and their ensuing exchange with Kasher and Yadlin, 2009.

[18] Ricoeur, of course, is not responsible for my remarks here.

[19] Jürgen Habermas, also using the notion of translation in the sense of making oneself intelligible to others, has reached a similar, but more fully articulated, conclusion; see Habermas, 2008, esp. pp. 137–47.

Chapter 10

Understanding the Body: The Relevance of Gadamer's and Ricoeur's View of the Body for Feminist Theory

Louise D. Derksen and Annemie Halsema

One of the contributions of feminist theory to contemporary intellectual thought is its reflections on the body and embodiment. While in the dominant Western philosophical tradition the body is either dismissed or absent—with some exceptions such as the philosophy of Nietzsche, Husserl, and the French existential phenomenologists—feminism has given attention to the body.[1] Feminists not only take the body as a subject of investigation, for instance by studying eating disorders and cosmetic surgery, but they also question the association of mind and body with masculinity and femininity, and explicitly criticize the dominant intellectual tradition for ignoring the body, or for considering it in a one-sided manner.[2]

Gadamer and Ricoeur are not among the continental thinkers in contemporary history, such as Merleau-Ponty, Sartre, Derrida, and also Husserl and Heidegger, who are much reflected upon within feminist philosophy.[3] In this chapter we shall ask whether or not this is a missed opportunity for feminist thought. We will start by sketching Gadamer's and Ricoeur's views of the body. These thinkers do not focus at length on the theme of the body, and their reflections are mostly only fragmentary. Therefore, in the first part of the chapter we will attempt to gather together these fragments. This part ends with a comparison of both views. In the second part, we will identify the elements in their thought that may contribute to feminist theory, but we will also note the limitations of their view of the body for feminism.

Gadamer's View of the Body as Constituting Our Being-in-the-World

Gadamer wrote a number of articles in which he develops notions concerning the body. The theoretical context for his analyses is the problem of the hermeneutics of the body, that is, understanding the body. These articles appeared from the 1960s through 1991 and were collected, translated into English, and published in the book *The Enigma of Health: The Art of Healing in a Scientific Age*. As the title makes clear, the example Gadamer uses of the problem of understanding the body is the relationship in which the physician attempts to understand the bodily state of the patient.

Within a broader philosophical context, Gadamer developed his view of the body within the phenomenological tradition inaugurated by Edmund Husserl and Martin Heidegger. Gadamer notes, however, that neither Husserl nor Heidegger developed an extensive or adequate theory of the body:

> Husserl's analyses concerning the kinesthetic constitution of our bodily being are of exquisite subtlety. However does not the real mystery of our body consist in this, that the actual being of the body is not an object of consciousness? (Vessey, 2000, p. 73)

With reference to Heidegger, Gadamer notes that even though Heidegger takes his point of departure in being-in-the-world, he was forced to admit to not having developed an analysis of the body (Gadamer, 1996, p. 70). As Heidegger states in *Being and Time*, "This 'bodily nature' hides a whole problematic of its own, although we shall not treat it here" (Heidegger, 2002, p. 143). Despite these shortcomings in the treatment of the body in the work of Husserl and Heidegger, their respective notions of the life world and the thrownness of our being-in-the-world are very useful for Gadamer as points of departure for thinking about the body.[4]

Gadamer argues that the human being, as bodily, finds itself taken up in larger meaning structures. Human existence takes place within historical, cultural, and linguistic contexts. These are not purely mental or ethereal, but are linked to very concrete factors that constitute our world. Gadamer speaks of the role of climate—that is, of weather, the seasons, and temperature—and of the environment—that is, of the need for water and general sustenance. He mentions the movement of the stars, the rise and fall of the oceans, and the living nature of the woods and fields (Gadamer, 1996, p. 115). All these elements make up the context of our lives. Gadamer describes this as a whole that includes and involves the entire life situation of a person (Gadamer, 1996, p. 41). This whole is the unity of being, itself, in which we live. To illustrate his view, he cites Socrates:

> Socrates . . . asks: "Do you believe that one can understand the nature of the soul without understanding the nature of the whole?" And his friend replies: "If we may believe Hippocrates the Asclepiad, then one cannot even understand anything of the body without this procedure." (Gadamer, 1996, p. 40)

Neither body nor soul functions in isolation from the totality of being.

Gadamer notes that being healthy is the capacity to function within the whole. Thus, health is not simply ascertained by introspection or by focusing on the individual. Speaking of human health, he states: "Rather, it is a condition of being involved, of being in the world, of being together with one's fellow human beings, of active and rewarding engagement in one's everyday tasks" (Gadamer, 1996, p. 113). Human beings are involved in their world and engage with other people. That bodily health is fundamental for this being-in-the world is shown by the fact that when people become ill they withdraw from the world and others. Their world becomes more confined (Gadamer, 1996, p. 42).

Our being-in-the-world means we not only live in a greater whole, but we live in harmony with it. This harmony is found in our own bodily existence. Gadamer goes so far as to define bodily existence in terms of harmony:

> The life of the body always seems to me to be something which is experienced as a constant movement between the loss of equilibrium and the search for a new point of stability. . . . This seems to me to be the fundamental model for our bodily, and not merely bodily, existence as human beings. (Gadamer, 1996, p. 78)

Thus, harmony is constitutive of our bodily being. Health as harmony is an ancient Greek notion that Gadamer takes up again. According to Gadamer, health is "the rhythm of life, a permanent process in which equilibrium reestablishes itself" (Gadamer, 1996, p. 114). He speaks of the processes of breathing, digesting, and sleeping: "The cycle of these three rhythmic phenomena helps to produce vitality, refreshment and the restoration of energy" (Gadamer, 1996, p. 114). Gadamer notes it is important to balance sleep and wakefulness (Gadamer, 1996, pp. 85–86). He speaks of mental health as a balance that can be disturbed by mental illness, and of health as a balance of the body that is lost when one is ill (Gadamer, 1996, pp. 59–60).

The notion that the body can only be understood in light of the whole— whether the whole of being, of nature, of our social environment, or of our lives—means the understanding of the body is a form of hermeneutical understanding. As Gadamer explains in *Truth and Method*, hermeneutics as the art of understanding always involves a consideration of contexts, of the whole. Hermeneutics of the text is the art of reading individual sentences in the context of paragraphs, paragraphs in the light of chapters, chapters in light of the whole book, the book in the context of the works of the author, the writings of the author in terms of cultural climate and historical contexts. Ultimately, the horizons of understanding expand into the dimensions of language and being. So, too, understanding our body is always contextual understanding.

The Physician's Art of Understanding the Body

In his book *The Enigma of Health*, Gadamer discusses the problem of understanding the body through an analysis of how a physician understands the body.

Two elements of this understanding are central to Gadamer's analysis—
the hermeneutical notions of understanding through dialogue, and that of
understanding the particular in light of the universal.

First, Gadamer sees communication as central for the understanding of the
bodily state of the patient. This communication is dialogical. Gadamer notes that
not all dialogue between physician and patient is ideally open. Doctors in their
practice may operate under the stress of time. In hospitals, they may be forced to
treat patients as numbers (Gadamer, 1996, p. 127). In addition, the relationship
between doctors and patients is not always an ideal one for dialogue. The patient
can feel uncertain, needy, or afraid, while the doctor can have an aura of authority that impedes conversation (Gadamer, 1996, p. 127). Yet, Gadamer notes that
dialogue, a central notion in his hermeneutics, also applies to the doctor-patient
relationship. This dialogue is one in which openness, respect, appropriate
distance, and mutual understanding all must play a role (Gadamer, 1996, p. 128).
He further states that even though the relationship between a doctor and patient
can have elements of tension, it is necessary to have the dialogue take the form
of a normal conversation as much as possible. The purpose is to have a meaningful dialogue in which true communication occurs. He describes the purpose of
the dialogue in these terms: "Genuine dialogue, rather, is concerned with creating the opportunity for the other to awaken his or her own inner activity—what
doctors call the patient's own 'participation'—without losing their way once
again" (Gadamer, 1996, p. 137). The patient must be able to express himself
or herself in the conversation. The goal of such a conversation, which Gadamer
calls the miracle of language, is finding "exactly the right word or . . . the perfect
expression in the words of someone else" (Gadamer, 1996, pp. 137–38).
Gadamer states that such a true conversation is possible because of attentiveness.
This attentiveness is the capacity to "sense the demands of an individual person
at a particular moment and to respond to those demands in an appropriate manner. It is in these terms that we must understand what is involved in therapeutic
dialogue" (Gadamer, 1996, p. 138).

Secondly, the physician can never simply apply the results of scientific research
to the body in a universal, abstract way. It is the task of the physician to explore
the individual aspects of illness and, by means of the aforementioned dialogue,
discover the contexts and specificities of a particular illness. Only then can a
proper diagnosis be developed and a therapy prescribed. The task of the physician is one of applying the universal principles of science to the particular situation of the patient (Gadamer, 1996, pp. 39–40). As such, the role of the
physician is more the application of art than it is the application of science
(Gadamer, 1996, pp. 31–44). What Gadamer means by this art of understanding can be illustrated by the example of the physician making a particular diagnosis. Science tells the physician what the general symptoms of a disease are.
This science of health is the science of general principles. But the physician is
confronted by concrete symptoms. A symptom can be common to many
illnesses. The physician must make a great number of artful decisions. Is the

symptom to be taken as a sign of a serious illness? Is further testing required? Does the patient have a history of such symptoms? Does this history explain the symptoms that have arisen? Are there factors in the personal situation of the patient which could account for the symptoms—medications used, lifestyle, diet, stress? The physician continuously makes such calls, and a good physician is a good diagnostician. Interestingly, Gadamer describes this process of coming to a diagnosis as not only intellectual and verbal, but also as manual: part of the process is that of the physician manually examining the individual patient (Gadamer, 1996, p. 99). Gadamer speaks of the integration of science and practical reason as a situation "in which diagnosis, treatment, dialogue and the participation of the patient all come together" (Gadamer, 1996, p. 138).

The art of the physician is the art of understanding the body in a hermeneutical sense (Gadamer, 1996, p. 104). In *Truth and Method*, Gadamer describes hermeneutical application as the art of applying general principles to particular situations. For example, in the case of legal hermeneutics, it is the task of the judge to apply laws that are universally applicable to individual situations. A law forbidding theft and prescribing penalties for this offence is applied by the judge to a particular situation—in light of the specific instance of theft and in consideration of the individual criminal history of the thief. Application of universal principles to particular situations also plays a role in theological hermeneutics.

If we can speak of a hermeneutical view of the body in the Gadamerian sense, it is a view of the understanding and interpretation of the body in light of the wider contexts in which the particular person lives, and in light of the application of dialogue, as well as of universal principles, to the observation of the particular situation of the person.

A Non-Objectifying Understanding of the Body

Gadamer contrasts his own view of the body to views less holistic than his. He criticizes the distinction between body and soul, as well as an instrumentalistic view of the body.

Gadamer agrees with the Aristotelian notion that the soul is the entelechy of the body. This means there is a fundamental unity between body and soul—the one cannot function without the other. In keeping with Aristotle, he regards the soul as that which gives life to the body—noting that the German words *Leben* (life) and *Leib* (body) should be linked to each other (Gadamer, 1996, pp. 142–43). The soul animates the body; it is the principle of self-movement. According to Gadamer, Descartes—in making a distinction between mind and body—sees the mind as pure self-consciousness and the body as objectified and as mechanical (Gadamer, 1996, p. 148). In Gadamer's view, life is more than mere mechanism—it is something that is experienced. Gadamer sees the living being as a unified organism, not just a collection of mechanical parts (Gadamer, 1996, p. 149).

Gadamer also argues that the body must not be seen in an instrumentalistic way. Modern science makes the body into an object which can be investigated by objectifying it. This does not do justice to the particularity of the body as the lived experience of a human being in the world. We can be studied as a *Körper*, as a bodily object, but we exist as *Leib*, as a living, bodily subject (Gadamer, 1998, p. 134). Our objectified body can be measured in the external sense of the term "measurement." But Gadamer states that this is only one meaning of the notion of measurement. The other meaning of the term measurement is that which is fitting. This measurement is from within (Gadamer, 1996, pp. 132–34). The nature and experience of the living body cannot be captured by objectifying means. As living bodies, we are all unique—living in our own bodies in particular "fitting" situations in the world.

This view of the body, as lived experience as opposed to being a mechanical object or an object of science, means the understanding of the body must be an understanding of the person as a living, embodied subject. Returning to the theme of the understanding of the body by the physician, this means the physician must see the person with whom he is speaking as an embodied subject—someone who lives subjectively in his body, who acts from out of his body, who stands in interaction with the world in a bodily sense, in short, a person who is his body.

The Enigmatic Nature of the Understanding of the Body

Gadamer describes health as enigmatic and the understanding of the body as limited. This is so for a number of reasons. Health can be called enigmatic because we cannot really grasp what it is to be healthy. We can only say we have the experience that we are functioning in such a way that we would describe ourselves as being healthy. Gadamer asks whether being healthy is even a state which we are in. He notes that well-being seems hidden from us, that we are not consciously aware of it, and that it seems to be only a condition in which nothing hurts (Gadamer, 1996, p. 130). We do not even reflect on our being healthy until we feel sick. Health is not something that can be defined.

The experience of health is, furthermore, not the same for all people. For example, a person with a chronic disease will describe himself as healthy in a very different way from someone who does not suffer from such an ailment. Gadamer notes that it is the task of the patient to make clear to the doctor what is wrong, to indicate in what sense the patient feels unhealthy or ill (Gadamer, 1996, p. 138).

Another sense in which knowledge of the body is enigmatic is that it is not always clear what type of pain we are feeling and where the pain is. Gadamer speaks of the self-concealment of pain (Gadamer, 1996, p. 131). It is, for example, very difficult to point to the exact tooth that hurts, or to know where exactly we are feeling pain in the chest. Sometimes pain can even be imaginary, as in the case of aching phantom limbs.

Lastly, the whole art of the physician to heal has an enigmatic aspect. This is because the physician does not really heal the patient; it is nature, Gadamer notes, that does the healing. In this sense, the relationship between patient and doctor is one that has an element that cannot be understood or controlled. The fact that nature heals us shows us the limits of our power over the body (Gadamer, 1996, pp. 32–36).

Ricoeur's Perception of the Body as "I Can" and Passivity

In Paul Ricoeur's oeuvre, the theme of the body is not systematically developed. But that does not imply it is absent from his works. For Ricoeur, we are beings who come into the world "in the mode of incarnation" (Ricoeur, 1992, p. 55). "Incarnation," a concept he derives from his teacher, Gabriel Marcel, represents the ontological unity of a human's being-in-the-world.

The notion of incarnation is already central in Ricoeur's doctoral dissertation, *Freedom and Nature* (1950, 2007a). In this phenomenological study of the reciprocal relationship between the voluntary and the involuntary, Ricoeur's view of the body is worked out in the most extensive manner of his entire oeuvre. About ten years later, in a short essay, "Wonder, Eroticism, and Enigma" (1964), Ricoeur reflects upon sexuality and the difference between eroticism and tenderness. The notion of sexuality in this essay also gives us an idea of his view on embodiment. He considers sexuality as an enigma and as irreducible to language. Thirty years later, in his synthesizing and summarizing study of the self, *Oneself as Another* (1992), the body reappears as the ontological status of the being that we are. Here, albeit very briefly, Ricoeur works out his ideas on the body that he developed in *Freedom and Nature*, and considers the body as both activity and passivity, and as flesh as well as body among other bodies. The notions of the body Ricoeur develops in these works will be outlined and related to each other in the following section.[5]

The Body as the Involuntary

In *Freedom and Nature*, the first volume of Ricoeur's philosophy of the will, the human body is introduced as the involuntary. "Man's body and the host of problems connected with it enters on the scene together with the involuntary," Ricoeur claims (2007a, p. 8). The involuntary has no meaning of its own. What is more, understanding proceeds from the voluntary and not from the involuntary. The involuntary gives motives and capacities, foundations and limits to the will, but can only be understood from the ordering principle of the will.

Ricoeur distinguishes between different types of involuntary structures related to the three moments of the will he analyses: the moments of decision, motion, and consent. Decision is based on motives. Voluntary motion implies preformed skills, emotions, and habit. To the "data" in the category of the absolutely involuntary—which takes the form of character, the unconscious, and biological—the individual consents.

In the case of motives that underlie decisions, Ricoeur discusses bodily needs and pleasures. Needs and pleasures do not in themselves explain why we decide to do something, but need to be appropriated by a will. As such, they are the involuntary underlying the voluntary. Nevertheless, the will also has a freedom with respect to these motives, and in that sense forms its own reason to make a choice.

Movement is perceived by Ricoeur as "the organ of Cogito's practical incarnation" (Kohak in Ricoeur, 2007a, p. xxiv). In movement, the person appears as the unity of the voluntary and involuntary. This is, here, more so than in the case of decision, which—as idea—seems distinct from action. Ricoeur carefully describes the spontaneity and availability of the involuntary in action as presented in preformed skills, emotion, and habit. In all these analyses, he shows they include voluntary acts. For instance, preformed skills, such as standing up or bending over, are not simply involuntary, since *whether* I stand up or bend over is a voluntary act. Something similar goes for emotions: they seem to be involuntary motives for my actions, but they include elements of valuation and judgment.

The will, however, not only encounters a relative involuntary in the sense just described, it also meets the absolutely involuntary of character type, the unconscious, and sheer biological life, birth and death. Can these given involuntary elements also be understood in terms of the will? Ricoeur here speaks of the will as *consenting* to the particulars that form my situation. Consent for him is "the ultimate reconciliation of freedom and nature" (Ricoeur, 2007a, p. 346), in that it pertains to actively accepting my situation as mine, instead of passively acknowledging it as necessity. In the end, this implies, not a surrender to, but a refusal of one's condition. Consent is won only from a refusal to be submerged in nature.

In *Freedom and Nature* the body and the fact that we are embodied form the necessary underpinnings of our existence. The body gives us the possibility of acting. It cannot be submitted to the human will and is not reducible to the will. As the involuntary, it stands in a dialectical relationship to the voluntary.

In the "general introduction" to the book, Ricoeur writes that the task of describing the voluntary and involuntary is "one of becoming receptive to Cogito's *complete* experience" (2007a, p. 8). He relates the body-will relationship to the Cartesian distinction between body and mind. In contrast to Descartes' separation of body and mind in the *Meditations*, Ricoeur takes his point of departure from the union between soul and body that Descartes describes in his letters to Princess Elizabeth. For Ricoeur, the Cogito is embodied, and we can only discover the body and the involuntary that it sustains in the context of the embodied Cogito. "The Cogito's experience, taken as a whole, includes 'I desire,' 'I can,' 'I intend' and, in a general way, my existence as a body" (Ricoeur, 2007a, p. 9). In this respect, Ricoeur also speaks of the "Cogito in the first person."

His notion of the body as the involuntary that stands in a dialectical relationship to the voluntary implies that the way in which experimental sciences understand the body, namely as empirical object, is a reduction of it. Ricoeur explains that involuntary elements, such as need and habit, cannot be understood in separation from the subject that experiences, intends, and refers to itself as an "I." Need is always "I have need of," and habit is "I have the habit of." Ricoeur, thus, objects to perceiving the involuntary as simply an empirical fact and the body as an object. Rather it is a "subject body" that is the source of motives, forms a cluster of capacities, and is nature.

Apart from refusing to understand the body solely as object, Ricoeur explains that the opposition between object body and subject body does not coincide with the opposition between two perspectives: toward other bodies outside of me and toward myself. Rather, both are different attitudes within two different frames of mind. Ricoeur considers the subject as both myself *and* yourself. The same can be said of the body: "[A] personal body (*corps propre*) is someone's body, a subject's body, *my* body, and your body" (Ricoeur, 2007a, p. 10). Consequently, Ricoeur not only comprehends the body as object *and* subject, but also understanding the body as subject is not limited to one's own body, but includes understanding the other's body. The body's subjectivity implies that I understand myself as embodied, *and* understand other human beings as embodied. In communicating with another, I do not reduce the other's body to an empirical object, but I read his or her body as "indicating acts which have a subjective aim and origin." "The you is another myself" (2007a, p. 11), writes Ricoeur, anticipating his book *Oneself as Another*, which he wrote 40 years later.

In short, in *Freedom and Nature* Ricoeur aims at what he (in line with Gabriel Marcel) calls the active participation in "*my incarnation as a mystery*" (2007a, p. 14). "Mystery" in this respect refers to what Ricoeur calls "the nourishing and inspiring spontaneity" of embodied existence. He opposes it to the self-positing consciousness and to a self that, in a "sterile circle," constantly returns to itself. In this early work, Ricoeur's perspective on the body is an existential phenomenological one. Distancing his perspective from how the sciences understand the body, and from how Husserl does, he writes that the body is "neither constituted in an objective sense, nor constitutive as a transcendental subject—it eludes this pair of opposites. It is the existing I" (Ricoeur, 2007a, p. 16).

Sexuality as Enigma

In the intriguing short essay, "Wonder, Eroticism, and Enigma," a similar notion of embodiment can be found. Even though Ricoeur does not speak of the body in this essay, but rather of sexuality, the essay is illustrative of his notion of the body.

Ricoeur describes sexuality as "impermeable to reflection and inaccessible to human mastery," and relates it to the mythical. Sexuality gives us the vivid and obscure feeling that we engage in the uniqueness *and* universality of life. It makes us experience that we engage in "the river of life" (Ricoeur, 1994, p. 83). Stronger than embodiment, sexuality makes us feel we take part in life and that it escapes us what precisely sexuality entails.

Ricoeur envisions sexuality as a human being's "other side," as that which is irreducible to language, tools (techniques), and institutions (such as marriage), all of which form "the trilogy which composes man" (ibid.). Sexuality does not belong to these central components that characterize humanity as such, but belongs to humanity's prelinguistic existence. When expressed in language, sexuality remains "an infra-, para, or superlinguistic expression. It mobilizes language, true, but crosses it, jostles it, sublimates it, stupefies it, pulverizes it into a murmur, an invocation" (ibid.).

Ricoeur refers to sexuality not only as that which cannot be completely articulated, which escapes linguistic articulation, but he more fundamentally perceives it as enigma. Sexuality partakes in a universe that is sunken within us, a "dislocated universe." It is accessible by hermeneutics, by exegesis of ancient myths for instance, but its organic side escapes from hermeneutics. Sexuality is enigmatic because it is irreducible to language, techniques and institutions. This enigmatic element can be symbolically represented but not absorbed in an ethic or technique.

Ricoeur's account of sexuality further explains his perception of embodiment as enigmatic. Embodiment can be articulated, but not completely, for Ricoeur names it a mystery that escapes language. As such, it reveals the limits of hermeneutics.

The Flesh as Intimacy to the Self and as Opening onto the World

In *Oneself as Another*, Ricoeur's notion of the body has characteristics similar to those in *Freedom and Nature*. But instead of speaking in terms of the voluntary and involuntary, freedom and nature, Ricoeur in this later work speaks of activity and passivity. The body appears at once as *I can* (1992, pp. 111–12, 323), but also as the fundamental passivity that opens the self ontologically to otherness. The enigmatic character of embodiment mentioned in *Freedom and Nature* and in the essay on sexuality does not return in *Oneself as Another*. Nevertheless, in the latter Ricoeur still considers human beings as incarnated, and his perspective on embodiment remains an existential phenomenological one. He further works out the themes of *Freedom and Nature* in the sense that he develops a notion of the self that forms an alternative to the Cartesian Cogito, namely, a self that is embodied, is part of the world, and engages with others. The body in this respect is important as the intermediate between self and world and as an encounter with otherness.

Ricoeur starts the development of his notion of the self in *Oneself as Another* with the philosophy of language. The first mention of the body appears in this context, but is not sufficient for Ricoeur. Instead of understanding the body from the limited perspective of the philosophy of language, he suggests that this understanding must be anchored within the phenomenological tradition in which mental and physical predicates are attributed to the twofold structure of the lived body: as observable reality and as "what is mine" (1992, p. 54). This implies that one's own body adheres to two domains at once: the domain of things and the domain of the self.

In the ensuing chapters on human action, Ricoeur claims it is only on the basis of belonging to the world as an embodied self that we can perceive human action as an event in the world *and* as having an author that is able to refer to him- or herself as agent. "One's own body is the very place (. . .) of this belonging, thanks to which the self can place its mark on those events that are its actions" (1992, p. 319).

Next, Ricoeur turns to the question of personal identity. Personal identity ties the corporeal and mental criteria of identity to the constancy of a self that finds its anchor in its own body. In this context, Ricoeur objects to identifications of the self with the psyche or mind and the body with the constancy of the self. He claims that he does not want to enter into discussions, like those in the analytical tradition, over the best criterion for identity: psychological or corporeal (1992, p. 128).[6] Also, the body does not form the permanent part of our being, does not remain "the same": "One only has to compare two self-portraits of Rembrandt," he writes (1992, p. 129).

Ricoeur considers human beings not only as active, but also as enduring, as suffering from the actions of others. The body in this respect appears not as the capacity for action, but as passivity. For instance, in the case of physical pain, the body forms a passivity. It prevents me from performing the actions I would like to undertake, and can make me experience that my self does not coincide with my body, in the sense that I want something else than my body allows me to do. As such, in Ricoeur's own words, the body "overlaps with the passivity belonging to the category of other people" (1992, p. 320). As that which can make the self suffer, the body stands phenomenologically on one level with other persons who make me suffer–albeit that for Ricoeur the lack of self esteem and hatred of others that can result from suffering caused by another person exceeds physical pain (ibid.).

Developed more extensively in the last chapter of *Oneself as Another*, is the notion of the body as passivity. Ricoeur distinguishes—as a working hypothesis, he adds—a triad of passivities, of phenomenological experiences of otherness, which relate to three ontological faces of otherness that are constitutive for the self. The triad consists of, first, "the passivity represented by the experience of one's own body—or . . . the flesh"; secondly, "the passivity implied by the relation of the self to the foreign," that is the other (than) self; and, thirdly, "the most deeply hidden passivity, that of the relation of the self to itself, which is conscience" (1992, p. 318).

In specifying the otherness of the body, Ricoeur takes his point of departure within the phenomenological tradition of thinkers such as Maine de Biran, Marcel, Merleau-Ponty, and Henry. He does not elaborate on their perspectives on the body, and he does not consider the differences between these philosophers, but only mentions a few central points of this tradition to clarify his perspective on the body. He starts with Maine de Biran who, writes Ricoeur, was the first philosopher to introduce one's own body "into the region of nonrepresentative certainty" (1992, p. 321). In other words, we have an assurance of our own body, but this certainty of our body is not symbolical and does not take the form of mental knowledge. Ricoeur relates it to "passivity," and he claims Maine de Biran describes different degrees of passivity. Embodiment entails activity: " 'I am' is to say 'I want, I move, I do,' " but also implies resistance that gives way to effort. Both form an indivisible unity. Furthermore, embodiment gives way to capricious humors, impressions of being content or discontent, and it encounters the resistance of external things. It gives the greatest certainty of one's own existence, but gives the greatest certainty of external existence as well. The body, in short, mediates between the intimacy of the self and the externality of the world (Ricoeur, 1992, p. 322).

Husserl's distinction between *Leib* and *Körper*, flesh and body,[7] as developed in his *Cartesian Meditations*, forms another major point of reference for Ricoeur's conception of the body. What Ricoeur finds inescapably developed in Husserl is an ontology of the flesh. Yet, Husserl is limited because of his emphasis on intention as the constitution of all reality in and through consciousness. He does not escape the philosophies of the Cogito that Ricoeur aims to evade. Ricoeur thinks Heidegger's *Being and Time* offers a more suitable framework, for it offers a break with our constitution on the basis of the intentionality of consciousness. Ricoeur states that Heidegger's "thrownness" comes closer than Husserl's idealistic notion of the body to the primary otherness that he aims at articulating (Ricoeur, 1992, pp. 322, 326–27). But Heidegger "did not allow an ontology of the flesh to unfold" (1992, p. 322).

Ricoeur takes his point of departure here in the Fifth of Husserl's *Cartesian Meditations*, where Husserl addresses the question of the constitution of a shared nature, of an intersubjectively founded nature. Husserl especially concentrates upon the creation of the distinction between flesh and body in this process. He suggests the transcendental ego constitutes other egos as equal partners in an intersubjective community, which founds the "objective," that is, intersubjective world. For Husserl, the constitution of the other as *alter ego* necessitates the methodological step of reduction to ownness (*Reduktion auf die Eigenheitssphäre*), in which all things in my experience are emptied of references to foreign subjectivities, that is, to other selves. Husserl explains the reduction to ownness as an abstraction, both from everything that gives humans and animals their specific sense as living beings with a sense of self, and from the environment as being there for anyone. What remains in this reduction, he says, is a sense of an "animated organism as uniquely singled out" (*Leib*). In this abstraction, my body is the sole object that I do not perceive as just body but as animate organism. It is something to which I ascribe "fields of sensation." It is the only object "in" which I "rule and govern" immediately (Husserl, 1995,

p. 99).[8] By means of this body, I perceive; it founds my capacities and my "world."

In interpreting this passage, Ricoeur shows that Husserl accomplishes the conceptualization of an ontological notion of flesh. Husserl's intersubjective constitution of nature obliges us to think of ourselves as flesh *before* the constitution of the alter ego (Ricoeur, 1992, p. 323). In explaining the otherness of the flesh, Ricoeur goes back to *Freedom and Nature*, in which he understood the body as an organ of desire and a support of free movement that is not the object of choice or desire. He claims it is this notion of the flesh that forms a "paradigm of otherness." In other words, he further develops the undifferentiated notion of the body in *Freedom and Nature*, and speaks of "flesh" as that which precedes the distinction between the voluntary and involuntary. It is the "I can" that precedes the "I want," he claims in *Oneself as Another*. "[The flesh] is the origin of all 'alteration of ownness.'" (Ricoeur, 1992, p. 324).

While developing an ontological notion of the flesh that is primordial and makes the world accessible to us, Husserl has difficulties thinking the body as part of the world, as objective *Körper*. For Ricoeur this aspect of embodiment is important, too. It is the observable reality of my body, of its being a thing that appears in the world among other things, body among bodies. Husserl helps us understand that my body is flesh, and that the bodies of others are *Körper*, but he has no answer to the question: "How am I to understand that *my* flesh is *also* a body?" (Ricoeur, 1992, p. 326, emphasis added). Here, phenomenology finds its limit. Husserl's "solution" to this problem is to make the flesh part of the world (*mondaneiser*), that is, to identify oneself with one of the things of nature, a physical body. Ricoeur claims, however, that the body can only function as such when it is flesh and body, and is perceived in this way *both* by me and the other:

> For my flesh appears as a body among bodies only to the extent that I am myself an other among all others, in the apprehension of a common nature, woven, as Husserl says, out of the network of intersubjectivity—itself, unlike Husserl's conception, founding selfhood in its own way. (Ricoeur, 1992, p. 326)

Ricoeur thus claims that the body's being one among others should be considered as no less primordial than its being flesh. The flesh should be thought of as both intimacy to the self *and* as opening onto the world. Here, again, Ricoeur refers to Heidegger, who with the notion of thrownness develops an existential category Ricoeur calls "especially appropriate to an investigation of the self as flesh" (1992, p. 327). In Ricoeur's interpretation this notion encompasses the strangeness of human finiteness, sealed by embodiment that can be called primary otherness (ibid.).

Ricoeur associates being a body among other bodies with "opening onto a world," "finding oneself in the world," and "appearing in the world" (1992, pp. 326–28). The body's being one among many makes apparent that I am part of the world, part of a community, and that others are similar to me—bodies that are flesh. In this way, Ricoeur connects the body's being flesh with its being a body among other bodies. The body that is the foundation for the acting self also forms the self's first encounter with otherness.

A Narrative of the Body

Ricoeur's phenomenological notion of the body entails that we understand ourselves and others as incarnated beings. The body constitutes our being-in-the-world, which for him implies an opening onto a world *and* mineness; passive reality *and* the possibility of action. These facets of his conception of the body underlie all of his works. In *Freedom and Nature* it is developed as the involuntary that in dialogue with the voluntary explains our decisions, movements, and the way we relate to what is fundamentally given: life, birth, death, the unconscious, and our character. In the essay on sexuality, it gives way to the enigmatic character of desire. And in *Oneself as Another*, the notion of the body is worked out as "I can" and the first passivity we phenomenologically encounter on an ontological level. For Ricoeur, embodiment thus includes the unity of human existence. Dichotomies such as subject and object, self and other, mind and body, are secondary to the ontological "oneness" that embodied existence implies.

Ricoeur's notion of the body as the unity of individual human existence underlies his notion of the self. This is the case, not in the sense that it forms an unvarying basis for the self—the body for Ricoeur is not something "the same" that lies beneath the changing self—but rather, the self is embodied. The body is not foreign to selfhood, because the self can claim: "this is my body." Given the physical changes in the body over time, the mineness of the body even forms "the most overwhelming testimony in favor of the irreducibility of selfhood to sameness" (Ricoeur, 1992, p. 128). The selfhood of the body is constituted by its belonging to someone who is capable of designating herself as the one whose body this is. The body thus co-constitutes "who" someone is, instead of only signifying someone's whatness. The whatness and whoness of the body show it belongs to the order of things as well as to the order of the self.

For Ricoeur, both aspects of embodiment can be narrated, and thus can be part of narrative identity. In *Oneself as Another* he develops a narrative notion of personal identity articulated within the context of a specific language and culture. Personal identity is a narrative because human life has a prenarrative capacity; it is prefigured narratively. We understand action and passion through the entire network of expressions and concepts offered us in language. Human action is embedded within a semantics of action that makes it understandable. Furthermore, human action is symbolically mediated; it is articulated in "signs, rules, norms" (Ricoeur, 1991, p. 28). Ricoeur summarizes the narrative quality of life as follows:

> Our life, when then embraced in a single glance, appears to us as the field of a constructive activity, borrowed from narrative understanding, by which we attempt to discover and not simply to impose from outside *the narrative identity that constitutes us.* (Ricoeur, 1991, p. 32)

We need to narrate who we are in order to understand ourselves, and we can only do so in a specific language and culture. Because we are embodied beings, narratives about the body are part of the narratives of our lives, and are culturally mediated as well. We can recall bodily experiences, explain what we feel and how it feels; we can objectify our body, speak about its characteristics and about what it shares with others. What can be expressed and articulated about the body thus forms a component of narrative identity. The self that tells its life story incorporates its body into its life story. But the self cannot express its body entirely. Embodiment also includes an enigma; even as it is expressed in language, it also escapes language.

Gadamer and Ricoeur in Dialogue: Understanding the Body

Although Gadamer and Ricoeur work out different perspectives on the body, they share the perception that the body constitutes our being-in-the-world. We have seen their notions of the body are strongly indebted to phenomenology, namely to the later Husserl and to Heidegger's notion of our thrownness into the world. Both Gadamer and Ricoeur take distance from Husserl's idealism and observe, in Heidegger's work, the lack of an elaboration of a concept of the body. From this starting point, the most important aspects they have in common regarding their concept of the body can be summarized as follows: the body enables humans to actively participate in the world, and the dichotomy of body and mind is an abstraction from the primordial unity of embodied existence.

The indebtedness to phenomenology of Gadamer's and Ricoeur's views of the body should not veil the fact that they take different positions with respect to the body. Ricoeur remains more in line with the phenomenological tradition, while Gadamer stands more firmly in the hermeneutical tradition. Ricoeur develops a phenomenology in order to understand the nature and experience of the body, while Gadamer focuses on the problem of the hermeneutical understanding of the body.

Other points of difference between Gadamer's and Ricoeur's perceptions on the body are ones of emphasis. First, their analyses concentrate on different aspects of embodiment. Ricoeur describes the two facets of embodiment, namely its being the basis for our actions *and* the passivity, or involuntariness, embodiment implies. In this sense, he analyses what it implies to have and be a body. Gadamer, however, sees embodiment mainly as active subjectivity, as a point of departure for engaging with the world. Passivity only plays a role in Gadamer's analyses in the case of illness, through which active participation in the world is curbed. Secondly, Gadamer analyses embodiment as the state of being in balance. This balance is not limited to the balance of functions in the individual body, but also belongs in a larger context, that is to say of lifestyle, environment, even the context of "the whole" of being. Ricoeur also sees embodiment as occurring in contexts, but his focus is on the question of what it means for individual people to be embodied.

Part of Gadamer's and Ricoeur's perceptions of the body is that they both speak of the limitations to understanding the body. Both believe there are aspects of bodily existence that are not fully accessible to abstract or theoretical thought. Ricoeur speaks of incarnation as a mystery not completely graspable by consciousness, a mystery that restricts the possibilities of consciousness returning to itself. Also, he describes the enigma of sexuality which, in turn, is an aspect of human embodiment. Sexuality is narratable (in ancient myths), and as such hermeneutically accessible, but it is not fully expressible. It is in that sense that our own body makes us encounter otherness and that it forms a passivity. Gadamer speaks of the enigma of health. We can only say we have the experience that we are functioning in such a way that we would describe ourselves as being healthy. We do not even reflect on our being healthy until we feel sick. Health is not something that can be defined, and the experience of our bodies can vary widely. Pain and healing in part also take place outside the realm of objectifying understanding.

Even though we cannot speak of identical approaches to the body in Gadamer and Ricoeur, both philosophers contribute to different aspects of the question of how to understand the body. They describe different levels of our understanding of the body. For Ricoeur, the focus is on the idea of understanding what it implies to be embodied, both as self and also in relationship to the other. The other partly becomes understandable because of having a body that is his or her own, just like my body. Gadamer is concerned with understanding the body on an experiential plane. In both cases, however, the body itself, even though it is symbolically representable, remains to a certain extent an enigma.

Limits for Feminist Theory of the Relevance of Gadamer's and Ricoeur's View of the Body

The question we posed at the beginning of this article is whether the ideas of Gadamer and Ricoeur about embodiment and the body can be of use for feminist theory. In this section we will start by delineating the limitations of their views of the body as far as feminism is concerned, only to conclude, in the final section, with a discussion of the remaining relevance of their views for feminism.

We just saw that Gadamer and Ricoeur have different approaches to understanding the body. Yet for both, cultural influences play an important part. For Gadamer, culture is an ever-present condition for understanding— all understanding is culturally influenced, including the understanding of the body. The same goes for Ricoeur. He considers identity as narrative, and narrative identity as articulated within the context of a specific language and culture. As embodied beings, we create narratives about the body. These narratives are part of the narratives of our lives, and are culturally mediated.

But, from a feminist perspective, it can be asked whether culture does not have much more of an influence on the way we perceive the body than Gadamer and Ricoeur realize. In the work of contemporary feminist thinker Judith Butler, a body notion is developed in which the body is seen as "materialized" in a specific cultural matrix. The body is not signified within a cultural context as a sort of material thing to which we add meaning. "Matter," in Butler's view, implies "a process of materialization that stabilizes over time to produce the effect of boundary, fixity, and surface we call matter" (Butler, 1993, p. 9). This implies the matter of the body is a cultural product as well. In other words, the way we perceive our bodies (for instance as female or male) is culturally constructed. In confronting Butler's view on the body with the views of Gadamer and Ricoeur, the question arises as to what extent embodiment is not only *mediated* by language and culture, as it is in the philosophy of Gadamer and Ricoeur, but more forcefully becomes *intelligible* through language and culture?

This problem leads to a second. Feminists have pointed out that any view of the body must entail a consideration of power structures. Bodies exist as empowered or powerless, and in society power is continually being exercised over the body. Female bodies are especially vulnerable to the exercise of power over them. In her book *Women and Human Development*, Martha Nussbaum points out that while bodily integrity is of fundamental importance for all people (2000, p. 78), it is not respected in all cultures, especially in the case of women. Forced marriages, laws legislating the frequency of sexual intercourse, and decrees and customs forbidding women to go outside the home are all examples of the imposition of power structures specifically on women's bodies. The philosophies of Gadamer and Ricoeur do not seem able to give an adequate account of such dynamics.

As a number of feminist critics have observed, one of the major drawbacks of Gadamer's philosophy for feminism is its lack of awareness of the working of power in processes of understanding (Code, 2003, pp. 10–27). It is notable, however, that in *Enigma of Health* Gadamer mentions Foucault. He states that Foucault showed mental illness and abnormality must be analyzed from a social and political point of view. Gadamer comments:

It cannot be denied that an awareness of social norms, as well as corresponding forms of behavior on the part of society as a whole, always contribute to the definition of such a concept of illness, and so render it problematic. (Gadamer, 1996, p. 169)

He notes that this applies to the definition of madness and normalcy. But beyond such remarks, Gadamer does not have an elaborate view of the role of power structures in relation to a view of the body. Gadamer's focus in this book is on threats to the notion of the body in the sphere of the objectification of the body by science.

Ricoeur also does not seem to take power processes into account in his writings on embodiment. Although, generally speaking, he cannot be accused of ignoring power,[9] he does not consider the uneven distributions of power and privileges often related to bodily differences such as gender, race, age, and health. He does not explicitly elaborate on the consequences of having a male or female body, a sick or healthy body, a colored or white body, or an old or young one. The specific forms of disrespect and discrimination related to bodily differences are not taken into consideration by him, even though it should be noted that on the basis of his reflections upon justice and recognition, these consequences could be worked out.

This brings us to the problem of the politics of the body. Gadamer has explicitly stated that philosophy should not concern itself with political issues (Code, 2003, p. 28). This has been a source of concern for feminists interpreting Gadamer. His philosophy does not strive for emancipation in a practical sense. Ricoeur's philosophy does not take into account the significance of being differently embodied and the power structures this entails in our society. This means he also fails to bring us further along in women's emancipation.

The next problem that can be noted is the importance of being able to think alterity. Many feminists believe one of the reasons for the lack of awareness of the female in Western society is the tendency to think of all people as the same, as male, or as having to conform to the same standard, that of maleness. In that respect the work of Luce Irigaray is illustrative. She claims sexual difference is irreducible. Between man and woman "there really is otherness: biological, morphological, relational" (1996, p. 61). For her, the ethical endeavor is to respect the other's otherness, or what she also calls transcendence. This interest in thinking alterity also applies to the body—the capacity of thinking and respecting the difference between male and female bodies and bodily experience.

To what extent can the philosophies of Gadamer and Ricoeur truly deal with alterity as it applies to the body? (Code, 2003, p. 28). Understanding is central to the hermeneutical endeavor, but it can be asked whether Gadamer develops a means of understanding that can incorporate the bodily experience of the other, in all his strangeness and otherness. The example Gadamer uses of the situation of understanding concerning the body is that of physician and patient—but the example he cites, of a gifted physician, is the prominent Viktor von Weiszäcker. Could his model also be applicable, as Lorraine Code questions, to the relationship between a less gifted physician and a female patient with ill-defined symptoms? (Code, 2003, pp. 29–30). Some feminists would argue that Gadamer's hermeneutics does not have the theoretical means to truly bring about understanding of radical alterity, because it always seeks to make that which is to be understood into something that fits into one's own horizons. They argue that even Gadamer's central notion of openness, that of asking questions, is one in which the presuppositions of the questions determine how that which is questioned will be seen (Code, 2003, p. 16). Some feminists suspect Gadamer's philosophy is embedded in a male, well-educated, middle class environment (Code, 2003, p. 15). This raises the issue as to what extent his philosophy can be used to understand the truly strange or different, including the feminine body and its relationships to the world and others.

Even though Ricoeur considers the self as ontologically open to otherness, and considers the other than the self as ethically primary to the self (1992, p. 168), it can be asked to what extent he is able to really engage with alterity. Because Ricoeur, in his account of the self-other relationship, stresses similarity. Ricoeur aims at respect for the other person, but by means of establishing *similitude* between self and other. The notion of similitude for Ricoeur explains the meaning of "oneself as another": I can only have self-esteem if I esteem others *as* myself. That implies that I consider others as capable as I am of starting something in the world, and of acting for a reason, of creating a hierarchy of priorities, evaluating the ends of actions, and esteeming themselves on that basis (1992, p. 193). Rather than basing his ethics upon the other's alterity, it is the other's similitude that, for Ricoeur, grounds his little ethics (see Halsema, 2005). From a feminist perspective, similarity is dangerous in that it engenders forgetting, or too quickly leaving aside, differences. The questions, then, that the confrontation between a feminist, such as Irigaray, and Ricoeur leaves us with are, first of all, whether understanding the other as similar to the self does not lead to sidestepping the differences between self and other—such as for instance sexual difference. Secondly, we can ask whether stressing similarity or difference is the best way to bring about respect for, and recognition of, the other.

To conclude, the relevance of Gadamer's and Ricoeur's notions of the body for feminism is limited primarily because of shortcomings in their notions of what factors play a role in understanding the body. Can they truly do justice to the materialization of bodies in language, to the power structures surrounding the understanding of the body, to a phenomenon such as sexual difference and to the existence of bodies that are significantly different?

The Relevance of Gadamer's and Ricoeur's Thought for a Feminist Notion of the Body

Do these limitations imply that Gadamer's and Ricoeur's ideas about the body have no relevance for feminist theory? In this section we will describe in what respect their reflections can be of help for feminists in understanding the body. Because there are differences in their approaches to the body, their relevance for feminism is not entirely identical.

Gadamer's view of the body is focused on the art of understanding the body. There are numerous concepts in Gadamer's philosophy that speak of the importance of coming to right understanding in a dialogue situation. Examples of these concepts are openness, questioning, respect for the other, doing justice to phenomena, the use of reason in understanding, understanding as the play of dialogue, and the fusion of horizons. Gadamer's philosophy of understanding is sympathetic, sophisticated, and is an expression of the value *Bildung*, having an educated perspective on matters. Gadamer describes language as listening to each other, as encompassing all reason and thought, as the universal dimension of hermeneutics. He states that the heart of philosophy is the pursuit of the logic of dialogue (Gadamer, 1996, pp. 166–67). From his book, *The Enigma of Health*, it is apparent Gadamer would like to apply his hermeneutical principles to the understanding of the body. This means the values represented in his hermeneutics are applicable to this endeavor.

As we have seen in the previous section, it is possible to argue that there are limitations to the notion of understanding Gadamer develops. It is, however, not possible to doubt the fact that Gadamer strives to create a view of the dialogue between physician and patient as a situation in which they attempt to do justice to the symptoms at issue. Gadamer admits the conversation may involve tension and insecurity on the part of the patient, authority on the part of the doctor, and problems in understanding the enigmatic aspects of bodily sensations. But, this does not mean the "miracle of language"—true understanding—cannot occur. Gadamer speaks of the special moments in which words are found to express what exactly one feels in one's body, when the patient is activated to participate in the process of describing the illness. For Gadamer, hermeneutics is an ongoing process. There are no guarantees that correct understanding will always take place. In this sense misunderstanding is always a hermeneutical possibility. But Gadamer's optimism is that we can strive to come to some type of understanding and communication about our bodies. This insight is relevant for feminism because it means a hermeneutical model of understanding the body may in fact work. Through the dialogical values Gadamer espouses, it may be possible to come to more understanding of the body within feminist theory.

This leaves us with another point of concern—that of the political contexts and implications of the dialogue concerning the body. Gadamer seems to have little consideration for these factors, but it could be argued that a successful dialogue itself has political implications. Lorraine Code argues that the example of physician and patient is "micropolitical" in the sense that there is politics in the relationship between physician and patient. There are power structures at work; there are social and political contexts for their conversation. But, at the same time, the example of the physician doing justice to the experience of the patient gives rise to empowerment that can initiate changes in the social order. These changes, however small, could lead to changes on a larger, "macropolitical" scale (Code, 2003, pp. 27–34). Even such a small, micropolitical moment of understanding in which the physician takes seriously a woman's symptoms may, in the end, lead to larger political changes. As numerous studies have shown, heart disease in women is different from that in men. Such an insight can only come about because of the awareness of differences between women and men.

Taking this notion of the possibility that small changes in a dialogical situation can be a means for changing larger political structures, it could be that Gadamer's view of the hermeneutical relationship between patient and physician might function as a model for communication between people about bodily experience. Perhaps, speaking and gesturing to each other about our bodies should occur within a relationship similar to the one Gadamer describes between physician and patient—one of hermeneutical understanding, in which listening and receptivity play an important role, and in which the process of understanding can indeed have an influence on power structures that play a role in the perception of the body.

As for Ricoeur, even though he does not explicitly reflect upon gender issues and the consequences of other embodied differences, his work offers several openings for feminist reflections. In the first place, the systematic way in which in *Oneself as Another* he works out a notion of the self that is ethical and ontologically open to otherness can enrich feminist notions of identity—in which, as noted, alterity plays an important part. Also, Ricoeur understands the subject as not only acting, but also suffering. He refers not only to the willing and acting subject, but also to the one who is excluded from action and who suffers from the other's acts. The fact he understands human subjects as active and passive, acting and suffering, opens his work all the more to comprehending disrespect, discrimination, and exclusion. Furthermore, the fact he considers the self as embodied in a phenomenological sense means his concept of personal and narrative identity is closer to feminist thought than theories of identity in which embodiment is not considered.

In his late work, Ricoeur is concerned with questions concerning justice and recognition, that are also central in feminist thought. His philosophy, even though not considering the difference between the sexes, is concerned with striving for just institutions. (Think of the self in *Oneself as Another* that strives for "the 'good life' with and for others, in just institutions" [Ricoeur, 1992, p. 172]). That means social and political change, the central characteristics of feminist philosophy, are considered in his philosophy as well.

With respect to the body specifically, there are also some interesting contributions Ricoeur can make to feminist theory. First of all, because it takes two perspectives into account, his notion of the body as the locus of activity, but also of passivity, enriches feminist discussions on how to relate to the body. For instance, in dealing with questions concerning cosmetic surgery and other improvements or adaptations to the body, Ricoeur's perspective helps us understand the urge to change one's body, to act on it as self, but this perspective also calls upon people to take their bodies for what they are, that is, to take them as the reality they are, passively. The double-sidedness of his perception of the body, as active and passive, can help feminist theory contradict accounts of embodiment that only consider it as a site of construction.

Next, Ricoeur provides us with a notion of embodiment that understands humans as not only having their bodies as "mine" in the phenomenological sense of the word, but also humans are situated in the world by means of their bodies. In its double structure the body constitutes my inextricable mineness as well as my own proper otherness that makes me appear in the world, and makes me part of it. This implies another double account of embodiment that can be enriching for feminist theorizing—for a feminist account of embodiment should include a perspective on what it implies to be situated in the world. The body is not only lived experience and a starting point for perceiving the world and others, as in Husserl's perception of the body but, in Ricoeur's view, it is also something that receives social meanings. It is the point where normative social structures cross, structures which situate the individual socially and influence her or his self-perception.

Gadamer's and Ricoeur's accounts of the body bring to the fore classical phenomenological and hermeneutical values, such as respect for phenomena and for other subjects, doing them justice, and having openness to them. Understanding the body in light of their philosophies amounts to respecting our embodiment in and for itself and to doing justice and having openness to the other's embodiment and the contexts in which embodiment takes place. Feminists could well be inspired by these aspects of the understanding of the body by Gadamer and Ricoeur.

Notes

[1] Feminist interest in the body shows itself, for example, in monographs on the body, such as Elizabeth Grosz's *Volatile Bodies* (1994) and Judith Butler's *Bodies That Matter* (1993), but also in the many volumes of collected essays on the body. To name a few: *Writing on the Body: Female Embodiment and Feminist Theory* (Eds. Conboy et al., 1996), *Feminist Theory and the Body. A Reader* (Eds. Price and Shildrick, 1999); *Feminism and the Body* (Schiebinger, 2000).

[2] See for a feminist perspective on cosmetic surgery Davis (1997). See for the association of mind-body with masculinity-femininity, for instance, Lloyd's *The Man of Reason* (1984) and Derksen's *Dialogues on Women* (1996). The feminist critique of the perception of the body in Western philosophy is described in the introductions of Grosz (1994), and Price and Shildrick, (1999). One of the most important sources for the feminist critique of ignoring the body in Western philosophy is Luce Irigaray. Important works in this respect are *Speculum of the Other Woman* (1985), *Ethics of Sexual Difference* (1993), and *To Be Two* (2000).

[3] Exceptions are the book edited by Lorraine Code, *Feminist Interpretations of Hans-Georg Gadamer* (2003), Morny Joy's (ed.), *Paul Ricoeur and Narrative: Context*

and Contestation (1997), and the Dutch dissertation by Nel van den Haak on Ricoeur and Kristeva (2001).

[4] The influence of Husserl and Heidegger on thinking about the body can be seen in authors varying from Merleau-Ponty to Michael Wheeler. For Wheeler's discussion on cognition as embodied and embedded, see Wheeler, 2005, pp. 225–48.

[5] The body is also mentioned in Ricoeur's exchange with Jean-Pierre Changeux, *What Makes Us Think?* (2000). In this dialogue, Ricoeur refers to the phenomeno-logical distinction between the body as object and the body as experienced, and he contrasts the phenomenological notion of the body to the scientific percep-tion of the body as object. The body concept Ricoeur refers to in *What Makes Us Think?* is not analyzed here, because he does not develop other philosophical perspectives on the body than the ones referred to in his earlier works.

[6] Ricoeur mainly mentions works from the 1970s by Amelie Rorty, John Perry, Sidney Shoemaker, and Bernard Williams; see note 19 in Ricoeur, 1992, pp. 128–29.

[7] Ricoeur translates the German *Leib* and *Körper* into French as respectively *chair* and *corps*. In the English translation, Kathleen Blamey speaks of "flesh" and "body." Even though the German *Leib* is commonly translated into English as "lived body," we will hold on to the terminology of the English translation in *Oneself as Another*.

[8] For the English translation of this passage, see: Ricoeur, 1992, p. 324.

[9] Especially in his late works Ricoeur explicitly reflects on political philosophical themes such as recognition and justice (Ricoeur, 2000, 2005, 2007).

Chapter 11

Thing Hermeneutics

David M. Kaplan

Neither Gadamer nor Ricoeur has anything original to say about technology. Gadamer affirms the familiar critique of technology as a form of dehumanizing, calculating rationality without adding much to it. Ricoeur sometimes characterizes technology as tool-usage, sometimes as a technique, and sometimes as a pernicious rationality that objectifies and homogenizes humanity. Neither is known for his work on technology; both rely heavily on the works of Heidegger and Marcuse. Yet, this reliance on others is unfortunate. Hermeneutic philosophies are quite helpful in addressing questions concerning technology—but only when technology is understood in the ordinary sense, not as a transcendental theory of technological experience. Recent philosophy of technology has taken a turn away from over-arching theories of rationality toward a more empirical examination of ordinary things in their actual-use contexts. The hermeneutic theories for Gadamer and Ricoeur are well-suited for this "empirical turn," given their orientation to particulars, to history, and to practice. They each have bearing on precisely what matters to a philosophy of technology: the meaning and nature of artifacts, the kind of reasoning relevant to their use, and how they mediate experience and self-understanding. Arguably, this attempt to construct a *thing hermeneutics* violates the very humanist spirit that animates the works of Gadamer and Ricoeur, but such is the fate of writing: texts can be interpreted in ways their authors never imagined (or even wished). The trick is to show the relevance of hermeneutics to the current issues in the philosophy of technology while, at the same time, respecting the integrity of their respective projects.

Old and New Philosophy of Technology

Old philosophy of technology is transcendental (in the Kantian, not phenomenological, sense). It lays out the conditions for technology, typically a form of rationality or social order (Marcuse, Ellul, Jaspers), or a way of understanding being (Heidegger); (Marcuse, 1964; Ellul, 1965; Jaspers, 1951, Heidegger, 1982).

This critique of technology was crystallized in the 1940s through the 1960s, in the aftermath of the European Holocaust and the atomic bomb. Philosophers joined with other critics (like Huxley and Orwell) to call attention to the dehumanizing effects of science and technology. These critics warned of the increasing autonomy of technology and decreasing freedom of people. Sometimes technology was seen as value-neutral (means are independent of ends); sometimes it was value-laden (means connected to ends). Technology was said to drive societies, not the other way around. On these models, technology was an independent force that followed its own imperatives. Humans merely respond, adapt, and conform. Technology imposed a way of life in which everything is based on efficiency, calculation, and manipulation. Everything can be managed like a technical problem, and any problem solved with a technical solution. This bleak assessment of technology is now commonplace in science fiction films, where future worlds are depicted as completely mechanized, rigidly ordered, and dehumanized. Everything in these future worlds is either technology or treated like technology; everything is uniform, homogenous, and part of a machinelike whole. The literary sci-fi future is meant to call attention to how our world is increasingly controlled by soulless, anonymous, technical forces.

The problem with transcendental theories of technology is they treat human-made things as if they are radically different from other socially constructed realities—like cultures, laws, and sports. This view takes the technical qualities of things to be their most important characteristic, and they overlook the obvious fact that if something is made and used by human beings then it cannot help but reflect human ends, values, and ideas. Technology cannot be value-neutral because people are not value-neutral; technology cannot determine history because it never is so independent from society to be in a position to cause it; and technology cannot be entirely good or bad because society is not entirely good or bad. Things can be neither entirely free from ends nor entirely shaped by a dominant end. Things are always open to interpretation: meanings vary by context and by observer. Often, users transform the meanings and uses of devices in spite of the designer's intentions (e.g., any media technology used for pornography). Meanings and uses are, therefore, relative, not fixed. Transcendental theories cannot make sense of these realities. They oversimplify. They define things entirely by their technical characteristics. They mistake the part for the whole. Ironically, transcendental theories take us so far away from ordinary things that it is not clear whether they are even about artifacts and machines at all.[1]

The advantage of viewing technology as a social construction is that it calls attention to how people, technologies, and environments are bound up together in relationships of mutual constitution. Humans and nonhumans fit together like pieces of a puzzle. Our identities are bound up together so much so that the story of one always involves the story of the other. Bruno Latour calls this phenomenon "imbroglios of humans and non-humans." People and machines exist together in what he calls "socio-technical collectives" (Latour, 1999, pp. 175–215). The virtue of constructivist theories is that they broaden our appreciation of how things function, how they figure into our lives, and how we influence one another. Things have (possibly universalizable) technical functions, to be sure, but they also have social meaning, historical significance, and an aesthetic dimension embodied into the materiality of things. That is to say, meaning is inherent in materials. Once we grant that the technical and social aspects of things are bound up together, we are less likely to treat technology as merely a form of rationality or technique. Philosophers today eschew these transcendental approaches. Glance at any recent program of the Society for Philosophy and Technology (www.spt.org) and you will scarcely find a mention of Heidegger or Marcuse. Instead you will see papers on converging and enhancement technologies, engineering ethics, design theory, and other topics, practical and political. Contemporary philosophy of technology is more normative than metaphysical. It is more concerned with technologies than technology as such.

Gadamer's Actual and Potential
Philosophy of Technology

Gadamer's criticism of the objectifications of the natural sciences as inappropriate for the human sciences is well known, and it is developed in tremendous detail in *Truth and Method*. But his references to technology are less common, aside from oblique references to applied science and the pairing of science-technology, as if they were indistinguishable from one another. One exception is his article, "What is Practice? The Conditions of Social Reason," in *Reason in the Age of Science*, where we find Gadamer waxing Heideggerian—and surprisingly Marcusean—about technological rationality. Gadamer begins this piece by (predictably) relating technology to modern science as the application of an abstract form of instrumental knowledge. Whereas premodern science was based on the "experienceable and familiar totality of our world," modern science has turned into a knowledge of "manipulable relationships by means of isolating experimentation" (Gadamer, 1981a, p. 70).[2] Technology (or rather, "the hour of technology") has arrived as a result of this understanding of science, which turns nature into an artificial construction.

> The ideal of construction implicit in the scientific concept of mechanics has become an arm prolonged to monstrous proportions. This has made possible the nature of our machines, our transformation of nature, and our outreach into space. (Ibid., pp. 70–71)

There are two consequences of the modern conjunction between "methodological construction" and "technological production." First, unlike premodern technology, which served the interests of its users, in contemporary societies "what has been artificially produced sets the new terms as consumer-awakening and need-stimulating industry is built up around us" (ibid., p. 71). That is to say, societies driven by technological growth reverse the relations of (technical) means and (human) ends. Now, our ends are driven by technology, not the other way around. Second, what is increasingly pervasive in this "ever more artificial world" is a "loss of flexibility."

> Whoever makes use of technology . . . entrusts himself to its functioning. It is by means of a primary renunciation of freedom in relation to one's own overall ability to act that one has come into the enjoyment of these astonishing comforts and enlargements of wealth that modern technology makes available to us. (Ibid.)

Unfortunately, it is not clear who—if anyone—benefits from these achievements. The crisis of our civilization is the eclipse of practical reason by expertise. Thanks to technical expertise that was once reserved for the mastery of nature but is now dedicated to the mastery of social life, modern societies are being determined by technology. The very fate of society is now handed over to the experts.

> This is the ideal of a technocratic society, in which one has recourse to the expert and looks to him for the discharging of the practical, political, and economic decisions one needs to make. Now the expert is an indispensable figure in the technical mastery of processes. (Ibid., p. 72)

Obviously, no experts can reasonably fulfill the expectation placed on them to manage society. Yet, the more we rely on experts for matters of basic self-governance, the more our ability to think and act practically and creatively degenerates. The main culprit is the mass media. The "technologizing of the formation of public opinion" is the most pernicious "technical penetration of society," which leads to "a more powerful manipulation of our minds" (ibid., p. 73). The more media power is concentrated and controlled, the less capable we are of independent thought.

> The individual in society who feels dependent and helpless in the face of its technically mediated life forms becomes incapable of establishing an identity. This has a profound social effect. Here lies the greatest danger under which our civilization stands: the elevation of adaptive qualities to privileged status. (Ibid.)

Social reason is replaced by social irrationality, creative thinking by conformity.

In another sustained analysis of technology, Gadamer again contrasts the technical knowledge of scientists and experts with the practical knowledge relevant to political life and humanities (Gadamer, 1996).[3] The argument is similar. Our present age is said to be characterized by the "scientific-technical mastery of nature"; the "artificial transformation of our environment" has lead to the "totalization of technical civilization"; the specialization and "business of research" has led to a "deluge of knowledge" and "loss of the whole," in which researchers "find themselves in need of orientation" and laypersons are "dependent on the correct functioning of technology"; and as "more areas of human life are subjected to technical domination," individual and group decision making is increasingly replaced by "rational automata" (ibid., pp. 6–8). Scientific-technical expertise is in tension with both inherent social practices and the very conditions that allow us to learn. As Gadamer inelegantly puts it: "The more strongly the sphere of application becomes rationalized, the more does proper exercise of judgment along with practical experience in the proper sense of the term fail to take place" (ibid., p. 17). In other words, science and technology are in conflict with human values.

If someone were to read these quotes passages to you, would you be able to tell they were written by Gadamer? Or would you guess someone else, such as Marcuse, Jaspers, or Horkheimer? There really is very little there that is unique to Gadamer, which is precisely why people do not read him for insights into technology. But they should. Although his actual take on technology is not very interesting, what his hermeneutic philosophy contributes to the conversation is. But only if technology is understood in the ordinary sense as something human-made, not in the transcendental sense of technical rationality. Three aspects of Gadamer's hermeneutics are particularly helpful for making sense of technology: interpretation, practical reason, and play.

First is the interpretive character of understanding. Reason, for Gadamer, is always tied to history, tradition, and prejudice. We "belong" to history and to our traditions prior to experience. They affect and influence us, shaping our prejudices. This is Gadamer's famous rehabilitation of authority and tradition: historically inherited prejudices are not obstacles, but conditions of understanding. Appropriate prejudices (from authority) produce truth and lets us understand; inappropriate prejudices (from over-hastiness) produce misunderstanding. History is effective, according to Gadamer. It determines both scientific and social understanding. The hermeneutic circle describes how we are always in a situation and never outside it. Our knowledge is never complete but, rather, partial and perspectival (Gadamer, 1989, pp. 267–305).

The role of interpretation in our experience with things should be patent. Any technology is open to interpretation. We encounter things in their particularity: with respect to particular uses, ends, and meanings. Historians and sociologists of technology have no shortage of examples of the contingent character of artifacts. Weibe Bijker's oft-cited analysis of Penny Farthing bicycles, for example, argues that social forces influence the design of artifacts more than technical imperatives. Bijker explains how the large front wheels of old-time bicycles were designed to be fast, dangerous, and showy for young, typically well-off men, who used them for sport and to signify their wealth and courage. By contrast, Safety Bicycles (chain driven, same-sized wheels) were designed for stability and security, with women users and urban settings in mind. One was designed for sport, the other for transportation. The eventual triumph of safety bicycles had nothing to do with (putatively necessary) technical superiority, but rather changing values and (contingent) social circumstances. Bijker's analysis shows technology, like any other constructed reality, to be shot through with social meaning (Bijker, 1995). When viewed historically, technology is clearly a matter of interpretation. Ironically, sociologists and historians analyze technology much more hermeneutically than even hermeneutic philosophers do.[4]

Gadamer's contribution is to provide a framework that describes what happens when sociologists and historians interpret artifacts. Hermeneutics can also account for notions of truth and objectivity in light of our historical situation. Hermeneutics claims universality: *all* understanding is language-bound, tied to a particular preunderstanding. Language is the *universal* medium in which understanding occurs. This interplay of universal and particular is lost on less subtle social constructionist theories of knowledge.[5]

Second is a theory of practical reason. Every interpretation, according to Gadamer, is a new *application* of understanding. We apply prejudices (and test them) by relating them to the present situation. Hermeneutics is an activity of applying knowledge, much like Aristotle's ethics: it is about knowing what to do in particular situations. And like ethical knowledge, understanding is learned, inculcated, and cultivated. It is closer to *techne* than *episteme*, more like *phronesis* than *sophia*. It requires social tact to know how to do it. And it takes practice (Gadamer, 1989, pp. 355–82). Hermeneutics *is* a practice, with both theoretical and practical meanings. As theoretical, it means interpretation, explication, and applied knowledge. As practical, it means reasonableness in making concrete decisions. Gadamer explains that "practice is conducting oneself and acting in solidarity. Solidarity, however, is the decisive condition and basis of all social reason" (Gadamer, 1981a, p. 87). In other words, our prior belonging to history together affects the character of experience and action (Gadamer, 1981b).

The design, development, use, and administration of artifacts is also a branch of applied knowledge: we learn how to act (with things) and what to do (with things) in particular situations. Technology is bound up with, not opposed to, practice—precisely the opposite of what Gadamer would have us believe. Philosophers today are well aware of this practical dimension of technology. For example, a research program at the University of Twente (The Netherlands) is devoted to examining the relationship between contemporary technologies and quality of life. Although references to Gadamer are scarce (compared to Heidegger and Aristotle), this project analyzes how artifacts impact daily life in terms of nonliberal normative frameworks, such as happiness and the good life (Brey et al., forthcoming). Another example is the research on "soft impacts" of technology on culture, ethics, and politics. Unlike "hard impacts" of safety, health, and environment, soft impacts are nonquantifiable and controversial, yet no less vital to responsible technological development. These wider concerns are evaluated on the basis of practical reason: interpretation, judgment, and practice.[6] Without knowing it, these research programs are doing something like a hermeneutic technology assessment. The key theme is appropriateness: the making and using of things should be appropriate, suitable, and fitting. Finding that fit is the art of practical reason.

What is this sense of appropriateness? For Gadamer it is "tact." It is a particular kind of social sensitivity to social situations and the judgment of how to behave in them. Tact is the tacit knowledge of appropriate action for a particular circumstance. It involves knowing what to say and do—and what not to say and do. Although not based on general principles or universal concepts, Gadamer maintains tact is a universal sense that requires of all that we remain both sensitive to particular situations, guided by the wisdom of the past, yet open to other points of view. Although it is difficult to prove any matter of tact conclusively, it is not an irrational concept; it is merely an acquired ability. How does one acquire it? Through education in culture, development, and self-cultivation in society. That is to say, *Bildung*. The only way to acquire interpretive tact is through practice. This connection between tact and practical wisdom has completely dropped out of the contemporary conversation of technology. But what is largely at issue in questions concerning the good life in a technological age is this notion of appropriateness in conduct. Technology is shot through with tact. It answers key questions, such as how things ought to be designed, how they should be used, how they should affect others, how they should be governed. Tact may not provide a precise answer to any of these questions, but if universalist and scientific concepts are ruled out (or not exclusively employed) then all that is left is practical wisdom, developed over time, through *Bildung*. After Gadamer, the notion of "appropriate technology" takes on a whole new dimension. New answers might be found to vexing practical questions concerning technology.

Third is the notion of play. Gadamer's phenomenology of play forms the basis for his analyses of history and language. It establishes the mode of being of the work of art and of the artwork-viewer relationship. Play, on Gadamer's reading, is serious. It only reaches presentation through the players if they lose themselves. Play has primacy over the consciousness of the player. The game itself masters the players and has its own spirit, which one enters into but never controls. In a theatrical play, players play roles as if in a game. In being played, the play speaks to the spectator through its presentation. In being interpreted, the work cannot be isolated from the conditions in which it appears. Part of the event of being occurs in presentation. Gadamer calls this the "non-differentiation" of work and interpretation: no independent subjects and no uninterpreted objects. Interpretation does not stand out apart from its object. It should fit. When an interpreter interprets, he or she is being interpreted—just as a player in a game is being played. The interpreter is affected, influenced, and transformed by the object (Gadamer, 1989, pp. 102–30).

There are echoes of Gadamer in contemporary analyses of technology and embodiment. Recent phenomenological studies of technology take tool usage as a fundamental, eidetic structure of human-technology relations. They typically rely on Heidegger's analysis of "worldhood" in BEING AND TIME (where things are encountered as equipment, not mere objects), and Merleau-Ponty's analysis of the "lived body" (where our bodies mediate our experience of the world). Don Ihde, for example, argues that in embodied experience of technology, artifacts "withdraw" and are "absorbed" into our activity, just as our activity is mediated by the artifact. In place of a single essence, a phenomenology of artifacts reveals different forms of experience of technology and the subtle ways in which technologies mediate our lives (Ihde, 1990, 2010). Peter-Paul Verbeek follows Ihde by examining the mediating role of material things for perception and action. Humans and things "co-shape" one another; neither is intelligible without reference to the other. Even the intentionality of consciousness and human freedom are joint products of humans and artifacts (Verbeek, 2005). And for many years Hubert Dreyfus has marshaled Heidegger and Merleau-Ponty in defense of an embodied understanding of human action against the claims of computer designers to have developed artificial intelligence and thinking machines. He argues that computers will never be able to equal (much less exceed) human intelligence because they do not think the way we do. People know through practice and experience based on our bodily capacity for understanding contextual meaning (Dreyfus, 1992). What all these thinkers of embodiment and technology share is the conviction that some kinds of knowledge and experience can be attained only through participation with things.

Gadamer's description of the kind of absorption and loss of self in game playing harmonizes with these phenomenological accounts of embodied experience. He is, at very least, a kindred spirit in these conversations. But hermeneutics does more than merely jibe with phenomenology and existentialism. It can add a dimension they lack, namely an internal relationship between the experience of involvement and the concepts of play, history, language. The crucial difference between hermeneutics and embodiment phenomenologies is that the experience of belonging, for Gadamer, is articulate. This experience can be brought to language. Play, for example, is not only about the experience of participation, but about *the play*. It detaches from players to become repeatable and permanent as a work. It achieves ideality intended and understood as play. This transformation is total; the new form lasts long after the original event passes. This pattern is repeated with history and language: the event passes, and the meaning remains. We belong to history, and we can be conscious of history's effects; we participate in dialogue, and things come to truth in language. Neither history nor truth is a possession but, like a game, it happens in us when we lose ourselves in language. Dialogue is the prime example of linguistic mediation between people and between language and the world. The very history we belong to enables understanding precisely because of the solidarity with others that enables and sustains it. This link between play and truth might be the most important contribution of hermeneutics to philosophy of technology. Our involvement with things does indeed absorb us, but the experience is no more or less enigmatic than linguistic experience. The meaning of such encounters with things and uses of tools is not merely a function of embodiment and practical know-how, but a matter that can be interpreted in the manner of a text, informed by the social consensus that always precedes us.

Ricoeur's Actual and Potential Philosophy of Technology

Ricoeur discussed technology on several occasions over his 70-year career, but never in a sustained way. His take on technology is not at all consistent. Sometimes he analyzes it in terms of tool usage; other times as a value-neutral and instrumental form of reason; still other times as a form of ideology that serves dominant group interests.

For example, in *Freedom and Nature* Ricoeur briefly discusses tools and instruments in his analysis of the role of the body in voluntary actions. He wants to distinguish the way we "use" our bodies from the way we use tools. The difference is the body is the "organ" of action, whereas an instrument is outside the body. It merely "prolongs" the organ. An instrument "represents a material rather than an organic mediation between myself and the action produced" (Ricoeur, 1966, p. 213). A technical, "artificial action" is work done with instruments. The "organ-plus-tool" relationship complicates the relationship between the will and the "pragma" (what is to be done by me). Unlike the simple "organ-pragma" relationship, the "organ-tool-pragma" relationship is not only internal and voluntary but also external and physical. On one hand, the tool is incorporated into action and extends it as an "organic mediator." One's attention is focused on the pragma, not on "the indivisible pair of organ and tool seen as an extension of the organ" (ibid.). On the other hand, the tool is entirely in the world, functioning like a natural force subject to the laws of physics. "The physical, industrial character of the relation of tool to work absorbs the organic character of man to the tool" (ibid.). The will-organ-tool-work relation is ambiguous because it can be read in two directions: from the will (and point of view of phenomenology) or the work (and the point of view of physics). The tool is "the point in which these two interpretations meet" (ibid.). A phenomenology of tool use reaches its limits in the objective characteristics of artifacts, which can only be explained in the manner of a thing not understood in the manner of experience. On Ricoeur's account, technology is a neutral means that extends, but does not modify, the will.

Elsewhere, he argues that neutral techniques of reason, not instruments, are the essence of technology. Artifacts and machines and the "technicity" they embody are mere means to an end. Ricoeur echoes Heidegger and includes skills, knowledge, and technique in general as forms of technicity. In *History and Truth*, for example, he writes: "The technical world of material tools and their extension into machines is not the whole of man's instrumental world. Knowledge is also a tool or instrument. . . . Knowledge becomes stratified, deposits of knowledge accumulate like tools and the worlds which result from them" (Ricoeur, 1965, p. 83). Ricoeur gives an instrumental—almost Deweyan reading—to Husserl's notion of "sedimentation." The quest for knowledge is like a "technical pursuit" that uses the acquired knowledge of the past "as a tool or instrument" to carry history forward (ibid.). For this reason we can speak of "technological revolutions" that propel societies forward, regardless of their particular cultures and traditions. The resulting "world-wide technics" helps developing nations "approach cosmopolitanism" (ibid., p. 272). Technology, on this reading, is the neutral instrument of historical progress. "It would be absurd to condemn machines, technocracy, administrative apparatus, social security, etc. Technical procedures and, in general, all 'technicity,' have the innocence of the instrument" (ibid., p. 107).

Elsewhere in *History and Truth*, though, Ricoeur warns about the dehumanizing effects of scientific-technological progress. Neutral, instrumental reason is homogenizing. For every advancement it brings about, it "at the same time constitutes a sort of subtle destruction . . . of the ethical and mythical nucleus of mankind" (ibid., p. 276). The kind of world civilization we are creating is "mediocre civilization" that is "wearing away" at the cultural resources of the "truly great civilizations of the world" by creating a uniform, standardized culture. Ricoeur notes that "everywhere throughout the world, one finds the same bad movies, the same slot machines, the same plastic or aluminum atrocities, the same twisting of language by propaganda, etc." (ibid., pp. 274–76). The triumph of such a conformist consumer culture, where everything is identical and everyone anonymous, would "represent the lowest degree of creative culture" and a danger "at least equal and perhaps more likely than that of atomic destruction" (ibid., p. 278). Sounds a lot like Marcuse.

I argue elsewhere that Ricoeur's work is relevant for the current philosophical conversation on technology in spite of his uninspired analysis of the subject (Kaplan, 2007). To continue this line of argument, three additional aspects of his work further contribute to a philosophy of technology: capabilities, testimony, and narration.

First is the notion of human capability or *l'homme capable*, what Ricoeur has called the "thin but continuous thread" running through his work and "the cornerstone of philosophical anthropology" (Ricoeur, 2002, p. 280). He analyzes our capabilities indirectly, through the ways the verb "I can" is modified and realized in the ways *I can speak, I can act, I can tell a story, I can be responsible*, and *I can remember*. By analyzing how these verbs can be imputed to individuals (and sometimes groups), we can trace out the contours of a subject to whom various predicates are attributed. Ricoeur notes our capabilities are always bound by limits that both enable and constrain us. In *Freedom and Nature*, our will is said to be limited internally (by the body) and externally (by the world).

In *The Course of Recognition*, Ricoeur argues that we have rights to capabilities, that these rights are bound up with social practices, and that capabilities imply responsibilities. Our capabilities are social and moral. They are also linked with a litany of constitutive forces: our bodies, the unconscious, language, memory, laws, institutions, and more. Yet, our capabilities are also fragile and fallible: we are not only capable, but incapable. We not only act, we suffer. Ricoeur calls it the "paradox of autonomy and vulnerability." "It is the same human being who is both of these things from different points of view. What is more, not simply opposed to each other, our two terms go together: the autonomy in question is that of a fragile, vulnerable being" (Ricoeur, 2007, p. 73). Our vulnerabilities are also tied to a litany of constitutive forces. Most are historic and contingent; some are universal and noncontingent. *L'homme capable* is, at the same time, *l'homme vulnérable* (Kaplan, 2010).

Although the relationship among capability, vulnerability, and technology seems rather obvious, philosophers only very recently have made the connection.[7] The intuition is that technology plays a vital role in expanding or hindering desired states (or "functionings," to use Sen's term) and capabilities (to attain valued functionings) (Sen, 1999). Technology also might create or eliminate barriers so people might realize freedoms. The capabilities approach in development ethics is well-suited to analyze how technology and innovation can improve the lives and alleviate the suffering of the poor. Ricoeur's contribution to this issue is twofold: (1) an expanded notion of capabilities (that far out-strips those proposed by either Sen or Martha Nussbaum [Nussbaum, 2001]); and (2) the pairing of capabilities with vulnerabilities. The task for technology development policy is not only to enhance capabilities but also to eliminate as many contingent, nonessential vulnerabilities as possible. If technological development policy is to succeed in contributing to the realization of capabilities and protection of vulnerabilities, it should take as its objectives to:

- enable user control and independence, rather than dependence;
- fit in appropriately with the values and political-economies of particular nations or groups;
- foster technical knowledge of, and participation in, technical infrastructures;
- employ a technological precautionary principle that requires development projects to be revisable and reversible;
- work to develop and support international political and regulatory authorities to foster technical independence in nations and protect underdeveloped nations from the depredations and policies of developed nations.

Arguably, we have a right to *techne*: the right to participate in technical processes; being able to choose, use, design, make, repair, and enjoy technical artifacts; the right not be made vulnerable, helpless, or unfree as a result of artifacts or technology policy. A richer notion of capabilities and vulnerabilities might help make this case.

Second is testimony. When I attest to something, I not only *believe that* but I also *believe in* something. It is both a statement of knowledge and certainty and a statement of confidence and conviction. There are two sides to a testimony: the assertion of truth of a reported event, and the presumed trustworthiness of one's experience. Only in a testimony is the "assertion of reality . . . inseparable from its being paired with the self-designation of the testifying subject" (Ricoeur, 2004, p. 163). When I testify, I commit myself and impute myself. I exist in my words when I ask that you *believe in* me. That is not to say the accreditation of testimony is arbitrary. One can always challenge the trustworthiness of a testimony, compare it to testimonies of others, and measure the reliability—the steadfastness—of the witness. The concept of attestation is crucial for moral, political, and legal judgments, where discourses are rational (even defeasible) but lacking the kind of verification available to the natural sciences. Even the study of history depends on testimony in the establishment of historical facts. One's (often unverifiable) experience is written down, archived, and later used as evidence by a historian. Without the concept of testimony we cannot fully make sense of who we are as individuals or groups.

The connection between testimony and technology might seem remote—especially in light of Ricoeur's technology-unfriendly Kantian conviction that one attests to persons but verifies things. There are, however, several ways in which attestation is vital to understanding technology. One is technology assessment for the sake of identifying existing and probable impacts of technological application. For example, some US regulatory agencies, such as the Food and Drug Administration, the Environmental Protection Agency, and the Federal Trade Commission, undertake technology assessments. The European parliament established its technology assessment office in 1990, modeled after the short-lived US Congressional Office of Technology Assessment (1974–95). The goal of these offices is to provide, for the sake of policy decisions, impartial information on the actual or possible social, economic, and environmental impact of new and emerging sciences and technologies. Technology assessment of this kind typically involves forecasting, economic analysis, systems analysis, risk assessment, and other methods that strive for objectivity. But assessments often also incorporate the testimonies of persons affected.

For example, the testimonies of victims of hazardous waste exposure near Love Canal, in western New York State, played a key role in eventual environmental policy changes (Newman, 2001). Often, in hazard assessments, vulnerable, disenfranchised individuals and communities have no other recourse to redress questions concerning environmental justice except their testimonies. For those lacking the resources to mobilize legal and scientific defenses, the validity of attestation is crucial. By simply telling their stories, individuals and groups can call attention to the ways in which a technological system affects users, environments, and communities. Often, such stories are effective in raising public awareness of a risk or hazard and play key roles in public hearings and civil lawsuits. It is often the only way for powerless people to have their voices heard and to contribute to the assessment of technological systems (Figueroa, 2006).

Third is narration. Ricoeur claims narratives capture the temporal, historical, and moral character of human experience better than any other epistemic or normative framework. The basic unit of a narrative is a plot, which unifies into a coherent unity the elements of a story—including the reasons, motives, and actions of characters, events, accidents, and circumstances. A plot synthesizes actions, events, and, ultimately, time into a unified whole that says something new and different than the sum of its parts. The thesis of *Time and Narrative* is that connection exists between the temporal character of human experience and the act of narrating a story. Temporal experience is expressed in the form of a narrative, which is able to reflect our social reality because it expresses temporal experience. A narrative creates the most comprehensive interpretation possible by synthesizing diverse plot elements into a meaningful story. Nonfiction relates events as they actually happened, fiction *as if* they happened. The central insight of narrative theory is that we interpret and evaluate the world through telling and reading stories (Ricoeur, 1984–88).

By the 1990s, narrative models became commonplace throughout the humanities and social sciences. But the "narrative turn" has had little effect on the philosophy of technology—and for good reason. Narrative theories are prejudiced in favor of persons over things. According to Ricoeur, only persons get have their stories told; mere things get explanations. Nonhumans, natural events, and artifacts are never the subject of their own stories but are often at best props or circumstances to be dealt with. As a result, the turn to narrative has not been used to examine the philosophical dimensions of technology.

But, in fact, narratives and technologies are not inimical. Stories about technologies do indeed exist. Turn on the television and you can easily find a documentary on a technology (usually a history-changing device or war machinery), or browse the shelves at a bookstore and find "microhistories" of various artifacts, significant and mundane. Historians, sociologists, anthropologists, and psychologists readily make use of narratives in their respective approaches to technology. Clearly human-made things are perfectly capable of being understood in terms of narratives; only the philosophers have been slow to recognize it. Something is amiss in narrative theory when it treats artifacts as incapable of narration; and something is missing in the philosophy of technology when it fails to avail itself of the methods and models of narrative theory. But if the bold premise of narrative theory is true—that *everything* has a story, *everything* a history, and *anything* that can be recounted can be explained in terms of a narrative and understood like a story—then there must be a way to make sense of how we narrate things. And Ricoeur must be wrong, for it is indeed possible for narratives to do what he says they cannot do: tell the story of things.

Sherry Turkle's work, *Evocative Objects*, is an example of how narratives of technology may call attention to otherwise hidden aspects of human-technology relations (Turkle, 2007). Edward Tenner's work, *Why Things Bite Back*, chronicles the unintended consequences of things by telling little known stories of the ranging effects of things (Tenner, 1997). Narrative theory—disabused of its humanist prejudices—can provide the theoretical foundations to make sense of these and other stories of artifacts. Different plots, tropes, and themes have the potential to shape our conceptual understanding and influence the political debates about technology. These stories pattern the way we think about and relate to technologies. Getting the story right—or disabusing our belief in misguided stories—can have lasting, even irreversible consequences. A profitable research project might be to analyze to ways in which stories and rhetorical devices have been used to shape popular opinion of technology and to drive policy making. We then might have a better understanding of what kind of work various stories do for us.

Thing Hermeneutics in Gadamer and Ricoeur

Of the two, I find Ricoeur to be more helpful when it comes to questions concerning technology. Gadamer's version of hermeneutics is transcendental. It analyzes what happens whenever we understand—anything. If Gadamer is right, then hermeneutics would, of course, be relevant to questions concerning technology. Artifacts and machines should pose no more, or fewer, problems than any other matter of interpretation. They should be capable of being understood in language, just like anything else. The question is whether philosophical hermeneutics is as exhaustive as Gadamer claims it to be. Does it obviate a phenomenology of human-technology relations? Does it account for the role of technology in the enrichment of human capabilities? Is an interpretation really the same as a narrative? The answer to each is, no: there is more to say about technology than that it is the play of history and language.

Ricoeur's work has always been more science and technology friendly—more amenable to the very things Gadamer worries are inimical to (or at least derivative of) hermeneutic experience. Throughout his career Ricoeur has incorporated various non-hermeneutic forms of knowledge into a general theory of interpretation, including methodological explanation, intentionality analysis, structuralist linguistics, and universal pragmatics. Each theoretical approach supplements hermeneutics. As a result, Ricoeur has more to offer because there is more to his work than simply a theory of the operation of understanding. There are more parts to work with—and we need these parts to analyze the countless ways technology figures in our lives. Minimally, a philosophy of technology needs theories of interpretation, practical reason, and history. Ideally, it would also have at its disposal a richer set of theoretical resources in order to answer the vexing questions posed by technology in our time: "how should things be designed?"; "how does technology affect social change?"; and "what role should citizens have in technical decisions?" Hermeneutics offers capable responses to these questions, provided it is conceived broadly to include capabilities, testimony, and narration. That is to say, more like Ricoeur's version than Gadamer's.

Notes

1. For a description of the empirical turn in philosophy of technology, see Achterhuis, 2001, pp. 1–9.
2. This chapter first appeared in German in 1977.
3. This first appeared in German in 1972 and in English in 1977.
4. For more examples of the socio-historical dimension to technical change, see Bijker et al., 1994; Oudshoorn et al., 2005; Oldenziel, 2004.
5. For example, the "strong programme" in the sociology of scientific knowledge claims all knowledge is intrinsically historical and social. See Bloor, 1976.
6. See "Responsible Innovation in Food Technology: About the Intricate Web of Soft Impacts (Ir)responsibilities, and Mutual Lack of Trust," a research project, led by Tsjalling Swierstra and Hedwig te Molder, funded by the Netherlands Organization for Scientific Research. (www.ethicsandtechnology.eu/research/projects/).
7. See, for example, the Dutch research program entitled, "Technology and Human Development: A Capability Approach," www.ethicsandtechnology.eu/research/projects/. See also Selinger, 2008.

Chapter 12

Gadamer's Philosophical Hermeneutics and New Confucianism

Kathleen Wright

A daring hypothesis: There is no major Western philosopher as close to Confucius's thinking as Gadamer.

Richard E. Palmer (2006, p. 82)

The title of this chapter should really end with a question mark. Better yet, it should be a longer title and chiasmatic, something like, "Thinking About Chinese Philosophy Through Gadamer: Thinking About Gadamer Through Chinese Philosophy." It seemed at first to be a welcome coincidence that some thinkers concerned with East Asia—thinkers within and outside China, including in the West—were drawn to Hans-Georg Gadamer's *Truth and Method* (Gadamer, 2006) at the same time as I was seeking to broaden my understanding of Chinese philosophy. I found myself then in considerable agreement with, for example, Steve van Zoeren, an East Asian scholar of reading, exegesis, and hermeneutics in traditional China, when he expressed his debt to Gadamer in the following words: "Although Gadamer writes from a Eurocentric perspective, his work has rich implications for those engaged in the study of culturally or historically remote works, and this study has been influenced and in a sense inspired by his insights" (Van Zoeren, 1991, pp. 5f.). So, too, I was heartened to read Rudolf G. Wagner's acknowledgement at the start of the first of his three books on Wang Bi (226–49) and Laozi, that he had learned so much from studying hermeneutics with Hans-Georg Gadamer (Wagner, 2000, pp. 1f.). These two scholars, who work closely with different kinds of texts (Confucian and Daoist) and problems (reading, exegesis, and commentary), gave me reason to believe that thinking about Chinese philosophy through Gadamer would broaden for me the way to Chinese philosophy.

However, I encountered other scholars concerned with East Asia—also within and outside China, including in the West—and also writing about Chinese philosophy through Gadamer, whose reception of Gadamer's philosophical hermeneutics was different from what I expected. It came as a real shock to find

Benjamin A. Elman, a professor of East Asian Studies and History at Princeton University, targeting Gadamer specifically for fostering the political ambitions of something called New Confucianism:

> [M]any "borderland" [Taiwan, Hong Kong, Singapore, South Korea, and Vietnam] students of Chinese philosophy increasingly rally around Gadamer's profound cultural conservatism as the means to reinvent China's classical hermeneutics . . . as the basis of the post-socialist future of New Confucianism. (Elman, 2002, p. 544)[1]

Some readers of Gadamer, I grant, might agree with Elman's characterization of Gadamer's position as "profound cultural conservatism" and not find this statement as exaggerated as I do. However, I think most readers of Gadamer would be as surprised as I was to find Gadamer being singled out as primarily responsible for the post-socialist aspirations of something called New Confucianism. What, I began to ask, was New Confucianism?

John Makeham has edited and contributed to a very helpful volume of essays entitled *New Confucianism: A Critical Examination*. In it, he starts with a relatively noncontroversial definition of New Confucianism. (Here and in the remainder of the chapter, my quotations will be of greater length in those cases where I presume less familiarity on the part of my readers with the sources I am using.) Makeham writes:

> Contemporary New Confucianism (*dangdai xin Rujia; dangdai xin Ruxue; xiandai xin Rujia; xiandai xin Ruxue*, hereafter New Confucianism) is a movement promoted and/or researched by prominent Chinese intellectuals based in China, Taiwan, Hong Kong, and the United States of America. (In English, the term "New Confucian" is to be distinguished from "Neo-Confucian," which refers to certain Confucian thinkers of the Song, Yuan, and Ming dynasties, in particular.) New Confucianism has emerged as a neo-conservative philosophical movement, with religious overtones, which claims to be the legitimate transmitter and representative of orthodox Confucian values. (Makeham, 2003, pp. 1f.)

Upon encountering this definition, I then began to wonder how Gadamer's philosophical hermeneutics could have become joined with New Confucianism. Elman specifically mentions Liu Shuxian and On-Cho Ng and their use of Gadamer when he criticizes Gadamer in relation to New Confucianism. In this chapter, I will argue that On-Cho Ng's teacher, the New Confucian philosopher, Chung-ying Cheng[2] of the University of Hawai'i at Manoa, plays the central role in the story about how Gadamer has come to be associated with the neoconservative Chinese philosophical movement called New Confucianism. Richard E. Palmer also plays a key role in the story that links Gadamer to New Confucianism. There are, however, two sides to this story. The first, told by Palmer, sets out to establish a link between Gadamer and a Confucius that is read through the

Analects. The second, told by Cheng, tells a tale about how the effective history of Gadamer's philosophical hermeneutics leads to his "onto-hermeneutics," a specifically Chinese form of philosophical hermeneutics that aspires to become not just one "world philosophy" but the one and only "world philosophy" (Cheng, 2006, p. 33).[3] Cheng, in contrast to Palmer, reads Confucius through the *Yijing* (the *Book of Changes*). After some background remarks about the meaning of the term "Chinese philosophy" in section one, I shall turn in sections two and three to these two sides of the story.

While I started this chapter "thinking about Chinese philosophy through Gadamer," I ended it "thinking *differently* about Gadamer through Chinese philosophy." I found myself returning to Paul Ricoeur and to the question he raised in 1973 about philosophical hermeneutics in "Gadamer and the critique of ideology" (Ricoeur, 1981, pp. 63–100): "Can Gadamer's 'receptive' hermeneutics be transformed into a 'critical' hermeneutics that is able also to include the 'critique of ideology'?" Ricoeur, a Protestant raised in Catholic France, knew, like the Protestant French pastor of the village of Le Chambon[4] before him, that times will come when one is called upon not to defer to but to differ with, and even to defy, authority. When invited in 1957 to travel to the China of Mao Zedong to report on the educational advances of the new People's Republic of China, Ricoeur returned filled with good will and admiration, yet also with some nagging suspicions. Perhaps the question he asks about Gadamer's philosophical hermeneutics in 1973 appears to be so very urgent, and indeed existential, because he is asking it against the background of the Cultural Revolution (1966–1976) then taking place within China (Ricoeur, 1956a, 1956b, and 1956c).[5]

"Chinese Philosophy"

The designation, "Chinese philosophy" requires some preliminary remarks. Like others trained only in Western philosophy, I had initially assumed that "Chinese philosophy" consisted of a number of "classical" texts, the two most prominent of which were Confucius's *Analects* and Laozi's *Daodejing*. Little did I know, for example, that before there were four Confucian "Books" there were five Confucian "Classics," and that the *Analects* was not among them (Nylan, 2001; Nylan and Wilson, 2010).[6] Nor did I know the *dao* that entitled Laozi, but not Confucius, to be called a "Daoist" was also at the heart of Confucius's concerns. Moreover, I was perplexed not to find Confucius and Laozi in *Three Ways of Thought in Ancient China*, Arthur Waley's introduction to ancient Chinese philosophy, and to meet instead Mencius, Zhuangzi, and Han Fei (representing the Realists). The title and, even more so, the contents of another introduction to ancient Chinese philosophy, A. C. Graham's *Disputers of the Tao: Philosophical Argument in Ancient China*, also caught me by surprise. Like many who could not forget Michel Foucault's striking account of the "Chinese

Encyclopedia" in the preface to *The Order of Things*, I had expected to find in classical Chinese philosophy a thinking "entirely devoted to the ordering of space" and one "most deaf to temporal events" (Foucault, 1970, p. xix). Instead, in the pages of Graham's *Disputers of the Tao*, I encountered three centuries of philosophy in ancient China (500–200 B.C.) overflowing with vigorous and impassioned "philosophical argument" among many completely divergent schools of thought. The Warring States Period of Chinese history (453–221 B.C.) was, it seemed appropriately, also called the One Hundred Schools (of Thinking) Period.

Although the Warring States Period ended violently, marked by massive book burnings and wide-scale execution of scholars by the founders of the Qin Dynasty (221–206 B.C.), a syncretistic philosophy that came to be called "Confucianism" gradually proved victorious over the many divergent schools of ancient Chinese philosophy during the course of the Han Dynasty (206 B.C. to A.D. 220). Graham succinctly explains how "Confucians" from the Han Dynasty on treated their philosophical opponents differently from the way philosophers, including Confucius (551–479 B.C.) and his defender, Mencius (fourth century B.C.), did in the pre-Han, classical period:

> The Confucians . . . treat their rivals not as wholly wrong but as one-sided, an attitude that would have been inconceivable to Mencius but is already assumed by Hsün-tzu [Xunzi] . . . Since the 3rd century B.C., there had been a general shift from "You are wrong. I'm right," to "You have a narrow view. I have a wide view." (Graham, 1989, p. 378)

Instead of sharpening conflicts over philosophical differences, as was the case in ancient Chinese philosophy, Confucianists compromised. They would rank "A above B rather than eliminate B," thereby "harmonizing" the competing schools of philosophy (or most of them) into one syncretistic philosophical system (Graham, 1989, p. 378).

Foucault, writing in 1966. and (unbeknownst to himself) on the eve of the Cultural Revolution, continues to conjure up a popular Western image of China during the last 2000 years of Confucianism as static and altogether outside history, a "privileged *site* of *space*[,] . . . we see it," he says, "spread and frozen, over the entire surface of a continent surrounded by walls. Even its writing does not reproduce the fugitive flight of the voice in horizontal lines; it erects the motionless and still recognizable images of things themselves in vertical columns" (Foucault, 1970, p. xix). But, just as Foucault is wrong here about the nature of Chinese writing, so too is he blind to the different historical epochs within "Confucianism" and to the discontinuities that lie between them. As Nathan Sivin, Emeritus Professor of Chinese Culture and the History of Science at the University of Pennsylvania, says: "It is hard to think of any idea responsible for more fuzziness in writing about China than the notion that Confucianism is one thing" (Sivin, 1984, p. xiii). Let me offer a brief overview of the history of

Confucianism, taking Bryan W. Van Norden's article, "America's Encounter with Confucian Thought: Three Trends," as my starting point (Van Norden, 2004).

The first distinction to be made is between Confucianism as a state ideology and Confucianism as a philosophy. Confucian ideology has dominated eastern Asia and remained virtually unchanged for two thousand years up until the founding of the Republic of China in 1911. Confucian philosophy has a history consisting roughly of three epochs, two before 1911 and one after. The first epoch of Confucian philosophy is retrospectively identified by members of the second epoch as *ancient* or *classical Confucianism*. The thinkers in this epoch are Confucius, Mencius, and Xunzi; the epoch is said to begin with Confucius and to end approximately six hundred years later when Indian Buddhism arrives in China in the first century A.D. The second epoch of Confucian philosophy is called *Daoxue* ("the study of the way") by the Chinese and *Neo-Confucianism* by English speakers (starting in the nineteenth century). Neo-Confucianism flourished during the Song (960–1279) and the Ming (1368–1644) dynasties. Zhu Xi (1130–1200), the Cheng brothers—Cheng Yi (1033–1107) and Cheng Hao (1032–85)—Wang Yangming (1471–1529), and Wang Fuzhi (1619–92) are recognized to be the most prominent Neo-Confucian philosophers. Although the general aim of Neo-Confucian philosophy is said to be conservative, namely, to revive "classical Confucianism" and defend it (although not always entirely successfully) against the powerful influence of Buddhism, the particular Neo-Confucian philosophies constructed by these philosophers differ from each other in significant ways. Zhu Xi is widely recognized to be the most important Neo-Confucian because he completely systematized Confucianism (Chan, 1986, p. 1). In ways reminiscent of Thomas Aquinas's systematic philosophy, Zhu Xi's vision of Neo-Confucianism became the "orthodox" version and as such was tested by the state administered examinations for entry into civil service up until 1911.

The third epoch of Confucian philosophy is called *New Confucianism*, and it is the one very much with us today, albeit in (at least) two quite different forms (Makeham, 2003).[7] Van Norden explains the complicated birth of the third epoch of Confucian philosophy as a reaction to the "May Fourth Movement" (1915 to the early 1920s). This movement, he explains, "blamed traditional culture, and Confucianism in particular, for making China backward and stagnant in comparison with other nations. In order for China to modernize, [the supporters of the May Fourth Movement] argued, China had to 'Destroy the shop of Confucius.'" (Van Norden, 2004) New Confucianism, Van Norden explains, is born in order to counter the attack on Confucianism by the pro-Western adherents of the May Fourth Movement. This first stage of New Confucianism is therefore reactive and conservative, but its aim is something other than simply the revival of "traditional" Neo-Confucian philosophy. As a philosophy that originated within the Republic of China after 1911, New Confucianism is post-imperial. It is and has to be a "modern" Confucian philosophy that conserves "traditional" Confucianism (Neo-Confucianism) even as

it defends Confucianism against a modern Western philosophy that threatens
to ignore it and thereby to destroy it.

Following the founding of the People's Republic of China in 1949, the
New Confucianism associated with the Republic of China enters a new stage
when it becomes identified with Taiwan, now a "borderland," like Hong Kong,
to the People's Republic on "mainland" China. As envisioned in what is commonly called "The New Confucian Manifesto" that is published in English in
Hong Kong in January 1958 ("borderland"), New Confucianism in Hong Kong
and Taiwan continues to define itself as a "modern" Confucian philosophy
even as it distinguishes itself from the Communism of "mainland" China. The
tenets laid out for New Confucianism within this document affirm, for example,
(a) the pro-democracy belief that Confucian philosophy can be made compatible with Western science and with democracy, along with (b) the pro-national-
ist (and therefore anti-internationalist) belief that Chinese culture is different
in essential ways from the diverse cultures of the West.[8]

In his discussion of the 1958 ("borderland") "New Confucian Manifesto" in
his invited lecture at the women's college, Bryn Mawr, in 2004, Van Norden
notes two missing elements. While the manifesto rightly recognizes that "China"
should learn "Western science, technology, capitalism and democracy" from
the West, it wrongly omits "feminism and 'pluralism' in Isaiah Berlin's sense of
that word" (Van Norden, 2004) from the list of things that can be learned from
the West. According to Van Norden, the cultivation of pluralism, in particular,
is needed if ("borderland") New Confucianism is to counter the longstanding
Chinese tendency to identify Chinese culture and Confucianism too "mono-
lithically" in terms of "one specific [Neo-Confucian] orthodox legacy going
back through at least some of the Neo-Confucian philosophers (such as Wang
Yangming) to Confucius himself" (ibid.). Makeham shares this same concern:
"Equally questionable are the proprietary claims over the entire 'orthodox'
Confucian tradition . . . " (Makeham, 2003, p. 44).

The picture of New Confucianism becomes more complicated and enters
another stage when the People's Republic of China turns conservative (Gan,
1998, pp. 55, 45–66) and embraces Confucianism seven years after the death of
Mao Zedong. It first establishes the Confucius Foundation in 1983. Then, in
October of 1989, just four months after the "Massacre at Tiananmen Square"
and upon the occasion of the celebration of the 2,540th anniversary of
Confucius's birth, Gu Yu declares that Confucianism is the essence of Chinese
tradition:

> As is known to all, the idea of harmony is an important component of
> Chinese traditional culture. As early as the last years of the West Zhou dynasty
> [1100–771 B.C.] three thousand years ago, ancient scholars elucidated the
> brilliant idea of "harmony making for prosperity." Later Confucians and
> the Confucian school put forward the proposition of "harmony above all"
> and established theories on the coordination of interpersonal relations, the

protection of the natural environment, and the maintenance of ecological balance. These thoughts not only made positive contributions to the prosperity of ancient Chinese society but also have profound practical significance for the survival and development of mankind today. (De Bary and Lufrano, 2000, pp. 582–83)

These are the last words of the last entry in volume two of *Sources of Chinese Tradition: From 1600 through the Twentieth Century*. The (unnamed) editor of this the last entry in the section called "The Continuing Critique of Tradition," adds the following *critical* remark:

By relying on the Confucian values of harmony and social discipline as the criteria for excluding decadent libertarian influences from the West, Gu would have China screen out the spiritual pollution that was responsible for the alleged unbridled disorders of Tiananmen Square. Understood as a call for compliance with direction from above, such harmony and discipline would yield the stability needed for economic progress. Nothing was said about the "harmony without conformity" spoken of by Confucius, much less the kind of political remonstrance advocated by Mencius. (Ibid., p. 582)

Among the several kinds of Confucian philosophy in China today there are (at least) two competing versions of New Confucianism and (at least) three visions of Confucius (counting the unnamed editor of Gu Yu's declaration). First, there is the version of a post-socialist New Confucianism that originates with Confucian scholars in the "borderlands" and is associated with Gadamer's philosophical hermeneutics. Second, there is the version of a socialist New Confucianism that goes together with the economic modernizations of Deng Xiaoping's China. Despite considerable differences in how they envision Confucius, both post-socialist and socialist New Confucians are in agreement that Confucianism is committed to "harmony above all." Finally, there are the memory and vision of a Confucius (and of his defender, Mencius), who would not be silenced and, instead, spoke truth to power.

What counts as Chinese philosophy, and whether New Confucianism will prevail over other contemporary forms of Confucian philosophy, are not just questions of interest only to academics[9] because China has spread its New Confucianism all around the world by founding Confucius Institutes. The first Confucius Institute opened in Seoul, South Korea, in 2004. Five years later, some five hundred new Confucius Institutes can be found around the world and five hundred more are scheduled to be in place by 2020. And, yet, these questions about Chinese philosophy and New Confucianism are also (and, I would argue, urgently) an academic matter and an issue for academics. A Confucius Institute differs in one fundamental respect from other institutes of language training and cultural exchange—such as the Goethe Institute, the

Alliance Française, and the British Council—in that a Confucius Institute must be affiliated with a university. This affiliation can have an effect on what aspects of Chinese culture are taught in the affiliated university and who teaches it. In the next two sections of this chapter, I shall take a closer look at how Gadamer has come to be associated with the post-socialist version of New Confucianism that today is increasingly present in, and influential within, "mainland" China, just as it is no doubt also present in, and influential within, Confucius Institutes abroad.

Gadamer and Confucius

Those who work on Gadamer in English will always owe a debt to Richard Palmer, whose 1969 book, *Hermeneutics: interpretation theory in Schleiermacher, Dilthey, Heidegger, and Gadamer,* first introduced English-speaking North Americans to Gadamer's philosophical hermeneutics (Palmer, 1969). Starting in 2001, Palmer once again began visiting universities to lecture on the thought of Hans-Georg Gadamer, but this time the universities were in the Republic of China (Taiwan) and in the People's Republic of China. Not only has he contributed to conferences on hermeneutics at East China Normal University in Shanghai and Anhui Normal University in Wuhu, China; he has also given the Taipei Lectures, a two-week, nine-day course in hermeneutics at Fu-jen Catholic University in Taipei, Taiwan. These lectures, as well as other of his recent works on Gadamer, have been translated and published in Chinese. It would be reasonable but wrong, as I shall argue here, to conclude that Palmer has had the most influence upon how Gadamer's philosophical hermeneutics is understood today in Taiwan and China.

In this part of my chapter, I will draw from two lectures Palmer gave in China in which he connects Gadamer's philosophical hermeneutics to the philosophy of Confucius. The first is "Seven Key Terms in the Philosophy of Hans-Georg Gadamer," which Palmer gave in Anhui in 2002, and which is available online (Palmer, 2002); this lecture forms the basis of the article, "Gadamer and Confucius: Some Possible Affinities," published by the *Journal of Chinese Philosophy* in its 2006 supplementary issue, entitled *Hermeneutical Thinking in Chinese Philosophy* (Palmer, 2006). Chung-ying Cheng, the New Confucian philosopher and teacher of On-Cho Ng, is the founder of the *Journal of Chinese Philosophy* as well its managing editor. The second is the revised version of a lecture given at the Hermeneutics Institute of the Anhui Normal University, also in 2002. It is now available under the title "Gadamer's Later 'Turn': From Heideggerian Ontology to Philosophical Hermeneutics Based on Anthropology," in *The Imperative of Understanding: Chinese Philosophy, Comparative Philosophy, and Onto-Hermeneutics,* a tribute volume edited by On-Cho Ng and dedicated to Professor Chung-ying Cheng in 2008 (Palmer, 2008).

In "Gadamer and Confucius: Some Possible Affinities," Palmer does not pretend to be engaged in a serious scholarly way in comparative East-West philosophy, and he openly concedes his linguistic limitations (he knows no Classical Chinese) and the general nature of his knowledge of Chinese philosophy (he has taught undergraduate courses (a) on Confucianism, Taoism, and Ch'an Buddhism, and (b) on the Confucian Classics: the *Yijing*, the *Analects*, the *Great Learning*, and the *Doctrine of the Mean*). His article is meant more to be a playful "experiment" offered "in support of a daring hypothesis: *There is no major Western philosopher as close to Confucius's thinking as Gadamer.*" Since it would be impossible, he readily admits, to prove this thesis conclusively, he instead sets out to "indirectly defend" his hypothesis by developing seven "thought-provoking affinities" between Gadamer's philosophy and that of Confucius. Even then, he adds, these are more "possible" affinities rather than definitive similarities and thus he invites "my readers [to] lend a helping hand to corroborate my thesis by adding examples to support it or, more likely, to refute my arguments with their more exact knowledge" (Palmer, 2006, pp. 33, 82). After presenting the seven affinities, I will take up Palmer's invitation to challenge his hypothesis. I shall do so indirectly since my primary concern is not to challenge what Palmer has to say about *Gadamer* but rather to raise questions about the New Confucian frame that shapes what Palmer has to say about *Confucius*. What then are the "possible affinities" between Gadamer and Confucius?

In the following, I will list each of these together with direct quotations from Palmer attesting to the possibility of affinities. The first six arise, Palmer says, when we compare what Confucius says in the *Analects* with what Gadamer writes in *Truth and Method*. The seventh, however, pertains to the value of human solidarity, something not mentioned at all in *Truth and Method*. To establish the basis of a possible affinity between Confucius in the *Analects* and Gadamer on solidarity, Palmer has to look to an unpublished "late" piece, "Artwork in word and image," published when Gadamer was 93. Palmer has more to say about Gadamer and Confucius on solidarity in the second lecture, published in the tribute volume in honor of Cheng, and so I will quote from "Gadamer's Later 'Turn'" when we come to solidarity.

1. Truth

Gadamer's definition of truth is not scientific, but humanistic. [It] is closely associated with what is right and also with beauty. I would say that this view is like what Confucius sees as in harmony with heaven, the way a true prince rules by the mandate of heaven, or the truth of the rectification of names. . . . It is a truth that grows out of the social fabric of the tradition in which one lives, a truth that one "recognizes" as true. It is this view of truth that is found in Gadamer's masterwork, *Truth and Method*. (Palmer, 2006, p. 83)

2. Textual Contemporaneity

The German word *Zeitlichkeit* in Gadamer refers to the fact that a text of poetry or philosophy or a great work of art speaks as vividly and compellingly today as when it was created—if it is truly poetry, truly philosophy, or truly art. . . . This is the reason why it is so important to preserve the great works of art, poetry, philosophy, and religion of the past. . . . Likewise, in Confucius's education to prepare a perfect Gentleman and civil servant, education trains a person not only in mathematics and logic, but also in the arts and poetry, in history, in literature. This is the fabric that humanizes and creates the Gentleman. Gadamer would agree. (Ibid.)

3. Practical Wisdom

For Gadamer, it is in the context of the social-historical-linguistic fabric of one's life (one's *"wirkungsgeschickliches Bewusstsein"* or "historically effected consciousness") that one makes wise judgments. The parallel in the Confucian tradition is the Gentleman (*junzi*) who thinks and lives well. Of course, the Gentleman has a piety for his parents and ancestors that is deeper than that of Gadamer. . . . But Gadamer's respect for culture, tradition, and authority sets him apart from most other Western philosophers. (Ibid., p. 84)

4. Application

To truly understand a text is [according to Gadamer] to see its application, its context, and direction of meaning. . . . It is how what is being said in the text applies to one's society and also to oneself. . . . Turning to Confucius, we find this process of application everywhere in his ethical writings. He is explicit in *Analects* [2:11]: "The Master said, 'He who by *reanimating the Old* can gain knowledge of the New is fit to be a teacher.'" The person who is reanimating the Old is applying it to a new situation [emphasis added by Palmer]. (Ibid., pp. 85f.)

5. Tradition

One should certainly try to become aware of one's prejudices and to purge those that are undesirable. . . . One should not [however] purge oneself of one's *tradition* but rather become conscious of its positive and negative sides, and try to overcome the undesirable prior beliefs. . . . Gadamer would agree with Shang Zhiying[10] that we should not just piously seek to restore the status of Confucius and the rest of antiquity, but rather to revitalize what is relevant today. (Ibid., 87f.)

6. *Conversation*

For Gadamer, experience and understanding are always dialogical, a matter of question and answer. . . . This masterwork [the *Analects*] is not just a series of comments and commentary by Confucius but a dialogue with his contemporaries and with his times. (Ibid., pp. 89f.)

7. *Solidarity*

Gadamer went back further culturally [than Heidegger] and found in the ancient Greek rites and festivals a deep bond of solidarity being celebrated among human beings *being with each other in community, in celebration.* But Confucius went before and beyond both of them [Heidegger and Gadamer] when, in the *Lun Yü* [the *Analects*], he spelled out the principles of *being with one another responsibly*: benevolence, respect, filial piety, sincerity, loyalty, leadership, fairness, inner strength, moral uprightness, cultural refinement and right attitude, all of which foster human solidarity and raise the quality of human life. (Palmer, 2008, p. 44)

In 2002, the same year that Palmer lectures at Chinese universities to "introduce" Gadamer's philosophical hermeneutics, Elman publishes "Rethinking 'Confucianism' and 'Neo-Confucianism' in Modern Chinese History" (Elman, 2002).[11] In this essay, as we recall, Elman criticizes and dismisses Gadamer's philosophical hermeneutics because it is connected to New Confucianism and specifically to the politically neoconservative New Confucianism professed by those who would have their "borderland" New Confucianism replace Marxism and Maoism in a post-socialist China. We find, however, no mention of New Confucianism in Palmer's 2002 lectures (or in the publications of these lectures in 2006 and 2008). Nor do we find the seventh affinity, solidarity, as Palmer presents it, to be indicative of Gadamer's "profound cultural conservatism" (Elman), which conservatism would attest to a *political affinity* between Gadamer and Confucius. Instead, the affinities Palmer finds between Gadamer and Confucius are all *ethical affinities.*

Makeham offers two observations that can explain why Elman connects Gadamer to New Confucianism, and why Palmer does not: "Despite the movement's importance, there is [in 2003] only one detailed study of New Confucianism written in English (Makeham, 2003, p. 2). By contrast, a tremendous amount of research and writing on the subject of New Confucianism has been done by Chinese (mainland and overseas) scholars over the last two decades [the 1980s on]" (ibid.).[12] On one hand, Palmer's side of the story about Gadamer's relation to Chinese philosophy through his affinity to the ideal "gentleman-scholar" (in Chinese, *junzi*), "Confucius," is ethical but not political, because in 2002 there was little about New Confucianism available in English for Palmer to read. On the other hand, Elman's identification of Gadamer's philosophical hermeneutics with the neoconservative philosophy of New Confucianism is based on a New Confucian version of Gadamer's philosophical hermeneutics that is already operative in China prior to Palmer's 2002 lectures on Gadamer. I will argue in the remainder of this chapter that the "reconstruction" or—to use one of the New Confucians' favorite descriptions— the "creative transformation" of Gadamer's philosophical hermeneutics that we that find in the onto-hermeneutical philosophy of Chung-ying Cheng is the ideal explanation for why Gadamer's philosophical hermeneutics has been associated with the political aspirations of the neoconservative "borderland" New Confucians.

Just as those who work on Gadamer in English owe a debt to Richard Palmer, so do those who work on Chinese philosophy in English owe a very considerable debt to Chung-ying Cheng for introducing them to a wide range of contemporary Chinese philosophers in his coedited book, *Contemporary Chinese Philosophy* (Cheng, 2002), and in his *Journal of Chinese Philosophy*. For Western philosophers unfamiliar with Chung-ying Cheng, let me introduce him using the words of his student, On-Cho Ng:

> Renowned as a leading representative of what has come to be known as "New Confucianism," Cheng is a systematic philosopher who, through his careful cross-cultural interrogations, is ultimately concerned with the possibilities of harmonization between the major traditions to yield a "world philosophy." Based on his understanding of Confucian ontology and Chinese philosophical texts, together with his sympathetic reading of Euro-American theories of hermeneutics, his thinking in recent years has coalesced into a coherent philosophical project that he calls "onto-hermeneutics"—his vision of a world philosophy. (Ng, 2008, pp. 1f.)[13]

Cheng's philosophy is based on the Confucian classic, the *Yijing* (the *Book of Changes*), which represents for him Confucius's ontology. In contrast, Palmer focuses on the ethical Confucius we know from the *Analects*. As I have noted, Cheng and/or his students facilitated the institutional setting for Palmer's lectures in China and Taiwan and for their subsequent publication. What I shall show in section three is that it is not Gadamer's philosophical hermeneutics per se but instead Cheng's ontological reconstruction of Gadamer's philosophical hermeneutics into his "onto-hermeneutics" that should really be the *primary target* of Elman's critical remarks about the post-socialist aspirations of Gadamer's hermeneutics. Palmer, we can infer from On-Cho Ng's words about

"Gadamer's Later 'Turn'" (his contribution to the tribute volume in honor of Cheng), is present at conferences and in publications associated with the New Confucian philosophy of Chung-ying Cheng, not so much to *introduce Gadamer* as to "*[underscore] the fruitfulness of Chung-ying Cheng's integrative onto-hermeneutics* (emphasis added)" (Ng, 2008, p. 4).

Gadamer and New Confucianism

In the 1970s, New Confucianism was introduced to the United States by Du Weiming and Chung-ying Cheng, the first generation of New Confucians working within American universities.[14] Both were born in China prior to 1949, both moved with their families to Taiwan; both studied first in Taiwan, and later at Harvard University for their doctorates; and both have had long and distinguished careers publishing and teaching at Harvard and the University of Hawai'i at Manoa, respectively. They differ, Chung-ying Cheng says, in the way they present New Confucianism to America: Du Weiming as a religion rather than as a philosophy; Chung-ying Cheng as a philosophy rather than as a religion (Cheng, 2002, pp. 361, 357).[15]

In keeping with his commitment to New Confucianism *as a philosophy*, Cheng founded the *Journal of Chinese Philosophy* in 1973 and the International Society for Chinese Philosophy in 1975. Cheng describes himself as first translating the word "hermeneutics" into Chinese (*quanshixue*) in the 1970s while in Taiwan and subsequently introducing "the central conception and theory of *benti-quanshixue* (onto-hermeneutics) in 1985 in China" (Cheng, 2006a, p. 2). Gadamer's *Truth and Method*, we should recall, was translated into English in 1975. In 2008, in his autobiographical essay in On-Cho Ng's tribute volume, Cheng characterizes Gadamer's philosophical hermeneutics in relation to his "onto-hermeneutics" in the following way: "In *reconstructing* such a new philosophical hermeneutics which I call Onto-Hermeneutics, I have *enlarged the scope* of Gadamer's hermeneutics by including the interpretation of ontology itself (emphasis added)" (Cheng, 2008, p. 18). What Cheng means here by "enlarging the scope" is that he has extended the process (the "event of understanding"), which Gadamer describes as a "fusion of horizons," to the level of cultures with different philosophical traditions or, more specifically, to the fusion of the different philosophical traditions identified with China and the West (Cheng, 2002, p. 402).

Cheng takes Gadamer's concept of the fusion of horizons to have world-historical consequences once it is "expanded" in his own onto-hermeneutics to the interpretation of the different philosophies (or "ontologies") of the East and the West. In his general introduction to the first supplement to *The Journal of Chinese Philosophy*, edited by L. Pfister and called *Hermeneutical Thinking in Chinese Philosophy*, Cheng adds the following remark:

It is through a conscious and conscientious onto-hermeneutical thinking today that Chinese philosophy in a contemporary sense will develop and grow into a powerful intellectual enterprise in which the past [the old Neo-Confucianism] will merge with the future [the New Neo-Confucianism/ New Confucianism] and the East (the Chinese) will merge with the West [this includes Chinese Marxism] *and vice versa* (emphasis added). (Cheng, 2006a, p. 2)

Cheng, if we read this closely, says only that "Chinese philosophy in a contemporary [New Confucian] sense" will grow into a "powerful intellectual enterprise" after "merging" with the West. He says nothing about what will happen to contemporary Western philosophy after "merging" with the East and his own Chinese philosophy. This omission tells us what "Chinese philosophy" does not mean in the names for the journal and the international society started by Cheng. The purpose of the *Journal of Chinese Philosophy* and the International Society for Chinese Philosophy is not, as their names might at first suggest, primarily to serve as settings for ongoing research into *a philosophy that is already Chinese.* Nor were they primarily instituted in order to establish a location, in print and at conferences such as the American Philosophical Association, to gather together those interested in *comparative East-West philosophy.* Both of these objectives are real, but secondary. Rather, the *Journal of Chinese Philosophy* and the International Society for Chinese Philosophy are founded primarily so that there can be a site for the emergence of the *Chinese philosophy of the future,* which will be *not one world philosophy among many but the one and only world philosophy.*[16]

I cannot discuss in this chapter Cheng's global aspirations regarding the merging of the "ontologies" of the East and the West and the future emergence of one world philosophy that would be Chinese. My primary goal is to understand how Gadamer's philosophical hermeneutics comes to be identified, by Elman, with the philosophy of the "borderland" New Confucians, who have political aspirations for "mainland" China. I have proposed that we look more closely at the "reconstruction" of Gadamer's philosophical hermeneutics in the onto-hermeneutical philosophy of one particular "borderland" New Confucian, namely Chung-ying Cheng.

The argument I will present in the remainder of this chapter leads to two conclusions. I will first demonstrate that Cheng's post-socialist political aspirations for New Confucianism develop initially in the form of a *dialectics* that is independent of Gadamer and of his *hermeneutics.* I find this demonstration does not, however, completely exonerate Gadamer's philosophical hermeneutics, since he bears an indirect responsibility insofar as his *philosophical hermeneutics* is linked to Cheng's *onto-hermeneutics.* Thus, what complicates an otherwise straightforward argument exonerating Gadamer's philosophical hermeneutics is, I shall show, the fact that Gadamer's hermeneutics lends itself to being reconstructed into Cheng's onto-hermeneutics in a way that, for example, Ricoeur's hermeneutics does not. Cheng's reconstruction of Gadamer's hermeneutics weakens the straightforward argument based on Cheng's dialectics because it exposes the incapacity of Gadamer's "receptive" hermeneutics to confront conflicting interpretations, or to critique claims that are ideological in nature. Cheng's onto-hermeneutics, therefore, strengthens the point Ricoeur makes in "Gadamer and the critique of ideology," that Gadamer's "receptive" hermeneutics needs something to replace "method" if the self-understanding Gadamer is concerned with is to be able to protect itself from ideological receptions. Let us look at the first part of my argument.

"Towards Constructing a Dialectics of Harmonization: Harmony and Conflict in Chinese Philosophy" was first published in 1977 in the *Journal of Chinese Philosophy* Cheng had recently founded, republished in 1991, and then republished prominently in 2006 in the *Hermeneutical Thinking in Chinese Philosophy*, the first supplementary volume to *The Journal of Chinese Philosophy*. This is a key text if we want to understand the political aspirations of Cheng's New Confucianism just after the end of the Cultural Revolution, and then just after the Chinese Communist Party publicly announces China's commitment to Confucianism in 1989, and finally now in the twenty-first century. In it we discover that Cheng's vision of a "Chinese philosophy of the future" rests ultimately on the "intellectual intuition" he has into a metaphysics (or ontology) of harmony and conflict which, he claims, is unique to Chinese culture. This Chinese metaphysics (or ontology) will prove superior, he argues, to the challenge to it by the West because the Chinese *dialectics of harmonization* that follows from this metaphysics will prove to be superior to the Western European *dialectics of conflict* (Hegel and also Marx) just as it has already proved to be superior to the Indian Buddhist *dialectics of transcendence* (Nagarjuna, 150–250).[17]

In "Towards Constructing a Dialectics of Harmonization," we encounter the kind of narrative of the history of Chinese philosophy that, in *The Postmodern Condition*, François Lyotard calls a "meta-narrative" (Lyotard, 1979). Starting with the historical fact that there has been "harmony and conflict among the schools of thought in Chinese philosophy," along with the fact that these different schools of thought conceive of harmony and of conflict differently, Cheng takes on the philosophical task of "pinpointing some underlying essential and unifying [metaphysical] structure of all major Chinese philosophical views of harmony and conflict" that can explain the emergence of different concepts of harmony and conflict as well as the dialectic of their subsequent harmonization (Cheng, 2006b, pp. 33, 25f.).

Not surprisingly, the two schools of thought he considers "foundational" for Chinese philosophy are the Confucian and the Daoist, and the Daoist texts Cheng considers (texts associated with the names of Laozi and Zhuangzi) are those one would expect. The texts he takes to be definitive of the Confucian school of thought—the *Yijing* (the *Book of Changes*, one of the five Confucian Classics), and especially the works of the Ming Neo-Confucian, Wang Yangming—have only recently been regarded as equally foundational. Wang

Yangming, it is important to know, is considered an "idealist" because of his concept of knowledge as innate and accessible through a form of intellectual intuition.

Drawing on the work of the Harvard Sinologist, Benjamin Schwartz, and others on "polarities" in Chinese thought (Schwartz, 1964 pp. 3–15), Cheng singles out the polarity between harmony and conflict[18] and makes the claim that it is the fundamental polarity behind all other polarities in the two foundational schools of Chinese thought. According to Cheng, the polarity of harmony and conflict constitutes a *metaphysics of harmony and conflict* that is uniquely Chinese. While the metaphysics of harmony and conflict is said by Cheng to be the "underlying and essential unifying structure" ever present, and thus constant, behind both Daoist and Confucian forms of Chinese thinking, a *dialectics of harmonization* is said to explain all the historical changes that have taken place throughout the long and complicated history of China:

> Notwithstanding that there may appear variation, difference, divergence, tension, opposition, and antagonism in the world, the Confucian insists [based on the *Yijing*] *that the overall tendency of social and cosmic processes as well as individual life conduces to unity and harmony.* (Cheng, 2006b, p. 28, emphasis added)

One may wonder why, for Cheng, the dialectics must be one of harmonization if harmony and conflict are complementary polar opposites. Why not a dialectics of conflict instead?

Although Cheng does not raise this question explicitly, he answers it implicitly when he accepts without question the logic of the following Confucian argument: "If harmony is identified with goodness, and if conflict, as the opposite of harmony, is identified with evil or badness, conflict then requires harmonization."[19] Although Cheng claims to base his understanding of the Chinese metaphysics of harmony and conflict, along with its "consequent" dialectics of harmonization, on his readings of Chinese texts—and specifically of the *Yijing*, of Wang Yangming, of Laozi, and of Zhuangzi—he relies, at times explicitly and more often implicitly, on an act of "intellectual intuition" (*guan* in Chinese, to see, to inspect) that he takes from the *Yijing* and also from the idealist epistemology of Wang Yangming.[20] Cheng cannot begin to question his own use of intellectual intuition if what the New Confucian, Mou Zongsan (1909–95), says holds true: "[I]f it is true that human beings cannot have intellectual intuition, then the whole of Chinese philosophy must collapse completely, and the thousands years of effort must be in vain. It [Chinese philosophy] is just an illusion" (Mou, 1975, p. 3; quoted in Tang, 2002, p. 333). Given Cheng's aim "to pinpoint some underlying essential and all unifying structure of all major Chinese philosophical views of harmony and conflict" throughout 2500 years of Chinese history, he has to resort to intellectual intuition as a "method" to access an "*a-historical problematic* that can be analytically studied" (Cheng, 2006b, pp. 26f.).

In "Toward Constructing a Dialectics of Harmonization," Cheng contrasts the dialectics of harmonization that he argues is uniquely Chinese with two alternative dialectics: the Western European dialectics of conflict found in Hegel and Marx, and the dialectics of transcendence found in the Indian Buddhist philosopher, Nagarjuna (known as Long Shu in Chinese Buddhism). Cheng says these two alternatives dialectics pose the most serious challenges to the Chinese dialectics of harmonization. Indian Buddhism, for example, challenged ancient Chinese Confucianism from the first century A.D. until Zhu Xi (1130–1200) ensured the final victory of Neo-Confucianism over Buddhism in the Song dynasty (960–1279) (Cheng, 2006b, p. 39). "In the present [twentieth] century," Cheng says, "we witness another encounter and an ongoing process of interaction between the native Chinese dialectics of harmonization and Western European views of harmony and conflict as embodied in the Hegelian-Marxist dialectics of conflict" (ibid.). For the "borderland" New Confucian philosopher, Cheng, the challenge to the "native Chinese dialectics of harmonization" that comes from a Western European dialectics of conflict is already actively operating in 1977 *within* mainland China:

> The introduction of the Darwinian "survival of the fittest" in the beginning of the twentieth century, the success of the 1949 Chinese Communist Revolution, and the subsequent propagandization of Marxist-Leninist ideology in mainland China all bear witness to the strength and influence of Western European dialectics of conflict in the development of modern Chinese society. . . . The Marxist-Leninist-Maoist campaign on the mainland against Confucius and Confucianism [i.e., the Cultural Revolution] acutely promoted a battle between the Confucian dialectics of harmonization and the Marxist dialectics of conflict, *a battle which must be fought on many fronts* (emphasis added). (Ibid., p. 40)

"Toward Constructing a Dialectics of Harmonization" is a telling piece of evidence for the purposes of defending Gadamer against the blame attached to his philosophical hermeneutics by Elman. We find no reference to Gadamer in this essay and, which is even more important, no mention of the word, hermeneutics. Instead, we find that Cheng's New Confucian philosophy already had post-socialist aspirations at a time, 1977, when he was writing about ontology or metaphysics only in relation to dialectics and not yet in connection to hermeneutics. This leads to the first of my two conclusions, which is that Cheng's philosophy (alone or together with that of other New Confucians) explains the post-socialist political aspirations of the neoconservative political movement called New Confucianism and not, as Elman maintains, Gadamer's philosophical hermeneutics per se.

The straightforward argument and clear-cut conclusion is weakened, however, when we ask the following question: "What is it about Gadamer's hermeneutics that invites Cheng to reconstruct it as opposed to a hermeneutical theory such as that of Ricoeur?" Let us be clear first about what Cheng understands himself to be doing by reconstructing Gadamer's philosophical hermeneutics. Cheng has told us that he formed his conception of onto-hermeneutics during the period between the early 1970s (and the Cultural Revolution), when he first translated the word "hermeneutics" into Chinese (*quanshixue*), and 1985 (after the death of Mao Zedong) at which time he first introduced the "central conception and theory of *benti-quanshixue* [onto-hermeneutics]" in China (Cheng, 2006a, p. 2). What Cheng accomplishes during this period is more than, as well as something other than, an "enlargement of the scope" of Gadamer's philosophical hermeneutics. It is, rather, the "reconstruction" (the so-called "creative transformation") of *one particular* Western European theory of hermeneutics, that of Gadamer, into an altogether new phenomenon, namely, the very first Chinese philosophy that claims to be a hermeneutics.[21] In order to make more transparent the steps involved when Cheng "reconstructs" Gadamer's Western European philosophical hermeneutics into a Chinese onto(logical)-hermeneutics, let us return to the story (the meta-narrative) that, in 1977, Cheng tells in "Toward Constructing a Dialectics of Harmonization" about the way the Chinese dialectics of harmonization came to prevail over the Indian Buddhist dialectics of transcendence.

To simplify this story,[22] let us recall A. C. Graham's succinct characterization of how rivals were treated differently by the adherents of the One Hundred Schools, and especially by Confucius and by Mencius, versus by the later Confucians. The Confucians, he says, treat their rivals not as wholly wrong ("You are wrong. I'm right.") but, instead, as one-sided ("You have a narrow view. I have a wide view."). In the first century A.D., the Chinese were confronted with a powerful philosophical tradition that came from outside the culture and philosophical tradition of China. The Indian Buddhist, Nagarjuna, we should remember, was primarily a formidable logician and philosopher. Instead of conflicts over philosophical differences that would (might?) lead to the elimination of the rival, B (here the philosophy of Indian Buddhism), Confucians, A (here the Neo-Confucians), harmonized by compromising and synthesizing. First, they creatively transformed Indian Buddhism into Chinese Buddhism (into Ch'an or what we call Zen Buddhism) and then they integrated it by subordinating Buddhism (B), now Chinese, to Neo-Confucianism, A, the one remaining elaborate philosophical system ("A above B"). The story Cheng tells about the past, how the Chinese (here the Neo-Confucian) dialectics of harmonization came to prevail over the Indian Buddhist dialectics of transcendence, is instructive because these same two actions later occur when Cheng "reconstructs" Gadamer's Western European philosophical hermeneutics. Like Indian Buddhism, Gadamer's philosophical hermeneutics (B) is first transformed by Cheng into a Chinese hermeneutics (onto-hermeneutics) and then integrated through subordination into Cheng's New Confucianism (A), thus implicating Gadamer with Cheng's New Confucian post-socialist aspirations ("A above B").

Against this background about how the Chinese dialectics of harmonization is said to function, let us look now at the steps involved when Cheng "reconstructs" Gadamer's hermeneutics into his own theory of onto-hermeneutics, the very first Chinese philosophy that explicitly claims to be a hermeneutics. Two important steps immediately come to mind: (a) the transformation of Gadamer's concept of horizon, and (b) the transformation of Gadamer's concept of understanding another as a fusion of horizons. These two transformations, I shall argue, "reconstruct" Gadamer's hermeneutics by taking the primacy of receptivity in Gadamer's philosophical hermeneutics to an unrecognizable extreme.

In their tributes to Cheng, his colleagues and students often write about the superiority of his onto-hermeneutics to Gadamer's philosophical hermeneutics (Goulding, 2008, p. 138; Flemming, 2008, p. 75), and so I shall rely on one such testimony as I discuss these two steps.

(1) Horizon: For Gadamer, as we know, the "horizon" of a text lets what the text claims to be the truth about some matter in question (*die Sache*) stand out as something different from what the reader/interpreter claims to be true from within his or her own horizon. Gadamer's concept of there being another horizon distinct from and over and against the reader/interpreter's own horizon is necessary for something that we read/interpret to challenge us to think differently about some matter we question. When we look at Cheng's onto-hermeneutics, though, we find the text is a manifestation of a "vague category" so that it no longer has a definite horizon. Robert Cummings Neville puts it this way:

> I would express Cheng's grasp of the texts to be in the form of what [Charles Sanders] Peirce and others call "vague categories." A vague category can be defined precisely in relation to other categories at its same level, but itself allows of being specified by versions of the category that contradict one another. For instance, both ZHU XI and WANG YANGMING affirm the centrality of Principle (*li*) yet have competing accounts of that; a vague category would say what they suppose in common prior to their differences. (Neville, 2008, p. 112)

In Cheng's onto-hermeneutics, then, a text such as the ancient classic, *Yijing*, or two Neo-Confucian texts from the same dynasty, one earlier and the other later, become "indefinite" or "vague" thereby leading a reader/interpreter to be able to discover only what he or she already has in common with the text. The first step, then, of Cheng's transformation of Gadamer's concept of "horizon" into his own concept of a "vague category" *harmonizes* by subordinating any differences between the (now indefinite/horizonless) "text" and the "reader/interpreter" to what they both "suppose in common prior to their difference." In effect, reading/interpreting a text grasped as a "vague category" takes away the matter in question, *die Sache*, and leaves no basis for disputing a claim or offering a conflicting interpretation.

(2) Fusion of Horizons: For Gadamer, the event of understanding that fuses the horizons of the text and of a reader/interpreter increases the self-understanding of the reader/interpreter and increases the being of the text (it comes

to mean more) (Wright, 1986). In this way, the history of the effects of texts
upon their reader/interpreters enriches the text, making more complicated
(a) the text, (b) our understanding of the text, and (c) our own self-understanding. Not so in Cheng's onto-hermeneutics in which, according to Neville:

> Cheng's interpretations of ancient texts, particularly the *Yi Jing*, is vague.
> It deliberately acknowledges the underdeterminateness of the text and pre-
> serves that. The themes or motifs of thought that he derives from the text can
> then be specified in many different, perhaps mutually contradictory, ways in
> the subsequent tradition. (Neville, 2008, p. 112)

Because the effective history of a text that is thought of in terms of a vague
category (rather than in terms of a definite/defining horizon as in Gadamer)
tones down variable, and even contradictory, readings/interpretations (such as,
for example, between Zhu Xi and Wang Yangming on *li*), there can be no real
matters of dispute (*die Sache*) at issue between an individual reader/interpreter
and the text; moreover, there can be no matters of dispute between two or more
readers/interpreters when they believe that they have understood one and the
same text differently. This second step in Cheng's transformation of Gadamer's
philosophical hermeneutics into his onto-hermeneutics also *harmonizes*, this
time by leading the readers/interpreters (in the plural) back to the indefinite
and vague, thereby subordinating any emerging differences or conflicts in
interpretation to what they "suppose in common prior to their differences."

Let us be clear about what Cheng has accomplished with these two steps.
First, he has transformed Gadamer's concept of the definite/defining horizon
of a text into the concept of a text as a vague category. Second, he has transformed Gadamer's concept of understanding another as a fusion of horizons
(the understanding of another/text as well as the understanding of another/
different, conflicting interpretations of a text) into understanding the vague
category held in common prior to differences. The outcome of the event of
understanding according to Cheng's onto-hermeneutics, namely, *understanding
the vague category held in common prior to differences*, is like the outcome of the
event of understanding according to Gadamer's philosophical hermeneutics,
namely, *understanding what we have in common*—but with this difference: Cheng's
onto-hermeneutics takes "what we have in common" to an extreme that conflates any and all difference(s). As Neville notes (approvingly): "Cheng can
romp gleefully through the Chinese tradition [and, he adds, also through 'a
wide array of Western traditions'], making the myriad schools all to be expressive of fundamental themes that they would not agree on articulating" (ibid.).
What Neville tells us in this tribute to Cheng helps explain why Gadamer's
receptive hermeneutics would recommend itself to Cheng rather than would,
for example, Ricoeur's hermeneutics. Among the Western European theories
of hermeneutics available to Cheng, Gadamer's "receptive" hermeneutics with
its aim set upon "what we have in common" is the one most capable of being

"reconstructed" into a hermeneutics that can be called "Chinese" because, to recall the words of Gu Yu, it subordinates any and all conflict to "harmony above all."

In this third section, I have presented two arguments in response to the charge leveled by Elman against Gadamer's philosophical hermeneutics—the charge that provoked this chapter. The arguments, however, reach conflicting conclusions. On one hand, a strong case can be made that Gadamer should in no way be the primary target of Elman's criticism, and that the post-socialist political aspirations (not to mention the global aspirations) of the neoconservative philosophical movement called New Confucianism can be traced back to Chung-ying Cheng's dialectics of harmonization and not to Gadamer's philosophical hermeneutics. On the other hand, a case can also be made that the value placed by Gadamer on receptivity and on arriving at "what we have in common" invites just the kind of transformation we find in Cheng's onto-hermeneutics, with its post-socialist and global aspirations. Although Gadamer's philosophical hermeneutics may be innocent of the charge as formulated by Elman, his philosophical hermeneutics remains suspect because, as it stands, it lends itself to being reconstructed and transformed into Cheng's onto-hermeneutics.

At the outset, I mentioned that by writing this chapter about thinking about Chinese philosophy through Gadamer, through Chinese philosophy I have ended up thinking differently about Gadamer. My second argument (guilty by association) has, I found, weakened my first argument and its clear-cut conclusion (not guilty). It has also strengthened the argument put forward in 1973 by Ricoeur in "Gadamer and the critique of ideology." That argument, let us recall, is that Gadamer's hermeneutics needs to be *developed* so that something can replace the concept of "method" Gadamer rejects if the self-understanding that Gadamer's philosophical hermeneutics is concerned with is not to fall prey to ideological receptions and self-deceptions.

Ricoeur speaks with manifest passion at the start of his essay about what *the fundamental gesture of philosophy* really is that is at stake behind the Gadamer-Habermas debate over the epistemology of the human sciences:

> [Is it to be] an avowal of the historical conditions to which all human understanding is to be subsumed under the reign of finitude? Or rather is it, in the final analysis, an act of defiance, a critical gesture, relentlessly repeated and indefinitely turned against "false consciousness," against the distortions of human communication which conceal the permanent exercise of domination and violence? (Ricoeur, 1981, p. 63)

After reading Chinese philosophy through Gadamer and after reading Gadamer through New Confucianism, these words by Ricoeur (as well as the logical structure of his essay) no longer seem to demand that we make a *choice* between the philosophical hermeneutics of Gadamer and the critical theory of Habermas. What Ricoeur seems to be calling for instead is to *refocus* the "critical gesture" *of* philosophical hermeneutics. Here the techniques and terminology of digital photography can help clarify the type of refocusing Ricoeur is suggesting. One way to refocus Gadamer's philosophical hermeneutics that Ricoeur would not be endorsing is that taken by Chung-ying Cheng who *enlarges its scope* by turning it into something panoramic, an onto-hermeneutics. In the technical process of digital photography, image editing software *refocuses* multiple pictures, each with their individual focus, by merging them together to create one continuous panoramic picture. Ricoeur would not support Cheng's panoramic way to refocus philosophical hermeneutics because it *blurs* its critical gesture.

A different way to refocus Gadamer's philosophical hermeneutics is to *lock onto* its critical gesture and the way that philosophical interpretation can expose not only one's own "false consciousness" but also "the distortions of human communication which conceal the permanent exercise of domination and violence." Put again in the technical terms of digital photography, locking onto the critical gesture of philosophical hermeneutics is like pointing the camera to the face or object that one is photographing and then holding the shutter button halfway down in a camera that has automatic focus. Locking the automatic focus in this way allows the photographer (not the camera) to actively *refocus* and recompose the picture before taking it by pushing the shutter button all the way down. So too locking onto the critical gesture of philosophical hermeneutics allows the reader in effect to become more active and in this specific sense less receptive in that she now takes the time to actively pose and repose her own challenging questions in response to the challenge of the text. This second way to refocus philosophical hermeneutics is, I believe, the one that Ricoeur would support because it *sharpens* the critical gesture of philosophical hermeneutics.

Notes

1   Elman, who takes the designation "borderland" (instead of using the more familiar "overseas") from Arif Dirlik, notes, "This notion of 'borderland' is sinocentric and should not be applied uncritically to Japan, or Vietnam, since it represents Chinese tributary conceits toward them" (Elman, 2002, p. 524 n.20). Elman also has in mind the neoconservative New Confucian philosophers, Chow Kai-wing and Huang Chun-Chieh. As a junior in college, Elman studied Chinese, classical Confucianism, and Neo-Confucianism with Chung-ying Cheng at the East-West Center at the University of Hawaii in 1966–67. The works by Chung-ying Cheng that I discuss in this chapter were all written in the 1970s and later.

2   In the following chapter, I preserve the Chinese way and order of designating names except when a person goes by a different name in English. I have also used pinyin Romanization for Chinese words except when the Wade-Giles Romanization appears in quotations. I have not changed well-known names such as Confucius into pinyin [Kongzi]. Lastly, I have left the Chinese characters out of the quotations I have used.

[3] I would like to take this opportunity to thank Professor Cheng publicly for his professional support of my work on the Neo-Confucian, Wang Fuzhi.

[4] For how the village of Le Chambon under the leadership of its Protestant pastor, Andre Trocme, defied the Nazis and saved around five thousand Jews, please see Hallie, 1979.

[5] I would like to thank my colleague in the French department, Koffi Anyinefa, for helping me with these articles.

[6] I would like to thank Michael Nylan for giving me very good advice about how to first approach Chinese philosophy.

[7] See also Bell, 2008, for a more popular introduction to New Confucianism in China today.

[8] Makeham evaluates and criticizes how this document has come to be considered such a defining document (Makeham, 2003, pp. 27–29).

[9] For an introduction to the variety of forms of Confucian thought that exist today within New Confucianism and outside it, both in China and the "borderlands," including North America, see Makeham, 2003, p. 44; Van Norden, 2004; and Cheng, 2002. I am particularly drawn to Makeham's suggestion (p. 44): "Rather than thinking of New Confucianism as a single line of intellectual orthodoxy, or even of a complex intellectual movement comprising many threads of thought, I would prefer to think in terms of twentieth-century Confucian or Confucian-inspired philosophy that embrace a variety of forms of intellectual expression. To privilege New Confucianism seems unjustified." Here, I would also like to recommend that we pay greater attention to the School of Evidential Scholarship that Elman has helped us reconsider; see Elman, 1984.

[10] Apparently a participant at the conference.

[11] See also Elman, 2006. This is a lecture he gave at the Colloquium on "Image of Philology," organized under the auspices of the History of Science Program at Princeton, NJ (February 16–17, 2006).

[12] He is referring to Bresciani, 2001. Since this book did not even have the words "New Confucianism" in its title, it would be unlikely for Palmer to have heard about New Confucianism from this work.

[13] I would like to thank James Gulick, the humanities librarian at Haverford College, for anticipating, even before I asked, my need to read this and other recent publications on New Confucianism.

[14] See Bresciani, 2001, for why Chung-ying Cheng and Du Weiming are considered "third generation" New Confucians in China and in Taiwan.

[15] Please note that Du Weiming might dispute this characterization of his position about Confucian thought.

[16] Philosophy, Cheng reassures us, will not stop when Chinese philosophy becomes world philosophy. Just as dominance of Chinese philosophy by Zhu Xi (1130–1200) caused the (old) Neo-Confucianism to continue to flourish until 1644, so too Chung-ying Cheng's New Confucian onto-hermeneutics will create "two areas of new philosophical thinking [that] will flourish as a consequence of conceiving of Chinese philosophy as world philosophy. One is interpretation across ontologies and methodologies and the other is globalization of ethics and epistemology"; see Cheng, 2002, p. 402.

[17] There appears to be, for Cheng, really only one metaphysics or ontology, namely, the Chinese metaphysics of harmony and conflict that is based on the *Yijing*. There are however three forms of dialectics. The Western European dialectics of

conflict and Indian Buddhist dialectics of transcendence will however prove to be not "untrue" but instead "narrower" than the dialectics of harmonization; see Graham, 1989, p. 378.

[18] Cheng defines harmony and conflict in the following way:

> For any two distinctive or coexisting forces, processes, or entities, if there is mutual complementation and mutual support between the two, so that each depends on the other for strength, actuality, productivity, and value, then we say that these two form a harmonious whole and an organic unity. In contrast, conflict means the absence of harmony between two distinctive, different or not-different, forces, processes or entities, to the extent that each tends to cancel out the other, contradict the other, harm the other, or even perhaps destroy the other. (Cheng, 2006b, p. 27)

[19] The text continues:

> [C]onflict is a matter of a people's inability to conform to reality. Conflict is therefore indicative of the weakness of an individual or a community of individuals in their failure to appreciate the intricacies of change and consequently to control or discipline themselves for making conformity to nature possible. [C]onflict can always be avoided if one strives to conform with nature by cultivating one's understanding and adjusting one's action in a proper way with respect to a propitious time. (Cheng, 2006b, p. 31)

[20] For more on "intellectual intuition," see also Flemming, 2008, pp. 73–106. Cheng's training in analytic philosophy and more specifically his study of the works of W. V. O. Quine and Charles Sanders Peirce may also play a role here.

[21] Wolfgang Kubin disputes the right for Cheng and those who follow him to talk at all about a Chinese "hermeneutics." See Kubin, 2005, pp. 311–20.

[22] I mean to take no stand here about the truth status of this story.

Bibliography

Chapter 1

Aristotle. (1962), *Nicomachean Ethics.* M. Ostwald (trans.). Indianapolis: Bobbs-Merrill.

—(1960), *Physics.* W. D. Ross (trans.). Oxford: Clarendon Press.

—(1954), *Rhetoric.* in *The Rhetoric and the Poetics of Aristotle,* W. R. Roberts (trans.). New York: Random House.

—(1933), *Metaphysics.* H. Tredennick (trans.). Cambridge, MA: Harvard University Press.

—(1926), *On Interpretation.* H. P. Cooke (trans.). Cambridge, MA: Harvard University Press.

Gadamer, H.-G. (1991), *Griechische Philosophie 2, Gesammelte Werke 7.* Tübingen: Mohr.

—(1989a), *Truth and Method* (2nd rev. edn). J. Weinsheimer and D. G. Marshall (trans.). New York: Crossroad.

—(1989b), "*Heideggers 'theologische' Jugendschrift* (Heidegger's youthful 'theological study')," *Dilthey-Jahrbuch* 6, 228–34.

—(1987), "*Kant und die hermeneutische Wendung* (Kant and the hermeneutical turn)," in *Neuere Philosophie 1, Gesammelte Werke 3,* H.-G. Gadamer. Tübingen: Mohr.

—(1986), *Wahrheit und Methode, Gesammelte Werke 1.* Tübingen: Mohr. Translated as Gadamer (1989a).

—(1985), *Griechische Philosophie 1, Gesammelte Werke 6.* Tübingen: Mohr.

Heidegger, M. (2002), *Grundbegriffe der Aristotelischen Philosophie.* Frankfurt: Klostermann.

—(1995a), "*Das Heimischwerden, die Sorge der Dichtung Hölderlins (Coming Home, the Concern of Hölderlin's poetry),*" in *Hölderlins Hymne "der Ister."* Frankfurt: Klostermann.

—(1995b), *Die Phänomenologie des religiösn Lebens.* Frankfurt: Klostermann.

—(1989), "*Phänomenologische Interpretationen zu Aristotles* (Phenomenological interpretations of Aristotle)," *Dilthey Jahrbuch* 6, 237–51.

—(1988), *Ontologie (Hermeneutik der Faktizität) (Ontology [The Hermeneutics of Facticity]).* Frankfurt: Klostermann.

—(1962), *Being and Time.* J. Macquarrie and E. Robinson (trans.). New York: Harper & Row.

—(1960), *Sein und Zeit.* Tübingen: Niemeyer. Translated as Heidegger (1962).

Kisiel, T. (1995), *The Genesis of Being and Time*. Berkeley: University of California Press.

Koch, W. (2009), "Heidegger's realist historicist answer to the problem of meaning," Ph.D. dissertation, University of South Florida.

Nietzsche, F. (1960), *Also sprach Zarathustra*, Part I, "Von den Verächtern des Leibes (On the Despisers of the Body)." Stuttgart: Kröner.

Plato (1961a), *Phaedo*. H. Tredennick (trans.), in *The Collected Dialogues of Plato*, E. Hamilton and H. Cairns (eds). Princeton: Princeton University Press, pp. 40–98.

—(1961b), *Philebus*. R. Hackforth (trans.), in *The Collected Dialogues of Plato*, E. Hamilton and H. Cairns (eds). Princeton: Princeton University Press, pp. 1086–1150.

Ricoeur, P. (1992), *Oneself as Another*. K. Blamey (trans.). Chicago: University of Chicago Press.

Smith, P. C. (2003), "*Phronêsis*, the Individual, and the Community," in *Gadamer Verstehen/Understanding Gadamer*, M. Wischke and M. Hofer (eds). Darmstadt: Wissenschaftliche Buchgesellschaft.

Virgil (1990), *Aeneid*. R. Fitzgerald (trans.). New York: Vintage Books.

Chapter 2

Aron, R. (1970), *Main Currents in Sociological Thought*. R. Howard and H. Weaver (trans.). Garden City: Doubleday.

Berger, P. and Luckmann, T. (1966), *The Social Construction of Reality*. New York: Doubleday.

Betti, E. D. (1980), "Hermeneutics as the general methodology of the *Geisteswissenschaften*," in *Contemporary Hermeneutics*, J. Bleicher (ed.). London: Routledge & Kegan Paul.

Derrida, J. (1992), "How to avoid speaking: denials," in *Derrida and Negative Theology*, H. Coward and T. Foshay (eds). Albany: SUNY Press.

—(1974, 1976), *Of Grammatology*. G. Chakravorty Spivak (trans.). Baltimore: Johns Hopkins University Press.

Dilthey, W. (1996), "The rise of hermeneutics," in *Hermeneutics and the Study of History*, vol. IV of *Selected Works*, R. A. Makkreel and F. Rodi (eds). Princeton: Princeton University Press.

—(1989), *Introduction to the Human Sciences*, vol. 1 of *Selected Works*, R. A. Makkreel and F. Rodi (eds). Princeton: Princeton University Press.

Ermarth, M. (1978), *William Dilthey: The Critique of Historical Reason*. Chicago: University of Chicago Press.

Gadamer, H-G. (1989), *Truth and Method* (2nd rev. edn). J. Weinsheimer and D. G. Marshall (trans.). New York: Crossroad.

—(1981), "What is practice? The conditions of social reason," in *Reason in the Age of Science*, F. G. Lawrence (trans.). Cambridge, MA: MIT Press.

—(1976a), "On the scope and function of hermeneutical reflection," in *Philosophical Hermeneutics*, D. E. Linge (trans.). Berkeley: University of California Press.

—(1976b), "The universality of the hermeneutical problem," in *Philosophical Hermeneutics*, D. E. Linge (trans.). Berkeley: University of California Press.

Habermas, J. (1980), "The hermeneutic claim to universality," in *Contemporary Hermeneutics*, J. Bleicher (ed.). London: Routledge & Kegan Paul.

—(1977), "A review of Gadamer's *Truth and Method*," in *Understanding and Social Inquiry*, F. R. Dallmayr and T. A. McCarthy (eds). Notre Dame: University of Notre Dame Press.

Habermas, J., Henrich, D., and J. Taubes (eds), (1971), *Hermeneutik und Ideologiekritik*. Frankfurt am Main: Suhrkamp.

Hegel, G. W. F. (1977), *Phenomenology of Spirit*. A. V. Miller (trans.). Oxford: Oxford University Press.

Heidegger, M. (1999), *Ontology: The Hermeneutics of Facticity*. J. van Buren (trans.). Bloomington: Indiana University Press.

Hirsch, E. D. Jr. (1967), *Validity in Interpretation*. New Haven: Yale University Press.

Kierkegaard, S. (1992), *Concluding Unscientific Postscript to Philosophical Fragments* (2 vols.), H. V. Hong and E. H. Hong (eds and trans.). Princeton: Princeton University Press.

Levinas, E. (1998), "The work of Edmund Husserl," in *Discovering Existence with Husserl*, R. A. Cohen and M. B. Smith (trans.). Evanston: Northwestern University Press.

Mannheim, K. (1936), *Ideology and Utopia: An Introduction to the Sociology of Knowledge*. L. Wirth and E. Shils (trans.). New York: Harcourt, Brace & World.

Merleau-Ponty, M. (1962), *The Phenomenology of Perception*. C. Smith (trans.). London: Routledge & Kegan Paul.

Ricoeur, P. (1986), *Lectures on Ideology and Utopia*. G. H. Taylor (ed.). New York: Columbia University Press.

—(1981), *Hermeneutics and the Human Sciences*. J. B. Thompson (ed. and trans.). New York: Cambridge University Press.

—(1974), *The Conflict of Interpretations*. D. Ihde (ed.). Evanston: Northwestern University Press.

—(1970), *Freud and Philosophy*. D. Savage (trans.). New Haven: Yale University Press.

—(1967), *Husserl: An Analysis of His Phenomenology*. E. G. Ballard and L. E. Embree (trans.). Evanston: Northwestern University Press.

Ricoeur, P. and A. LaCocque (1998), *Thinking Biblically: Exegetical and Hermeneutical Studies*. D. Pellauer (trans.). Chicago: University of Chicago Press.

Rorty, R. (1979), *Philosophy and the Mirror of Nature*. Princeton: Princeton University Press.

Weberman, D. (2002), "Gadamer's hermeneutics and the question of authorial intention," in *The Death and Resurrection of the Author?* W. Irwin (ed.). Westport: Greenwood Press.

Westphal, M. (2002), "Kierkegaard and the anxiety of authorship," in *The Death and Resurrection of the Author?* W. Irwin (ed.). Westport: Greenwood Press.

—(2001), "Totality and finitude in Schleiermacher's hermeneutics," in *Overcoming Onto-theology*. New York: Fordham University Press.

—(1999), "Hermeneutics as epistemology," in *The Blackwell Guide to Epistemology*, J. Greco and E. Sosa (eds). Oxford: Blackwell.

—(1998), *Suspicion and Faith: The Religious Uses of Modern Atheism*. New York: Fordham University Press.

Chapter 3

Cameron, W. S. K. (1996), "On communicative actors talking past one another," *Philosophy Today* 40, 1, 160–68.

Derrida, J. (1989), "Three questions to Hans-Georg Gadamer," in *Dialogue and Deconstruction: The Gadamer-Derrida Encounter*, D. P. Michelfelder and R. E. Palmer (eds). Albany: State University of New York Press, pp. 52–54.

Foucault, M. (1972), "The Discourse on Language," in *The Archaeology of Knowledge*. R. Sawyer (trans.). New York: Pantheon Books, pp. 215–37.

Gadamer, H.-G. (1994), *Truth and Method*. (2nd rev. edn.) J. Weinsheimer and D. G. Marshall (trans.). New York: Continuum.

—(1967), *Philosophie, Hermeneutik* (vol. 1 of *Kleine Schriften*). Tübingen: Mohr.

Grondin, J. (1994), *Introduction to Philosophical Hermeneutics*. New Haven: Yale University Press.

Habermas, J. (1997), "A Review of Gadamer's *Truth and Method*," in *Understanding and Social Inquiry*, F. R. Dallmayr and T. McCarthy (trans. and eds). Notre Dame: University of Notre Dame Press.

Howard, R. J. (1982), *Three Faces of Hermeneutics. An Introduction to Current Theories of Understanding*. Berkeley: University of California Press.

Laden, A. S. (2001), "Legitimate differences: interpretation in the abortion controversy and other public debates," *The Philosophical Review* 3, 431–33.

Ricoeur, P. (1991), *From Text to Action. Essays on Hermeneutics II*. K. Blamey and J. B. Thompson (trans.). Evanston: Northwestern University Press.

—(1986), *Lectures on Ideology and Utopia*. G. H. Taylor (ed.). New York: Columbia University Press.

Warnke, G. (1999), *Legitimate Differences. Interpretation in the Abortion Controversy and Other Debates*. Berkeley: University of California Press.

Chapter 4

Abizadeh, A. (2007), "On the philosophy/reason binaries: or, is Habermasian discourse motivationally impotent?" *Philosophy and Social Criticism* 33, 4, 445–72.

Anderson, H. (1997), *Conversation, Language, and Possibilities: A Postmodern Approach to Therapy*. New York: Basic Books.

Arthos, J. (2007), "The hermeneutic version of the rhetorical turn, or Heidegger and Gadamer in the recuperation of a humanist rhetoric," *Philosophy Today* 51 (Supplement), 70–81.

Dockhorn, K. (1980), "Hans-Georg Gadamer's *Truth and Method*," M. Brown (trans.), *Philosophy and Rhetoric* 13, 3, 160–80.

Dostal, R. J. (2002), "Gadamer's relation to Heidegger and phenomenology," in *The Cambridge Companion to Gadamer*, R. Dostal (ed.). Cambridge: Cambridge University Press, pp. 247–66.

D'Souza, K. (2006), "Ricoeur's narrative hermeneutics in relationship with Gadamer's philosophical hermeneutics: continuity and discontinuity," in *Issues in Interpretation Theory*, P. Vandevelde (ed.). Milwaukee: Marquette University Press, pp. 137–66.

Eskridge, Jr., W. N. (2006), "No frills textualism," *Harvard Law Review* 119, 7, 2041–75.

—(2001), "All about words: early understandings of the 'judicial power' in statutory interpretation, 1776–1806," *Columbia Law Review* 101, 5, 990–1106.

—(1994), *Dynamic Statutory Interpretation*. Cambridge, MA: Harvard University Press.

—(1990), "Gadamer/statutory interpretation," *Columbia Law Review* 90, 3, 609–81.

—(1987), "Dynamic statutory interpretation," *University of Pennsylvania Law Review* 135, 6, 1479–1555.

Eskridge, Jr., W. N. and Frickey, P. (1990), "Statutory interpretation as practical reasoning," *Stanford Law Review* 42, 2, 321–84.

Gadamer, H.-G. (2006a), "Classical and philosophical hermeneutics," *Theory, Culture & Society* 23, 1, 29–56.

—(2006b), "Looking back with Gadamer over his writings and their effective history: a dialogue with Jean Grondin (1996)," *Theory, Culture & Society* 23, 1, 85–100.

—(2005), "Heidegger as rhetor: Hans-Georg Gadamer interviewed by Ansgar Kemmann," in *Heidegger and Rhetoric*, D. M. Gross and A. Kemmann (eds), L. K. Schmidt (trans.). Albany: State University of New York Press, pp. 47–64 (Interviews conducted 1999–2001).

—(1998), "Science and the public sphere," in *Praise of Theory: Speeches and Essays*, C. Dawson (ed. and trans.). New Haven: Yale University Press, pp. 62–70 (1977 lecture).

—(1997a), "Reflections on my philosophical journey," in *The Philosophy of Hans-Georg Gadamer*, L. E. Hahn (ed.), R. E. Palmer (trans.). Chicago: Open Court, pp. 3–63.

—(1997b), "Reply to Donald Phillip Verene," in *The Philosophy of Hans-Georg Gadamer*, L. E. Hahn (ed.), M. Lütkehermölle and D. J. Schmidt (trans.). Chicago: Open Court, pp. 154–55.

—(1992a), "The expressive power of language," *Publications of the Modern Language Association of America* 107, 348–52.

—(1992b), "Interview: writing and the living voice," in *Hans-Georg Gadamer on Education, Poetry, and History: Applied Hermeneutics*, D. Misgeld and G. Nicholson (eds), L. Schmidt and M. Reuss (trans.). Albany: State University of New York Press, pp. 63–71.

—(1992c), "The diversity of Europe: inheritance and future," in *Hans-Georg Gadamer on Education, Poetry, and History: Applied Hermeneutics*, D. Misgeld and G. Nicholson (eds), L. Schmidt and M. Reuss (trans.). Albany: State University of New York Press, pp. 221–36.

—(1989), *Truth and Method*. (2nd rev. edn). J. Weinsheimer and D. G. Marshall (trans.), New York: Crossroad.

—(1986), *The Relevance of the Beautiful and Other Essays*. R. Bernasconi (ed.), N. Walker (trans.). Cambridge: Cambridge University Press.

—(1984), "The hermeneutics of suspicion," in *Hermeneutics: Questions and Prospects*, G. Shapiro and A. Sica (eds). Amherst: University of Massachusetts Press, pp. 54–65.

—(1981a), "Hermeneutics as practical philosophy," in *Reason in the Age of Science*, F. G. Lawrence (trans.). Cambridge, MA: MIT Press, pp. 88–112.

—(1981b), "Hermeneutics as a theoretical and practical task," in *Reason in the Age of Science*, F. G. Lawrence (trans.). Cambridge, MA: MIT Press, pp. 113–38.

—(1976), "On the scope and function of hermeneutical reflection," in *Philosophical Hermeneutics*, D. E. Linge (ed.), G. B. Hess and R. E. Palmer (trans.). Berkeley: University of California Press, pp. 18–43.

Gonzalez, F. (2006), "Dialectic and dialogue in the hermeneutics of Paul Ricoeur and H.-G. Gadamer," *Continental Philosophical Review* 39, 3, 313–45.

Mootz III, F. J. (2006), *Rhetorical Knowledge in Legal Practice and Critical Legal Theory*. Tuscaloosa: University of Alabama Press.

—(2000), "Psychotherapeutic practice as a model for postmodern legal theory," *Yale Journal of Law & the Humanities* 12, 2, 299–395.

Ricoeur, P. (2004), *Memory, History, Forgetting*. K. Blamey and D. Pellauer (trans.). Chicago: University of Chicago Press.

—(1997), "Rhetoric-poetics-hermeneutics," in *Rhetoric and Hermeneutics in Our Time: A Reader*, W. Jost and M. J. Hyde (eds), R. Harvey (trans.). New Haven: Yale University Press, pp. 60–72.

—(1986), *Lectures on Ideology and Utopia*. G. H. Taylor (ed.). New York: Columbia University Press.

—(1983), "The conflict of interpretations," in *Phenomenology: Dialogues and Bridges*, R. Bruzina and B. Wilshire (eds and trans.). Albany: State University of New York Press, pp. 299–320.

—(1981a), "The task of hermeneutics," in *Hermeneutics and the Human Sciences*, J. B. Thompson (ed. and trans.). Cambridge: Cambridge University Press, pp. 43–62.

—(1981b), "Hermeneutics and the critique of ideology," in *Hermeneutics and the Human Sciences*, J. B. Thompson (ed. and trans.). Cambridge: Cambridge University Press, pp. 63–100.

—(1976), *Interpretation Theory: Discourse and the Surplus of Meaning*. Fort Worth: Texas Christian University Press.

Ritivoi, A. (2006), *Paul Ricoeur: Tradition and Innovation in Rhetorical Theory*. Albany: State University of New York Press.

Schneider, D. M. (2001), "Empirical research on judicial reasoning: statutory interpretation in federal tax cases," *New Mexico Law Review* 31, 2, 325–58.

Shapiro, S. E. (1994), "Rhetoric as ideology critique: the Gadamer-Habermas debate reinvented," *Journal of the American Academy of Religion* 62, 1, 123–50.

Chapter 5

Bruns, G. L. (1992), *Hermeneutics Ancient and Modern*. New Haven: Yale University Press.

Dosse, F. (2008), *Paul Ricoeur: Les Sens d'une Vie (1913–2005)* (rev. edn.). Paris: La Découverte.

Eberhard, P. (2004), *The Middle Voice in Gadamer's Hermeneutics*. Tübingen: Mohr Siebeck.

Frey, D. (2008), *L'Interprétation et la Lecture chez Ricoeur et Gadamer*. Paris: Presses Universitaires de France.

Gadamer, H.-G. (1996), "Die Welt als Spiegelkabinett: Zum 350. Geburstag von Leibniz am 1. Juli 1996 (The World as a Room Full of Mirrors: On the Occasion of Leibniz's 350th Birthday)" (radio broadcast).

—(1992), *Hans-Georg Gadamer on Education, Poetry, and History: Applied Hermeneutics.* D. Misgeld and Graeme Nicholson (eds), L. Schmidt and M. Reusss (trans.). Albany: State University of New York Press.

—(1989), *Truth and Method* (2nd rev. edn). J. Weinsheimer and D. G. Marshall (trans.). New York: Crossroad.

—(1980a), "Anschauung und Anschaulichkeit," *Neue Hefte für Philosophie* 18/19, 1–14.

—(1980b), *Dialogue and Dialectic: Eight Hermeneutical Studies on Plato.* P. C. Smith (trans.). New Haven: Yale University Press.

Grondin, J. (2007), "L'art comme présentation chez Hans-Georg Gadamer: portée et limites d'un concept," *Études Germaniques* 62, 337–49.

—(2005), "La fusion des horizons: la version gadamérienne de l'adaequatio rei et intellectus?" *Archives de Philosophie* 68, 401–18.

—(2003), *Hans-Georg Gadamer: A Biography.* New Haven: Yale University Press.

Jervolino, D. (2008), "Rethinking Ricoeur: the unity of his work and the paradigm of translation," in *Reading Ricoeur*, D. M. Kaplan (ed.). Albany: State University of New York Press, pp. 225–35.

Kearney, R. (2006), "Introduction: Ricoeur's philosophy of translation," in *On Translation*, P. Ricoeur, E. Brennnan (trans.). London: Routledge.

Lakoff, G. (2002), *Moral Politics: How Liberals and Conservatives Think* (2nd edn). Chicago: University of Chicago Press.

Lambert, C. (2007), "Le Professeur," *Harvard Magazine*, July–August, 32–34.

Mootz, F. J. III (2006), *Rhetorical Knowledge in Legal Practice and Critical Legal Theory.* Tuscaloosa: University of Alabama Press.

Ricoeur, P. (2006), *On Translation.* E. Brennan (trans.). London: Routledge.

—(2004), *Memory, History, Forgetting.* K. Blamey and D. Pellauer (trans.). Chicago: University of Chicago Press.

—(1988), *Time and Narrative* (vol. 3), K. Blamey and D. Pellauer (trans.). Chicago: University of Chicago Press.

—(1984), *Time and Narrative* (vol. 1). K. McLaughlin and D. Pellauer (trans.). Chicago: University of Chicago Press.

—(1981a), "Appropriation," in *Hermeneutics and the Human Sciences*, J. B. Thompson (ed. and trans.). Cambridge: Cambridge University Press, pp. 182–93.

—(1981b), *Hermeneutics and the Human Sciences.* J. B. Thompson (ed. and trans.). Cambridge: Cambridge University Press.

—(1978), *The Philosophy of Paul Ricoeur.* C. E. Reagan and D. Stewart (eds). Boston: Beacon Press.

—(1977), *The Rule of Metaphor.* R. Czerny (trans.). Toronto: University of Toronto Press.

—(1976), *Interpretation Theory.* Fort Worth: Texas Christian University Press.

Rosen, S. (1997), "Horizontverschmelzung," in *The Philosophy of Hans-Georg Gadamer*, L. E. Hahn (ed.). Chicago: Open Court, pp. 207–18.

Stout, J. (2004), *Democracy and Tradition.* Princeton: Princeton University Press.

Tannen, D. (1990), *You Just Don't Understand: Women and Men in Conversation.* New York: Morrow.

Taylor, C. (1994), "The politics of recognition," in *Multiculturalism*, A. Gutmann (ed.). Princeton: Princeton University Press, pp. 25–73.

—(1990), "Comparison, history, truth," in *Myth and Philosophy*, F. Reynolds and D. Tracy (eds). Albany: State University of New York Press, pp. 37–55.

Taylor, G. (2010), "Legal interpretation: the window of the text as transparent, opaque, or translucent," *Nevada Law Journal* 10, 700–18.

—(2006), "Ricoeur's philosophy of imagination," *Journal of French Philosophy* 16, 93–104.

Vessey, D. (2010), Gadamer and the Fusion of Horizons," *International Journal of Philosophical Studies* 17(4), 526–36.

Warnke, G. (1987), *Gadamer: Hermeneutics, Tradition and Reason*. Stanford: Stanford University Press.

Weinsheimer, J. (1991), *Philosophical Hermeneutics and Literary Theory*. New Haven: Yale University Press.

—(1985), *Gadamer's Hermeneutics: A Reading of Truth and Method*. New Haven: Yale University Press.

Chapter 6

Dilthey, W. (2002), *The Formation of the Historical World in the Human Sciences*. R. A. Makkreel (ed.). Princeton: Princeton University Press.

D'Souza, K. (2006), "Ricoeur's narrative hermeneutics in relationship with Gadamer's philosophical hermeneutics," in *Issues in Interpretation Theory*, P. Vandevelde (ed.). Milwaukee: Marquette University Press, pp. 137–66.

Gadamer, H.-G. (2007), "The artwork in word and image: 'So true, so full of being!' " in *The Gadamer Reader*, R. Palmer (ed. and trans.). Evanston: Northwestern University Press, pp. 192–224.

—(1997), "Wort und Bild," in *Gadamer Lesebuch*. Tübingen: Mohr Siebeck, p. 176.

—(1993a), *Truth and Method* (2nd rev. edn). J. Weinsheimer and D. G. Marshall (trans.). New York: Continuum.

—(1993b), "Wort und Bild, so wahr, so seiend!" in *Gesammelte Werke 8*. Tübingen: J. C. B. Mohr, pp. 373–99.

—(1990), *Wahrheit und Methode*. Tübingen: J. C. B. Mohr.

—(1986), *Relevance of the Beautiful*. Nicholas Walker (trans.). Cambridge: Cambridge University Press.

—(1977), "The Western view of the inner experience of time and the limits of thought," in *Time and the Philosophies*, H. Aguessy (ed.). Paris: UNESCO, pp. 33–48.

—(1972), "The continuity of history and the existential movement," Thomas Wren (trans.), *Philosophy Today* 16, 3, 230–40.

—(1970), "Concerning empty and ful-filled time," *Southern Journal of Philosophy* 8, 4, 341–53.

Heidegger, M. (1971), *Poetry, Language, Thought*. A. Hofstadter (trans.). New York: Harper & Row.

Kosman, L. A. (1969), "Aristotle's definition of motion," *Phronesis* 14, 40–62.

Petrarca, F. (1966), *Letters from Petrarch*. M. Bishop (trans.). Bloomington: Indiana University Press.

Ricoeur, P. (1996), "Reply to Ted Klein," in *The Philosophy of Paul Ricoeur*, L. E. Hahn (ed.). Chicago: Open Court, pp. 367–70.

—(1992), *Oneself as Another*. K. Blamey (trans.). Chicago: University of Chicago Press.

—(1991a), "The human experience of time and narrative," in *A Ricoeur Reader*, Mario J. Valdés (ed.). Toronto: University of Toronto Press, pp. 99–116.

—(1991b), "Mimesis and representation," in *A Ricoeur Reader*, Mario J. Valdés (ed.). Toronto: University of Toronto Press, pp. 137–55.

—(1991c), *From Text to Action: Essays in Hermeneutics 2*. K. Blamey and J. B. Thompson (trans.). Evanston: Northwestern University.

—(1991d), "Narrated time," in *A Ricoeur Reader*, Mario J. Valdés (ed.). Toronto: University of Toronto Press, pp. 338–54.

—(1988), *Time and Narrative, vol. 3*. K. Blamey and D. Pellauer (trans.). Chicago: University of Chicago Press.

—(1985), *Time and Narrative, vol. 2*. K. McLaughlin and D. Pellauer (trans.). Chicago: University of Chicago Press.

—(1984), *Time and Narrative, vol. 1*. K. McLaughlin and D. Pellauer (trans.). Chicago: University of Chicago Press.

Ross, S. (2006), "The temporality of tarrying in Gadamer," *Theory, Culture and Society* 23, 1, 101–23.

Sachs, J. "Aristotle: motion and its place in nature," *The Internet Encyclopedia of Philosophy*, available at www.iep.utm.edu/a/aris-mot.htm (accessed December 15, 2010).

—(1995), *Aristotle's Physics: A Guided Study*. New Brunswick: Rutgers University Press.

Chapter 7

Gadamer, H.-G. (2007), "Hermeneutics and ontological difference," in *The Gadamer Reader*, Richard Palmer (ed.). Evanston: Northwestern University Press, pp. 356–71.

—(2004), *Truth and Method* (2nd rev. edn). J. Weinsheimer and D. G. Marshall (trans.). New York: Continuum.

—(2000a), "Phenomenology of ritual and language," in *Language and Linguisticality in Gadamer's Hermeneutics*, Lawrence Schmidt (ed.). Lanham: Lexington Books, pp. 19–50.

—(2000b), "Subjectivity and intersubjectivity; subject and person," *Continental Philosophy Review* 33, 275–287.

—(1991), *Plato's Dialectical Ethics*. R. M. Wallace (trans. and intro.). New Haven: Yale University Press.

—(1987), "Ich und du (Löwith)," in *Gesammelte Werke, vol. 4*. Tübingen: Mohr Siebeck, pp. 234–39.

—(1985), "Praktisches wissen," in *Gesammelte Werke, vol. 5*. Tübingen: Mohr Siebeck, pp. 230–48.

—(1980), "Religious and poetical speaking," in *Myth, Symbol and Reality*, A. Olson (ed.). Notre Dame: University of Notre Dame Press, pp. 86–98.

—(1976), "The universality of the hermeneutic problem," in *Philosophical Hermeneutics*, D. E. Linge (trans. and ed.). Berkeley: University of California Press, pp. 3–17.

Honneth, A. (2003), "On the destructive power of the third: Gadamer and Heidegger's doctrine of intersubjectivity," *Philosophy and Social Criticism* 29, 1, 5–21.

—(1996), *The Struggle for Recognition*. Boston: MIT Press.

Kojève, A. (1969), *Introduction to the Reading of Hegel*. New York: Basic Books.

Plutarch. (1992), "On how to tell a flatterer from a friend," in *Essays*. London: Penguin Books, pp. 51–112.

Ricoeur, P. (2005), *The Course of Recognition*. D. Pellauer (trans.). Cambridge, MA.: Harvard University Press.

—(1988), *Time and Narrative, vol. III*. K. Blamey and D. Pellauer (trans.). Chicago: University of Chicago Press.

—(1981), "Appropriation," in *Hermeneutics and the Human Sciences*, J. B. Thompson (trans. and ed.). Cambridge: Cambridge University Press, pp. 182–94.

Theunissen, M. (1984), *The Other: Studies in the Social Ontology of Husserl, Heidegger, Sartre and Buber*. Cambridge, MA: MIT Press.

Chapter 8

Aeschylus (1942), *Aeschylus I: Agamemnon, The Libation Bearers, The Eumenides, Prometheus Bound*. D. Green and R. Lattimore (eds). New York: Modern Library.

Allen, C. W. (1989), "The primacy of 'phronesis': a proposal for avoiding frustrating tendencies in our conception of rationality," *Journal of Religion* 69, 359–74.

Annas, J. (1995), "Prudence and morality in ancient and modern ethics," *Ethics* 105, 241–57.

Aristotle (1998) *The Nicomachean Ethics*. J. L. Ackrill and J. O. Urmson (eds), David Ross (trans.). Oxford: Oxford University Press.

Bauman, Z. (2005), *Liquid Life*. Cambridge: Polity Press.

Benhabib, S. (2001), "Judgment and the moral foundations of politics in Hannah Arendt's thought," in *Judgment, Imagination, and Politics: Themes from Kant and Arendt*, R. Beiner and J. Nedelsky (eds). Lanham: Rowman & Littlefield, pp. 183–204.

Blum, L. A. (1994), *Moral Perception and Particularity*. Cambridge: Cambridge University Press.

Brague, R. (1988), *Aristote et la Question du Monde*. Paris: Presses universitaires de France.

Caputo, J. D. (2003), "Against principles: a sketch of an ethics without ethics," in E. Wyschogrod and G. P. McKenny (eds), *The Ethical*. Oxford: Blackwell, pp. 169–80.

Depew, D. (2004), "Review of *Prudence: Classical Virtue, Postmodern Practice*. Ed. Robert Hariman," *Philosophy & Rhetoric* 37, 167–75.

Dostal, R. J. (2002), "Introduction," in *The Cambridge Companion to Gadamer's Hermeneutics*, R. J. Dostal (ed.). Cambridge: Cambridge University Press, pp. 1–12.

—(1992), "Friendship and politics: Heidegger's failing," *Political Theory* 20, 399–423.

Dunne, J. (1993), *Back to the Rough Ground: Practical Judgment and the Lure of Technique*. Notre Dame: University of Notre Dame Press.

Eagleton, T. (2003), *Sweet Violence: The Idea of the Tragic*. Oxford: Blackwell.

Ewen, S. (1990), *All Consuming Images: The Politics of Style in Contemporary Culture* (revised edn). New York: Basic Books.

Gadamer, H.-G. (1994), "The Marburg theology," in *Heidegger's Ways*, H.-G. Gadamer, J. W. Stanley (trans.). Albany: State University of New York Press, pp. 29–45.

—(1992), *Truth and Method* (2nd revised edn). J. Weinsheimer and D. G. Marshall (trans.). New York: Crossroad.

Gadamer, H.-G. and McCumber, J. (1989), "Back from Syracuse?" *Critical Inquiry* 15, 427–30.

Geiman, C. P. (2001), "Heidegger's Antigones," in *A Companion to Heidegger's Introduction to Metaphysics*, R. Polt and G. Fried (eds). New Haven: Yale University Press, pp. 161–82.

Gellrich, M. (1988), *Tragedy and Theory: The Problem of Conflict Since Aristotle*. Princeton: Princeton University Press.

Gillespie, M. A. (2000), "Martin Heidegger's Aristotelian National Socialism," *Political Theory* 28, 46–66.

Groth, M. (2001), "Review [of Polt and Fried (2001)]," *Review of Metaphysics* 56, 452–55.

Guigon, C. (2001), "Being as appearing: retrieving the Greek experience of '*phusis*'," in *A Companion to Heidegger's Introduction to Metaphysics*, R. Polt and G. Fried (eds). New Haven: Yale University Press, pp. 34–57.

Hariman, R. (ed.) (2003), *Prudence: Classical Virtue, Postmodern Practice*. University Park: Pennsylvania State University Press.

Heidegger, M. (2009), *Basic Concepts of Aristotelian Philosophy*. R. D. Metcalf and M. B. Tanzer (trans.). Bloomington: Indiana University Press.

—(2002), *Grundbegriffe der Aristotelischen Philosophie*. M. Michalski (ed.). Frankfurt: Vittorio Klostermann. Translated as Heidegger (2009).

—(1997), *Plato's Sophist*. R. Rojcewicz and A. Schuwer (trans.). Bloomington: Indiana University Press.

—(1995), *Aristotle's Metaphysics Theta 1–3: On the Essence and Actuality of Force*. W. Brogan and P. Warnek (trans.). Bloomington: Indiana University Press.

—(1992a), *Parmenides*. A. Schuwer and R. Rojcewicz (trans.). Bloomington: Indiana University Press.

—(1992b), *Platon: Sophistes*. Frankfurt: Vittorio Klostermann. Translated as Heidegger (1997).

—(1984), *Hölderlins Hymne "Der Ister."* Frankfurt: Vittorio Klostermann.

—(1981), *Aristoteles Metaphysic Theta 1–3. Von Wesen und Wirklichkeit der Kraft*, (Gesamtausgabe 33). Frankfurt: Vittorio Klostermann. Translated as Heidegger (1995).

—(1968), *An Introduction to Metaphysics*. R. Manheim (trans.). New Haven: Yale University Press.

—(1966), *Einführung in die Metaphysik*. Tübingen: Niemeyer Verlag.

—(1963), "Preface," in *Heidegger: Through Phenomenology to Thought*, W. J. Richardson. The Hague: M. Nijhoff, pp. viii–xxiv.

—(1962), *Being and Time*. J. Macquarrie and E. Robinson (trans.). New York and Evanston: Harper & Row.

Ichheiser, G. (1966), "Social perception and moral judgment," *Philosophy and Phenomenological Research* 26, 546–60.

Kant, I. (1954), *Critique of Judgement.* J. C. Meredith (trans.). Oxford: Oxford University Press.

Kelly, K. (2010), "From print to pixel," *Smithsonian* 41, July/August, 122–28.

Kyte, R. (1996), "Moral reasoning as perception: a reading of Carol Gilligan," *Hypatia* 11, 97–113.

Larmore, C. (1987), *Patterns of Moral Complexity.* Cambridge: Cambridge University Press.

Levinas, E. (1989), "As if consenting to horror," P. Wissing (trans.), *Critical Inquiry* 15, 485–88.

Lingis, A. (1994), *The Community of Those Who Have Nothing in Common.* Bloomington: Indiana University Press.

McNeil, W. (2001), "The time of contributions to philosophy," in *Companion to Heidegger's Contributions to Philosophy,* C. Scott, S. M. Schoenbohm, D. Vallega-Neu, and A. Vallega (eds). Bloomington: Indiana University Press, pp. 129–49.

Nonet, P. (2005), "Antigone's Law," http://escholarship.org/uc/item/5480b45q (accessed December 15, 2010).

Nussbaum, M. (1990), "The discernment of perception: an Aristotelian conception of private and public rationality," in *Love's Knowledge: Essays on Philosophy and Literature.* Oxford: Oxford University Press, pp. 54–105.

—(1986), *The Fragility of Goodness.* Cambridge: Cambridge University Press.

Polanyi, M. (1983), *The Tacit Dimension.* Gloucester: Peter Smith.

Ricoeur, P. (2007), *Reflections on the Just.* D. Pellauer (trans.). Chicago: University of Chicago Press.

—(2000), *The Just.* D. Pellauer (trans.). Chicago: University of Chicago Press.

—(1998a), *Critique and Conviction.* K. Blamey (trans.). New York: Columbia University Press.

—(1998b), "Philosophy after Kierkegaard," in *Kierkegaard: A Critical Reader,* J. Reé and J. Chamberlain (eds). Oxford: Blackwell, pp. 9–25.

—(1995), "Hope and the structure of philosophical systems," in *Figuring the Sacred: Religion, Narrative and Imagination,* D. Pellauer (trans.) and M. I. Wallace (ed.). Minneapolis: Fortress Press, pp. 203–16.

—(1992), *Oneself as Another.* K. Blamey (trans.). Chicago: University of Chicago Press.

—(1991), *From Text to Action: Essays in Hermeneutics II.* K. Blamey and J. B. Thompson (trans.). Evanston: Northwestern University Press.

—(1988), *Time and Narrative,* vol. 3. K. Blamey and D. Pellauer (trans). Chicago: The University of Chicago Press.

—(1984), *Time and Narrative,* vol. 1. K. McLaughlin and D. Pellauer (trans.). Chicago: University of Chicago Press.

—(1969), "Preface," in *Elements for an Ethic,* J. Nabert, W. J. Petrek (trans.). Evanston: Northwestern University Press, pp. xvii–xxviii.

—(1967), *The Symbolism of Evil.* E. Buchanan (trans.). Boston: Beacon Press.

—(1963), "Philosopher après Kierkegaard," *Revue de Théologie et de Philosophie* 13, 303–16. Translated as Ricoeur (1998).

Rorty, A. O. (1980), "The place of contemplation in Aristotle's Nichomachean Ethics," in *Essays on Aristotle's Ethics,* A. O. Rorty (ed.). Berkeley: University of California Press, pp. 377–94.

Scarry, E. (1985), *The Body in Pain: The Making and Unmaking of the World.* Oxford: Oxford University Press.

Schmidt, D. J. (2001), *On Germans and Other Greeks: Tragedy and Ethical Life.* Bloomington: Indiana University Press.

Schoenbohm, S. (2001), "Heidegger's interpretation of phusis," in *A Companion to Heidegger's Introduction to Metaphysics,* R. Polt and G. Fried (eds). New Haven: Yale University Press, pp. 143–60.

Scott, C. (1991), "Heidegger's rector's address: a loss of the question of ethics," *Graduate Faculty Philosophy Journal* 14, 237–64.

Segal, C. (1964), "Sophocles' praise of man and the conflicts of the 'Antigone,'" *Arion* 3, 46–66.

Sontag, S. (2003), *Regarding the Pain of Others.* New York: Farrar, Straus and Giroux.

Sophocles (1954), *Sophocles I: Oedipus the King, Oedipus at Colonus, Antigone.* D. Green and R. Lattimore (eds). New York: Modern Library.

Steiner, G. (1984), *Antigones.* New Haven: Yale University Press.

Tabachnik, D. E. (2004), "Phronesis, democracy and technology," *Canadian Journal of Political Science/Revue canadienne de science politique* 37, 997–1016.

Taminiaux, J. (1991), *Heidegger and the Project of Fundamental Ontology.* M. Gendre (trans. and ed.). Albany: State University of New York Press.

—(1989), *Lectures de l'Ontologie Fundamental. Essais sur Heidegger.* Grenoble: Jerome Millon. Translated as Taminiaux (1991).

Warren, R. P. (1985), "The corner of the eye," in *New and Selected Poems: 1923–1985.* New York: Random House, pp. 103–04.

Chapter 9

Abel, O. (2005), "Paul Ricoeur's hermeneutics: from critique to poetics," in *Reading Ricoeur,* David M. Kaplan (ed.). Albany: SUNY Press.

Arendt, H. (1958), *The Human Condition.* Chicago and London: University of Chicago Press.

Aristotle. (1962), *Nicomachean Ethics,* M. Ostwald (trans. and intro.). Indianapolis: Bobbs-Merrill.

Dauenhauer, B. (2007), "Responding to evil," *The Southern Journal of Philosophy* 45, 207–22.

—(2005), "The place of hope in responsible political practice," in *Interdisciplinary Perspectives on Hope,* J. A. Elliott (ed.). New York: Nova Science Publishers, pp. 81–97.

—(2002), "Paul Ricoeur and the tasks of citizenship," in *Paul Ricoeur and Contemporary Moral Thought,* J. Wall, W. Schweiker and W. D. Hall (eds and intro.). New York: Routledge, pp. 233–50.

—.(1998), *Paul Ricoeur: The Promise and Risk of Politics.* Lanham: Rowman & Littlefield.

Dauenhauer, B. and Wells, M. (2001), "Corrective justice and constitutional torts," *Georgia Law Review* 35, 903–29.

Davion, V. and Wolf, C. (2000), "Introduction: from comprehensive justice to political liberalism," in *The Idea of a Political Liberalism.* Lanham: Rowman & Littlefield, pp. 1–15.

Dworkin, R. (2006), *Is Democracy Possible Here?* Princeton and Oxford: Princeton University Press.

Gadamer, H-G. (1989), *Truth and Method* (2nd rev. edn). J. Weinsheimer and D. G. Marshall (trans.). New York: Crossroad.

—(1976), "On the scope and function of hermeneutical reflection," in *Philosophical Hermeneutics*, D. Linge (trans. and ed.). Berkeley and Los Angeles: University of California Press, pp. 18–43.

Griswold, C. L. (2007), *Forgiveness: A Philosophical Exploration*. Cambridge: Cambridge University Press.

Habermas, J. (2008), "Religion in the public sphere: cognitive presuppositions for the 'public use of reason' by religious and secular citizens," in *Between Naturalism and Religion*, C. Cronin (trans.). Cambridge: Polity Press, pp. 114–48.

Harent, S. (1939), "Espérance," in *Dictionnaire de Théologie Catholique*, 5, part 1, A. Vacant and E. Mangenot (eds.). Paris: Librarie Letouzey et Ané, pp. 609–11.

Heaney, S. (2005), *Finders Keepers: Selected Prose 1971–2001*. New York: Farrar, Straus, Giroux.

Husserl, E. (1970), *The Crisis of European Man and Transcendental Phenomenology*. D. Carr (trans.). Evanston: Northwestern University Press.

Jaspers, K. (1947), *The Question of German Guilt*. E. B. Ashton (trans.). New York: Dial Press.

Jervolino, D. (2008), "Rethinking Ricoeur: the unity of his work and the paradigm of translation," in *Reading Ricoeur*, D. M. Kaplan (ed.) Albany: SUNY Press, pp. 225–36.

Kasher, A. and A. Yadlin (2009), "Israel and the rules of war: an exchange" (with a response by A. Margalit and M. Walzer), *The New York Review of Books* 56, 10, June 11, 77, available at: www.nybooks.com/articles/archives/2009/jun/11/israel-the-rules-of-war-an-exchange/ (accessed December 15, 2010).

Kearney, R. (2006), "Introduction: Ricoeur's philosophy of translation," in *On Translation*, P. Ricoeur. New York: Routledge, pp. vii–xx.

Kennedy, E. M. (Senator) (2006), "We can't ignore Iraq's refugees," *The Washington Post*, December 30, A 21.

Linge, D. (1976), "Editor's introduction," in *Philosophical Hermeneutics*, H.-G. Gadamer, D. E. Linge (ed. and trans.). Berkeley and Los Angeles: University of California Press, pp. xi–lviii.

Margalit, A. and Walzer, M. (2009), "Israel: civilians and combatants," *The New York Review of Books* 56, 8, May 14, available at: www.nybooks.com/articles/archives/2009/may/14/israel-civilians (accessed December 15, 2010).

Ricoeur, P. (2006), *On Translation*. Eileen Brennan (trans.). London and New York: Routledge.

—(2004a), *Memory, History, Forgetting*. K. Blamey and D. Pellauer (trans.). Chicago and London: University of Chicago Press.

—(2004b), "Epilogue: difficult forgiveness," in *Memory, History, Forgetting*, K. Blamey and D. Pellauer (trans.). Chicago and London: University of Chicago Press, pp. 457–506.

—(2002), "Ethics and human capability," in *Paul Ricoeur and Contemporary Moral Thought*, J. Wall, W. Schweiker, and W. D. Hall (eds). New York and London: Routledge.

—(2001), "Introduction," in *Le Juste 2*. Paris: Editions Esprit, pp. 7–51.

—(2000a), "Interpretation and/or argumentation," in *The Just*, D. Pellauer (trans.). Chicago and London: University of Chicago Press, pp. 109–26.

—(2000b), "The act of judging," in *The Just*, D. Pellauer (trans.). Chicago and London: University of Chicago Press, pp. 127–32.

—(2000c), "Sanction, rehabilitation, pardon," in *The Just*, D. Pellauer (trans.). Chicago and London: University of Chicago Press, pp. 133–45.

—(1998), *Critique and Conviction*, K. Blamey (trans.). New York: Columbia University Press.

—(1996a), "From metaphysics to moral philosophy," *Philosophy Today* 40, 443–58.

—(1996b), "Le destinaire de la religion: l'homme capable," *Archivio di Filosofia* 64, 19–34.

—(1996c), "Préface," in *Code de déontologie médicale*, L. René (intro. and commentary). Paris: Éditions du Seuil, pp. 9–25.

—(1995a), "Le pardon peut-il guérir?" *Esprit*, mars-avril, 77–82.

—(1995b), "A philosophical hermeneutics of religion: Kant," in *Figuring the Sacred*, D. Pellauer (trans.), M. I. Wallace (ed.). Minneapolis: Fortress Press, pp. 75–92.

—(1995c), "Reflections on a new ethos for Europe," *Philosophy and Social Criticism* 21, 5, 3–13.

—(1995d), "Fragility and Responsibility," E. Iwanowski (trans.), *Philosophy and Social Criticism* 21, 5, 15–22.

—(1994), "Entretien," in *Éthique et responsabilité, Paul Ricoeur*, J.-C. Aeschlimann (ed.). Neuchâtal: Baconnière, pp. 11–37.

—(1992a), "Fragilité et responsabilité," in *Eros and Eris: Contributions to a Hermeneutical Phenomenology*, P. Van Tongeren, P. Sars, C. Bremmers, and K. Boey (eds). Dordrecht: Kluwer, pp. 295–304.

—(1992b), *Oneself as Another*. K. Blamey (trans.). Chicago and London: University of Chicago Press.

—(1992c), "Quel éthos nouveau pour l'Europe?," in *Imaginer l'Europe*, P. Koslowski (ed.). Paris: Éditions du Cerf, pp. 107–16.

—(1991a), "Éthique et politique," in *Lectures I*. Paris: Éditions du Seuil, pp. 233–38.

—(1991b), "Explanation and understanding," in *From Text to Action*, K. Blamey and J. B. Thompson (trans.). Evanston: Northwestern University Press, pp. 125–43.

—(1991c), "Practical reason," in *From Text to Action*, K. Blamey and J. B. Thompson (trans.). Evanston: Northwestern University Press, pp. 188–207.

—(1991d), "Hermeneutics and the critique of ideology," in *From Text to Action*, K. Blamey and J. B. Thompson (trans.). Evanston: Northwestern University Press, pp. 270–307.

—(1991e), "Ethics and politics," in *From Text to Action*, K. Blamey and J. B. Thompson (trans.). Evanston: Northwestern University Press, pp. 325–37.

—(1987), "The fragility of political language." *Philosophy Today* 31, 35–44.

—(1986), "Foreword," in *The Politics of Hope*, B. Dauenhauer. New York and London: Routledge and Kegan Paul, pp. ix–xvi.

—(1981), *Hermeneutics and the Human Sciences*. J. B. Thompson (ed. and trans.). Cambridge: Cambridge University Press.

—(1978), "The problem of the foundation of moral philosophy," *Philosophy Today* 22, 175–92.

—(1973), "The task of the political educator," *Philosophy Today* 17, 142–52.

—(1968), "Tasks of the ecclesial community in the modern world," in *Theology of Renewal II*, L. K. Shook (ed.). New York: Herder and Herder, pp. 242–54.

—(1965), "The political paradox," in *History and Truth*, C. A. Kelbley (trans.). Evanston: Northwestern University Press, pp. 247–70.

Taylor, G. H. (2011), "Understanding as metaphoric, not a fusion of horizons," in this volume.

Walker, M. U. (2006), *Moral Repair: Reconstructing Moral Relations after Wrongdoing*. Cambridge: Cambridge University Press.

Walzer, M. (1977), *Just and Unjust Wars* (4th edn). New York: Basic Books.

Weber, M. (1978), "Politics as a vocation," in *Max Weber: Selections in Translation*, E. Matthews (ed. and trans.). Cambridge: Cambridge University Press.

White, J. B. (1990), *Justice as Translation*. Chicago and London: University of Chicago Press.

Wills, G. (2009), "The Voice of the Eagle," *The New York Review of Books* 56, 8, May 14, available at: www.nybooks.com/articles/archives/2009/may/14/the-voice-of-the-eagle (accessed December 15, 2010).

Chapter 10

Butler, J. (1993), *Bodies That Matter: On the Discursive Limits of "Sex."* New York and London: Routledge.

Code, L. (ed.) (2003), *Feminist Interpretations of Hans-Georg Gadamer*. University Park: Pennsylvania State University Press.

Conboy, K., N. Medina and S. Stanbury (1996), *Writing on the Body: Female Embodiment and Feminist Theory*. New York: Columbia University Press.

Davis, K. (ed.) (1997), *Embodied Practices: Feminist Perspectives on the Body*. London: Sage.

Derksen, L. D. (1996), *Dialogues on Women*. Amsterdam: VU University Press.

—(1983), *On Universal Hermeneutics: A Study in the Philosophy of Hans-Georg Gadamer*. Amsterdam: VU University Press.

Gadamer, H.-G. (1996), *The Enigma of Health. The Art of Healing in a Scientific Age*. J. Gaiger and N. Walker (trans.). Cambridge: Polity Press.

—(1995), *Truth and Method* (2nd rev. edn). J. Weinsheimer and D. G. Marshall (trans.). New York: Continuum.

Grosz, E. (1994), *Volatile Bodies: Toward a Corporeal Feminism*. Bloomington and Indianapolis: Indiana University Press.

Halsema, A. (2005), "Reflexionen über Identität in einer multikulturellen Gesellschaft —Ein Dialog zwischen Ricoeur, Irigaray und Butler," in *Feministische Phänomenologie und Hermeneutik, Reihe Orbis Phaenomenologicus*, S. Stoller, V. Vasterling, and L. Fischer (eds). Würzburg: Königshausen & Neumann, pp. 208–34.

Heidegger, M. (2002), *Being and Time*. John Macquarrie and Edward Robinson (trans.). Malden: Blackwell.

Husserl, E. (1977), *Cartesianische Meditationen*. Hamburg: Felix Meiner.

Irigaray, L. (2000), *To Be Two*. M. M. Rhodes and M. F. Cocito-Monoc (trans.). London, New Brunswick: The Athlone Press.

—(1993), *An Ethics of Sexual Difference*. C. Burke and G. C. Gill (trans.). Ithaca: Cornell University Press.

—(1985), *Speculum of the Other Woman*. G. C. Gill (trans.). Ithaca: Cornell University Press.

Joy, M. (ed.) (1997), *Paul Ricoeur and Narrative: Context and Contestation*. Calgary: University of Calgary Press.

Lloyd, G. (1984), *The Man of Reason: Male and Female in Western Philosophy.* London: Methuen.

Nussbaum, M. (2000), *Women and Human Development: The Capabilities Approach.* Cambridge: Cambridge University Press.

Price, J. and Shildrick, M. (eds) (1999), *Feminist Theory and the Body: A Reader.* Edinburgh: Edinburgh University Press.

Ricoeur, P. (2007a), *Freedom and Nature. The Voluntary and the Involuntary.* E. V. Kohák (trans. and intro.), D. Ihde (foreword). Evanston: Northwestern University Press.

—(2007b), *Reflections on The Just.* D. Pellauer (trans). Chicago and London: The University of Chicago Press.

—(2005), *The Course of Recognition.* D. Pellauer (trans.). Cambridge, MA, and London: Harvard University Press.

—(2000), *The Just.* D. Pellauer (trans.). Chicago and London: The University of Chicago Press.

—(1994), "Wonder, Eroticism, and Enigma," in *Sexuality and the Sacred. Sources for Theological Reflection,* J. B. Nelson and S. P. Longfellow (eds). Westminster: John Knox Press, pp. 80–84 (originally published in *Cross Currents* 14, 2, 1964).

—(1992), *Oneself as Another.* K. Blamey (trans.). Chicago and London: University of Chicago Press.

—(1991), "Life in Quest of Narrative," in *On Paul Ricoeur: Narrative and Interpretation,* David Wood (ed.). London and New York: Routledge, pp. 20–33.

Ricoeur, P. and J.-P. Changeux (2000), *What Makes Us Think? A Neuroscientist and a Philosopher Argue about Ethics, Human Nature, and the Brain.* M. B. DeBevoise (trans.). Princeton and Oxford: Princeton University Press.

Schiebinger, L. (2000), *Feminism and the Body.* Oxford Readings in Feminism. Oxford and New York: Oxford University Press.

Van den Haak, N. (2001), *Metafoor en filosofie, Studie naar de metaforische werking in de filosofie aan de hand van Julia Kristeva en Paul Ricoeur.* Best: Damon.

Vessey, D. (2000), "Gadamer and the Body Across Dialogical Contexts," *Philosophy Today* SPEP Supplement, 70–76.

Wheeler, M. (2005), *Reconstructing the Cognitive World.* Cambridge, MA and London: MIT Press.

Chapter 11

Achterhuis, H. (ed.) (2001), *American Philosophy of Technology.* Bloomington: Indiana University Press.

Bijker, W. E. (1995), "King of the road: the social construction of the safety bicycle," in *Of Bicycles, Bakelight, and Bulbs: Toward a Theory of Sociotechnical Change.* Cambridge, MA: MIT Press, pp. 19–100.

Bijker, W. E. and J. Law (eds) (1994), *Shaping Technology/Building Societies: Studies in Sociotechnical Change.* Cambridge, MA: MIT Press.

Bloor, D. (1976), *Knowledge and Social Imagery.* Chicago: University of Chicago Press.

Brey, P., Briggle, A., Spence, E. (eds) (forthcoming), *The Good Life in a Technological Age.* London: Routledge.

Dreyfus, H. (1992), *What Computers Still Can't Do: A Critique of Artificial Reason.* Cambridge, MA: MIT Press.

Ellul, J. (1965), *The Technological Society.* New York: Knopf.

Figueroa, R. M. (2006), "Evaluating environmental justice claims," in *Forging Environmentalism: Justice, Livelihood, and Contested Environments,* J. Bauer (ed.). Armonk: E. M. Sharpe, pp. 360–76.

Gadamer, H.-G. (1996), "Theory, technology, praxis," in *The Enigma of Health,* J. Gaiger and N. Walker (trans.). Stanford: Stanford University Press, pp. 1–30.

—(1989), *Truth and Method* (2nd rev. edn). J. Weinsheimer and D. G. Marshall (trans.). New York: Crossroad.

—(1981a), "What is practice? The conditions of social reason," in *Reason in the Age of Science,* F. G. Lawrence (trans.). Cambridge, MA: MIT Press, pp. 69–87.

—(1981b), "Hermeneutics as a theoretical and practical task," in *Reason in the Age of Science,* F. G. Lawrence (trans.). Cambridge, MA: MIT Press, pp. 113–37.

Heidegger, M. (1982), *The Question Concerning Technology and Other Essays.* New York: Harper Perennial.

Ihde, D. (2010), *Embodied Technics.* New York: Automatic Press.

—(1990), *Technology and the Lifeworld.* Bloomington: Indiana University Press.

Jaspers, K. (1951), *Man in the Modern Age.* London: Routledge & Kegan Paul.

Kaplan, D. M. (2010), "Paul Ricoeur and development ethics," in *A Passion for the Possible: Thinking With Paul Ricoeur,* B. Treanor and H. I. Venema (eds). New York: Fordham University Press, pp. 112–28.

—(2006), "Paul Ricoeur and the philosophy of technology," *Journal of French Philosophy* 16, 42–56.

Latour, B. (1999), *Pandora's Hope: Essays on the Reality of Science Studies.* Cambridge, MA: Harvard University Press.

Marcuse, H. (1964), *One-Dimensional Man.* Boston: Beacon Press.

Newman, R. (2001), "Making environmental activism: women and Love Canal activism," *Women's Studies Quarterly* 27, 65–84.

Nussbaum, M. (2001), *Women and Human Development.* Cambridge: Cambridge University Press.

Oldenziel, R. (2004), *Making Technology Masculine: Men, Women, and Modern Machines in America 1870–1945.* Amsterdam: Amsterdam University Press.

Oudshoorn, N. and Pinch, T. (eds) (2005), *How Users Matter: The Co-Construction of Users and Technology.* Cambridge, MA: MIT Press.

Ricoeur, P. (2007), "Autonomy and vulnerability," in *Reflections on the Just,* D. Pellauer (trans.). Chicago: University of Chicago Press, pp. 72–90.

—(2005), *The Course of Recognition.* D. Pellauer (trans.). Cambridge, MA: Harvard University Press.

—(2004), *Memory, History, Forgetting.* K. Blamey and D. Pellauer (trans.). Chicago: University of Chicago Press.

—(2002), "Ethics and human capability: a response," in *Paul Ricoeur and Contemporary Moral Thought,* J. Wall, W. Schweiker, and W. D. Hall (eds). New York: Routledge, pp. 279–90.

—(1984–88), *Time and Narrative* (vols 1–3). K. Blamey and D. Pellauer (trans.). Chicago: University of Chicago Press.

—(1966), *Freedom and Nature: The Voluntary and the Involuntary.* E. Kohak (trans.). Evanston: Northwestern University Press.

—(1965), "Christianity and the meaning of history," in *History and Truth,* C. A. Kelbley (trans.). Evanston: Northwestern University Press, pp. 81–97.

Selinger, E. (2008), "Technology transfer and globalization: a new wave for philosophy of technology?," in J. Olsen, E. Selinger, and S. Riis (eds), *New Waves in Philosophy of Technology*. New York: Palgrave Macmillan, pp. 267–91.

Sen, A. (1999), *Development as Freedom*. New York: Knopf.

Tenner, E. (1997), *Why Things Bite Back: Technology and the Revenge of Unintended Consequences*. New York: Vintage Press.

Turkle, S. (ed.) (2007), *Evocative Objects: Things We Think With*. Cambridge, MA: MIT Press.

Verbeek, P.-P. (2005), *What Things Do: Philosophical Reflections on Technology, Agency, and Design*. University Park: Pennsylvania State University Press.

Chapter 12

Bell, D. A. (2008), *China's New Confucianism*. Princeton and Oxford: Princeton University Press.

Bresciani, U. (2001), *Reinventing Confucianism*. Taipei: Taipei Ricci Institute for Chinese Studies.

Chan, W.-T. (ed.) (1986), *Chu Hsi and Neo-Confucianism*. Honolulu: University of Hawaii Press.

Cheng, C.-Y. (2008), "On entering the 21st century: my philosophical vision and my philosophical practice." in *The Imperative of Understanding: Chinese Philosophy, Comparative Philosophy, and Onto-Hermeneutics*, O.-C. Ng (ed.). New York: Global Scholarly Publications, pp. 14–28.

—(2006a), "General introduction," *Journal of Chinese Philosophy*, L. Pfister (ed.), Supplement 1 *Hermeneutical Thinking in Chinese Philosophy* (December), 33, 1–2.

—(2006b), "Toward constructing a dialectics of harmonization: harmony and conflict in Chinese philosophy," *Journal of Chinese Philosophy*, L. Pfister (ed.), Supplement 1 *Hermeneutical Thinking in Chinese Philosophy* (December), 33, 25–59.

—(2002), "An onto-hermeneutic interpretation of twentieth century Chinese philosophy: identity and vision," in *Contemporary Chinese Philosophy*, C.Y. Cheng and N. Bunnin (eds.). Malden and Oxford: Blackwell Publishers Ltd, pp. 365–402.

Cheng, C.-Y. and N. Bunnin (eds) (2002), *Contemporary Chinese Philosophy*. Malden and Oxford: Blackwell Publishers Ltd, pp. 365–404.

De Bary, W. T. and R. Lufrano (2000), *Sources of Chinese Tradition* (2nd edn), vol. 2 *From 1600 Through the Twentieth Century*. New York: Columbia University Press.

Elman, B. A. (2006), "Philology and its enemies: changing views of late imperial Chinese classicism." Lecture prepared for a colloquium on "Image of Philology," organized under the auspices of the History of Science Program at Princeton, NJ (February 16–17, 2006).

—(2002), *Rethinking Confucianism: Past and Present in China, Japan, Korea, and Vietnam*. Los Angeles: University of California Press.

—(1984), *From Philosophy to Philology: Intellectual and Social Aspects of Change in Late Imperial China*. Cambridge, MA: Harvard University Press.

Flemming, J. (2008), "The onto-hermeneutics of *guan*," in *The Imperative of Understanding: Chinese Philosophy, Comparative Philosophy, and Onto-Hermeneutics*, O.-C. Ng (ed.). New York: Global Scholarly Publications, pp. 73–106.

Foucault, M. (1970), *The Order of Things: An Archaeology of the Human Sciences*. New York: Vintage Books.

Gadamer, H.-G. (2006), *Truth and Method* (2nd rev. edn). J. Weinsheimer and D. G. Marshall (trans.). London and New York: Continuum.

Gan, Y. (1998), "A critique of Chinese conservatism in the 1990s," *Social Text* 55 *Intellectual Politics in Post-Tiananmen China* (Summer), 45–66.

Goulding, J. (2008), "Cheng Chung-ying's onto-cosmology: Chinese philosophy and hermeneutic phenomenology." in *The Imperative of Understanding: Chinese Philosophy, Comparative Philosophy, and Onto-Hermeneutics*, O.-C. Ng (ed.). New York: Global Scholarly Publications, pp. 135–55.

Graham, A. C. (1989), *Disputers of the Dao: Philosophical Argument in Ancient China*. La Salle: Open Court.

Hallie, P. P. (1979), *Lest Innocent Blood be Shed*. New York: Harper & Row.

Kubin, W. (2005), "Chinese 'hermeneutics'—a chimera?: preliminary remarks on differences of understanding," in *Interpretation and Historical Change: Chinese Hermeneutics in Historical Perspective*, C.-I. Tu (ed.). New Brunswick: Transaction Publishers, pp. 311–19.

Lyotard, J. F. (1984), *The Postmodern Condition: A Report on Knowledge*. Minneapolis: University of Minnesota Press.

Makeham, J. (ed.) (2003), *New Confucianism: A Critical Examination*. New York: Palgrave Macmillan.

Mou, Z. (1975), *Xianxiang yu wuzishen* (Phenomenon and noumenon). Taipei: Student Book Company.

Neville, R. C. (2008), "Cheng Chung-ying's constructive philosophy," in *The Imperative of Understanding: Chinese Philosophy, Comparative Philosophy, and Onto-Hermeneutics*, O.-C. Ng (ed.). New York: Global Scholarly Publications, pp. 107–21.

Ng, O.-C. (ed.) (2008a), *The Imperative of Understanding: Chinese Philosophy, Comparative Philosophy, and Onto-Hermeneutics*. New York: Global Scholarly Publications.

—(2008b), "Preface," in *The Imperative of Understanding: Chinese Philosophy, Comparative Philosophy, and Onto-Hermeneutics*. New York: Global Scholarly Publications, pp. 1–13.

Nylan, M. (2001), *The Five "Confucian" Classics*. New Haven: Yale University Press.

Nylan, M. and T. Wilson (2010), *The Lives of Confucius: Civilization's Greatest Sage Through the Ages*. New York: Doubleday.

Palmer, R. E. (2008), "Gadamer's late 'turn': from Heideggerian ontology to a philosophical hermeneutics based on anthropology," in *The Imperative of Understanding: Chinese Philosophy, Comparative Philosophy, and Onto-Hermeneutics*, O.-C. Ng (ed.). New York: Global Scholarly Publications, pp. 29–46.

—(2006), "Gadamer and Confucius: some possible affinities," in L. Pfister (ed.), *Journal of Chinese Philosophy* Supplement 1 *Hermeneutical Thinking in Chinese Philosophy*, December, 33, 81–93.

—(2002), "Seven key terms in the philosophy of Hans-Georg Gadamer," www.vahidnab.com/key.htm (accessed December 15, 2010).

—(1969), *Hermeneutics: Interpretation Theory in Schleiermacher, Dilthey, Heidegger, and Gadamer*. Evanston: Northwestern University Press.

Ricoeur, P. (1981), "Gadamer and the critique of ideology," in *Hermeneutics and the Human Sciences*, J. B. Thompson (ed.). Cambridge: Cambridge University Press, pp. 63–100.

—(1956a), "Certitudes et incertitudes d'une revolution," *L'Esprit*, January, 5–28.

—(1956b), "L'enseignement dans la Chine nouvelle," *Foi-Education*, 26/34, 25–30.

—(1956c), "Note critique sur 'Chine ouverte,'" *L'Esprit*, June, 897–910.

Schwartz, B. (1964), "Some polarities in Confucian thought," in *Confucianism and Chinese Civilization*, A. Wright (ed.). New York: Athenaeum Press, pp. 3–15.

Sivin, N. (1984), "Foreword" to Elman, B. A., *From Philosophy to Philology: Intellectual and Social Aspects of Change in Late Imperial China*. Cambridge, MA: Harvard University Press, pp. xiii–xviii.

Tang, R. (2002), "Mou Zongsan on intellectual intuition," in *Contemporary Chinese Philosophy*, C.-Y. Cheng and N. Bunnin (eds). Malden and Oxford: Blackwell Publishers Ltd, pp. 327–345.

Van Norden, B. W. (2004), "America's encounter with Confucian thought: three trends," http://faculty.vassar.edu/brvannor/ThreeTrends.pdf (accessed December 15, 2010).

Van Zoeren, S. (1991), *Poetry and Personality: Reading, Exegesis, and Hermeneutics in Traditional China*. Stanford: Stanford University Press.

Wright, K. (1986), "Gadamer: the speculative structure of language," in *Hermeneutics and Modern Philosophy*, B. Wachterhauser (ed.). Albany: SUNY Press, pp. 193–218.

List of Contributors

John Arthos, Associate Professor of Rhetorical Studies, Denison University. He has published numerous essays on hermeneutics in journals such as *Philosophy Today*, *International Philosophical Quarterly*, *Rhetoric Society Quarterly*, *Philosophy and Rhetoric*, and *American Catholic Philosophical Quarterly*. Recently published is *The Inner Word in Gadamer's Hermeneutics* (2009).

Bernard P. Dauenhauer, University Professor of Philosophy (Emeritus), University of Georgia. Among his publications are: *Paul Ricoeur: The Promise and Risk of Politics* (1998); *Citizenship in a Fragile World* (1996); *The Politics of Hope* (1986); and *Silence: The Phenomenon and Its Ontological Significance* (1980).

Louise D. Derksen, Assistant Professor of Philosophical Anthropology, Free University, Amsterdam. Her publications include: *On Universal Hermeneutics. A Study in the Philosophy of Hans-Georg Gadamer* (1983) and *Dialogues on Women. Images of Women in the History of Philosophy* (1996). She has also published articles in the areas of hermeneutics, philosophy of mind, women's studies, and philosophical anthropology.

David H. Fisher, Professor of Philosophy, Ruge Distinguished Teaching Fellow, North Central College. His research specializes in ethics, philosophy of law, and the history of ideas. His writings on Ricoeur include: "Doing justice to justice: Paul Ricoeur," "Work of mourning," "Waiting on Ricoeur: Ricoeur on tragedy," "Ricoeur's c*linamen*," and "Just Ricoeur." He is on the editorial board of the journal of the Association for the Study of Law, Culture and the Humanities.

Annemie Halsema, Assistant Professor of Philosophy, Free University, Amsterdam. Her recent research focuses on the relationship between hermeneutics and feminist philosophy. English publications include: "The gift of recognition: self and other in the multicultural situation," in H. Fielding, G. Hiltmann, D. Olkowski, A. Reichold (eds), *The Other. Feminist Reflections in Ethics* (2007) and "Horizontal transcendence. Irigaray's religion after ontotheology," in H. de Vries (ed.), *Religion: Beyond a Concept* (2008).

David M. Kaplan, Assistant Professor of Philosophy, University of North Texas. He is the author of *Ricoeur's Critical Theory* (2003) and editor of *Reading Ricoeur* (2008). His writings on Ricoeur include "Paul Ricoeur and the philosophy of technology," in F. Erfani (ed.), *Paul Ricoeur (1913–2005): Remembering a Life, Continuing the Work*, (2011); "Paul Ricoeur and development ethics," in B. Treanor and H. I. Venema (eds), *A Passion for the Possible: Thinking with Paul Ricoeur* (2010); "Paul Ricoeur and the Nazis," in *Research in Phenomenology* (2007); "Ricoeur's theory of truth: from phenomenology to communicative action," in A. Wiercinski (ed.), *The Hermeneutic Turn in Phenomenology* (2005); and the "Paul Ricoeur" entry in the *Encyclopedia of Philosophy*, 2nd edition (2006).

Francis J. Mootz III, Associate Dean for Research and Faculty Development, William S. Boyd Professor of Law, William S. Boyd School of Law, University of Nevada—Las Vegas. A leading theorist of the relationship of Gadamer's philosophical hermeneutics to jurisprudence and legal philosophy, Mootz is the author of *Rhetorical Knowledge in Legal Practice and Critical Legal Theory* (2006), editor of *On Philosophy in American Law* (2009) and *Gadamer and Law* (2007), coeditor of *Nietzsche and Law* (2008), and author of numerous articles in law reviews and peer-reviewed journals. He is a member of the Organizing Committee of the Association for the Study of Law, Culture and the Humanities, and an editor of the *International Journal for the Semiotics of Law*.

Andreea Deciu Ritivoi, Associate Professor of English and Rhetoric, Carnegie Mellon University. Her work includes: *Paul Ricoeur: Tradition and Innovation in Rhetorical Theory* **(2006);** *Interpretation and Its Objects: Studies in the Philosophy of Michael Krausz,* **editor (2003); and** *Yesterday's Self: Nostalgia and the Immigrant Identity* (2002).

P. Christopher Smith, Professor of Philosophy (Emeritus), University of Massachusetts Lowell. He is a former student of Gadamer and the author of *The Hermeneutics of Original Argument: Demonstration, Dialectic, Rhetoric* (1998) and *Hermeneutics and Human Finitude* (1991). He is also the translator of Gadamer's *The Idea of the Good in Platonic-Aristotelian Philosophy* (1986); *Dialogue and Dialectic* (1980); and *Hegel's Dialectic* (1976).

George H. Taylor, Professor of Law, University of Pittsburgh. A former student of Ricoeur, he has edited Ricoeur's *Lectures on Ideology and Utopia* (1986). His articles applying Ricoeur's hermeneutics to legal interpretation have appeared in such journals as the *New York University Review of Law & Social Change, Boston University Law Review, Michigan Journal of Race & Law, Chicago-Kent Law Review,* and the *Cleveland State Law Review*. He is also the author of such articles as "Ricoeur and the distinctiveness of legal hermeneutics," in *Ricoeur Across the Disciplines*, S. Davidson (ed.) (2010) and "Ricoeur's philosophy of imagination," in *Journal of French Philosophy* (2006). He is the past president of the Society for Ricoeur Studies.

David Vessey, Assistant Professor of Philosophy, Grand Valley State University. His many writings on Gadamer and on hermeneutics include: "Relating Levinas and Gadamer through Heidegger," *Levinas Studies* (2008); "Hermeneutics," in *American Philosophy: An Encyclopedia* (2008); "Deriving Gadamer's account of intersubjectivity from his account of dialogue," in *Sprache ist Gespräch—Gadamer's Understanding of Language as Conversation*, A. Wiercinski (ed.) (2009); "Who was Gadamer's Husserl?," in *The New Yearbook for Phenomenology and Phenomenological Philosophy* (2008); "Engaging across traditions: Royce and Gadamer on interpretation," *Issues in Interpretation Theory*, P. Vandevelde (ed.) (2006); and "Hermeneutics and pragmatism," *The Blackwell Companion to Pragmatism* (2006). He has translated several of Gadamer's essays into English, and is a member of the Executive Board, North American Society for Philosophical Hermeneutics.

Merold Westphal, Distinguished Professor of Philosophy, Fordham University. He is the author of *Levinas and Kierkegaard in Dialogue* (2008); *Transcendence and Self-Transcendence: An Essay on God and the Soul* (2004); *Overcoming Onto-Theology* (2001); *Becoming a Self: A Reading of Kierkegaard's Concluding Unscientific Postscript* (1996); *Suspicion and Faith: The Religious Uses of Modern Atheism* (1993); *Hegel, Freedom and Modernity* (1992); *Kierkegaard's Critique of Reason and Society* (1991); *God, Guilt, and Death: An Existential Phenomenology of Religion* (1984); and *History and Truth in Hegel's Phenomenology* (1979). He has served as president of the Hegel Society of America and of the Soren Kierkegaard Society and as executive co-director of the Society for Phenomenology and Existential Philosophy (SPEP).

Kathleen Wright, Professor of Philosophy, Haverford College. She is a former student of Gadamer and has edited *Festivals of Interpretation: Essays on Hans-Georg Gadamer's Work* (1990). Her writings on Gadamer include: "Engendering dialogue: Gadamer's philosophical hermeneutics and feminist thought," in *Rereading the Canon: Hans-Georg Gadamer*, Lorraine Code (ed.) (2003); "Hans-Georg Gadamer," in *Routledge Encyclopedia of Philosophy*, T. Baldwin (ed.) (2001); "The fusion of horizons: Hans-Georg Gadamer and Wang Fu Chih," in *Continental Philosophy Review* (2000); "Gadamer: the speculative structure of language," in *Hermeneutics and Modern Philosophy*, B. Wachterhauser (ed.) (1986).

Subject Index

Name Index

Made in the USA
Las Vegas, NV
13 November 2021

34370278R00168